DIVIDED SOUL

The Life of MARVIN GAYE

ALSO BY DAVID RITZ

Biography: *BROTHER RAY (with Ray Charles)*

Novels: *SEARCH FOR HAPPINESS*

THE MAN WHO BROUGHT THE DODGERS BACK TO BROOKLYN

DIVIDED
SOUL

The Life of
MARVIN GAYE

DAVID RITZ

MCGRAW-HILL BOOK COMPANY

New York St. Louis San Francisco
Toronto Hamburg Mexico

1 2 3 4 5 6 7 8 9 D O C D O C 8 7 6 5

ISBN 0-07-052929-9

LIBRARY OF CONGRESS CATALOGING IN PUBLICATION DATA

Ritz, David.
   Divided soul.
   Discography: p. 341
   1. Gaye, Marvin. 2. Singers—United States—Biography.
I. Title.
ML420.G305R6   1985   784.5′5′00924 [B]   84-28856
ISBN 0-07-052929-9

Book design by Patrice Fodero

For my father, with love

CONTENTS

Part Two

Part Three

THANKS

To God.

To my mother; my heavenly wife Roberta and daughters Allison and Jessica, who keep me company and keep me sane; sisters Esther and Elizabeth; Gary, Jennifer, Sarah, Julia, Gabriel, Marc, Brad, and Florence and Mannie Plitt.

To Aaron Priest, skillful agent and loyal friend; to Marc Staenberg, Barney Karpfinger, Molly Friedrich, Jessica Lehman, Jim Henke, Audrey Edwards; and to Gladys Justin Carr, Chairman, McGraw-Hill Editorial Board, and Leslie Meredith, Editor, who sponsored and edited this work.

To those who sat with me, sometimes for days, and answered my questions: Mrs. Alberta Gay, Marvin Gay, Sr., Jeanne Gay, Frankie Gay, Irene Gay, Dave Simmons (for assistance beyond the call of duty), Art Stewart, Ray Baradat (for his scholarship and sensitivity), Cecil Jenkins, Jewel Price, Curtis Shaw, Reese Palmer, Sondra Lattisaw, Ken Grant, Kim Weston, Richard "Do Dirty" Bethune, Etta James, Clarence Paul, Beatrice Carson, Bishop S. P. Rawlings, Mrs. S. P. Rawlings, Estella Mayberry, Ed Eckstine, Quincy Jones, Maurice King, Thomas "Beans" Bowles, Bishop Harold Solomon, Geraldine "Peasie" Adams, Barry White, Herb Fame, Gene Page, Jeff Wald, Les Moss, Lawrence Berry, Charles Davies, Dewey Hughes, Tahira Hylton, Liz Moran, Maxine Powell, Billie Jean Brown, Curtis McNair, Marcus Belgrave, Ted Harris, Glenn Leonard, Otis Williams, Dennis Edwards, Tom Noonan, Ralph Seltzer, Gene Byrd, Freddy Cousaert, Maggie and Donald Pylyser, John Cammon, Ed Townsend, Leon Ware, Renaldo Benson, Mel Farr, Chuck Barksdale, Mary Turner, Fred Ross, Jr., Fred Ross, Sr., Jeffrey Kruger, Rob Cohen, Gil Askey, Shelley Berger, Dave Harris, Johnetta Anderson, Randall Wilson, and Gwen McClendon.

To those writers whose work guided me: Herb Boyd (Dean of Detroit), Charles Keil, Alan Abrams, Merlene Davis, Miles White, Courtland Milloy, Nelson George, Gerri Hirshey, Peter Benjaminson, Ted Fox, the authors of *The Rolling Stone Illustrated History of Rock & Roll*, Arnold Shaw, Michael Goldberg, Chris Salewicz, David Morse, John Keats, Percy Bysshe Shelley, John Donne, T. S. Eliot, S. T. Coleridge, Carl Jung, and Dante.

To the authors whose muscular, rhythmic prose inspired me most deeply: Leslie Fiedler, Harold Robbins, and W. Somerset Maugham.

To my songwriting partners: Patrick Henderson, Ray Kennedy, Wayne Arnold, Fred White, and Robin Swados.

To Lewis MacAdams for his translations from the French of Marvin Gaye interviews; and Richard Freed, Alan Eisenstock, Susan Teegardin, June Massell, and Dick Sinreich.

To the staffs of the Los Angeles Public Library and the Music Library of U.C.L.A.

And finally to Marvin Pentz Gaye, Jr., for lessons of praise and hymns of hope.

PREFACE:
MEETING
MARVIN

This is not the book that Marvin Gaye and I had planned.

When we met in 1979, we were excited about each other's work and immediately decided to collaborate. In a letter to the *Los Angeles Times*, I had called his album, *Here, My Dear*, a masterpiece, arguing with critics who'd dismissed it as self-indulgent. Marvin had just read *Brother Ray*, which I'd written with Ray Charles, and said he wanted to do a similar book with me. At the time, I was in the middle of a novel based upon a childhood fantasy—*The Man Who Brought the Dodgers Back to Brooklyn*—but put the project aside. Working with Marvin was an even greater fantasy. We became fast friends.

Separated from Janis, his second wife, Gaye was staying with his parents on Gramercy Place. I was living only two miles away, in the same Crenshaw-Wilshire district of Los Angeles, close to his private recording studio on Sunset Boulevard in Hollywood. These were the two locales where we did most of our talking. His bedroom at home—the same room where five years later he would meet his tragic end—and the apartment he kept atop the recording studio were the places he felt most secluded and comfortable. We also spent time on his estate in Hidden Hills in the San Fernando Valley where he had lived with Janis and their two children. For a while, I went on tour with him, traveling in his customized Greyhound bus.

Two years of pulling information out of Ray Charles proved to be the right sort of training for dealing with Marvin. There were great similarities between the two men. Both were brilliant, moody, and self-absorbed. But there were also differences: Charles was a disciplined businessman, a dependable partner who jealously guarded his time. Gaye hated business—we never discussed terms or contracts for the book—and had no more regard for keeping appointments than for meeting deadlines. I'd have to catch him whenever I could. When we did speak, though, the conversation could go on for days.

Often we spoke before concerts. Afraid of performing, he'd reflect on his childhood when he should have been dressing and heading for the stage. Sometimes he'd interrupt or end a recording session to tell anecdotes about his early Motown days or expand upon his views of heaven and hell. We'd read poetry together—I convinced him that he was spiritually related to Dante, Donne, Shelley, and Keats—or we'd talk all night, seated in the back of his limo as his chauffeur slowly drove along the San Francisco Bay till break of dawn. Alternately merry and melancholy, Marvin had an urgent need to talk—and to be understood. Our discussions were almost always probing, sometimes turning to debate or prayer. Marvin Gaye was not a man given to superficiality, especially when discussing himself.

Although Ray Charles and I finally became friends, I could never help but see him as an authoritative uncle or father. Because Marvin and I were closer in age, and because he was a remarkably candid man, our relationship was far more relaxed and included warm feelings of brotherly love. Self-analysis did not come easily to Ray; with Marvin it was second nature. He was a reflective artist who wrote and sang about personal feelings. He saw the events of his life as an extraordinary work of art which he evaluated with remarkable objectivity, much as he might evaluate one of his recordings.

Through Marvin, I met and interviewed his family and became friends with his brother Frankie, his sister Jeanne and his mother, in whose bedroom I attended occasional prayer meetings on Saturday afternoons. Gaye was reluctant to have me meet his father, though finally, through my own insistence, I managed to do so.

One afternoon Marvin and I were talking in the house on Gramercy Place, discussing Mr. Gay, whom I knew to be just down the hall in the bedroom where he stayed by himself. Marvin was saying how important it was to love one's father.

"Do you love yours?" I asked him.

"Yes," Marvin answered.

"Why don't you tell him?"

"Why don't you tell *your* father?" Marvin challenged.

"I will if you will."

"You go first."

I met the challenge by calling my father in Dallas. But when it was Marvin's turn, he backed out. "I can't do it. I can't go in to see him."

"Can I? If I'm going to write this book, I need to meet your father."

"You can try."

I succeeded in conducting a series of interviews with Mr. Gay, a slight man with delicate fingers and inscrutable eyes who, at five feet eight and 150 pounds, looked petite next to his athletic six-foot-tall son. I did not, however, succeed in completing my literary project with Marvin.

Toward the end of 1979, he was going through another series of crazy crises. He was displeased with a new album I had watched him record. More seriously, his second marriage had collapsed and he was being cornered by an angry army of creditors and hounded by the IRS for millions of dollars in back taxes. He was fleeing, and invited me to go overseas with him. Reluctant to leave my family for an indefinite period of time and unwilling to chase Marvin halfway across the world, I stayed home, banking on the fact that eventually he'd be drawn back to Los Angeles and his mother.

He'd been gone two and a half years when, in 1982, I found an excuse to visit him in Belgium. Together for two weeks, we renewed our friendship and our project. In his apartment in Ostend, in the recording studio in Ohaine, walking through the great squares of Brussels, he described his exile and patiently filled in the gaps I'd found in the information he'd previously given me. "We can't start writing the book now," he said. "I have to get this new record out. But someday soon."

Our literary relationship deepened when, during this same trip, I named and wrote lyrics for the song that would become "Sexual Healing." After seeing my work, Marvin urged me to become a full-time songwriter, just as he had always urged me to become a

Christian. He also tried to cure my stutter. Unfortunately, our musical collaboration spelled the end of our friendship. Once the tune was a hit and Marvin found himself back in America, we fought over credit and money.

The last time I spoke with Marvin was in 1983 at a hospital in Los Angeles, just hours after the birth of his brother Frankie's daughter, April. There was obvious tension between us. Our argument hadn't yet reached the lawsuit stage, though we were well on our way. In spite of the mounting distrust, Marvin said goodbye in the same manner he had said hello when we had met four years earlier. He asked that we silently meditate for a few moments. Afterward, we embraced as he whispered, "God bless you." We never spoke again.

In late March of 1984, our mutual friend Dave Simmons, determined to bring us together, forced Marvin to reread a long and admiring article I'd written about him in 1979. "Read this," Dave urged him, "and you'll see that Ritz really loves you." According to Dave, Marvin read the article and remembered the good feelings between us.

Two days later, he was shot to death.

Even before I met Marvin Gaye I had been convinced that I was chosen—by fate or God or the power of my own passion—to write about his life and music. What I thought would be a joint effort has now become a solitary work. Either way, this is a book I've had to write. As a creative character, both mythic and real, Marvin has haunted and thrilled my imagination since I was a teenager.

I've based this biography not only on months of private interviews with Marvin, but on twenty years of studying, listening, and dancing to his music. In addition, I've made research trips to his homes—in Washington, D.C., Detroit, and Europe—and to the childhood home of his father in Lexington, Kentucky. I've spoken to dozens of Marvin's friends and acquaintances from every period of his life, as well as to his preachers, teachers, managers, producers, lawyers, and adversaries. I've also been privileged to amass a complete collection of his recordings, which include a wealth of unreleased material given to me by Marvin and his colleagues. Finally, I've examined everything I could find that's been written on Gaye since he stepped into the spotlight in the early sixties.

Marvin Gaye hated hypocrisy. In spite of a vicious streak of self-destructiveness which, I believe, led to his own demise, he was a man—an enormously complicated man—who revelled in candor. He pleased himself and those who were curious about him with outrageous disclosures. He loved to surprise and shock. "If I can't be honest about myself," he told me, "I can't be honest about anything." Above all, he strove to tell the truth about the conflicts between his body and his soul. This is the spirit in which I offer this book, hoping that it not only informs the reader but satisfies Marvin Gaye's courageous notion that painstaking revelation is a way of growing closer to God.

PART
ONE

1

IN THE BEGINNING

Marvin's father—Marvin Pentz Gay, Sr., the third of thirteen children—was born on a farm along Catnip Hill Pike in Jessamine County, Kentucky, on October 1, 1914. Pentz was the name of the German doctor who delivered him. In the early twenties, the family eventually moved to Charles Avenue in west Lexington, Kentucky. (Marvin Jr. added the "e" to the family name after going into show business.)

Gay's parents had been sharecroppers, and his mother broke sharply from the rest of the black community by joining what seemed to her neighbors an eccentric church—the House of God. Mamie Gay was said to be the first female member of the Pentecostal sect. According to Bishop Simon Peter Rawlings, chief apostle of the church and for years Marvin Gay, Sr.'s closest associate and friend, the movement was founded in 1918 by R. A. R. Johnson, a black man, from New Bern, North Carolina.

The long, official name is a combination of quotes from the Old and New Testaments, Isaiah and First Timothy: *The House of God, the Holy Church of the Living God, the Pillar and Ground of the Truth, the House of Prayer for All People.*

Similarly, the church is a bizarre mixture of orthodox Judaism and Pentecostal Christianity.

"If you want to understand my religion and the spirit I received as a child," Marvin Jr. once instructed me in his high-pitched, sad-

3

edged voice, "then you must begin by talking to Bishop Rawlings. He's the man."

"If you want to understand our church," Bishop Rawlings told me, "come to our services. Our building is somewhat larger these days, but we worship God as we always have—and always will."

On Georgetown Road, on the other side of the tracks in the shadow of downtown Lexington, Sabbath services at the House of God begin at three o'clock on Saturday afternoon.

First you notice the women, dressed dramatically in white. Such is the dress code from Passover to Harvest Festival. This is a Christian church where only Old Testament holidays are honored.

"We follow Biblical instructions," says Bishop Rawlings, "and the Bible does not ask us to celebrate Jesus' birth or the Crucifixion. Christmas and Easter are holidays that some might even view as pagan, and we feel obligated to ignore them."

The dogma is strict, the male hierarchy is evident—the elders and deacons refer to one another by title—but the sight of the women in white is touching. Their heads are covered with white pillbox hats, lace flowing from the back, the crowns adorned with pale blue Stars of David. Their young daughters wear black velvet skullcaps with Stars of David embroidered in white.

"Not long ago," says Estella Mayberry, Marvin Jr.'s first cousin and long-standing member of the Lexington church, "the women wore full white headdresses. They still do in many of the Houses of God today."

The feeling is warm and maternal. The women take on the appearance of spiritual nurses, and it's easy to see why a young Marvin Jr. was so deeply comforted by the church.

"The church women!" he remembered. "Oh, how they loved it when I sang. They'd hug me and smother me in their huge breasts. I liked the way that felt—being able to please them with my voice, reaching to God, feeling their satisfaction. I could always please Mother by singing."

The gospel music in the House of God is traditional, wildly emotional, loose, and free: wailing saxophones, tambourines, organ, piano, guitars, trumpets, call-and-response, hand claps, and dancing in the aisles. The mood is electric, ecstatic. "The only musical obligation," explains Bishop Rawlings, "is that we make a joyful noise. And we further believe that music should not be used for secular purposes."

The pulpit is adorned with a large Star of David carved in wood. Twin sets of the Ten Commandments, in extra-large print, are set in frames facing the congregation. At the start of service, the worshippers read the commandments out loud.

"We observe the dietary laws of the Old Testament," instructs Bishop Rawlings. "No shellfish, no pork. We believe in divine healing. On the Day of Atonement we fast and stay in church from sundown to sundown, twenty-four straight hours, much like the Orthodox Jews. On Passover, we eat unleavened bread. If a brother or sister among us is moved to speak in tongues—which happens on occasion—we have absolute respect for that process."

"I loved my father's religion," Marvin Jr. told me. "At a very early age, I realized I was born into a very rootsy church, and I found it exciting. The idea of tarrying thrilled and fascinated me. That's where you wait for the Holy Ghost, where you repeat over and again, 'Thank you, Jesus, thank you, Jesus, thank you, Jesus, thank you, Jesus,' until the spirit arrives. It can take minutes, or hours. Later I'd understand that it was similar to the way Eastern religions use mantras. We were tapping an energy force in the universe."

Marvin Sr. followed his mother into the church and became an active member at an early age. While still a teenager, he began traveling through the South with evangelist Sister Fame. Marvin Sr.'s uncle, James Gay, recalled how his nephew and Sister Fame "made a tour, begging gas, tires, and anything else along the way."

"I was enraptured with God and all He could give," Marvin Sr. related to me when I first met him in 1979. In describing his childhood, he spoke eloquently, his voice tinged with an accent that sounded slightly affected, slightly aristocratic. "Because of the work I had to do to survive—on truck farms and tobacco fields— my work for Jesus was that much sweeter. The Depression nearly destroyed us."

"Our ministers," Bishop Rawlings explained, "were not formally trained. Mr. Gay, like myself, was divinely inspired to serve God. We were ordained through the spirit of God."

In 1934, Gay met his wife-to-be, Alberta, in Washington, D.C., where he had come to preach.

"There was tragedy in my younger life," Mrs. Gay had told me in her kitchen in Los Angeles in 1979 as she fixed Marvin lunch. "My father, for instance, was a violent man who once shot my mother. Mama survived, but the fear still lives inside me. My father died in a hospital for the insane. I never really had a father and they didn't put me in school till I was eight."

"When I met my husband," Mrs. Gay told me during one of our long conversations, "I had just come from Rocky Mountain, North Carolina. I also had an infant son, Michael. I knew nothing about the city and city life. Mr. Gay and Mr. Rawlings both courted me. I believe they both wanted to marry me. Sometimes the three of us would go out together and I'd kiss them on the cheek goodnight and wonder which man I liked better. Mr. Gay seemed more powerful.

"Only later on did I learn about the awful violence of the Gay family back in Lexington. There were stories of shootings—Gays against Gays."

On July 2, 1935, Marvin Sr. and Alberta were married in Washington, D.C., where they found an apartment in the southwest projects at 1617 First Street, only a few blocks from the Anacostia River. Not wanting to raise the child as his own, Father Gay sent Michael to live with Alberta's sister Pearl in the same city. Two years later their first child was born. They named the girl Jeanne.

"It was important that I have a male child," Mr. Gay said in the living room of the Gramercy Place home when I interviewed him, with his wife by his side, in 1982. In her husband's presence, Mrs. Gay appeared almost a different person from when she'd spoken to me alone. Before she was anxious to discuss her country upbringing. Now she was remarkably reticent, saying only a few words, while her husband spoke for hours. "A namesake is what I wanted," Father continued. "The day he was born, I felt he was destined for greatness. I thanked God for the blessing of his life. I thanked God for Marvin. I knew he was a special child."

"My husband never wanted Marvin," Mrs. Gay told me. "And he never liked him. He used to say that he didn't think he was really his child. I told him that was nonsense. He *knew* Marvin was his. But for some reason, he didn't love Marvin and, what's worse, he didn't want *me* to love Marvin either. Marvin wasn't very old before he understood that."

The tragic triangle was established at birth—Father and Son competing for Mother's love—a tension that only grew over the years, finally exploding in two angry blasts of gunfire.

2

ORIGINAL SIN

Marvin Pentz Gaye, Jr. was born at Freedman's Hospital in Washington, D.C., on April 2, 1939, a Sunday, the same day of the week he died.

In the same city, exactly one week later, the great black contralto, Marian Anderson, barred from singing at Constitution Hall by the Daughters of the American Revolution, would perform at the Lincoln Memorial before seventy-five thousand spectators on Easter morning, thanks to the intervention of Secretary of the Interior Harold Ickes.

"My father told me the story," Marvin remembered as an adult, "and it made a deep impression upon me. I felt a kinship to Miss Anderson, just as I'd always feel a great kinship with Mahalia Jackson. These were triumphant women. They were among the greatest singers the world had ever known. My father himself had a great voice and the capacity to become a great singer. Early on, I realized—largely through dreams—that I, too, was destined to be such a singer."

Marvin had precise recollections of childhood dreams, but were these dreams engendered while awake or asleep?

"Both," he replied with an inflection both regal and street. "They were more visions than dreams. Visions of myself on stage, while all the world watched and waited for me to sing something so stupendous that life as we know it would be forever altered. I was brought here to make a change."

He was unable to lose the feeling that the world revolved around him; a spiritual, childlike egocentricity would be one of Marvin's lifelong characteristics.

His father shared the same quality of self-centeredness.

"I knew my powers as a man of God were extraordinary," said Gay Sr. one afternoon as we sat in his bedroom on Gramercy Place and listened to gospel tapes while he pontificated on his past. "I believed that there was nothing I couldn't do. I had the power to heal."

"Ask Father," Marvin demanded, his dark eyes flashing when I told him what Mr. Gay had told me, "how he lost that power."

The elder Gay was irritated by such a question and instead talked about his early history with the church. "In 1936, I had my first mission in Northtown, Pennsylvania. When we moved to Washington, services were conducted in our home. We were joined by another family, the Solomons, who actually lived with us, and a few others. Our house *was* the church, which was the reason my children received such strong religious preparation."

"Seemed like Mrs. Gay's mother lived there too," remembered Howard Solomon, now a bishop at the House of God on East Capitol Street in Washington. "My wife Maude and our two children made up the congregation. There was a time when Bishop Gay had a little mission, and I'll never forget Marvin Jr. playing the piano and singin' 'bout 'I must see my Jesus some day.' "

In his early life, Marvin had access to the keyboard, which he learned totally by ear. Even as a pre-teen, he had developed into a fine two-fisted country-church pianist. He could also play heartfelt blues. Music was the joyful part of services in the House of God which, in other ways, bound its members to an unbending code.

"In the early days," explained Jeanne Gay, now an insurance executive in Los Angeles, "the Solomons and the Gays were the only two families in the church. Father's church was extremely hard on young people, especially women. We couldn't wear sleeveless dresses, nylons, lipstick, or nail polish. We couldn't show our hair or even wear open-toe shoes. No dancing was allowed and, for a long time, no movies or television."

"The Sabbath was strange," said Marvin. "We were forced to cut off the outside world. Come Friday night at sundown, everything stopped for us. We weren't allowed to play. We couldn't even ride the bus. All we could do was pray and praise God. Father instructed us on the exact interpretation of the Bible. He was a theologian of great integrity. Even though he taught that Christ was the answer, he believed that Jews were blessed. We were drilled and tested on the Old and New Testaments. We kept the Sabbath in the purest sense. Father anointed converts with olive oil and baptized them in the river. The Sabbath was his day, it was God's day, and it was also a day for singing. Every member of our family was blessed with a good voice. The joy of music was the joy of God."

Little joy, however, existed between Marvin and his father.

"Seemed like Mr. Gay had a grudge against his son. He had expectations which were too high for a little boy to reach," observed Mrs. Beatrice Carson, a distant cousin of Alberta Gay's from Nashville, North Carolina. Mrs. Carson came to live in the Gay apartment with her own infant son in 1946 and stayed for five years. By then, the Gays had two other children besides Jeanne and Marvin—Frankie, three years younger than Marvin, and Zeola, nicknamed Sweetsie, three years younger than Frankie.

"In those years," Mrs. Carson said, "me, Jeanne, and my son Lenwood were sharing one bedroom, Frankie and Marvin were in another, and Mr. and Mrs. Gay had Sweetsie in with them.

"When I arrived, it hurt me to see what was happening. Little Marvin would wet his bed and his father would beat him unmercifully. Me and Jeanne and Babe—that's what I call Mrs. Gay, who's as close to me as a sister—we'd all get on our hands and knees and pray for him to stop beating the child. We believed in prayer, and we believed in mercy, but it seemed like that man had it in for the child. He frightened him to death."

"It wasn't simply that my father beat me," Marvin confessed one April night in Belgium in 1982 as he peered from his huge apartment window down into the dark North Sea, his back turned to me, "though that was bad enough. By the time I was twelve, there wasn't an inch of my body that hadn't been bruised and beaten by him. But Father did something else far worse. You see, he's a man with a subtle mind. He understood that if you're interested in inflicting pain, prolonging the process adds to the excitement. He'd say, 'Boy, you're going to get a whipping.' Then he'd tell me to take off my clothes and send me to the bedroom I shared with

Frankie. Frankie was smarter; he placated him. But I felt I had to challenge Father, and he repaid me with his belt. It wouldn't have been so awful if he had hit me right away. But Father liked mind games. He'd play with me. He'd make me wait an hour, or even more, all the while jangling his belt buckle loud enough so I could hear. The only way to short-circuit the agony was to provoke him even more and just get the beating over with. When he finally struck me, I knew—children know these things—that something inside him was enjoying the whole thing."

"All four of us had bed-wetting problems," Jeanne Gay told me with a candor reminiscent of Marvin. "That should tell you something about the nervousness and fear that existed in the household. Father hit us all and demanded that we be naked for the whippings. Then he'd get his strap or switch and beat us till he saw welts on our skin. He wouldn't be satisfied until he saw those welts. In his mind, that meant we'd learned our lesson.

"Once when I was eleven, I wet my bed. I made the bed up anyway, hoping not to be discovered. When I got home from school and saw that Father had put the mattress out on the porch to dry, I was petrified. He told me to get undressed and wait for him. I was filled with shame and embarrassment because my body had already started to bud. Luckily, Mother interceded and stopped him. That was one of the rare times she was able to do so.

"Marvin was never so lucky. He constantly provoked Father. He'd disappear on Saturday mornings when it was time to go to church. He'd use Father's hairbrush, not bother to clean it, and leave it in a place where he knew he'd be caught. Against Father's orders, he'd wander off after school and come home late. All these things Marvin did over and over and over again, knowing he'd be beaten, almost asking to be beaten. From the time he was seven until he became a teenager, Marvin's life at home consisted of a series of brutal whippings."

Certain he could never win Father's approval, Gaye sought his attention through antagonism. For the rest of his life, Marvin would express his need for affection through provocations of violence, the perverse pattern of behavior which would literally kill him.

"All the children were very scared of him," Mrs. Gay told me. "I tried to protect them as best as I could, but I was very frightened myself. My husband was a fearful man. I was afraid he'd beat me. When I'd try to take the switch out of his hand, he'd push me back and then go in and give them an even worse whipping—just 'cause I tried to stop him."

Did she ever think of leaving him?

"Yes," Mother Gay answered, "but I didn't because I felt a loyalty and responsibility. I also felt sorry for him. I knew he needed help. So I stuck with him. Now I realize that he could have done without our children back then. He wasn't ready for children. He didn't understand how to treat them."

Mrs. Carson tells me the story about how Michael, Mrs. Gay's first child, once told an eight-year-old Marvin that he thought the family shouldn't put up with Mr. Gay's violent ways. Marvin told his father what Michael had said. Father's response was to ban the boy from his home. Soon afterward, Michael was sent to Detroit to live with his Aunt Zeola.

Jeanne Gay remembered it differently. "Michael always wanted to live with us, but he'd been led to believe that Aunt Pearl was his mother. Mother wanted to tell him the truth, but Father didn't. Michael finally discovered the truth when he became a teenager, and Father responded by sending him to Detroit where he lived with Aunt Zeola, another sister of Mother's."

"Mr. Gay's violent streak," Mrs. Carson said, "was especially sad and hurtful, because he'd tell me how his own father, back in Kentucky, would beat his wife, Mr. Gay's mother. He'd describe the blood and the horror he saw."

"Living with Father was something like living with a king," Marvin observed, "a very peculiar, changeable, cruel, and all-powerful king. You were supposed to tip-toe around his moods. You were supposed to do anything to win his favor. I never did. Even though winning his love was the ultimate goal of my childhood, I defied him. I hated his attitude. I thought I could win his love through singing, so I sang my heart out. But the better I became, the greater his demands. I could never please him, and if it wasn't for Mother, who was always there to console me and praise my singing, I think I would have been one of those child suicide cases you read about in the papers."

What about normal childhood activities?

"The word 'normal' could never describe my childhood," Marvin claimed. "First of all, I knew we didn't live in a normal neighborhood. I was brought up in a slum, the part of town we called Simple City. It seemed half-city, half-country. I never lived in a high-rise

or a tenement like you see in Harlem. It was definitely funky—
some people had outhouses—but there were also trees and grass.
Still, I knew we were living on the bottom.

"Because my father was a preacher, I felt even less normal. And
the kind of preacher he was—keeping the sabbath on Saturday and
ignoring Christmas while everyone else was exchanging gifts—well,
that separated us from the rest of the blacks, even the other Pentecostal black families. You should have seen the faces of the Jewish
store owners in our neighborhood when we went to buy matzos
for Passover."

"The average person in Washington, even the average Christian,"
Father Gay told me, "did not accept our kind. We received no
respect and were considered the backwash of society."

"We were constantly branded," Bishop Rawlings reiterated, "and
looked upon as peculiar. But because we consider ourselves special
people, it was part of the burden we accepted."

"There were times," Marvin said, "when my religion made me
feel elite and terribly blessed. But there were other times when in
my heart I yearned to play with the other kids on Saturday. Always
being reminded that I was different was no picnic. We had our
dignity, but no status."

"There was a stigma to living in the ghetto," Jeanne Gay observed. "All during our childhood we felt that stigma very strongly."

As early as age five, Marvin was traveling with Father. Bishop
Rawlings' wife, Mary, remembered little Marvin at a church convention. "He sang 'Precious Lord' with such beautiful feeling that
there could be no doubt of the boy's spiritual gift."

"I was flattered to go along on my father's religious missions,"
Marvin said. "Sometimes on those trips I'd see things which weren't
always purely religious. The gospel circuit was filled with temptations, and many of the performers fell to sin. But the devotion
to Jesus was real. The spirit was there, in the room and in the
songs. The spirit enraptured me. The strength of my singing surprised me. That's how I found the courage to sing according to
feeling. I let my voice do things choir teachers would never allow.
I realized my voice was a gift of God and had to be used to praise
Him. Sometimes I wondered, though, whether Father was jealous
of my voice. At gospel meetings, for example, when I pleased all
the women, he'd look at me like I'd done something very bad. He
hated it when my singing won more praise than his sermons."

Father Gay's relationship with the church had undergone several changes. In the late forties, the House of God split. A faction of its membership, including Mr. Gay, followed Henry Ferguson and his newly formed House of the Living God.

"The division," said Bishop Rawlings, "was caused by a disagreement over the name. We couldn't accept a change in the original name. Though Mr. Gay went with the new group, there really wasn't any congregation for him to lead in Washington. He was a lay person with a title. In 1949, when I was named bishop of the House of God, he rejoined us, and in the early fifties he headed our Board of Apostles."

Mr. Gay spoke to me of a church he had on East Capitol and Seventeenth Street in northeast Washington, D.C., but Mrs. Carson and Jeanne Gay claimed that when Father was still preaching, he did so only at home or in small storefronts, rented for single Saturday afternoons.

"By the mid-fifties," Bishop Rawlings remembered, "Mr. Gay had grown disenchanted with the church and went into seclusion. He never did much after that."

"My husband and Bishop Rawlings were extremely close friends when they were young men," Mrs. Gay mentioned, "but they were also competitors."

Jeanne Gay claimed the real reason her father left the church was because Bishop Rawlings, and not the Reverend Marvin Gay, had been named chief apostle. "His ego couldn't take it. For four or five years after that," said Jeanne, "Father weaned himself away from the church until he'd dropped out completely."

Bishop Solomon also remembered a time, after a convention, when both he and Mr. Gay came back to Washington to find themselves vying for the same tiny congregation.

"By the time I was a teenager—all during the fifties," Marvin said, "Father's relationship with the church had faded. That seemed to make him even angrier. And more secretive. That's when he lost his healing powers.

"Father always taught us that Jesus forgave, but there was also a punishing side to God. You were expected to fast, deny, and sacrifice your comforts to the point of physical pain. Those sacrifices became too much for Father, and in his heart, I believe, he punished himself for being weak."

"Reverend Gay had been our teacher," Bishop Solomon stated,

"and it saddened me to see him leave the church. I couldn't help but think of I Timothy, chapter 4, verse 1: 'Now the Spirit speaketh expressly, that in the latter times some shall depart from the faith, giving heed to seducing spirits, and doctrines of devils.' "

Thus, as a child and adolescent, Marvin Gaye witnessed his father abandon his spiritual obsessions for other, more worldly matters. Gay Sr. was a divided soul. As an adult, Marvin mirrored the same division. During half his son's childhood, Father fervently preached; during the other half, he turned into an entirely different sort of man.

Marvin lived in fear of becoming his father, of taking on Father's characteristics.

"The perfect relationship," the singer said, "is the one between Jesus and his heavenly Father. That's the example all human relationships must follow. They were different, but Jesus and his Father were also the same. They transmitted to each other pure, divine love."

The absence of such a love from his earthly father became one of the towering frustrations of Gaye's life. Because Father had fallen from grace, Marvin, even as a boy, was afraid that he, too, would fall. As his life unfolded before him, the inevitability of that fall became clearer, and the fear more intense.

3

SEXUAL CONFUSION

Feelings of sexual inadequacy permeated the life of Marvin Gaye, Jr. Complicating matters even more was his father's sexual ambivalence. Both men saw sex as a dangerous force that threatened and finally destroyed their peace of mind and the virtuous life they aspired to lead.

Dewey Hughes, now an entertainment business executive, went to Randall Junior High School with Marvin and lived in the same neighborhood. He knew him well between the ages of twelve and fourteen.

"Like many of us, Marvin was a boy in pain. He was into singing—that was something you could never kid him about—and he was also very shy, very afraid of girls. He wore his sensitivity on his sleeve. I don't think there's any doubt that he was ashamed of his father. We'd never be invited inside Marvin's home, no matter what. It was evident to us that Mr. Gay was a flamboyant and extremely effeminate man. Marvin was kidded about that by the older kids. To be called a sissy or have your father called a sissy was the lowest insult. In the ghetto, the cats were the cruelest. Putting you in the Dozens—those games of verbal abuse—triggered bloody fights. But Marvin wasn't a fighter. Rather than express his anger, he absorbed it."

A strong sexual ambiguity surrounding Mr. Gay was something

I'd noticed the first time I met him in 1979. Though at the time Marvin was forty, in his reluctance to have me knock on his father's bedroom door I sensed the same shame Dewey Hughes mentioned in describing Marvin at twelve. In each of our interviews, Mr. Gay wore at least one unusual article of clothing—a lacy blouselike shirt or a pair of flowery socks. His speech and body language were soft and overtly feminine.

"Mr. Gay," said Dewey Hughes, "was definitely a show. He sought and liked attention."

"My father," Marvin told me in Europe in 1982 during a discussion of "Sexual Healing," "likes to wear women's clothing. As you well know, that doesn't mean he's homosexual. In fact, my father was always known as a ladies' man. He simply likes to dress up. What he does in private, I really don't know—nor do I care to know. You met him at a time when he was relatively cool about it. There have been other periods when his hair was very long and curled under, and when he seemed quite adamant in showing the world the girlish side of himself. That may have been to further embarrass me. I find the situation all the more difficult because, to tell you the truth, I have the same fascination with women's clothes. In my case, that has nothing to do with any attraction for men. Sexually, men don't interest me. But seeing myself as a woman is something that intrigues me. It's also something I fear. I indulge myself only at the most discreet and intimate moments. Afterward, I must bear the guilt and shame for weeks. After all, indulgence of the flesh is wicked, no matter what your kick. The hot stuff is lethal. I've never been able to stay away from the hot stuff."

Shame and guilt haunted Marvin as a child. "I wanted to beat the shit out of the guys when they teased me about Father," Marvin said. "I wanted to smash their faces and cut their throats, but I was afraid. I suppose I was afraid that I was just like him—that I was too much of a woman to fight back. Instead of taking my blows like a man, I ran. My main memories of growing up have to do with running. And, believe me, I was fast. I loved sports, and I always felt that I had great athletic ability—football, basketball, you name it—but I was scared of the confrontations, so I backed off."

Did he believe his father was homosexual?

"I didn't know. I didn't want to know. I just drove the thought out of my mind."

I asked Mrs. Gay the same question about her husband.

"I'm not certain. I do know that five of his siblings were homosexual. And it's true that he liked soft clothing. Soft things of all kinds attracted him. He liked to wear my panties, my shoes, my gowns, even my nylon hose. Marvin would see him like that sometimes."

Confusion about manhood would become another great theme in Marvin Gaye's life. His search for strong male role models led him into boxing rings and onto football fields while he fought to prove, fought to deny, fought to win his self-respect—gallant attempts which proved futile.

He was also convinced that he had inherited what he considered Father's streak of laziness. Gay Sr.'s chronic unemployment was another reason Marvin was so frustrated and angry with his father.

"I worked for the postal office," Mr. Gay told me, "as well as the Air Force and Western Union. But a back injury laid me off early. And I left Western Union because I absolutely refused to work on Saturday, the Sabbath."

Bishop Rawlings's memory was that Mr. Gay worked very little. And according to Beatrice Carson, it was Mrs. Gay who supported the family:

"Babe and I both worked as domestics. We'd cook and take care of the kids, we'd mop and clean and do whatever was needed. During the winters, we'd stand on the corner when it was fifteen degrees with freezing sleet and snow coming down while we waited for the bus to take us to Maryland or Virginia. I never did know Mr. Gay to work."

"I'd wake up four or five in the morning to go out to work," Mrs. Gay remembered, "while my children and husband stayed in bed. I didn't have any choice. I had to bring in the food, and I did. I'm proud of myself. I kept my family alive."

"My mother used to tell me a story," Frankie Gay remembered, "about two mice drowning in a cup of milk. One complained and panicked and screamed and finally went under. The other one calmly kept kicking and kicking until the milk turned to cream and the cream turned to butter and the little mouse just walked on out. Mother had faith. She believed in hard work. Father didn't."

"I remember Mr. Gay telling me of a job he had held for a very short time," said Bishop Solomon. "He said he worked as a chauffeur for the government. I never will forget the reason he gave for leaving. He told me he had very tender feet."

"All told," Jeanne Gay remembered, "I don't think Father worked for much more than three years—if that much."

"Among the several sins I got from Father," Marvin stated, "is a love of loafing. Neither of us particularly likes to work. The difference is, I finally made money while nothing—not even the sight of Mother cleaning rich people's toilets for slave wages—could ever motivate Father to abandon his life of leisure. Oh, he had it made! The king! The king and his secret life!"

If Marvin saw Father as a king, he quickly began perceiving himself as a prince.

"Did Babe spoil Marvin?" Mrs. Carson asked herself. "I know we all tried our best to protect him from his father. He needed a lot of affection, that boy did, and I don't see how his mother could have done anything else but smother him with love. Besides, Marvin was the kind of boy you couldn't help but love."

"Mother was a devout church member," Jeanne said. "She believed those teachings of the House of God which insisted that a woman be submissive to her husband. Her religious convictions obligated her to obey Father, no matter what."

"Mother was caught in between," Marvin explained. "She was too afraid of Father to openly defy him. He might strike her. He might put her out. But as time went on, she quickly saw that I was going to be able to do something for her that Father couldn't—give her money. As a kid, I thought of robbing banks so she wouldn't have to work night and day to provide for us. But I couldn't do that. I wasn't raised that way. You must understand that I was a good boy. In Simple City the Gays might have been perceived as strange, but we were looked up to. We lived by principles. Mother especially. Her kindness and generosity were legendary. She took in people and fed neighbors, even when we were still dirt poor. The woman suffered so, and yet her suffering seemed to make her stronger. The older I've gotten, the more I've wished that all women could be like my mother."

A fixation on Mother remained a permanent part of Gaye's psyche. To please, support, and protect her was a need and desire that dominated every phase of his life. Marvin measured all other women against Mother, whom he saw as purity and perfection. In his sight, no other woman, save his father's wife, would ever make him happy.

His search for the ideal female, someone whose patience and approval of him knew no limits, dominated Marvin's romantic imagination. At the first sign of a woman's imperfection, Gaye despaired, often growing violent, unable to accept the fact that his view of the mythically untainted woman was shattered.

4

STIMULATION

As an adolescent, Marvin was stimulated by the overriding powers of sex and singing. Those two preoccupations often merged into a single psychological force which brought both pleasure and fear as Marvin sought the courage to move from fantasy to performance.

Singing was something that pleased his mother. She was far more tolerant than her husband of secular music, and, throughout her son's life, she encouraged his singing and approved of his ambition to become a popular recording artist.

On the other hand, though Father appreciated blues and jazz, he considered it devilish. His church had absolute views on the subject. "The House of God," he told me, "can never really approve of any music that does not praise God."

Marvin's first forays into nonreligious singing were, at least in part, a defiance of Father. As a preacher's son, Gaye felt alienated from the normal world of teenagers who played baseball in sandlots and kissed girls on park benches. Music was a way for Marvin to ease into that world, to gain acceptance while expressing his romantic soul.

"Junior high," remembered Dewey Hughes, "was when the serious singing began. In the hallways, between classes, all the time. There was a fascinating relationship between sex and singing. Those of us who were musically inclined were looked upon with suspicion.

A lot of the guys thought we were sissies. They were also jealous that our singing attracted the girls. It was pretty singing, very soft and melodic. In our neighborhood, when cats no older then eleven used to boast that they were already going all the way with girls, Marvin and I were still virgins when we started school—though we'd never admit it."

"Around the ages of twelve and thirteen," Marvin reflected, "I became fascinated with masturbation. Naturally, this was normal, though at the time I didn't know that. I didn't compare notes with the other boys, but I've a feeling I was a much heavier masturbator than the average teenager. I'd try to get myself to stop, but once I discovered how fantasy feeds feeling, I was gone. I knew it was wrong, and I promised God I'd never touch myself again. The promises never lasted more than a day. I remember feeling the shivering release of my first orgasm and understanding that in my life the pleasures of the devil were going to give the joys of God some mighty stiff competition."

In 1954, the Gays made their first move. The buildings around First Street were being torn down, and the family was sent to a new group of projects in the far northeast quadrant of the city, smack against the Maryland district line—the East Capitol Dwellings.

The two-story apartment at 10 Sixtieth Street was somewhat nicer than what the Gays had known before, certainly newer, and built in the same red-brick garden-court style. But their level of income hadn't risen. Mrs. Gay still worked as a domestic while her husband stayed home.

Geraldine Trice Adams, called Peasie, lived down the street and became a close friend and protector of Marvin's.

"It didn't look like Marvin's daddy ever worked too much," said Peasie. "He'd sit on the porch and water the lawn. He was a little snarly and Lord knows he stayed on Marvin's case. Seemed like Mr. Gay was riding the gravy train. Just to pass the time during the days, he'd ride the bus all the way to the White House and back. Sometimes he'd bring Kool Aid to the construction workers or bus drivers. He was definitely the neighborhood character, always dressed sharp, sometimes in wigs, sometimes in shorts and V-neck T-shirts. Not that he didn't have class. We always thought that the Gays—all of them—were very classy, educated people.

They stood out, they spoke well, and Marvin's mama had an especially kind heart.

"I remember how Mr. Gay used to kick Marvin out of the house. Happened all the time. Marvin became a floater. He'd hide out and you'd never be sure of where he was staying. Sometimes he'd come stay with us. Well, his mama would be so worried that she'd slip me money for Marvin. 'Don't tell his daddy,' she'd say, 'but just make sure my boy gets this.' "

"By the time I was ready to start high school," Marvin said, "things between me and Father turned from bad to worse. I'd reached physical maturity. Even though I'd grown taller and stronger than Father, he was still beating me. I wanted to strike back, but where I come from, even to raise your hand to your father is an invitation for him to kill you. Father became stricter, demanding that I conform to his ridiculous curfew rules. If I came home a minute late, it was like I'd defied all ten commandments. The more demanding Father became, the more rebellious I grew."

"In the fifties," Mrs. Gay told me, "my husband started drinking heavily. That didn't help him get along any better with Marvin. He never did develop any love for the boy."

"He often threatened to disown me," Marvin remembered, "or ban me from the house. I retaliated by reminding him that the apartment really belonged to Mother, since she was the one paying the rent. He hated hearing that. 'You're running around with bums,' he'd say, 'and you're going to wind up a bum.' Actually, the bums he referred to were other kids who loved to sing. But Father knew how to touch a nerve. You see, I've always admired bums. Bums are able to forget all sense of responsibility. People laugh when I tell them I've always wanted to be a bum. It's just that certain things got in the way. I might have been a bum if I wasn't so determined to be a pop singer," said Marvin, who sometimes referred to his father as a bum.

What happened to the spiritual singing, to Marvin's sense of himself as a divine messenger?

"I've often wondered about that. Perhaps if Father had stayed in the church, I would have stayed with him. But I don't want to blame him. The biblical information he taught us would always stay with me. By the time I was thirteen or fourteen, I still felt the call, I still believed in Jesus, but by then so many sorts of music were buzzing in my ear. Other musical voices were stronger."

Thus Marvin, somewhat guilty about leaving church music behind, stepped out into the fifties, into a world of secular singing. One word describes the bewitching style which, together with gospel, blues, and jazz, would shape the future course of Marvin Gaye's music: doo-wop.

In August 1949, a new chapter in the history of black music began when Sonny Til and his Orioles played a smash two-week engagement at the Apollo Theatre in Harlem. Originally known as the Vibranaires, the five-man group renamed itself after the local ball team, the Orioles, thus starting a decade-long fad of bird names. They were from Baltimore, just up the road from D.C., and Marvin cherished memories of listening to them chirp on their home turf.

Influenced by the Ink Spots before them, the Orioles were nonetheless original and harmonically far more complex than the popular black groups—the Mills Brothers, the Cats and the Fiddle, the Ravens—who preceded them. Their singing also displayed great emotional depth.

The fifties would develop comical groups like the Robins and the Coasters. Rhythmical, soaring singers such as the Drifters would have an enormous impact on Marvin. His lifelong penchant for dazzling, dense harmonies, however, was born out of the pioneering work of the Orioles and later singers like the Capris, the Cadillacs, and Lee Andrews and the Hearts.

It wasn't only for technical reasons that these innovative groups excited Marvin's musical imagination; it was also their melancholy which touched his soul. The emotions in the music corresponded to Gaye's decidedly sultry moods; the ultrasensitive songs spoke to his own loneliness, his pained alienation from his family, and, most of all, his sense of unrequited love, a theme which would haunt him until the day of his death.

Doo-wop, with its sparse instrumentation—the Orioles accompanied themselves with simple guitar and soft string bass—mirrored the bare bones of teenage hurt, fear, and innocence. Twin themes ran through this music, both of which made Marvin realize that popular singing could serve as an outlet for his own unarticulated yearnings: the hope for pure, untainted love and, correspondingly, the desire to elevate such a love, to sanctify it with a divinity which transcended sex.

"Beyond sex," Gaye loved to say, "is God."

In Marvin's mind, God was also the force that blessed romantic singing.

"We had a little neighborhood vocal group," said Marvin's friend Peasie from the East Capitol projects, "and the song Marvin always asked me to sing was 'Heavenly Father,' a big hit then by Edna McGriff."

" 'God Only Knows' by the Capris," Marvin recalled, "nearly killed me. It was a monster. It fell from the heavens and hit me between the eyes. So much soul, so much hurt. I related to the story, to the way that no one except the Lord really can read the heart of lonely kids in love. It wasn't that I was in love with a particular girl. I wasn't. I was still too shy to approach girls and still too afraid they didn't like me. I was in love with the idea of love. I'd fantasize."

Marvin entered the Church of Holy Doo-Wop, where he prayed at the altar of pure love, love removed from the stress of the material world. His devotion was absolute. The virtues of faith and fidelity could be felt in the Capris' "She Still Loves Me Because Heaven Tells Me So," "Bless You for Being an Angel," and in the words of the Orioles' "Crying in the Moonlight," where the devoted lover waits for his woman until "moonlight turns to dust."

"Lonely Room" by Lee Andrews and the Hearts, another song Marvin mentioned, expressed the intensely depressive nature which characterized a great deal of doo-wop. "Abide by the Golden Rule" by the same group showed what Gaye found so attractive about this rich vein of music—the exact enunciation, the plaintive phrasing, and the yearning for God.

"Remember the Turbans?" Marvin asked, chuckling at the memory. "These cats actually wore turbans and sang up a storm. They had this one song, 'Please Let Me Show You Around My Heart,' with lyrics comparing an empty house to an open heart. That's when I understood language. It wasn't anything they tried to teach me in high school. Language was true feelings, coming from kids like us who really believed that one wonderful girl would make us happy for the rest of our lives. We worshipped her with our singing. If we didn't already have her, we prayed for her. What was Percy Mayfield's prayer? 'Please Send Me Someone to Love.'

"It isn't that I wasn't interested in sex. I was. But women were meant to be put on a pedestal. Back then sex wasn't as free as it is today. The fifties messed up a lot of men. Things were tight. Morality was strict. And besides, Father's church was always there to show me the straight and narrow path."

Though Marvin no longer attended services at the House of God, he worshipped elsewhere, before a secular shrine: the Church of Holy Doo-Wop, a baroque cathedral which housed a wealth of important stylistic differences. There was Southern doo-wop, New York doo-wop, a Los Angeles sound, and a distinct Washington style.

"The thing about D.C. doo-wop," explained singer Herb Fame, who grew up in the District in the same era as Marvin, "is that we were a combination of that thick, molasses Southern style—like the Five Royales—and that tougher but still polished New York thing being done by the Solitaires. D.C. is on the borderline, and everything and everyone passed on through. We're right there by the Mason-Dixon Line where North meets South. We were blessed to pick up the best of everything."

The hybrid combination of styles that would typify Marvin Gaye's work can be heard in another Washingtonian, another complex musical figure who came forty years earlier and played and wrote everything from jump tunes and blues to pop ballads and sacred suites. Like Marvin, Duke Ellington's creativity was singular, yet his most brilliant work was achieved through collaboration. Much the way Ellington's band would be characterized by the strong bottom of Harry Carney's booming baritone sax, so would D.C. doo-wop carry the same identity.

"You knew our groups by the powerful bass," reported Lawrence Berry, a lifetime Washington resident, singer, local musical historian, and friend of Marvin's from the old days. "The bass had to be true. A lot of groups in New York did doubling—two singers singing the same notes. But down here we had five singers singing five different notes. Maybe it's all these churches around here or maybe it's 'cause Washington is the capital. We've always had a dignity about our music. It could never be simple. We heard too much to ever compromise."

"I had a group called the Dreamtones," said Herb Fame whose successful singing career with Peaches and Herb in the midsixties would parallel Marvin's romantic duets with Tammi Terrell. "Man, there were more groups than birds in the trees. The Clovers came out of Washington, and so did Van McCoy. He was one of the main men behind the disco craze in the seventies. Back in the fifties, he had a group called the Starlighters. The competition was thick enough to cut with a knife."

Reese Palmer was also a neighbor of Marvin's in the East Capitol projects and soon became his best friend. "I read somewhere that Marvin began in the Rainbows," Reese said. "That's not true. Don Covay and James Nolan—he'd wind up singing with us—came out of the Rainbows, but not Marvin."

"People say I'm an old doo-wopper, and it's certainly true," Marvin commented. "Just don't forget, though, that of the four singers who influenced me most, only two could be considered group singers.

"The big four were Rudy West, Clyde McPhatter, Little Willie John, and Ray Charles.

"Now Rudy, who sang the ballads with the Five Keys, was the cat who sang 'Out of Sight, Out of Mind.' He had a pure, satin style that thrilled me. McPhatter was an all-around master. I first heard him do 'Harbor Lights' when he was with Billy Ward and the Dominoes. That destroyed me. His voice had a power and beauty I greatly admired. Little Willie John, who wasn't associated with a group, cut the original on 'Fever.' He had this silky edge of sexy danger which I dug. Ray Charles reminded us all where we came from. Of course his early hits, like 'I Got a Woman,' were nothing but church. I liked that. I liked the sweat in his voice, and I liked his raw soul. But don't make the mistake of thinking that my musical background was all black. I'm sensitive to every sound around, and there was nothing I heard that didn't influence me."

"One of my earliest memories," said Reese Palmer, "is Marvin in the projects recreation center singing 'Cry' and doing a near-perfect imitation of Johnnie Ray. First time me and Marvin started talking about singing he said he wanted to do pop, like Sinatra, and he never did change his mind."

"My dream," Marvin confessed, "was to become Frank Sinatra. I loved his phrasing, especially when he was very young and pure. He grew into a fabulous jazz singer and I used to fantasize about having a lifestyle like his—carrying on in Hollywood and becoming a movie star. Every woman in America wanted to go to bed with Frank Sinatra. He was the king I longed to be. My greatest dream was to satisfy as many women as Sinatra. He was the heavyweight champ, the absolute.

"Now this is going to surprise you, but I also dug Dean Martin and especially Perry Como. They weren't monster singers, but I liked their relaxed presentation. Perry had a great attitude. When I finally got some money together over at Motown in the sixties, I used to sport Perry Como sweaters. I always felt like my personality and Perry's had a lot in common."

The female singer who made the deepest impression upon him was Billie Holiday.

"Her pain is what got to me," Marvin said. "Billie turned herself inside out, all in the name of love. She was deeper than sex. The hurt she felt was the hurt of all humanity. Great artists suffer for the people. The greatest artist was Jesus, and the rest of us can only imitate his perfect suffering.

"I remember listening to Billie's album *Lady in Satin* with tears rolling down my cheeks. I memorized every last lick. She phrased like a jazz horn, and that intrigued me. Somewhere in the fifties I also got hooked on Miles Davis, especially the way he played ballads through his mute. His 'It Never Entered My Mind' killed me. Miles cried like a singer, and Billie sang like an instrumentalist, and everything they both did was wrapped in the blues."

Gaye's appreciation of jazz and Jesus would help mold his artistic identity. His musical sophistication, his ear for the subtleties of jazz phrasing, distinguished him from his colleagues, just as his identification with Jesus—the loving Jesus, the suffering Jesus—deepened his emotional range.

Reese and Marvin went to Cardoza High School together where they formed their first group, the D.C. Tones. Their lead singer was Sondra Lattisaw, whose daughter Stacy is today a successful pop vocalist.

Sondra's dark eyes smiled when she remembered the Marvin Gaye she knew in high school:

"He was different. You sensed that right away. Extremely sensitive and very lonely. Marvin was definitely a loner. No girlfriends, and not the kind of fella who'd hit on girls either. He had fine manners, and you could tell he had real breeding. He used to wear his pants real baggy—I remember that—and he was always neat and well-groomed. He was a gentleman. Fact is, all the time he was in our group I didn't know he could sing, 'cause he was strictly playing piano. Marvin had a perfect ear and played just beautifully. I suppose he was too shy to sing."

Among the black kids back in the neighborhood, the fifties in D.C. was an age of hot curlers, outrageous conks, and do rags. The crowd was greasing up and straightening out their hair. It was a time when Little Lord Fauntleroy Bandy ruled the airwaves at WUST, when the gang spent Saturday night at the Kalarama Road Skating Rink or Wilmer's Park or the Booker T. Movie Theater or Sparrow's Beach in Maryland. The city's great cultural cathedral was a small, intimate movie house that also featured live musical revues. The Howard Theater, at Seventeenth and T, was part of the first-run show circuit that included the Apollo in New York and the Regal in Chicago.

"The Howard," Marvin explained, "was my real high school. I studied the singers like my life depended on it. When I saw Sam Cooke and Jesse Belvin I'd try to avoid my friends and family for days. I didn't want to talk or be talked to 'cause I was busy practicing and memorizing everything I heard those singers do. The shows were knockouts. Cats like the Cadillacs could really step. James Brown was opening for Little Willie John in those days, and between James and Jackie Wilson, I knew I could never be a sure-enough stage performer."

"We were just living to sing back then," said Reese Palmer. "We didn't even know the first thing about dope. Worst thing me and Marvin used to do was smoke cigarettes. He taught me on Viceroys. There were fights, and you knew not to go into strange neighborhoods, but there wasn't the kind of killing you see today.

"There was a bully on our block, Donald Morgan—we called him Zoot—and he 'bout scared Marvin to death. 'Don't worry about Zoot,' I'd tell Marvin, 'just keep singing.' With all these other groups making moves around us, we had to keep rehearsing and learning new tunes off the radio."

"Feeling inadequate has always been my biggest problem." Marvin was able to analyze himself with the objectivity of a clinical psychologist. "My voice is basically created in my throat, and there I was, surrounded by full-bodied singers, boys who could sing from their diaphragms. If you'd ever teach these cats Italian, they'd be opera stars. Billy Stewart, for instance, the guy we called Fat Udy, well, he and his brother John had incredibly full voices. At a very young age, Billy owned a wholly original style, almost a way of stuttering, jazz-like, through a song. I was always afraid that I had no style. Compared to the other fellas on the street, my voice sounded small. It took me a long time just to open my mouth, and when I did, I was sure I'd be slapped down by the singer next to me. Besides, the kind of vocalist I wanted to be—pure pop—was almost always a baritone. All the famous ones, like Tony Bennett and Nat Cole, had deeper voices than mine."

Insecurity was the flip side of Marvin's megalomania. His feelings of inadequacy, especially in relation to other men, often involved size. In some part of his mind, he equated musical masculinity with vocal muscle—the deeper, the bigger, the better. In truth, though, his own voice was flexible enough to achieve the he-man sound he sought. At the same time, his singing could be gentle and flowery. The one constant element in all Gaye's styles, however, was the presence of pain.

"Pain," Marvin liked to say, "is just another word for fear. True believers have no fears. That means not doubting yourself or your God. When I was a kid, my doubts were greater than my beliefs. Maybe that's why today I have this bleeding heart."

Pain permeated his music, just as it permeated his life. The pain of his childhood—the physical pain of Father's beatings, the emotional pain of feeling unloved and unwanted by Father—left Marvin scarred and, in many ways, incapable of dealing with the spectacular success he fought so hard to achieve. Finally, ironically, he rebelled against his own success just as passionately as he rebelled against his own father.

5

COMING OF AGE

By age fifteen, Marvin was growing restless. He was developing a sensitive awareness and distinct skepticism about the city and society in which he lived. He no longer took things for granted. He no longer believed what he was taught. He began to understand that racial discrimination surrounded him, and, with greater frequency, he rebelled against the society that permitted it.

Academically, he did considerably poorer in high school than junior high, where, according to his teacher Mary Turner, he'd sung in the boys choir and been a member of the honor society.

"I couldn't concentrate any longer," Marvin said. "Nothing seemed more important than music. I didn't want to listen to my teachers. I started challenging their authority. I was tired of being a goody-goody. I'd wait for the bell to ring at the end of the class, jump up and sing my way down the halls with the other guys. We'd be jamming in the lunchroom, in the playgrounds, and on the bus home. Man, we'd skip school all the time just to hang out and sing. School was jail. Learning all the supposedly wonderful lessons of American history, and knowing deep inside that they're lies."

"Growing up black in Washington," Marvin's friend, Dewey Hughes, pointed out, "was a unique experience. Unlike other ghettos, ours was backed up to all the buildings and institutions dedicated to lofty American principles. That drove us a little crazy. From our junior high school, you'd see the Capitol dome and be reminded of what it stood for. Then after school, Marvin and I would be chased from a public playground by an official screaming, 'Get out! This is for whites only!' "

From the windows of Cardoza, Marvin had a commanding view of the city's major monuments. "Schoolkids in D.C. were taken on tours of all those places," Marvin explained. "I remember visiting the Washington, Lincoln, and Jefferson memorials at different ages. I could appreciate the grandeur of the architecture. But I had the distinct feeling that these marvelous treasures belonged to white people. It was as though we could look but not touch, and never, never own. Coming up when I did, it was tough not to be cynical about America. The Washington schools were segregated and so were the restaurants and movies. I don't remember ever having a white teacher. How's the average black kid supposed to buy the Bill of Rights when he sees on the street that his own rights aren't worth shit?"

Marvin's antagonism toward the government began at an early age. In time, his sense of political alienation would intensify to the point where he refused to pay taxes. Along with his wives and father, the U.S. government—especially the IRS—would become one of his chief adversaries.

"I wouldn't say Marvin was angry in high school," Reese Palmer observed. "I'd call him shrewd and very aware. I guess we both considered school a waste of time. Marvin and I should have graduated in 1956. Instead, we both quit after the eleventh grade. I worked and Marvin did something that surprised a lot of people. But you know Marvin, he was always full of surprises."

Gaye's relationship with official America took a new turn when he decided to enlist.

"Why did I run off and join the Air Force?" Marvin asked himself, pausing before answering the question. "I suppose I thought I was being bold. I fancied myself a flyer—like Errol Flynn with an ascot tied around his neck—but oddly enough I've always been petrified of flying. Perhaps this was the ultimate dare. Anyway, I was sick to death of Father's household. I had to get out. Besides, I didn't have the concentration to make it through high school. I was afraid of failing. I knew I couldn't live up to Father's standards."

Gay Sr. would later tell a different story. He claimed that he gave his son an ultimatum: either join the armed service or finish high school and start college.

"It was my dream," Gay Sr. told me, "that Marvin become a lawyer. It was a dream that I once had for myself. I could see myself arguing before a jury or even going before the Supreme Court. Maybe it's my religious background, but I've always been interested in the interpretation of law. Marvin has the mind of a lawyer, and if he hadn't been distracted he could have made an outstanding attorney. That would have been a first for our family. Short of that, I didn't want him on the streets. I insisted that he enlist."

According to Marvin, though, enlisting was an act of defiance, not obedience.

"There have been times," said Gaye, "when I laughed about Father's expectations and times when I've cried. How could I even think about being a lawyer when I didn't even have the chops to finish high school? It was ridiculous. On the other hand, Father was right. He knew that he and I had similar dispositions. Throughout my career, I've been drawn to legal issues. I can study them like the Bible. My father taught me how to read carefully and interpret moral law. By the time I left Motown, I had learned to negotiate for myself. Nothing against any of the lawyers, but I felt like my legal skills were as great as theirs. The only man I've met who's a sharper negotiator may be Berry Gordy, and on good days, I might give Berry a run for his money. All negotiation means, of course, is getting the best of your opponents. These are the games that men play."

Marvin did have a keen analytical mind, though he exaggerated his—and Father's—erudition. Both men expressed a certain intellectual arrogance, overcompensating for their lack of formal education by claiming expertise in a wide range of subjects, from politics to philosophy. "My father is a know-it-all," Gaye once said to me, "and I'm afraid I'm no different."

Feeling guilty and ashamed for not finishing high school, Marvin saw the Air Force as an easy escape. It wasn't; it was a disastrous experience. Marvin not only failed to adjust but found himself in open rebellion against authority. His extreme sensitivity smashed against a brick wall of regimentation.

"I felt betrayed," he said. "I went in to learn to fly and wound up peeling potatoes on some God-forsaken bases in Kansas, Texas, and Wyoming. The recruiting sergeant promised I'd be in the special services. He didn't tell me I'd be doing menial tasks. I wasn't made for menial tasks. I was completely unprepared and found it impossible to take orders from pompous assholes with nothing better to do than humiliate me. I felt like I'd been tricked. KP became an issue. They said I had to do it. I said I'd think about it and maybe do it tomorrow. Since no one talks that way in the service, they called me crazy. It became a nightmare. They'd say cough, and I'd shout. They'd say sit, and I'd stand. Instead of flying airplanes, I was washing 'em and filling 'em with gas. I thought those jobs were beneath me, and I told them so. I even wrote my superior officer a long letter about everything that was wrong with the Air Force. He flipped. Oh man, the way I carried on in the Air Force was ridiculous! They threw cold water on me, they threw me in the can, they stayed on my ass. After eight or nine months, I thought, 'To hell with this shit; I'm going home.' It wasn't that easy, though. I had to prove I was crazy. I began by faking a crazy attitude, but in the end, believe me, it was no act. My discharge was honorable, although it plainly stated, 'Marvin Gay cannot adjust to regimentation and authority.' "

His military experience showed, as Marvin later admitted, how spoiled he was. Whether he actually defied his commanding officers with the daring he claimed is uncertain. What's clear, though, was his absolute inability to fall in line.

"I couldn't wait to get out of the service," he said. "I can't think of one good thing that happened to me in the Air Force with the exception of finally getting laid. And even that was freaky."

Marvin lost his virginity to a prostitute, and thus ignited an obsessive interest in what he liked to call "love for sale."

"There was a crummy little cathouse outside the base. Four hookers for two thousand men. I was shaking in my boots and scared shitless about being able to get it up. It didn't help that the girl was fat. She was also impatient. She wanted me in and out in a hurry. I tried to tell her that I was a cherry, but words failed me. I can't even remember whether I actually got hard. I know I tried to fight my way through her fatty flesh, but then my mind won't remember any more. I felt betrayed. Sex was crude and frightening. Suddenly I could see a world of pure sex where people turned off their minds and fed their lusts, no questions asked. The concept sickened me, but I also found it exciting."

"Every man carries within him," wrote psychologist Carl Jung, "the eternal image of a woman, not the image of this or that particular woman, but a definitive feminine image. This image is fundamentally unconscious, an hereditary factor of primordial origin engraved in the living organic system of the man, an imprint or 'archetype' of all the ancestral experiences of the female, a deposit, as it were, of all the impressions ever made by woman. . . . Since this image is unconscious, it is always unconsciously projected upon the person of the beloved, and is one of the chief reasons for passionate attraction or aversion."

Marvin's archetypal woman was part holy, part corrupt, reflecting his own divided nature. The whore, both real and imagined—along with her counterpart, the idealized mother-madonna figure—would live at the center of his erotic imagination and later in his most serious musical work.

"I need prostitutes," Marvin confessed to the French magazine *Actuel* in 1983. "Prostitutes protect me from passion. Passions are dangerous. They cause you to lust after other men's wives."

A year before, in 1982, he claimed to have come close to actually marrying a prostitute while in Europe. At that time, he'd convinced himself that she alone could resolve his mushrooming sexual anguish.

Back in D.C. in 1957, Marvin was forced to return home from the Air Force a failure.

"At first I couldn't walk into Father's house. The situation hadn't changed. He wasn't working and Mother was and I hadn't done anything to help. I knew what he'd say. I knew how he'd laugh. So I just lived on the outside, crashing on friends' couches. When it became clear that I had to follow fate and sing for a living, there was even more reason to avoid Father. He'd see it as proof positive of my being a bum. As a man, I still hadn't made it. I was back on the streets of Washington, but my hustle vibe was serious. This show business thing had to work for me. I had nothing else."

The Marquees were formed just around this time and became Gaye's first singing venture as an adult.

"When Marvin returned from the Air Force in the summer of 1957," Reese remembered, "me, him, James Nolan, and Chester Simmons started the Marquees. Chester had just graduated from Cardoza. He sang bass. Nolan sang baritone, I was first tenor and Marvin second tenor. But Marvin also sang beautiful baritone harmony. Marvin could sing anything."

To some degree, the Marquees modeled themselves after the Moonglows, whose 1955 "Sincerely" was a doo-wop classic. Gaye claimed that the Marquees were named after Marquis de Sade. "That's the root of my sadomasochism," he joked. The truth, though, Marvin later confessed, is that in the fifties he hadn't heard of de Sade.

"In my adult life," he said, "the Marquis would become a fascinating character of evil. I identified with his wicked ways. He had a power to raise the blood pressure. He fulfilled fantasies. As prince of darkness, he wasn't afraid of the hot stuff. There were days—nights, weeks, months—when, I, too, played the role. But God had blessed me with a voice to touch the hearts of people. I'd been instructed to spread love, not lust. And in those days, my innocence kept me away from evil."

"We played sock hops, school assemblies, anywhere we could," Reese explained. "Once we even went on the Milt Grant Show, one of those TV teen things. Nothing really happened, though, until we met Bo Diddley."

"I introduced the boys to Bo," said Peasie, who proved to be not only a devoted friend but valuable connection for the Marquees. "Bo used to run through the projects, eating those shelled pecans, and I told him, I said, 'Bo, we got some boys around here who can shout a little.' "

"We used to go down to Bo's basement over there on 2600 Rhode Island Avenue and jam like crazy," Reese remembered. "Bo was just the man we needed."

Marvin called Bo Diddley the first genuine star he ever knew. His real name was Ellas McDaniel, he hailed from Mississippi, and his main model was Muddy Waters. "I'm classed as a Negro but I'm not," Bo once said. "I'm what you call a black Frenchman, a Creole. All my people are from New Orleans, the bayou country. I like gumbo. Hot sauces, too. That's where my music comes from, all the mixture." His scorching midfifties hits "I'm a Man" and "Bo Diddley" startled an "I Like Ike" culture lulled to sleep by Mantovanni and "How Much Is That Doggie in the Window?"

"I loved Bo," Marvin told me, an open smile playing upon his lips as he told the story. "Meeting him was a very important moment in my life. Bo was a rhythmic genius. Like James Brown, he was a certified witch doctor. He was also able to write out of his own experiences. His songs said exactly what he was thinking. I admired that, and I admired his manliness. Bo had a kind of swampfire fever. He was a tower, and we were grateful to God that he decided to live in the District for a hot minute."

Like Louis Armstrong joining King Oliver, Marvin's relationship with Bo Diddley would critically alter his musical being. Diddley was one of the great root sources of American music. His brilliant rock and roll primitivism—the sensual shout, the blistering beat— strengthened Marvin's ties to the country church and blues tradition.

"Bo produced our first record date," Reese recalled. "He took us to New York where the Marquees cut our one and only single— 'Wyatt Earp' and 'Hey, Little School Girl'—for Okeh, which was part of Columbia. I wrote 'Wyatt' and sang lead on both songs. Bo brought his band from D.C. with Billy Stewart, also one of Bo's discoveries, on piano. The New York people didn't like the sound, so we recut it with some heavy cats like Sam the Man Taylor and Panama Francis. Didn't matter, though, 'cause the Silhouettes came out with 'Get a Job' that year and buried us."

Heavily influenced by the Robins and the Coasters, these songs are the essence of undistinguished fifties black rock and roll— whimsical, upbeat, and spirited. "Hey, Little School Girl" is a bouncy expression of high school horniness, while "Wyatt Earp," a novelty, pays tribute to the era's great TV hero.

"Marvin and me," Reese said, "would sit up in front of a television set for hours. Matter of fact, that's how he wrote his first song, 'Barbara.' He stole the melody from the theme of *The Perry Mason Show*."

From the start, Gaye admitted, there was no doubt that he wanted to steal the Marquees show. Sharing the spotlight was always painful for Marvin, and in these early years he resented being simply one of the singers. During live performances, for example, James Nolan sang lead, much to Gaye's chagrin. As a result, a deep and bitter rivalry developed between them.

"I'd been wanting to sing lead since we started the group," Marvin admitted. "I was never the team member I should have been. Given my nature, it's impossible for me not to compete with other singers, even if they are my partners, and especially if they're good. James Nolan was good."

The group itself was good. Why, then, did their initial recording fail? It may have been due to the unoriginality of their material and also because of the direction in which Bo Diddley was pushing them. For all his musical acumen, Diddley tapped the group's least powerful energy—their rhythmic drive. Bo had the Marquees rocking, and the Marquees, as time would prove, would make their mark crooning. They were melodists and harmonizers, and it would take a different kind of producer to push them into the national spotlight.

The record failed commercially. Chester Simmons left the group to become Bo Diddley's driver. Gaye's frustrations grew. His pride was wounded. There was no hit song for his father to hear, no money earned. He and Palmer were forced to find menial labor—first as stockboys, then dishwashers at People's Drugstore. The lunch-counter dishwashing job was especially demeaning, since the eating area was for whites only. Marvin and Reese were told to eat their lunch outside on a bus bench.

"I hated Washington," said Marvin, who would later disown the city. "The place filled me with a feeling of hopelessness. Nothing happened in Washington. Nothing was made or produced or sold. It was all government, papers, bureaucrats, and bullshit. Here was a city blessed with musical talent and no place to record, no real labels or promoters or distributors."

By 1958, Gaye and the Marquees were itching for a chance to escape the District. They were ready to play in the major leagues. And with just as much desire, Marvin dreamt of fleeing from his father.

"The thing with Father grew worse by the day. I'd sneak home for a day or two, grab some food or money from Mother, and then slip out again. He didn't want to see me and I didn't want to see him. Mother believed in my singing. Father was waiting for me to fall on my ass."

Lack of confidence would always remain one of Marvin's biggest problems. He spent his life looking for his Father's blessing. Because the blessing was denied, he could never have enough love. Certain that girls found him strange—as strange, he feared, as his own father—he hid behind a shyness which, ironically, women found seductive.

"Girls loved Marvin's style," Reese said. "When he sang the Spaniels' 'Baby, It's You,' they nearly tore him apart. In his own quiet way, he drove the girls crazy."

"It was a power that frightened me," Marvin recalled. "I didn't know I had it, because, to be truthful, it didn't happen by design. I'm a sensualist by nature. As a kid, I didn't really get any girls, but I bragged. I even lied about it. My singing covered up for the action I wasn't getting. It always has. If I'm a sexy singer, though, I think it has to do with something deeper than sex. I saw that I was reaching these girls on a mystical level. Almost like I was one of them."

The quality of female vulnerability is a key, I believe, to a great deal of Marvin Gaye's vocal success. Part of his musical psyche identified with the robust machismo of Bo Diddley. But the finer side of his sensibility, the subtle side, identified with women. Like many pop singers before him—Sam Cooke and Frankie Lymon, Johnny Mathis and Jesse Belvin—his sweetness, to turn around a Barry White phrase, was women's weakness. Softly and gently, he won their hearts, matching their emotional sensitivity with his own. In fact, Marvin often sounded like a woman; he was a vocalist who, by exposing his vulnerability, reached into the souls of women.

Once I told him that I thought the woman within him was the true artist. He blanched and replied, "I don't like that idea."

The notion of possessing female qualities, even positive ones, irritated Gaye by bringing Father to mind.

"There's a difference," he continued, "between reaching a woman with your song and reaching her with your body. One is fantasy and the other's reality. If you're a singer who's also a sex symbol, you're likely to confuse the two. When I was a kid, if I was singing to a room full of girls, I could work it so any one of them—every one of them—could be mine. That was a heavy burden to bear."

Successfully seducing women was one thing, but satisfying them sexually was another. Early on, Gaye saw himself as a Superman who was afraid of flying. Yet once established, he felt compelled to maintain his image as the ultimate lover. He convinced himself that it was the only way women would accept him.

"I used to call Marvin a red-boned specialist," Reese said. "He liked high-yellow women. That was the thing back then."

"My mother is light-skinned and quite beautiful," Marvin believed. "No other woman ever looked as good to me as Mother. It was very hard breaking away from her. Slowly, as I stepped out and saw the world, I'd start having girlfriends. It was never serious, though—not while I was still in Washington. Because I'd been so

terribly lonely and afraid as a child, I clung to that loneliness like
an old teddy bear. My sexual technique left lots to be desired. In
those days, I assumed that all the other guys knew more than me.
I talked big, 'cause I didn't want anyone accusing me of being a
sissy. It wasn't just about Father, it had to do with my brother
Frankie. Not only was his sexual apparatus a lot larger than mine,
he also had a very good voice. His size worried me, and there was
no telling how big his talent might be."

"I was always asking Marvin to let Frankie sing with us, but
Marvin never would," Reese reported. "He was scared Frankie
could outsing him."

"The one memory of growing up with Marvin which keeps coming back," Frankie Gay told me, "happened in the bedroom we
shared in D.C. I'd only have one pair of clean underwear left, but
before I could turn around, Marvin would slip them on, get dressed
and be dancing down the street, with me yelling after him to bring
back my shorts. Marvin was like that. He also never let me become
friends with his friends."

Gaye suffered from this sibling rivalry. He was frightened that
Frankie was not only a better musician, but also a better athlete.
He couldn't bear the thought of being bested by his own brother.
In truth, Frankie's talent was great, though he lacked Marvin's
drive. For a short period in the seventies, Gaye let Frankie sing
with his backup vocalists. The arrangement, however, made Marvin uncomfortable. Frankie also wrote a successful movie score,
but he never released a record of his own. Marvin died with the
unfulfilled promise of introducing his brother as a featured singer
on his next album.

The tension, though, between Marvin and Frankie was subtle.
Both boys were reluctant to discuss it, and years passed without
either of them mentioning the matter. It was a sore point for them,
but a small one in contrast to the gaping psychological wounds
Marvin and Father continued to inflict upon one another. To escape
the pain, Marvin required outside help, a savior, a man with a plan.

That man was Harvey Fuqua. In Marvin's eyes he appeared to
be a combination father figure and musical master.

Like Gay Sr., Fuqua was an ambitious Kentuckian. Eleven years
older than Marvin, Harvey had been instrumental in forging new
combinations of sounds and styles in American popular music. He'd

written "Sincerely" along with his writing partner, disc jockey Alan Freed, and Fuqua's Moonglows had backed Bo Diddley on "Diddley Daddy" and "Diddy Wah Diddy." His romantic ballads, along with those of the Flamingos ("I'll Be Home"), helped Chicago-based Chess Records broaden their black base, even though, as was customary then, the McGuire Sisters' white version of "Sincerely" sold four times as many copies as the original.

Fuqua had a knack for reading trends and moving into the thick of things, especially as teenage music started fermenting in the late fifties and early sixties. He was Marvin Gaye's mentor. He was there at the beginning and at the end, twenty-four years later, when he co-produced his student's final album, *Midnight Love*, and sang background on "Sexual Healing."

Marvin idolized Harvey. He respected him not only for his string of Moonglow hits—"Most of All," "See Saw," "Please Send Me Someone to Love"—but also for the lilting romanticism which characterized the group. Besides his talent for writing and arranging, Fuqua was also a strong, smooth tenor, having sung the lead on "Ten Commandments of Love," a song which Marvin had been doing with the Marquees. What's more, Harvey was a brilliant original. He trained the Moonglows in what became known as "blow harmony," an exclusive sound, forged by Fuqua, which differentiated his group from all others.

"Harvey also had guts," Marvin said, "and I admired that. He was out there in the world. He'd been around, and I was still in the crib. I needed to see the world. I thought that's what the Air Force would be, but the Air Force was prison. Harvey's world was filled with cool times and hot women. I was ready for a taste of the big time. I saw myself singing before thousands of women, making them swoon, choosing any one of them for the mere asking. That was my destiny, and the sooner the better."

By metamorphosing into the Moonglows, Marvin and the Marquees were convinced they'd soon find national fame. It wouldn't be that easy.

"In November of 1958," Reese Palmer remembered, "Chester Simmons, who used to sing with the Marquees, was still with Bo Diddley. Bo and Harvey were on the same bill somewhere up in Canada, and Harvey said he might be looking for some new Moonglows. He was having problems with Bobby Lester, his lead tenor.

Naturally Chester mentioned us, and when the Moonglows came to the Howard Theater that same year, we were ready.

"Harvey was staying at Cecelia's, a little joint right next to the theater. It was a bar and restaurant, and upstairs they had rooms. That's where the new Moonglows were born. Even though he was performing with the old Moonglows at the Howard, he let us know that right after this gig they were out and we were in. Harvey was sneaky like that. Between shows, he'd be rehearsing us to death. We thought we were hot shit, but Harvey showed us what real-life five-part harmony was all about."

"I loved Harvey," Marvin said. "I felt like a small-time piano player who suddenly became a student of Rubinstein's. Harvey was interested in the songs' stories only in terms of what would sell. But his technical interests went far beyond commercialism. Harvey was a perfectionist, and he brought out the perfectionist in me. One moment my life seemed helpless. In spite of cutting a record, the Marquees looked like every other group around D.C. I didn't think we'd ever get out. Then one day this Harvey Fuqua came along. The clouds broke and the sun started shining. Not only were we being groomed for the road, but the quality of sound surrounding me became incredibly sophisticated.

"Harvey used to make fun of the doo-woppers. He'd call them 'gang groups.' Harvey would tell us, 'Look, the other cats are singing *doo-doo-doo*. It ain't *doo*, it's *who*.' He'd show us how to fix our mouth muscles to get all sorts of other sounds, mainly *who-who-who*. That was his 'blow harmony.' He taught us to make our breath part of the phrasing, even part of the sound. It was an eye-opening, or should I say a mouth-opening, experience.

"All my life I've thought of myself as an elitist. Father felt the same way. Maybe that's because we came out of an elitist church. Anyway, Harvey's style was elite. He made me feel special."

Fuqua's "blow harmony" was a dramatic refinement of popular black singing. It gave the human voice a reedlike quality, a hollow, breathy sound, rich in timbre and romantic in feeling. The technique became an important, permanent part of Marvin Gaye's bag of vocal tricks.

In early 1959, nineteen-year-old Marvin Gaye left home and headed to Chicago with the newly formed, newly named Harvey and the Moonglows.

"I can't say whether it was more difficult saying good-bye to Mother or Father. I didn't want Mother to think I was deserting her. I promised her I never would. I told her that I was doing this for her. She believed me, and she told me that she knew I'd make it. I wanted to tell Father that I wished never to see him again. I wanted to forget everything he'd done to me as a child, but that wasn't possible. We just looked at each other. I think we were both afraid of what we might say. Father and I had special ways of hurting each other. If I could have spoken my heart, I'd have said, 'Please love me.' But I didn't say a word, and neither did he. We both realized that this was it. I was going out on my own, and there was nothing in hell he could do about it.

"I drove away in Harvey's car—I'd signed with Harvey for life—and I was happy to be leaving, hoping never to come back to these bad, sad memories again."

6
BREAKOUT

Marvin's search for an understanding, supportive father was a source of deep frustration. He never found what he was looking for— acceptance without authority, approval without discipline, love without demands.

"I thought I had escaped. I thought Father's prison was behind me," Marvin recounted. "What I didn't know, though, was that life is about finding different taskmasters. If you want to grow, you gotta go up against these tough teachers. Harvey was cool, but, believe me, he also broke our balls. I thought our training had been strenuous in Washington. But when we settled in Chicago in 1959, the real woodshedding had just started. Harvey was a slave driver. He wouldn't put up with no sloppy singing. He and I did a lot of fighting."

"Harvey was a little slippery," said Reese Palmer. "He'd take me to the side and say, 'Look, I'm going to pay you a little more than the other boys.' Then he'd tell each of them the same thing. Far as money goes, we got room and board and not much else."

In Chicago, Harvey asked Chuck Barksdale, who'd been singing with the Dells, to join the Moonglows, thus turning the group into a sextet. Fuqua was featured on most of the leads, James Nolan on others, Marvin and Reese sang tenor, and Chester Simmons and Chuck duplicated the bass parts, giving the group an extraordinarily fat bottom.

By finding fresh young Moonglows and putting himself out front, Fuqua had what he wanted.

The group lived at Fifty-seventh and Woodlawn, apartments owned by the Chess brothers, the same men who owned the recording label for which the Moonglows recorded. The winter was freezing, made even colder by Fuqua's musical demands: He was a perfectionist, a master craftsman of the art of doo-wop. Even a master, though, makes mistakes. During this same winter, Fuqua rejected David Ruffin as a Moonglow, the same Ruffin who would lead the Temptations through their phenomenal period of sixties hits. Marvin would later acknowledge Ruffin as one of the Motown artists he admired most. Harvey's standards may have been too strict.

"When it came to business and music, Harvey was as strict as Father," said Marvin. "He saw me as a pain in the ass. I was always complaining about not singing enough leads. Fact is, if I hadn't been so in love with show business, I'm sure I would have popped him. A couple of times we came to blows. No matter how much he was teaching me, I still couldn't stand taking orders. He would have dumped me, except for my talent. I know I can get away with throwing temper tantrums because of my talent. My talent means money, and Harvey knew that, too."

"Marvin wasn't easy to deal with," Reese recalled, "and once he and James Nolan got into a fist fight. Another time down in Florida, Harvey and Marvin went after each other. But you got to remember that when he wanted to be, Marvin was one of the nicest, warmest cats you'd ever want to meet. He had this low-key ability to make people like him, just by being relaxed and natural. He also loved to laugh. Marvin had a lot of sides to him, but his good side was golden."

Gaye's drive was unrelenting. He still strove to be the star, and singing simply as one of the boys would never be enough. He required more attention: his talent, his ego, his charm demanded it.

The original Moonglows had recorded for Chess, and Harvey had established a long-time working relationship with the label. Phil and Leonard Chess had started out in the forties hustling records out of the trunk of their car. Somehow they managed to tap a main vein of black music—the deep funk of country blues, electrified by the city lights of Chicago's South Side. At one time or another, the Chess brothers recorded Bo Diddley, Willie Dixon, Sonny Boy Williamson, Howlin' Wolf, Muddy Waters, John Lee Hooker, and Chuck Berry. This was the red-hot recording environment into which Marvin was thrown.

Later in 1959, Harvey and his new Moonglows went into the Chess studios. They recorded "That's What Girls Are Made For" and "Love, I'm So Glad I Found You," which were never released. A while later, Harvey recorded the same songs, this time on his own short-lived label, with vocals by the Spinners. The Moonglows did, however, sing on some hits. Marvin Gaye, along with his colleagues, sang harmony on Chuck Berry's irresistible "Back in the U.S.A." and "Almost Grown." Etta James, rough-and-tumble rhythm and blues pioneer and Janis Joplin's musical mama, also sang on those sides.

"In those days," Etta told me, "I was another Chess slave."

The Moonglows accompanied Etta on "Chained to My Rocking Chair," while Etta and Harvey also sang a few duets under the pseudonyms Betty and Dupree for Kent Records. For a while, Etta and Harvey were sweethearts.

"Harvey was the one who showed me," said Marvin, "that romance could do you a world of good in business. The aim was to use all your assets and come out on top. He was the first big-time operator I saw up close, and I admired his style. Harvey could lay his sweet harmony on anyone and wind up a winner."

Harvey and the Moonglows only recorded a few songs, and Marvin Gaye sang the lead on only one: "Mama Loochie." A lively romp written by Gaye and Fuqua, the song had Marvin slipping and sliding, falling from falsetto crescendos, dabbling in word play—"my Mama Loochie, she's a brand-new coochie."

When I asked Marvin what the tune was about, he thought for a moment and said, "The perfect mother and perfect wife."

Though Gaye had an analytical mind, as a creative artist he worked instinctively. Only afterward did he become reflective about his creations. In the sound of his voice and the songs he sang, his method was simply to express his true-life feelings.

The story line of "Mama Loochie," for instance, revolved around the theme of marrying, settling down, and raising a family. Characteristically, Marvin's lead-vocal debut reflected a personal desire. Here he yearned for domestic happiness, the one thing he sought throughout life and the one thing which continually eluded him.

It's also telling that, for all Marvin's ambitions to be a balladeer, Fuqua saw the singer's primary strength in dance songs. Gaye had a syncopated pull, a sexy, light-hearted sway. Marvin's future managers would see that same quality and successfully sell it: time after time, Marvin would be haunted by his inevitable success with sensuous rhythms. Gaye's singing would always be closely tied to the act of dancing, though as an observer, a voyeur, and not as a participant. Marvin hated to dance, though he'd always be inspired by the sight—and fantasy—of bodies gracefully undulating to the sounds of seductive music.

"If you listen closely to 'Mama Loochie,' " said Chuck Barksdale, whose career with the Dells, aside from his nine-month Moonglows stint, would span three decades, "you'll hear that it's not a typical song of the times. The musical changes are very advanced."

On "Twelve Months of the Year," an attempt to echo the previous success of the old Moonglows hit, "Ten Commandments of Love," Marvin can be heard singing baritone harmony. He also recited the song's opening and closing rhymed couplet. Melodramatically spoken lines had been a black group tradition since the Ink Spots. Marvin took the role seriously. You hear not the quiet melancholy and sweet depression which typified Gaye's speaking voice but also a distinct British accent, one of his favorite ploys. He loved the aristocratic flavor of Old World English and would sometimes, in more pretentious moments, draw out the "a," pronouncing "rather" as "rahhther," for example.

None of these tunes were hits. In fact, in spite of Harvey's attempt to revitalize his Moonglows and feature himself, musical trends were working against him. The doo-wop era was fading, and the best Fuqua could do was book a final run around the chittlin circuit. For the very first time, Marvin Gaye was going on the road.

Sexually and musically, Marvin was being tested. With women drawn to his good looks and smooth manner, he found himself weak before their advances. While he could never approach a girl with great confidence, he was unable to resist when the proposal was directed at him. He toyed with sleeping with two women at once, he told me, and then three. Finally, the question became, "How many women can one man please?" Throughout his life, Marvin felt sexually obligated to every one of his female fans, a pressure great enough to destroy any man. The irony was that he found himself playing the role of Dionysus, god of indiscriminate sex, when all the while he only wanted to be Apollo, god of song.

"Actually, the more I sang the hot stuff," Marvin continued, speaking of himself as a twenty-year-old, "the more I was convinced that my original dream was right. I just wanted to wear a tux, sit on a stool, and sing love songs. The road was glamorous for a hot minute. Then it was just one raunchy club and dirty dance hall after another. Somewhere along the way, Bobby Lester, Harvey's original lead tenor, rejoined the group, and that killed my chances for singing more leads. I was terribly jealous of Bobby, but I couldn't help but love the way he sang 'Blue Velvet.' "

"We were touring down South with Big Joe Turner and Etta James," Reese Palmer said. "Sleeping in a station wagon, trying to keep our process jobs together. Ran into all kinds of racist shit. Some white folks didn't like the way we wore our hair."

"I'm one of those entertainers," Marvin told me, "who felt the indignity of being refused lodgings because of the color of my skin. In Southern cities we couldn't get rooms. Sometimes there weren't even segregated accommodations for us. We had nothing except the back seat of the car or the cold, hard ground. I thought about Joseph and Mary being turned away, but that wasn't comfort enough. Jesus turned over the tables in the temple, and I was ready to break down the doors. Remember, this was when the white South was going through its agony, hating the changes it was being forced to make. Suffering and injustice are things which I've always felt deep in my soul, and I wondered what I was doing singing rock and roll in some dive instead of leading the marchers. I know I had that ability, but that wasn't my role. My role was to sing. Years later when Bob Marley came around, I saw that both things were possible. His music caused political change, and that's why he'll occupy a high place in history."

From an early age, Marvin had been well aware that his musical contribution could also be of historical significance. He was blessed with an understanding of music's limitless potential to do good. He often wondered what kind of singing voice Jesus himself might have had. Marley came closest to achieving what Gaye considered the ultimate—using songs to raise the consciousness of his people and improve their lot in life. It was important for Gaye to be great, but just as important to be famous. From time to time, he'd proclaim his destiny.

"One day in Louisville, Chester Simmons and I were rooming with Marvin," Chuck Barksdale told me. "You gotta understand that it'd been a rough tour. The crowds were small and Harvey paid us practically nothing, though I was grateful for the crumbs. Now on this particular afternoon we were sitting around when Marvin walked over to the window and just stood there, staring outside. Then he announced, calm as could be, 'I'm going to be a big star one day.' 'What about us?' we wanted to know. He smiled but didn't say anything. At first I was mad, but then I realized that he was right. His ego was huge, but he could get away with it.

"As a musician and singer, he was far beyond us. Harvey saw Marvin's genius, I believe, before Marvin did. Anyway, from the day he made that statement, his attitude changed. In spite of all the anxious moments—we never knew from day to day whether we'd have enough bread to eat—I could see Marvin's mind going places. He was sprouting his wings. We all knew that we were in the presence of a talent that comes along once every forty or fifty years. I don't mean he wasn't a human being. Marvin did some obnoxious things out there, but hell, we all did. When you're poor, you act funny. We had more adventures in those nine months than most people have in a lifetime."

"We got busted on that tour," Reese recalled. "It happened in Beaumont, Texas, and we got thrown in the can—me, Marvin, Harvey, Etta James—the whole show.''

"I was there for that Beaumont bust," Etta James told me between sets at the Vine Street Bar and Grill in Hollywood. Etta's a straight talker and a soul shouter in the Bessie Smith–Dinah Washington–Aretha Franklin tradition. She told the story of how, at the time she knew Marvin, she was in love with Harvey Fuqua.

"He was my first boyfriend," Etta said. "I was this chubby little singer—an original groupy—and strung out on Harvey until I was buying the boy rings and hi-fi sets."

Harvey eventually broke Etta's heart. In fact, later she'd record a song called "All I Could Do Was Cry." The song was about a girl who watches her man marry someone else. Amazingly, one of the tune's co-composers, Gwen Gordy, turned out to be the very woman Harvey Fuqua married.

The Beaumont bust was caused by Titty Tassel Toni, a shake dancer on the show. Marijuana joints fell from her bra at a gas station, an attendant called the cops, and the entertainment troupe was arrested. One of the girls in the show claimed the pot was hers, thus saving the others. Marvin never served time in jail.

His prison was a mental one. He was trapped in his own cage of sexual confusion. Extreme by nature, he chose women as the objects of absolute good or absolute corruption. Thus his fascination with bought love. According to Etta James, Toni was a professional prostitute and Marvin was in love with her. Their relationship was marred by sudden spurts of anger and jealousy on his part. One night they fought their way into a ditch, where Toni took a bite out of Marvin's stomach. Violence would always be a part of his dealings with the women he desired most.

He also started dealing with the world through the smoke screen of marijuana. That would inevitably alter his perceptions, intensifying both aspects of his personality—his smooth, mellow side and his sharp paranoia.

"Reefer is an interesting thing," Marvin once told me in the late seventies as he took a strong toke from the joint he was smoking. He was high during almost all our interviews. "I *stay* high," Marvin said. "I respect reefer. If you're an artist, you'll recognize its creative possibilities. In those early days especially, I was trying hard to listen to myself as I sang. That's something I've always tried to do. Herb seemed to enhance that process. I've always listened to natural sounds—like gusts of wind or raindrops falling to the ground— and grass helped me listen closer. In Jamaica I learned that the Rastas use pot for religious purposes, and I can see that. I've had my share of smoky visions. But to be frank, I don't think I started for any of those lofty reasons. I started because I hated drinking— I still do—and if you want to be hip, what else is there? Slowly you see the world through this fascinating filter, and slowly you decide you'd rather live your life stoned than straight. You know it's not good for you, you know it'll cause you to make mistakes, but it's too late. You're a pothead."

Drugs weren't a product of Gaye's childhood, but part of his initiation into professional music. He experimented with pot only after he hit the road with the Moonglows. His relationship to dope was intense and complex. He started through peer pressure but soon discovered that smoke, and later coke, gave him an otherworld feeling he found irresistible.

In the summer of 1960 the Moonglows passed through Washington, D.C., playing first at Wilmer's Park in Brandywine, Maryland, and then in the city at the Howard Theater on the same bill as Mary Ann Fisher—once a featured vocalist with Ray Charles—the Fiestas, and Bobby Freeman.

"Now that was a touch of heaven!" Marvin recalled. "On the stage of the Howard! Strange, but I don't remember Father coming. I don't even remember asking him. Mother was there, I'm sure, but somehow I didn't even want to include Father. From the moment I saw a glimpse of stardom, I had a strong desire to wipe out my past—every last bit of it. Singing with the Moonglows at the Howard, I returned home a conquering hero. At the same time, though, I pretended that this was just another city, just another audience, and I was an entertainer merely passing through. Aside from Mother, if I could forget everything about my past, I'd be a happier person."

By the end of the fifties, the old musical configurations were changing. The Eisenhower age was ending, and the curtain was coming down on groups like the Moonglows. Different sorts of sounds—from Ray Charles and Jackie Wilson, the Chantels and the Shirelles—were attracting a different generation of teenagers. The Moonglows weren't hitting, and Fuqua knew that something had to be done.

"The new Moonglows began crazy and ended crazy," said Chuck Barksdale. "Even the beginning was leading to the end, though we didn't know it. Here's what happened: Leonard Chess loved Harvey and wanted to help him in any way. Billy Davis, Leonard's A&R [artists and repertoire] man, was going with Gwen Gordy, who had good connections. Leonard thought it was a good idea if Harvey met Gwen, so he set the thing up. Harvey took it from there. We all saw the handwriting on the wall."

"I suppose Harvey and I are both hustlers," Marvin commented through his sly-fox smile. "We've always had a sixth sense about when to make a move. We'd been talking among ourselves, away from the others, about what to do. Going out alone, without the group, seemed right. Harvey was convinced I could be a solo artist. That's why I was ready to follow him to the ends of the earth. Remember, I'd signed with him for *life*. That's how much I trusted him.

"Somehow we wound up in Detroit, just the two of us. The Moonglows had gigged there, and I'd been noticed by a couple of interesting people. For a while, Harvey ran back and forth between Chicago and Detroit, trying to make up his mind. Detroit won out. He liked the music vibe there. He was also starting to realize that his performing days were numbered.

"Harvey needed me and I needed him. He was still my guide through the back alleys and over the snake pits. Harvey protected me and taught me about the wild, wicked world out there. He also saw he could make a fortune off me.

"We agreed that with the right push I could still make it as a black Sinatra. With Harvey in my corner, I found the guts to step out and try. I also saw that pleasing women meant pleasing your bank account. Sex and money and music were all tied up together. I thought I was cool, I thought I could handle anything, but, oh man, I didn't know what I was in for. Detroit did turn out to be heaven, but it also turned out to be hell."

In moving to Motor City, Marvin was running from a past he needed to forget, straight ahead into a future of great wealth but even greater pain.

7

MOTOWN

Berry Gordy, Jr., was the boss. Ten years older than Marvin, Gordy was born into a family of extraordinary entrepreneurs. One of eight siblings, he'd inherited the restless energy of his light-skinned father, who pursued four careers at once (plasterer, grocer, contractor, and salesman), and his mother, who worked in real estate and politics. The Gordys had immigrated to Detroit from Sandersville, Georgia, in the twenties.

"I loved Pops Gordy," Marvin said. "He had a big heart and a beautiful soul, but Mom Gordy was the real power. She was the forceful lady who ran the show."

Like Marvin, Berry Jr. had dropped out of high school. His model had been Detroiter Joe Louis, the heavyweight champ. By 1950, Gordy had boxed his way to a respectable record for a five-foot six-inch flyweight/featherweight.

"Berry had a short man's complex," Marvin observed. "That's one of the reasons he was so competitive and tough. I respected him for his guts, but even in the beginning I knew we were destined to clash. At the same time, I was awed by him. BG—that's what we called him—was also the coolest dude I'd ever met. Had women like you wouldn't believe. Beautiful, world-class women. In his time, Berry's gone with Miss Universe herself. Combine that with a talent for making millions—all in the music business—and you get some idea of the impact this guy had on me. Harvey was terrific, but Berry had a wider worldview. This cat was serious."

Gordy replaced Harvey Fuqua as the major male role model in Marvin's life. Rejecting his own father, Gaye was deeply influenced by strong men. Sometimes these men were his managers, sometimes his mentors, or sometimes, later in his life, simply professional athletes. Gordy had a powerful influence on Marvin, especially as a businessman. Gaye admired Berry's cunning in the vicious marketplace of pop music. He also viewed Gordy's ability to combine finance and romance as the essence of cool.

It took Gordy ten years—the decade of the fifties—to get down to the serious work of building his empire. He spent three years in the Army, went to Korea, and returned home in 1953, the year he married Thelma Louise Coleman and opened the 3-D Record Mart. Two years later, the store, specializing in jazz, threw Gordy into bankruptcy. His customers wanted Ruth Brown, not Thelonius Monk. From then on Berry's musical mind turned toward mass marketing. Although he could neither read nor write music, melodies danced through his dreams and he was still convinced he could make money in the record business.

But how? By 1956, he had three children to support and a failed marriage. He took whatever work he could find, helping his father on plastering jobs and working on an automotive assembly line, where he slapped chrome trim on the side of Lincolns and Mercurys. But the rhythm in Gordy's soul didn't stop as the cars rolled by, and after work he'd drop into Morris Wasserman's Flame Show Bar at the corner of Canfield and John R, where he'd catch Billie Holiday or Della Reese, another Detroiter, and chat with his buddies Maurice King, the bandleader, and Thomas "Beans" Bowles, the baritone saxophonist. Within a few years, both men would be working for Gordy as teachers and musicians.

Berry's sister Gwen and brother Robert were also at the Flame, working the large room with their photography concession, selling pictures of the patrons at fifty cents a pop. Gwen and her sisters Anna, Esther, and Loucye had inherited their parents' business acumen. Gwen was especially motivated and had already started making records.

Berry couldn't take the assembly line for long. He left his job in July 1957, determined to salvage himself through songwriting. By

1958 he had a hit. Tunes he'd written for his close chum Jackie Wilson took off. One song, "Lonely Teardrops," was a smash.

Significantly, Berry didn't write alone. In a creative environment, he functioned more as editor than initiator. His first tunes were written with Gwen's boyfriend, Billy Davis, who, under the pen name of Tyrone Carlo, cocomposed "Teardrops," "To Be Loved," "That's Why," "I'll Be Satisfied" and "Reet Petite"—all Jackie Wilson hits for the Brunswick label.

Gordy did not, as critics have claimed, begin with the notion of producing whitewashed black music. In fact, it was his displeasure with the white way Jackie Wilson was being produced—Brunswick Records was drowning Jackie in a sea of syrupy strings—that helped convince Berry to produce his own songs.

Gordy was disposed to mix business and love. His new girlfriend, Raynoma, who would become his second wife in 1959, also helped him produce artists on their primitive Webcor tape recorder when they lived at 1719 Gladstone. (Artists wanting to sing paid Berry and Raynoma to record them.) Like other women in Gordy's life, Raynoma would prove to be a profitable asset.

Meanwhile, Berry kept writing—with Janie Bradford, Barrett Strong, Eddie Holland, and his sister Gwen, who recently became interested in a man who boasted an impressive track record of his own in the music business: Harvey Fuqua. Like brother Berry, Gwen tended to combine business and romance.

After coming to Detroit in 1960, Harvey had started a small label. Still pushing his name, he called it Harvey Records and had signed tenor saxophonist Jr. Walker, a group called the Quails, and the singer he'd brought from Washington, Marvin Gaye.

"Everything started coming together," Marvin remembered. "Harvey Records hooked up with Anna Records, which belonged to Gwen. Gwen had the Spinners, Lamont Dozier, Joe Tex, and Barrett Strong. Suddenly Anna Records was called Anna-Tri Phi— there was also Miracle Records that had Jimmy Ruffin and the Temptations—and just as suddenly Berry was in the middle of it all with a label called Tammi. It didn't take me long to realize that even though I'd signed with Harvey for life, Berry was about to buy me. Since Harvey needed the cash, I knew it was going to happen. As soon as Berry saw how big my talent was, he made a bid—and that was it. Harvey sold him his whole roster. I don't know how much Berry paid for me, but I'm sure the low figure would embarrass me."

In truth, the transaction hurt Marvin, who had looked to Harvey as a true and constant father. But as he did with so many other men in authoritative positions, Gaye couldn't help but fight with Fuqua, even as he hungered for his love and approval. Berry would become the new father.

"Berry was cool, Berry was cold, Berry was a lot of things," said Gaye. "I've always fancied myself as a good reader of people, and I saw right off that, after his mom, he was the power. I knew I needed him, and I knew I wanted to stay around. He was another guide, teacher, a cat who knew more than I did. Meanwhile, Detroit was jamming. People were turning out cars and making records and I was ready. After all, one of my idols, Little Willie John, came from Detroit. Yes sir, Detroit was live."

Like Washington, Detroit was fertile ground for music. It was here where the Reverend C. L. Franklin's young daughter, Aretha, had been thrilling the parishioners at his New Bethel Church with her impassioned voice. It was also here that Smokey Robinson had been struggling with his vocal group, the Miracles, since 1955. Smokey was convinced that he needed production and promotional help from his close friend Berry Gordy and was one of the people most responsible for persuading Gordy to finally take the plunge into management.

On the royalties earned from "Lonely Teardrops," and a few hundred dollars borrowed from his family, BG began his great adventure into the music business at about the same time young Jack Kennedy moved into the White House. Berry moved his business into a modest house on West Grand Boulevard, which would soon contain offices and a primitive studio. He called the place Hitsville, U.S.A.

America wanted a new sound. Youth was in power. Music was changing. Berry Gordy's Motown would not only emerge as a feisty giant killer in a white-controlled industry, it would grow to become the biggest black-owned industry in the annals of American business. "Money" was the name of the first Motown hit. "Money," wrote Berry Gordy, "is what I want."

"I once wrote two lines that I never recorded," Marvin Gaye said, recalling the early Motown days. "I should have, because they tell the whole story: 'There were roads leading to nowhere that I chose to follow/ I didn't have to, but I worshipped the mighty dollar.'

"I thought it was going to be easy. I actually believed I was through paying dues. All I had to do was slip into my solo thing and be a star. Lord have mercy, was I ever wrong!"

In the beginning, Marvin scuffled along with everyone else, hanging out, hanging on.

"There were a lot of people ahead of me on line. That was the real problem," Marvin explained. "Smokey, for instance, was not only a good singer and a great writer but extremely tight with Berry. Their friendship went back a long way, and I couldn't expect to cut in front of Smokey. Even if I tried, it wouldn't have worked."

In early 1961, the Miracles' "Shop Around," written by Smokey and Berry, became Motown's first million-selling single.

"Far as business went," Marvin remembered, "Berry had the publishing wrapped up from the beginning. You could write songs at Motown, but you'd never own any of your copyrights. Berry was a strong businessman who understood that the key to his personal wealth would be the accumulation of valuable copyrights. You'd get paid as an employee—paid very little—but no one except Berry kept any ownership of the songs. We were all helping Berry build his catalogue."

"Just about everyone got ripped off at Motown," Clarence Paul told me. He was there at the beginning, as a writer, producer and conductor-caretaker for Little Stevie Wonder. Eleven years older than Marvin, CP, as Gaye called him, remained one of his closest friends until the very end.

"The royalty rates were substandard," Clarence claimed. "Motown had their own song-writing contracts, which were way below the rest of the industry. Tunes were stolen all the time, and often credit wasn't properly assigned."

"Berry's way," said Marvin, "was to take as much as he could. He wasn't any different from any other businessman trying to make money in music. As far as negotiating goes, he was the master. Somehow he wound up with everything. I couldn't have asked for a better trainer."

In a 1983 series in *The Metro Times* of Detroit, scholar Herb Boyd cited a series of alleged song thefts in the early days of Motown.

"I wrote 'Come to Me,' but Berry put his name on it," Marv

Johnson told Boyd. Johnson was the singer who cut the first Motown single. Beans Bowles—Johnson's first manager—made similar claims about the way some of his songs were swiped.

Bowles played baritone sax and flute on many of the early Motown hits and acted as road manager for the early Motown Revues. He was fourteen years older than Gaye, and the young singer often confided in him.

"Marvin was a troubled boy from the first day I met him," Bowles told me. "He was a beautiful human being beneath all his complexes, but, believe me, he had lots of complexes. The biggest was about his name. That was the root of the whole thing."

Beans was referring, of course, to "Gaye." Marvin was burdened with a continuing crisis in self-identity. He didn't want to be what he was—the son of a sexually ambiguous man. He didn't want to be a Gay. Yet adding the "e" didn't solve the problem.

"All someone has to do with my name," Gaye said, "is put an 'is' in front of it. 'Is Marvin Gaye?' Man, I can't tell you how many guys have asked me that."

Try as he might, Marvin could never escape from the cruel irony of the matter. He was attached to his father's name, branded for life.

"He fought it," Bowles said. "The cats would kid him about being gay, knowing he wasn't, but knowing how he hated hearing about it. We called him Gayesky. That bugged him too. He'd tell 'em that one day he was going to play professional football or box, but the cats would say, 'Yeah, Marv, but some of those guys are the biggest fags around.' Later Marvin saw that for himself.

"I tried to counsel Marvin as best as I could, but I don't think anyone could really help him. I did encourage him with his music. His real idol was Ray Charles. He'd go crazy listening to what Ray did with his voice. I told him he was in the same class, but I'm not sure he believed me. Not believing in himself is what tripped him up."

Marvin often spoke with confidence, convinced that his power was unlimited. But deep down, his fear outweighed his faith. Beans Bowles' sensitivity allowed him to see the real Gaye.

"Marvin was always trying to figure out the best kind of music to do," said Bowles. "He was afraid of deciding. Marvin was a little afraid of making decisions of any kind."

The early musical decisions were being made by Berry Gordy, who had put together an assortment of musicians responsible for creating what was soon called the Motown sound, a distinguishable, easily digestible, and always danceable recipe for pop success. Gordy's singers were not asked, but told what to sing. Gordy and his producers made the decisions. Marvin would fight that system and, though it would take him a decade, he'd win.

The emergence of a Motown sound was not immediate. The initial releases by Mary Wells—the label's first certified star—were tough-minded rhythm-and-blues Berry Gordy productions in the no-nonsense Etta James tradition. "Bye Bye Baby" is a classic example. The same is true of the Contours' early screamer, "Do You Love Me?" sung in the feverish Falcons' mode. There was fresh, vibrant energy—always a Motown trademark—but no distinguishable style.

"Berry was an experimenter," Marvin said. "He'd like to combine styles. 'I wonder what a Smokey Robinson song,' he'd ask himself, 'and a Smokey Robinson production on Mary Wells would do?' Well, 'My Guy' zoomed to the top.

"Berry also liked to play mind games. He was like me and Father in that regard, a manipulator who loved stoking competitive fires. You can't imagine what a hotbed of competition that little bungalow on West Grand was like. It was beautiful because we were young and talented and willing to help each other. But people being people, everyone was out for Number One. Berry first and foremost. He established himself as king. He owned us. So there was this mad scramble for position. We were all a bunch of ghetto kids looking to break out, and Berry was the cat with the key to the recording studio.

"The object of the game was to get in that little studio. A lot of the girls, like Martha Reeves and Diana Ross, would work in the office just to be close to the studio. I got in by telling 'em I was a drummer. I really wasn't, but I proved that I really was. I never learned to read music, although all the instruments come easy to me, 'specially drums and piano. I played drums for all the early acts. But I really wanted to get next to Smokey 'cause Smokey was next to Berry. That's how I became a drummer for the Miracles, getting paid maybe five dollars a session, and traveling with them on the road. Least I was in.

"As a writer, Smokey taught me a lot. More as a lyricist than anything else. Smokey has a melodic mind, though if he could play a whole instrument—he really plays only part of the piano—his songs wouldn't all sound the same. But who cares what I think when he's written so many hits? Anyway, I think Smokey's one of the greatest poets. He has an ability to make simple words rhyme until the meaning is clear to everyone. Smokey will say things like, 'I'm a choosey beggar, baby.' Marv Tarplin, Smokey's guitar player, also deserves credit. Smokey's done some of his best writing teamed up with Marv. Strange that Smokey and I never really wrote together. Anyway, we became friends, close friends, and he helped me. But I needed more than professional help. I needed a little personal help with the king.

"Now King Berry didn't have one queen, he really had four. His four sisters. They were all real smart chicks. Esther was the oldest and the most educated. She married a politician and had a lot of class—all the Gordys did—and wound up taking care of the artists and damn near running the shop. Loucye was another doll. When she died in 1965, it broke my heart. Loucye was this bubbly, vivacious girl, the fox of the family, and a beautiful lady. She came in the office and figured out a way to collect money from the distributors. BG used to say if it wasn't for Loucye he'd never be able to keep the doors open. Gwen and Anna were the prima donnas. They had a hell of a reputation for being party girls. They were physical—that's true of all the Gordys—and spoiled. Gwen and Anna were glamorous, always dressed to the teeth and interested in beauty. They were also fiercely loyal to their brother. I admired that. Fact is, the Gordys were the tightest family I'd ever seen. I never saw rivalry between them. No one could break into the circle, though I probably came as close as anyone."

How did the Marvin/Anna romance begin?

"I know what you're going to say," Gaye said to me. "You're going to play shrink and say that I really married my mother. Well, you're not the first to hit me with that. When you go with a woman seventeen years older than you, people start talking. In the beginning, though, the age difference between Anna and me didn't seem that important. She was thirty-seven, I was twenty and still a very lonely little boy. Aside from silly flings that never lasted, I never had a real girlfriend before, especially someone who cared about me like Anna did. There was real passion between us. Anna was more experienced than me, and I needed a loving teacher. Every man does. From a professional point of view I have to say—and I hope this doesn't sound too cold—that I knew just what I was doing. Marrying a queen might not make me king, but at least I'd have a shot at being prince. Besides, Anna was into my music more than any woman I'd ever known. She'd beg me to play and sing and write, and because she had wonderful ears, she appreciated my every move. She complimented me. She called me her fine young thing. She was more forward than I was. She knew she wanted me and she got me. But I also knew what I wanted; I wanted her to help me cut into that long line in front of the recording studio."

Marvin did look at Anna much the way he looked at Mother—as a woman who supported his music and boosted his confidence. Theirs was a romantic relationship in which the woman—older, wiser, and worldier—enjoyed the upper hand. Gaye both relished and resented the situation. The Machiavellian side of his political character was excited by the prospect of moving into the center of power. He followed his instincts and achieved his goal. Anna led him to stardom. In a matter of a few short years, though, he found himself rebelling against Anna's—and her brother's—authority, just as he would rebel against all authority figures throughout his life—father, managers, wives, the U.S. government. The single exception was Mother, who never quite exerted her authority, thus preserving her relationship with Marvin.

Even more painful than his bouts with his bosses were his constant self-doubts. Because of the critical role Anna and Berry played in Marvin's career, he never believed he could have done it on his own. In Marvin's mind, it was his romantic and political maneuvering which brought him success, not the quality of his artistry.

On the other hand, to the outside world he appeared cool and confident. Gaye had an ability to mask his uncertainties. For moments, hours, even days, he was able to shed those insecurities and play the part of the suave crooner displaying the Como-Crosby-Sinatra side of his personality. This, I believe, was the most natural Marvin, the calmest, the wisest, the most relaxed. This was the Marvin who understood the power of his talent—to please people with his voice—and knew there was no need to worry. His was a confidence of unnatural magnitude, equalled only by his enormous self-doubts.

"His problem was insecurity," Beans Bowles added. "He was this very shy guy who worried all the time. That's why he took to Anna. She helped him, and he genuinely loved her. Anna was good for Marvin—up to a point. Afterward, it was clear that no one could have been any better. Same was true with Marvin and Berry. BG understood Marvin. Knew how to handle him. Marvin, though, was paranoid about Berry. He didn't trust him one hundred percent, and with good reason. You see, Berry had control of Marvin through Anna.

"Anna wanted two things, money and Marvin, and she got both. She was in control of Marvin's money, and in one way that was good. At least she kept him together. But Marvin was the kind of cat who wanted control. Being I was with an older woman too, I could advise Marvin about what to expect. He listened and he didn't. He felt like he was being had. I knew what he meant. My own theory was that Berry wanted all his stars to marry into the family. That way BG could control everything."

Marvin's courtship with Anna was further complicated by the effect he had on the young girls at Motown. They were wild for him. Still shy and sexually unsure of himself, he did little fooling around. He knew, though, that his popularity with women gave him leverage with Anna. She was older and not nearly as pretty, in many eyes, as Mary Wilson or Martha Reeves.

"He [Marvin] was so handsome and so soulful," Mary Wilson of the Supremes told writer Gerri Hirshey, "about the most soulful singer that company ever turned up. And we just sat there in a trance. I mean, I fell in love with him, and so did Florence and Diana [Ross]. He knew we all had crushes on him."

Yet Marvin stayed away from the girls, partly out of fear of losing Anna and partly because he still saw himself as a one-woman man. He clung to the dreams expressed in the songs of his childhood; he still envisioned his one true love waiting in a quiet chapel by the moonlight.

Meanwhile, Harvey Fuqua was deepening his relationship with sister Gwen. There was talk of marriage. Gaye still studied his mentor with great care. From Harvey, he learned the principle of combining the personal and professional—a typical Motown motif.

But also, in typical Motown fashion, these pragmatic romantic relationships would eventually sour.

"Harvey had it figured a little differently," Clarence Paul told me. "He thought he'd hook up with Anna and put Marvin with Gwen. It didn't work out that way. Anna liked Marvin. 'He's green,' I told her. 'I'll teach him,' she told me. And she did."

8

SOUNDS COMING 'ROUND

By the early sixties the power in teenage music was falling into the hands of writer-producers. Just as Phil Spector was packaging a sound for the Crystals, just as Carole King and Gerry Goffin were creating "The Locomotion" for Little Eva, Berry Gordy was engineering a half-dozen different trains on a half-dozen different tracks.

"Berry thought like an oil man," Marvin once said. "Drill as many holes as you can and hope for at least one gusher. He wound up with a whole oil field."

As a one-time retailer, songwriter, and producer, Gordy had the right combination of experience. At first he was happy to do a large part of the writing and producing himself. But because his deepest desire was to build an empire, he soon understood that as emperor he needed time for deliberation. Delegation was the key. Berry created teams of writers and producers, talents like Eddie and Brian Holland, Lamont Dozier, William Mickey Stevenson, Norman Whitfield, Ivy Hunter, Hank Cosby, and Clarence Paul. He paid them little, challenged them to come up with hits, and pitted them against each other. With only a handful of writer-producers, Motown would soon surpass the commercial achievement of an institution as formidable as New York's Brill Building, which, in 1965, housed 165 different music firms.

"All us producers were in there writing tunes," Clarence Paul explained. "BG had this policy—get the tune to the artist it fit. An artist might come by—Marvin or the Temps or Gladys—and hear something in the song they could relate to. That 'something' let them pour themselves into the performance. Berry's way was to get the artist into the studio—that afternoon, within the hour—and strike while the iron was hot. That was his genius. Go for spontaneity. Catch that urgency. No matter what the release schedule might be, if you produced a hotter song, it'd get out there right away. I mean within days! That's how we flooded the streets and filled the charts. That's how I once put three tunes in the Top Ten in the same week.

"Now Marvin was a good drummer back then. Good piano player, too. I used him on most of the early things I did for Stevie. Marvin had more talents than anyone else up there. He was deep. In that early Marvin Gaye Revue, when he went out on the road with the Spinners and Hattie Little, I used to say, 'Marvin, you don't want to perform, you want to write.' "

The boss was also pushing Gaye in that same creative direction.

"Berry knew I could write," Marvin said. "He knew I could produce. He saw that from the beginning. But I resisted. I didn't want to be one of the cats behind the scenes. I was determined to get out front. I wound up working on tunes like 'Dancing in the Streets' for Martha and the Vandellas. In those days, even if I did most of the writing and my partners might only contribute a word or a note, I'd share the credit with them equally. I didn't have eyes to compose. I was afraid that my writing talent was so great, I'd get distracted from singing."

Gaye's egotism, as pervasive as it might be, could be balanced by a cool objectivity. To successfully push his case for a splashy Motown singing career, Marvin needed help. He was quick to recognize those best equipped to assist him.

"Smokey was smarter than I was," he admitted. "Not only was he a slicker politician, he wound up performing *and* writing *and* making more money than me. I suppose you could say I was stupid. Or maybe it was just that I didn't want to work that hard."

Marvin also refused to be treated like the other singers, pawns who performed at the producers' pleasure.

"I saw what BG was doing," said Gaye. "He was trying to get the most out of everyone, like a general training his field sergeants. It was a little like the Air Force, and that was the part I hated. I hated the discipline and all the demands. The more hits Berry had, the tighter he ran the ship. Soon Motown was like the gestapo. It was a loving gestapo—because Berry is a loving cat—but it was still the gestapo. I was the one guy crazy enough to argue with BG. Though we were fighting on the same side, I resented his power. He was trying to help me, but I was too defiant to accept his help. I have to say that Berry was patient with me. He understood me because he has a split personality like mine."

"Berry Gordy," said Rob Cohen, who headed the Motown film division in the seventies, "is half teddy bear, half grizzly bear. He's absolutely wonderful, or absolutely frightening. You never know which Berry you're going to get."

"Berry's a fascinating man," Marvin said, "with a lot of angles to him. He's a compulsive gambler, for instance. Berry's such a hard-core better that if you were in his office and it was raining, he'd pick out two raindrops that hit the window at the same time. He'd take one, you'd take the other, and he'd bet you ten bucks that his raindrop would slide down and hit the bottom of the window before yours. He had to be betting all the time.

"Same way with women. Couldn't stay away from them, especially petite, light-skinned women. Berry was the horniest man in Detroit. He married blacks and fooled around with whites. You'd think he was working, but he might be freaking with some chick right up there in his office. Say whatever you want to about Berry, though, but if it wasn't for him, you wouldn't have heard of any of us. BG had the vision."

Gordy's behavior, business and otherwise, continued feeding Marvin's own fantasies. He, too, yearned to become an international playboy, to oversee a vast entertainment empire in which he could play God, toying with employees as though they were so many rooks and knights on a chess board.

"Berry had this trick," explained a former Motown executive, "of turning people against each other. He encouraged infighting as a way to protect his money. He figured if two guys were battling, they'd squeal to him and he'd catch the thief. All through the years he had a lot of thieves up there in high positions. Later when Marvin went on his own, he followed Berry's example—playing advisers against each other, seeing how dishonest people could be. Berry had a distinctive way of doing business."

Imitating Gordy's willful ways would finally do Marvin little good. An extraordinarily good singer, Gaye was an extraordinarily poor businessman. He had a knack for losing money.

Back in the sixties, though, Berry was doing more than building profits; he had finally nurtured a distinctive sound.

"I'd attribute the Motown sound to Jamie Jamerson's busy bass," said Maurice King.

Once King left the Flame Show Bar, he became Motown's main maestro, the man in charge of the Supremes' early stage shows, conductor for Gladys Knight and the Pips, and an important musical instructor to all the acts. A silver-haired and distinguished gentleman, Daddy King, as his students called him, explained the creation of the Motown sound as we lunched in Detroit.

"Jamerson was an inventive bassist who gave the instrument a new dimension. None of the arrangers wrote out the bass lines. Jamie improvised, and many of the best charts were built around his improvisations. Teenage dance music is based on rhythm, and the Motown rhythm section was the Rock of Gibraltar. They called themselves the Funk Brothers—Earl Van Dyke, the leader, on keyboards, Robert White or Joe Messina on guitar, Benny 'Papa Zita' Benjamin on drums, and Jamie on bass. Down there in Studio A, they laid the foundation for Berry Gordy's fortune. We'd add other important elements like tambourines and saxes and strings. Paul Riser's arrangements—seems like he arranged eighty percent of the records—really set the standards and created the overall sound. There was also a strong old-time gospel feel woven in there. But the basis was rhythm, a beat kids danced to, and that beat was largely the invention of Jamie Jamerson who influenced generations of bass players to come."

Beans Bowles agreed with Daddy King: "No doubt Jamie was the man. He came out of Washboard Willie and the Super Suds of Rhythm. He set the tone, he laid down the lines."

"Jamerson was a genius," Marvin told Nelson George in a *Musician* magazine interview in 1983. "The little group that they had there was the Motown sound, and half the credit for productions should go to the musicians . . . they didn't get enough credit."

When George asked Gaye why, he replied, "Because they didn't make it happen. You give your input out of love and expect nothing or you give it and sign a contract. If you want something, you say, 'I'm not giving it up until I sign something and get something for it.' "

"We were doing more on the job than we thought we were doing," Jamerson told Nelson George, "and we didn't get any songwriting credit. They didn't start giving musicians credit until the seventies."

James Jamerson died in 1983. During one of Marvin's final performances, he stopped his "Sexual Healing" show at the Greek Theater in Los Angeles and prayed to Jesus for the bassist's soul.

In those early years, Marvin was experimenting with his own sounds and image. He was trying to fit in and stand out, all at the same time.

"I was playing a game," Marvin commented. "And I had to be careful about making that first move. I enjoyed being a good boy— a drummer, a piano player, a cat who could help out with writing. But when my thing with Anna was tight, I could finally go for what I wanted. My first request was a big one because I didn't know whether I'd ever get a second chance. I wanted to do a jazz-pop album. Anna convinced Berry to let me do it. All this rhythm and blues was cute, but I wasn't interested."

How did Marvin differentiate rhythm and blues from pop?

"Strictly the market. Pop meant selling whites, and R&B or soul meant selling the sisters and brothers back in the neighborhood. Everyone wanted to sell whites 'cause whites got the most money. Our attitude was—give us some. It's that simple."

In spite of the fact that many fans and critics now consider Gaye a "pure artist"—Gordy's description of his former brother-in-law at the time of Marvin's death—the singer was nonetheless obsessed with sales. A part of Marvin considered the music business, along with the rest of human activity, a fascinating game. And he was determined to win. Winning in American enterprise meant expanding your markets—to every age group and color—as ultimately achieved by entertainment geniuses like Walt Disney and Michael Jackson. Success on that level would elude Marvin whose heart remained divided even with his final album in 1983: Should he be true to himself or please his public? Which came first—art or business?

His first album tried to accomplish both goals. Gaye attempted to satisfy his notion of himself as a pure pop singer while aiming for a large crossover market. The effort didn't work. Produced by Gordy himself, *The Soulful Moods of Marvin Gaye* from 1961 featured a wistful cover photograph of the twenty-two-year-old singer, his hair greased and waved in the style of the times. "I had some conks in those days," Marvin remembered, "that looked like ice sculpture."

His debut album was the point at which Gaye officially added the "e" to his name. In addition to wanting to distance himself from Father, he also thought the extra letter lent a certain class. "I was aware that Sam Cooke had done exactly the same thing," he said. "If it worked for Sam, why wouldn't it work for me?"

From the opening piano chords on "The Masquerade Is Over"— a quote from Thelonious Monk's introduction to "Round 'Bout Midnight"—the mood was unsustained. The instrumentation was eerie and sparse, with Marvin sounding unsure of himself. His vibrato was exaggerated, his phrasing wobbly. Supported by a jazz rhythm section, he vacillated between the pop sensibility of Jesse Belvin and the blues-drenched depression of Billie Holiday. He wound up in no-man's-land, a singer in search of a style.

The songs were mostly standards. "I sang 'Witchcraft,' " Marvin admitted, "because Sinatra sang it, and 'You Don't Know What Love Is' because of Lady Day's version. Miles had a thing out on 'My Funny Valentine' which moved me to record the song. I was always fascinated by the theme of 'Love for Sale' and promised myself to put that tune on my first album."

Ironically, the most satisfying vehicles were the only two non-standards. The first, "Let Your Conscience Be Your Guide" by Berry Gordy, had a mournful Ray Charles rhythm-and-blues flavor which suited Marvin's melancholy to a T. The other, "Never Let You Go (Sha-Lu-Bop)," written by Harvey and Anna, had Marvin reaching for his falsetto in a strangely effective stop-and-stutter Jerry Lee Lewis mode. Logically enough, "Conscience" was released as a single, Marvin's first. It failed, as did the album.

"Motown never really wanted me to be a pop singer," Marvin insisted in later years. "They undercut my efforts and never gave me the promotion or push I needed."

When asked for specific examples of how he was undone, Marvin would say, "It was something I felt." When asked why Motown would work against their own artist, he answered, "They were afraid I'd run too far ahead of the rest of the pack."

But the evidence is overwhelming that Motown did, in fact, try to sell Marvin as a new Nat Cole. Over the next four years, he'd record no less than half a dozen albums aimed at a white pop market.

They simply didn't sell. Gordy wanted nothing more than a black Sinatra in his stable, with all the profits and prestige which would accompany such a coup. It's not clear whether the failure was due to Motown's inability to reach that market or because Marvin's voice lacked the emotional authority demanded of experienced balladeers. Probably both.

Either way, Marvin found it especially difficult, if not impossible, to admit this or any other failure. His inflated but frail ego couldn't accept the notion that the public had rejected him. Typically, he made excuses and lay the blame elsewhere.

How did Gaye get away with such conceit? By counterbalancing it with quiet charm and disarming candor. His soft-spoken ways, his laughing eyes, his seductive sincerity, his warmth, wit, and little-boy sweetness gave him considerable power as a personality. People naturally sought Marvin's company and friendship. You couldn't help but love him. He was fun, funny, and, to colleagues and friends, a fascinating man. Gaye used his charisma as expertly as his singing voice. As time went on, he honed his social skills, turning himself into a unique blend of diplomat and prince.

Nonetheless, he worried about his future.

"Down at the studio you couldn't help but be nervous 'cause acts were exploding all around you," Marvin remembered. "You'd come in on a Monday morning and boom! The new *Billboard* was talkin' 'bout a new Marvelettes' smash called 'Please Mr. Postman.' That was Motown's first Number One pop hit, so everyone was jumping up and down. Smokey was hitting and Mary Wells was crossing over with 'You Beat Me to the Punch.' At some point, I realized that doing ballads and singing jazz was cool, but I wanted a hit, too. Without a hit, even if you were going with the boss' sister, your ass would be out of there in no time. Motown wasn't about art. It was about hits."

Marvin's next two singles—a strangely syncopated suger-coated cover version of "Sandman" and the unconvincing military-romantic-patriotic "Soldier's Plea"—also flopped. Both songs were emotionally and musically limp.

"I started to panic," Marvin explained. "It looked like everyone was getting out there with hits and I was stalled at the starting gate. Harvey married Gwen, and he was writing and producing and doing great. If it hadn't been for Anna, I might have skipped out. But she never stopped encouraging me. We were living together then, and it was wonderful because she was always urging me to sing. Anna kept saying that it was only a matter of time before I'd have a hit, and it sure didn't hurt that she was telling Berry the same thing."

Still convinced that the power to succeed came from outside forces—and not from his own talent—Marvin pressed on, motivated to get money for Mother, to show Father he was a winner, to prove himself, to score any way he could.

9
SCORING

The origins of Gaye's first hit were personal, the lyrics, as so often with Marvin, autobiographical.

"Anna was always telling me how stubborn I was," he explained. "I'm an Aries, which helps explain it. I believe in astrology. We know the moon affects the oceans, and since we're mainly water, why wouldn't we be affected by heavenly bodies? Anyway, this 'stubborn' idea was floating around my brain while Mickey Stevenson and I started jamming. We'd come up with a basic jazz feeling, when Berry walked by, heard what we were doing, sat down at the piano and said, 'How 'bout trying these chords? Put these chords in there and I think you'll sell some records.' That was Berry's genius—just a few chords, and I was gone."

"Stubborn Kind of Fellow" with Martha and the Vandellas singing background and Beans Bowles on flute, was infectious, sexy, straight-ahead rhythm and blues, light years away from Marvin's peaches-and-cream balladry. He coated the dark middle range of his voice with gravel and grit. Because it was a hit—a black hit— the song changed the course of Marvin Gaye's career. Not white people, as Marvin had hoped, but black people represented his primary market. They demanded of him, just as they had demanded of Ray Charles (who had begun his career by imitating Nat Cole), that he sing his color.

"I wanted a hit, and I got one," Marvin told me. "I had to be happy. But I also felt out of control. I felt Berry was the pilot and I was the plane. I watched the song climb up the R&B chart. It made the Top Ten, but I knew it wouldn't cross over to the white chart. And it didn't. At that point I knew I'd have to travel the same road as all black artists before me—establish a soul audience and then reach beyond that. Looking back, it was probably good for me. It kept me honest and forced me back to my roots, but it also frustrated me. It meant I'd have to get out there and shake my ass like everyone else."

Gaye was pushed back out on stage, a reluctant and frightened performer. Yet no matter how strong his fear of singing live, his drive to become a star was even stronger. When the bus pulled out, he was on it.

The first Motortown Revue hit the road in 1962, the same year James Meredith was finally admitted as the first black student into the University of Mississippi. The Contours, Supremes, Marvelettes, Little Stevie Wonder, Mary Wells, the Miracles, and Marvin Gaye were on the tour, which opened, ironically, at the Howard Theater at Washington, D.C. From there they went to the Midwest, through the Deep South, and after dozens of grueling one-nighters, wound up at the Apollo for a week. The results can be heard on *Recorded Live at the Apollo, Volume 1*.

The concert sounded crude. The famous Motown performance polish had yet to be applied. The acts were still struggling. Searching for their first hit, the Supremes featured Diana Ross singing in a rough, gruff style outside her element. Little Stevie did a studied imitation of Ray Charles, duplicating Ray's "Don't You Know" lick for lick. The big stars on the bill, the Miracles and Mary Wells, sang with surprising gospel fervor.

Listening to the record with Marvin, I watched him smile while he put his hands over his ears. "That's the Apollo, all right," he laughed. "The audience was right up in your face, the women be screaming at you, grabbing at you, and I was scared out of my wits. I liked the shows later on when Jr. Walker opened the bill with that signifyin' sax of his."

Marvin's Apollo performance was an illumination of the twin-image bind in which he found himself.

He opened with "What Kind of Fool Am I?", his attempt to establish his ballad-pop persona. His voice, though, was filled with fear. His phrasing was so unsteady that for a second it didn't seem like he could finish the song. As on his first album, he sounded lost and afraid. A few swoons from female admirers gave him a bit more confidence, but, singing the chorus a second time, he was still shaky. On the final chorus, like a boxer down for the count, Marvin realized he was about out. How could he recover? How could he stay on his feet? By invoking the muse of Ray Charles. Suddenly Gaye interrupted his ballad with a church cry: "I want to tell y'all, just like Uncle Ray would say right here," he sang before moaning and groaning his way to a satisfying emotional conclusion. He was on his feet again as he smoothly switched gears, bouncing into "Stubborn Kind of Fellow," a song that sat firmly upon the rock of the country-church tradition.

"You can't imagine how important Ray Charles was for us," Marvin told me. "We all idolized him—me, Smokey, Stevie, Berry, Beans, CP, all the cats who really knew music. Ray had crossed over by being his bad self, and that impressed us. Berry's aim was to sell white people, and Ray had already accomplished that. Matter of fact, in my opinion he went too far. Ray got funny when he started using white background vocalists, instead of Raelettes, to sing his country shit. Black folk resented that. They'll always honor and love him, but he quit them, and they knew it. Rest of his career, Ray had to sell white people. He tried to sing ballads and had some success, but I don't think Ray's a ballad singer. He's a blues singer. Just like Nat Cole couldn't sing no blues, Ray Charles can't sing no ballads. Me, I knew I could go both ways.

"Commercially, though, I learned quickly that it was primarily my people who were going to support me. I vowed always to take care of them—give 'em the funk they wanted. It wasn't my first choice, but there's integrity in the idea of pleasing your own people. Secretly, I yearned to sing for rich Republicans in tuxes and tails at the Copacabana. No matter, I listened to Smokey Robinson, a very smart cat, when he told me, 'Treat your fans right. Respect them and they'll respect you.' Fans are funny. Leave them once, and they'll never forgive you.

"You have a relationship with your fans, especially your female fans, just like you have a relationship with a woman. They feel like they know you, and they do. You've exposed your deepest emotions to them. You can tease 'em, you can please 'em, you can leave 'em, or you can drive 'em wild. I've done all those things to my fans, but they've stuck with me 'cause they feel my sincerity. When I'm happy, I sing about it. When I'm not, they know about that, too. The act of singing to people is just as strong as screwing—sometimes stronger. The emotions are just as big as the money you're making. It's risky."

Gaye was learning how to excite an audience. The link in his mind between singing and sexual intercourse was a recurring theme. He was insecure about both acts, never quite certain how long his power would last. For Marvin, sex and public performances were troublesome tests of his masculinity. He would refine his skills at stimulating women during live concerts, but the price was guilt and self-scorn. As hard as he tried, he could never convince himself that celebrating the flesh was anything less than devilish. He yearned to be off the road, where he could concentrate on composing and recording at home with some degree of calmness.

According to his friend Beans Bowles, "If it hadn't been for Stevie, Marvin probably never would have been a star. You see, we'd always put Stevie on before Marvin, 'cause Stevie was about energy. Stevie would get out there and carry on. He didn't give Marvin any choice. After what Stevie did, Marvin had to come out there steamin' or he'd lose the crowd.

" 'Why you always puttin' that little blind sucker on before me?' Marvin would ask me. He really loved Stevie, but that's how he talked.

" 'Cause that's the only way we got of getting you to really sing,' I'd tell him.

"Touring back then was murder. Berry packed far too many people on the bus—we were always overcrowded—and he booked way too many dates. The strain was bad. We had a bad accident in November of '62—my driver was killed—and we were lucky not to have others. There might have been a little weed around, but no coke. Who had the money? The pay stunk. I don't think Marvin was getting more than $60 a week back then, even when he had his own band with Eddie 'Bongo' Brown. Everyone was always complaining. You see, in order to protect the singers and musicians, we'd put part of their money in an escrow account. Most of them were under eighteen, and if we hadn't done that, they'd have blown all their bread before we'd get back to Detroit. The problem was that Berry kept those accounts going for too long. He didn't know when to stop treating people like kids. They wanted to be respected as adults."

Marvin's songwriting talents resulted in a major hit for the Marvelettes. Marvin, George Gordy, and Mickey Stevenson wrote "Beechwood 45789" which ran up in the charts in the summer of 1962.

At the beginning of 1963 Gaye wrote a road song, "Hitch Hike," with Mickey Stevenson and Clarence Paul, a former vocal duo. This was when Stevenson, who'd once sung with Lionel Hampton's Hamp-Tones, and CP comprised the Motown A&R department.

" 'Hitch Hike' was Marvin's concept," said Clarence. "He had the groove worked out when we started helping him. That's him playing drums and piano on the track."

Marvin also claimed, justifiably, that he invented the thumbs-out arms-extended dance called the Hitch Hike.

"Dick Clark started having me on his show," Marvin remembered. "He saw that I'd started this Hitch Hike craze, and he got a kick out of watching me stumble around the stage."

In old concert film clips, like the teen T.A.M.I. shows, Marvin appeared as a surprisingly relaxed and polished dancer. Though nothing fancy, his steps were consistently smooth. He possessed a subtle grace. To see him dance so deftly, you can't help but wonder why he was frightened of the act.

"I don't know," he said. "Maybe it has to do with school dances and never having the guts to ask the girl to dance. I was afraid I'd step all over myself. That feeling never went away. Besides, if you're a black dancer—a black male dancer—you're moving in James Brown's territory. There's room for only one champ. I knew I didn't have a shot. Perhaps I could be Number One with my voice, but never with my feet. Michael Jackson became James' successor. Watch Michael dance and you'll understand why I'd rather be singing while sitting on a stool."

"Hitch Hike," in which Gaye quoted from Ray Charles' "What I Say," became a dance smash, a gospel shuffle with Marvin referring to his congregation as 'chillin'." Mick Jagger soon sang a painfully pale cover version with the Rolling Stones.

"All these songs were naturals," Marvin said. "It was like they wrote themselves."

In June 1963, "Pride and Joy" became the first of Marvin's songs to cross over. It made the Top Ten on the pop chart, establishing Marvin Gaye as something more than a rhythm-and-blues star. Now white kids were dancing to his music. His commercial value had risen dramatically. For most artists this would be a moment of great jubilation. Unable to enjoy his success, Marvin grew anxious.

"In my mind I started worrying—how long could I last? Stars, you see, are merely leaping from hit to hit. Below us, the public watches and waits for us to fall on our ass. But if we don't keep leaping, we fade and die. That's the sort of pressure I faced."

Some of the worry was assuaged through his marriage later that year to Anna. "Pride and Joy" coincided with their legal union. Gaye wrote the song with Mickey Stevenson and Norman Whitfield, who, later in the sixties, would become Marvin's nemesis as well as producer. From the bright opening riffs of light jazz piano and walking bass, the mood was merry.

"When I composed 'Pride and Joy,'" Marvin said, "I was head over heels in love with Anna. I just wrote what I felt about her, and what she did for me. She was my pride and joy."

In the song, Gaye referred to himself as Anna's "baby boy," saying how he worked for her night and day, how he gave her all his pay, and how she rewarded him by breaking his depressions. He remembered the parties they attended, and her flamboyant dresses designed to "shake up" the city's high society.

"Anna would love to get dressed up for those affairs," Marvin said. "God bless her. She had to be the snazziest dresser in Detroit. When Anna got decked out, I mean she got decked out. Whenever I wasn't working—and that wasn't too often—we'd be partying."

The song, Gaye's most powerful performance to date, had him pumping the call-and-response pattern like a natural-born preacher. His voice dipped down to a surprisingly deep Brook Benton bottom as he utilized more of his three-octave range. He was confident and happy, providing for two women—the wife he called Mama and the lady back in Washington he called Mother.

Clarence Paul attended Anna and Marvin's wedding and described the party which followed:

"The reception was in the shop downstairs, at Farnsworth and St. Antoine, the place where Anna Records used to be. All the Motown people were there—the singers, musicians, everyone from the office. Anna and Marvin got into a big fight—right there at the party. Anna hit him in the head with a shoe heel. Me and Fuqua, we nearly fell down laughing."

Marvin's family in Washington, D.C., had been moved out of the East Capitol Dwellings into still another project, this one on Allison Street. Shortly after his marriage Marvin moved them out of the projects altogether and bought them a large house on the corner of Fifteenth and Varnum, in the black middle-class section of northwest Washington.

Mother was finally able to stop working and enjoy the security of owning a home. The house, with its large outside porches, was roomy and comfortable. The neighborhood was tree-lined and green, with spacious parks nearby. The house on Varnum would be the Gaye family home for the next decade. It was here where Marvin would periodically visit his mother, visits which would have been more frequent were it not for the presence of Father.

Marvin was still ashamed of his father and determined to relegate Washington to his past. His unhappy memories of growing up, his sibling rivalry with Frankie and sister Jeanne—herself as independent and feisty as Marvin—kept him far away from the District. Gaye's shame concerned more than his father, though; he was just as ashamed of his remembered self as a kid—a frustrated athlete, a reluctant fighter, a boy painfully shy with girls. He wanted to forget it all.

"We knew Marvin was doing well," said Jeanne Gay, "because he sent us money. He kept us far from the Gordys, though. He didn't want us involved in his Detroit life. He never wanted us to know the Gordys."

In the Gordy family, Marvin felt protected and loved. In Pops Gordy, he found a father of deep compassion and acceptance, qualities which, Gaye maintained, his own father lacked. In Mom Gordy, he found a mother who wasn't the least afraid of men. He was comforted by her strength and ability to hold the family together. To the third generation of Gordys—the children of Berry and his siblings—Marvin was the cool uncle, a man who loved and understood kids. In Gaye's mind, he had been adopted and saved from a past of rejection and pain. No wonder he wanted to forget Washington.

"When Marvin started having hits," said Peasie, his neighbor from the East Capitol projects, "seems like he turned his back on D.C. I heard him say in interviews that he didn't like Washington. Then he started telling everyone that he came from Detroit."

"When Marvin left," his old friend Reese Palmer recalled, "he left without looking back . . . that hurt a lot of us."

"I'm a little like that song the Five Keys used to sing," Gaye said. " 'Out of Sight, Out of Mind.' "

Marvin's attempts to forget his past would never succeed. His deep-rooted affection for Mother always brought him home. He would always be close to his mother, and this would be intensified in the late sixties when his relationship with Anna began to collapse. Soon after his marriage he would grow jealous of Anna's closeness to Berry, just as he was jealous of his own mother's relationship with his father. "Anna never had the love for me that she had for her brother," Gaye claimed.

Yet for some time Marvin found comfort in the arms of his wife. He was nurtured by a strong Gordy clan whose loyalty to one another was absolute. His ambition was perfectly matched by their appreciation for his talent and their desire to make money on music. In the beginning, it was a fruitful marriage—emotionally and creatively. The fact that the Gordys—Anna and Berry especially—were also noted for a degree of sexual liberalism served both to excite and confuse a twenty-four-year-old Marvin Gaye, who was still filled with fears of the ways of the material world.

10

GAIN AND STRAIN

For a while, it seemed as though Gaye had found a measure of domestic happiness.

"Marv and Anna were a beautiful couple," Renaldo "Obie" Benson of the Four Tops told me. "In the early years when I was knowing them it seemed like a very sweet marriage. Marvin was one of the most mellow cats I'd ever met. There was a little friendly competition between him and the Tops, but it was good for us. We all knew we could sing, and we brought out the best in each other. I saw Marvin's happy side, the Marvin that liked to play ball in the park all afternoon and laugh till his sides split. I spent lots of good times with Marv and Anna, especially when they were living in their first place over on St. Antoine and Farnsworth."

St. Antoine and Farnsworth has mythical significance in the history of the Gordy family. The intersection represents the very heart of the family enterprise.

"It all began there," Esther said wistfully. "Berry Gordy grew up on that corner. It's where we should really build a museum."

In the original office on West Grand, Esther Gordy Edwards, the family historian, displayed a photograph of Berry Gordy as a kid, climbing atop the street sign of that very corner where Pops Gordy had his print shop and grocery store. At this same locale, in their little apartment, Anna gave Marvin the push—just as her parents had pushed Berry—to go out and conquer the world.

* * *

Back in the studio in 1963, after his marriage, Marvin had begun pacing the pack. He not only caught up with the others but jumped out ahead, with one significant exception.

In June 1963, the same month that Medgar Evers was murdered in Mississippi, Motown had celebrated its second Number One pop song, the best-selling record in the country. Little Stevie Wonder's "Fingertips, Part 2," co-written by Stevie and Clarence Paul, was all the more unusual because it was a live recording, a virtual revival meeting.

"When they put the record out," Clarence said, "Berry Gordy was listed as producer. He wasn't even in town when we did it."

"You really had to start paying attention to Stevie after 'Fingertips,' " said Gaye, who, with his pal Paul, had written "Soul Bongo," an early jazz percussion showpiece for Stevie. "No matter what else you might be doing, you'd always know that Stevie had a superior musical intelligence and was learning just as fast as you."

Like Marvin, Stevie was also a drummer and had all the advantages of being a percussive vocalist, a singer especially sensitive to rhythmic nuances.

In July, Wonder released his first album, recorded before "Fingertips," in which he was called an "11-year-old musical genius." The record, *Tribute to Uncle Ray*, introduced Stevie as the next Ray Charles who, according to Billie Jean Brown's liner notes, was Wonder's idol. The album arrived in the stores within days of the March on Washington, when over 210,000 civil rights demonstrators converged to witness the "I Have a Dream" sermon of Martin Luther King, Jr., whose most inspired speeches were recorded and sold on Motown Records. (Earlier in the summer, Dr. King, with the Reverend C. L. Franklin by his side, had led a massive rally down Woodward Avenue in Detroit which some called the prototype for the March on Washington. Two decades later Wonder would honor his political hero by successfully leading a campaign to make King's birthday a national holiday.)

Meanwhile, in the summer of 1963, Motown's response to "Fingertips" was typical—crank out more of the same. If the gospel feeling was selling, then pour it on. By November, Holland-Dozier-Holland, Motown's most successful producer-writer team, had written "Can I Get a Witness?" whose title revealed its holy roots. Marvin recorded the tune minutes after hearing it the first time. The song, a particular favorite of John Lennon's, was a hit. Gaye's popularity was on the rise.

"The civil rights movement was really happening," Marvin remembered, "and I think a lot of the hipper white kids were tired of the old folks' prejudices. They liked our stuff 'cause we expressed real feelings. We also turned out the best dance music. If America would judge its music on merit, blacks would dominate the industry. The music biz would start looking like the National Basketball Association. Back in the sixties, the white folks felt guilty for a few years, and they gave us a little coin. Then the killings started—Jack Kennedy, Malcolm, Martin, Bobby—LBJ bought the Vietnam bullshit and everything got fucked."

The movement of Marvin's career was swift, but Gordy wanted him moving even faster.

"Berry was crazy back then," Marvin said. "Hard work is one thing. I can dig the Gordy family approach—work keeps you straight—but Berry carried it too far. Berry had us working till we dropped. There was a lot of mental pressure and not everyone could handle it. Berry found people to teach us to dress and speak and perform at nightclubs, but he also might have thought a little about our mental state. Some of us—though we'd never admit it—might have needed help. Show business means working eighteen-hour days, with a million phone calls and interviews and rehearsals and recordings, all with the aim of pleasing people. At some point you gotta go off and cool out or you'll crack."

As a member of the family, couldn't Marvin make that point to Gordy?

"Berry didn't understand the concept. He pushed us as far as human beings could be pushed. If we weren't touring we were cutting sides, and if we weren't promoting we were learning our dance steps."

At a certain point, though, Marvin rebelled against Gordy, just as he'd rebelled against Father.

A disc jockey tells the story of a midsixties night at the Twenty Grand, a Detroit night spot, when Gaye was due to perform while Gordy was seated out front. Marvin simply refused to go on, saying he was too frightened. Burning with anger, Berry went backstage and smacked Marvin in the mouth, then began cursing him. The disc jockey said he'd never seen anyone reprimanded with such vehemence. Marvin took the punishment and, a few minutes later, performed.

Usually, though, his rebellion was not derailed.

"Soon as I had a couple of hits, I said, 'No, I don't want no charm school, I don't need no charm school, and no one's going to make me go.' Being married to Anna, I got away with that attitude. Now I regret my arrogance because I think teachers like Miss Powell really had something to teach."

Maxine Powell headed the Motown finishing school. She dressed and groomed the Supremes. From a Broadway stage in 1977, Diana Ross introduced her as "the woman who taught me everything I know."

After a formal banquet in Detroit during which Esther Gordy Edwards acknowledged Miss Powell's seminal contribution to the company's success, I met with Maxine. Privately, she was embittered that Motown hadn't provided for her retirement, though she spoke of her service with quiet pride.

"I taught them discipline and also how to handle people. My philosophy was, don't antagonize the enemy, obligate him. The kids had three main teachers. Maurice King taught them music two hours a day. Cholly Atkins taught them dancing for two hours, and I taught them manners. Be warm, I told them, be natural, be poised, and be positive. I gave them stage presence. I taught them how to walk, how to talk, how to hold a microphone. I explained that body communication is an art. Mr. Gordy was interested in giving these young artists class. They were kids who didn't even know how to shake hands or look someone directly in the eye— eye contact is so important—or say please and thank you. The Temptations and Supremes were good students, though in the beginning Diana tried too hard to make funny faces and play with her eyes. That was phony, and she finally stopped. Marvin Gaye would argue with me. I'd tell him to keep his eyes opened when he sang, and he'd refuse. He also didn't like coming to class, but in his case I don't think it mattered much. Marvin had fine manners and poise. He was a person of breeding. My biggest responsibility was with the girls, and when the Supremes became an international sensation, I went on the road with them. I served as their chaperone, polishing and dying their shoes, even mending their dresses. For all that, I have years of memories and nothing else."

Abandonment is a common cry among the Motowners who remained in Detroit.

At the end of the sixties, when Berry Gordy deserted the city by moving his operation to Los Angeles, he provoked the sort of bitter resentment Brooklynites express over their long-lost Dodgers. To many it seemed wrong, unfair, even immoral. They argued that the soul of his empire—and his music—was in the streets of Detroit.

In the beginning Gordy depended upon strict teachers like Powell, King, and Atkins to give his student singers a brand of professionalism geared to eliminate the smell of the streets. The instructors were twenty years older than their pupils and seasoned pros themselves.

"We didn't stand for a bit of nonsense," Maurice King told me. "No drinking, no pot. We worked the kids until they became pros. When we were through with them, they could play any supper club in the country and shine."

Committed to the American work ethic and a policy of upward mobility, Gordy's corporate slogan became "The Sound of Young America." The label that Marvin would record on—from his first Motown record in 1961 to his last, some thirty albums later in 1982—was Tamla, inspired by Berry Gordy's favorite Debbie Reynolds movie, *Tammy*. Emerging out of the turbulent and angry sixties, Berry Gordy's black acts were nonetheless exciting throwbacks to early Negro show business. Gordy produced entertainers in the grand old style reminiscent of Duke Ellington in top hat and tails, his orchestra outfitted in dazzling white tuxedos.

Doubly ironic was the fact that although Gordy's crossover marketing strategy benefited from a civil rights–minded period in history, the company, at least in its music, ignored the social revolution which was partially responsible for its spectacular success. Not until the late sixties did Motown catch up with the rest of soul music in interjecting racial consciousness into its songs. As a good businessman, Berry was far more interested in preparing his performers for the high-priced white clubs. He accomplished that with exceptional class. Marvin was convinced he could do the same, but only according to his own artistic vision. He insisted that he have a show of his own.

Typically, Gaye went from an extreme reliance on his mentors— Fuqua and Gordy—to a fiery declaration of independence. Marvin was ready to break out in his own style. His ambivalence toward record executives, managers, and lawyers would increase as his career prospered. He resented needing them. Even more, a distinct sense of mistrust, which ultimately turned to blatant paranoia, became a permanent part of his attitude toward nearly everyone with whom he did business.

Marvin Gaye, Live on Stage documented his 1963 show, recorded just before the assassination of President Kennedy. Twelve months and three hits after his floundering performance at the Apollo, he sounded like a different man.

"There's nothing like singing a string of your own hits," he said. "The audience response is immediate."

By the time Marvin sang "Hitch Hike," he had the audience in his pocket. They knew all the lyrics. Singing along, they became his church choir. His version of "Days of Wine and Roses" proved he hadn't given up his ballad ambitions, just as "You Are My Sunshine" showed that Ray Charles' comforting spirit was still close to Gaye's heart.

Marvin's confidence grew with leaps and bounds. Being part of a troop of highly driven performers helped keep him sharp. He and his colleagues competed with one another, but they also enjoyed a strong solidarity. Caught in the same upward spiral, whirling toward success, they leaned on one another for moral support. At the same time, though, having married into the Gordy inner circle, Marvin was always one step ahead of the others.

In 1964, Gaye was filled with praise and gratitude for the woman who had given him his advantage, Anna Ruby Gordy Gaye. In turn, Holland-Dozier-Holland gave Marvin "You're a Wonderful One," which hit the charts in February.

The song's simple story concerned a woman who gave her man courage through "words of confidence," who lifted his spirit and pushed him ahead in an otherwise burdensome world.

"I sang all these songs for Anna," Marvin said. "Before we actually married, I had struggled with the decision. It was something we both wanted, but also a situation where we could see the dangers. Anna and I were hot characters with hot ambitions. Because her ambition was directed on me, it seemed cool. And once I started selling, I was overjoyed. Our plan seemed to be working. I was going to be the biggest star, and Anna would get to be the biggest star's glamorous wife. Her thing was being Mrs. Marvin Gaye. She was pushing me to be the champ.

"Around this time, Muhammad Ali knocked out Sonny Liston in seven rounds. Ali was really the champ I wanted to be. I knew he was a fighter who would last for years. Consistency—that's the quality I respect the most. Ernie Banks, Hank Aaron, Jim Brown—those were the big-name cats who were proving something."

The Motortown Revue souvenir program from 1964 awarded Gaye top billing, an indication of his standing with Motown management at the time. His picture came before anyone else's. While all the other singers—Little Stevie, the Supremes, the Marvelettes, the Temptations, Martha and the Vandellas—had single-page photographs, Marvin was the only artist with two full pages devoted entirely to him. He was shown in a suave dinner jacket posing like Sinatra—sitting on a stool while lighting a cigarette. "This personable showman," the blurb read, "is appealing to adults as well as teens."

"We tried to market Marvin to as broad-based an audience as possible," said Alan Abrams, Motown's original public relations man. Even though Gaye argued otherwise, it's hard to understand why Motown would go against itself and *not* try to make Marvin into a superstar. Gaye's attitude was more a result of paranoia than fact.

In April 1964, Mary Wells' "My Guy" crossed over and became Motown's third Number One pop hit. Marvin benefited from the success because he'd just recorded an album of duets with Mary—*Together*—his first in what would be a succession of musical pairings with women.

Gaye's duets had enormous impact on his career. They elicited another side of his musical personality. He became the young black boy every young black girl wanted to date and love.

"White girls also got off on that stuff," Marvin said, "but the times wouldn't let them admit it. I've always thought my white female following was extremely strong, though dormant."

Women of all shades started falling for Marvin in greater numbers not only because of his clean-cut pretty-boy looks, but also because of the peculiarly personal nature of the love songs he sang with lady singers. With this visibility, however, came problems.

"I suppose you could say that the duets were not great for my marriage," Marvin said.

"We both were young and attractive people, so it started gossip," said Mary Wells. " 'Are they going together?' "

"Anna was the jealous type to begin with," Marvin remembered. "I guess I didn't make it any easier for her. I had all these hits, and maybe I was feeling a little bit more confident. I was starting to feel my oats. After all, when women are yelling for you night after night, that does something to your head. Temptations were on the rise. I fell into the habit of taking a handkerchief, mopping my brow, and throwing it into the audience. I loved watching the women fight over my sweat. It gave me a funny feeling, a thrill and a fear, because I saw how much they really wanted me. Sometimes one of those women would actually run up on stage and throw herself at me. People laugh, but being sexually assaulted by a half-crazed woman is no laughing matter."

The more success Gaye enjoyed with female fans, the more his old childhood fears of women—and his inability to satisfy them— resurfaced. It was a trap he would never escape and the reason he often made the statement that he hated womankind. Pleasing women was a chore he approached with suppressed anger which manifested itself in his sadomasochism, in rituals which allowed him to inflict pain upon his sexual partners, thereby punishing them for their insatiable demands.

A note of discord slipped into the early duets. Appropriately enough, the big Marvin-and-Mary single was "What's the Matter With You, Baby?" his first hit in which romantic quarreling cropped up as a theme. The flip side—"Once Upon a Time"—co-written and produced by Clarence Paul, invoked the fairy-tale tone which typified many of Marvin's duets.

Marvin Gaye and Mary Wells were Motown's premier singers in May 1964. Only two months later, though, the situation shifted.

In July, the Supremes' "Where Did Our Love Go?" and the Four Tops' "Baby, I Need Your Loving" crossed over and ushered in a new era for Motown. Sales went from good to phenomenal. White people in droves were picking up the Motown groove, and for the next several years, the Supremes and the Tops would lead the way to the bank.

Though somewhat less spectacular, Marvin's hits didn't stop.

"Try It Baby" climbed the charts, black and white, in the summer and fall of 1964. In this same period, Marvin heard the rolling thunder of a new soul singer, Otis Redding, whose muscular style influenced Gaye's second 1964 hit, "Baby Don't You Do It."

A few months later, Holland-Dozier-Holland borrowed a line from Jackie Gleason and gave Marvin "How Sweet It Is." The tune was Gaye's biggest seller to date, reaching Number Six pop and consolidating his consistency as a crossover artist. Marvin saw the lyrics as another loving tribute to Anna and his dependence upon her. In the song, sung in his bounciest happy-go-lucky mood, he admitted he'd be nowhere without his wife in his life.

"I was glad it was a big hit," he said, "but very disappointed that it didn't reach Number One. That was a dream I still couldn't give up."

Nor had he given up his dream of becoming a crooner. In addition to *How Sweet It Is*, an album featuring his rhythm-and-blues hits, Gaye also released *When I'm Alone I Cry*, another attempt to crack the pop market with standards and strings. Compared to the bare-bones arrangements on Marvin's 1961 *Soulful Moods* album, the orchestrations were extravagant and lush.

"I did the tracks in New York and Chicago," said Clarence Paul who produced the work. "Marvin was out on the road, and I called him to get the right keys. Then I had first-rate jazz arrangers—Jerome Richardson, Melba Liston, and Ernie Wilkins—write the charts. Everything was done by the time Marvin got back to Detroit. At Motown, you'd be working your butt off on the road, and the minute you hit Detroit, you'd be recording vocal overdubs. From the road to the studio back to the road again, with no time to catch your breath."

Still infatuated with Billie Holiday's *Lady in Satin*, Marvin asked Clarence to include two of its songs, "You've Changed" and "I'll Be Around." There were also songs associated with Ray Charles and Frank Sinatra. You can feel the seriousness of Marvin's effort. If anything, he tried too hard, enunciating like Nat Cole, slurring like Sinatra. His ballad style remained self-conscious and restrained. He held back feelings in favor of what he considered "correct" interpretations. The results were flat, though on the up-tempo numbers he swung effortlessly, demonstrating his natural feel for jazz. Marvin's musical craft showed signs of refinement.

Still, the album failed commercially, while his first collection of *Greatest Hits*, released a month afterward, sold briskly.

Nineteen sixty-four was the year that Dick Gregory, a later friend of Marvin's, led demonstrations in Atlanta, three civil rights workers were killed in Mississippi, Martin Luther King, Jr. won the Nobel Peace Prize, and the Civil Rights Act was passed. Meanwhile, the music business was going through monumental changes of its own: The Beatles were arriving in America.

"The Beatles and Motown had something of a friendly rivalry," according to Marvin. "Historical battles fascinate me, and this was a big one. The English were invading our shores. Even though at first it sounded like they were just singing watered-down versions of Chuck Berry and Isley Brothers songs, they had the style and the sales. No matter, Berry was prepared to hold his ground. When everyone else in America got scared off by the big British wave, when everyone in the music business was screaming that American pop was through, Motown had the guts to hold firm. Not only that—BG fired back. He made Motown big in England. Ever see that picture of Berry over his mantle when he moved into the mansion on Boston Boulevard? It's BG dressed up as Napoleon. You got to hand it to him—Berry was a fearless warrior."

The Beatles arrived in America for the first time on February 7, 1964. LBJ bombed North Vietnam in August. On November 21, *Melody Maker* in England carried a story stating that "Tamla Motown star Marvin Gaye was due to fly into London on Tuesday for six days of television and radio dates." The Beatles were back home—"I Feel Fine" went on sale the week Marvin was in town—and Marvin, along with his wife Anna and Gwen and Harvey Fuqua, had come to boost his career in Britain.

"I was enthralled," the singer said. "The English people and I shared an immediate rapport. There was a very soulful thing between us. They brought out the aristocrat in me, and they could see how much I love listening to them speak. When I looked at Trafalgar Square the first time, I swore I'd come back to England to live. Like everything else I've ever wanted, I achieved that goal, though under highly unusual conditions."

In the November 28, 1964, issue, *Melody Maker* explained the real purpose behind Marvin's trip: "Marvin Gaye, aged 24, has not had a hit in Britain. . . . Marvin was in Britain last week for TV and radio appearances. He took time off to review some of the latest pop singles for *Melody Maker* and proved an intelligent, analytical commentator."

Gaye was played records and asked to guess who was singing. He correctly identified Johnny Rivers and the Four Seasons—he liked them both—but confused the Honeycombs for the Rolling Stones. He was quick to analyze trends, revealing his interest in music marketing. He also voiced his opinion on current English tastes. "I think the British people right now prefer rhythm and blues," he told the press.

At the end of 1964, with "How Sweet It Is" a hit on both sides of the Atlantic, Gaye returned to Detroit, flushed with success and grateful to Anna that his star was in ascension, but dangerously distracted by the screams of his female admirers, the women pulling at him from the first row. He feared them, he hated them, he sang to make them happy. He realized that they were the key to his fortune and the path to his ruin. By winning the hearts of women—his primary market—Marvin Gaye was making money.

"Sometimes I felt like a kept man," Marvin reflected, "but prostitution is a matter of deep personal interest to me. Heat rises when money is involved. Mixing money and sex makes for a sizzling erotic stew."

The restless energy of America's black masses could be felt in the pounding, relentless rhythms of Motown's hard-working music. Black people had always loved Motown. They responded to its authenticity. Now white people were buying the sound, just as Berry Gordy was wrapping his artists in the most attractive, brightly colored packages he could devise.

The corporate public relations program was in full swing. Articles placed from coast to coast perpetuated the Motown myth. Diana Ross and her sister Supremes were photographed skipping through the Brewster Projects. Motown wanted America to believe Diana's rags-to-riches story, while, in truth, she'd been brought up thoroughly middle class: her father had been a successful mid-level factory supervisor.

On the deepest level, though, the myth was true. Motown was a miracle. It wasn't the squeaky-clean company described in *The*

New York Times Magazine article entitled "The Big, Happy, Beating Heart of the Detroit Sound." Yet with all its secret anxieties, its back stabbing and feuds, the company had become a powerfully independent black-owned force in a white-controlled industry.

In the midst of Motown's spectacular rise, Marvin Gaye blew into the mid-sixties on a whirlwind of bewildering success.

11

SUPREME WEALTH

The explosive success of the Supremes set Motown on its ear, changing the very nature of the company, turning it from an oddity to a major factor in international pop music.

"Berry Gordy was already getting rich," Marvin said, "but in '64–'65 the Supremes made him super rich."

That was the period when the group owned the charts, scoring five Number One songs in a row: "Where Did Our Love Go?" "Baby Love," "Come See about Me," "Stop! In the Name of Love," "Back in My Arms Again," all written and produced by Holland-Dozier-Holland. The Supremes became the most popular American entertainers of the day. Only the Beatles made more money.

"Holland-Dozier-Holland," said Billie Jean Brown, who had become Berry Gordy's executive assistant, "really warmed up on Martha and the Vandellas. When they started producing the Supremes, they hit their prime."

"At Motown, stars had little power," Kim Weston told me in Detroit as we sat in the office from which she ran a mayor's arts program for underprivileged children. A woman with alluring eyes and shapely hips, she was the sixties Motown singing star who had followed Mary Wells as Marvin's duet partner.

"In those days," Kim said in her soft, sultry voice, "the producer had the power. I was married to Mickey Stevenson, the A&R director, and I saw how things worked. Diane—that's what we called her back then—did anything the producers asked. She was especially close to Brian Holland. She was very aggressive and not always popular with her co-workers. Diane was lucky someone didn't kick her ass.

"Dick Clark is the one really responsible for the Supremes phenomenon. They had gone on his 'Cavalcade of Stars' revue at the last minute as substitutes. Because of the impact of Dick Clark's show, 'Where Did Our Love Go?' became a hit while they were on the road. It was an accident of history. But it was no accident the way Diane catered to Berry, and later got Berry to cater to her."

"No one was prepared for the Supremes," Marvin said. "It flipped Berry out, like he was playing the slot machines in Vegas and three cherries came up ten times in a row. He was gone. The rest of us felt his interest turn. Professionally he turned toward the Supremes and romantically he hooked up with Diana. Everyone saw it coming. I had predicted it and was definitely aware of being jealous of Diana. She had a power I lacked. I had Anna to talk to Berry, but Diana had Berry himself. For years, I was obsessed with Diana's stardom. I resented the attention BG lavished upon her. But how could I blame him? The Supremes were making him a fortune. Besides, with Diana's drive and class, he knew this was only the beginning."

"Diana Ross," Gil Askey told me, "had an ideal commercial voice. When she had to, she could go out and get the butter." Askey travelled for years as musical director of the Supremes and was one of Motown's most respected musicians. His big-band arrangements were the highlights of Ross' first film, *Lady Sings the Blues*.

"Motown understood the transistor radio," said Marvin. "Back then transistors were selling like hot cakes, and Motown songs were mixed to sound good on transistors and car radios. Diana's voice was the perfect instrument to cut through those sound waves.

"I appreciate Diana's trip and Diana's talent. She's worked hard for everything she's achieved. If she had been white like Barbra Streisand, it would have been a hundred times easier for her. Diana's always measured herself against Barbra. Her older sister's name is Barbara. She's also very pretty and smart and Diana's had to compete against that.

"Even with Berry's help, Diana hasn't reached Streisand's position, though she deserves it. Diana's about business. She'll out-rehearse you, outdress you, and outperform you, so you best stay out of her way. We were always very cautious of each other. Everyone said that Diana was Berry's puppet. But I know women, and I knew it was only a matter of time before Diana would get what she wanted. I watched her consolidate her power. Any woman who gets involved with Berry Gordy—and hangs in like Diana did—must be made of steel."

Was Motown's reputation for a loose sex-in-the-office policy justified?

"Yes and no," Marvin observed. "Berry liked to play, and since Berry was the leader, we followed the leader. There were dozens of little affairs between this singer and that producer, but no more so than probably any other show business situation. Show people tend to be sensualists. It's not our fault. Much of what we sell is sexual, and our personal lives are influenced by that. Since Motown made party music, you'd expect that we were party people.

"On the other hand, Berry was strict when it came to public behavior. He was image-conscious. In that way, I'd have to say he was hypocritical. When the girls went on tour—the Vandellas, Marvelletes, Supremes—he protected them like daughters. They used to bitch about it all the time—how they couldn't even meet men on the road, much less date them. BG was scared the girls would get pregnant, so he did everything but put chastity belts around them. The girls were too afraid of Berry to fight back.

"I wasn't. I began seeing myself as an artist whose sensitivity and talent required respect. 'Why are you going to produce me?' I'd ask Holland-Dozier-Holland, 'why don't you produce Shorty Long?' He was this beautiful cat who had two hits, 'Function at the Junction' and 'Here Comes the Judge,' and then got ignored. I fought for guys like Shorty and vocal groups like the Andantes, who were probably the best girl group at Motown, except no one ever pushed them."

Marvin liked supporting underdogs. There were a few instances when he later helped young artists—the Originals, Frankie Beverly and Maze—but ultimately his compulsive self-concern fixed his concentration on his own career and no one else's. Moreover, down deep he *was* afraid of Gordy, just as he feared his own father. But to prove he wasn't afraid of their rejection, he overcompensated through senseless rebellion, provoking the very men whose love and approval he so desperately needed.

*   *   *

The Beatles were crying "Help!" and the Beach Boys were singing "California Girls" when, in 1965, Motown's Temptations broke
through. "My Girl," written and produced by Smokey Robinson,
hit Number One on the soul and pop charts. Along with Levi
Stubbs of the Four Tops—their "I Can't Help Myself" reached
the top in May of the same year—the Temptations' David Ruffin
established himself as one of the great Motown shouters.

"David had all the characteristics of a true artist," Marvin believed. "So did Levi. I heard in their voices a strength my own
voice lacked. Listening to these singers every day inspired me to
work even harder on my natural midrange—my tough-man voice.
I developed a growl. The Temps and Tops made me remember
that when a lot of women listen to music, they want to feel the
power of a real man."

This was also the time when Anna and Marvin adopted a child.
According to Clarence Paul, Anna was unable to have children.

"I was thrilled," Marvin said. "Our marriage was strained, and
I thought this would cool us out. Anna and I have always loved
kids. Besides, she was insecure, and she sensed her hold on me
loosening. A child might bring us together. I was on a star trip—
what 26-year-old guy wouldn't be?—and my behavior was strange,
to say the least. Anna and I started developing ways to play on
each other's fears. It was a game we perfected. Anna proved to be
a strong opponent. I'd met my match. In fact, Anna's one of the
world's toughest women. When Marvin III came along, I saw the
chance for a happy family life. I would have liked that. And there
were periods of time—long months—when we actually pulled it
off. It just didn't last."

The *Washington Evening Star*, now defunct, published a feature
article on Gaye in its November 27, 1965, edition. A photograph
shows a smartly coiffed, smiling Anna—new mother and model
wife—dressed in a long-sleeved lacy blouse, pouring coffee for her
man, dutifully serving an especially youthful-looking Marvin his
breakfast as he read the morning paper. In the article, Gaye mentioned that his father was unhappy with his decision to leave Washington five years ago, "but things are rather peaceful now. If a man
is a respectful and God-fearing man, then it doesn't matter what
you do as long as you include God in it, and I do."

For a short time, while enjoying his early successes, Gaye felt reasonably comfortable with his relationship with Father, largely because the two had very little contact. Even more, his new son, as is so often the case, became a catalyst for warm family feelings.

"Anna and I saw that our child was a blessing," Marvin told me. "It was a quiet moment in the midst of a storm."

Why did he name his son, who came to Anna and him in November 1965, Marvin Pentz Gaye III?

"I was torn. I liked the tradition of naming my son after me, but I also didn't want to be reminded of my father. When Marvin arrived, I made the decision: Tradition had to be upheld. That's what we learned from the Old Testament. I was also determined to avoid the pitfalls of Father in raising my son. Some I did avoid. Others I didn't. A child is a great source of joy, though I didn't realize how much little Marvin would dominate his mother's attention. I could see why Father had been jealous of me. I felt jealousy rising up within me."

Rather than attempt to reconcile with his father, Gaye always kept his distance.

As a man who loved children, Marvin was well-motivated to be a good father. When I was with the two of them in the late seventies—Marvin III was 13 then—I felt, beyond the apparent tension, a strong bond between them. Marvin couldn't resist teasing his son, playing mind games, which were much milder throwbacks to the mental warfare introduced by Marvin Sr. back in D.C. But as hard as he tried, in the sixties Gaye's time with little Marvin was restricted.

"I was still out there chasing the almighty dollar, flying out on tours, recording all night, worrying that I'd fall behind in the fool's footrace that had me running at a pace faster than my natural speed," he said. "By nature, I'm a midtempo man. I like to sing ballads at achingly slow rhythms. Back then, though, I was sprinting, going against myself and losing the natural balance of the real me."

His stage fright continued to plague him. In the book *Showtime at the Apollo*, Bobby Schiffman, who owned the theater, tells of going to the airport to pick up Marvin for his sold-out weekend engagement. Gaye wasn't on the plane. He finally called Schiffman to say, "Bobby, I couldn't do it. I came to New York, got off the plane, and was so scared I got on another plane and went back to Detroit. . . . I can't help it. . . . I'm afraid." The dates were cancelled.

The erratic patterns of Marvin's life became set during these early career years. Like most people, he would never change. Later he would emerge from long periods of virtual inactivity by going on high-powered fast-moving tours, sometimes appearing, sometimes ducking out at the last minute. The road would drain him dry, and his recovery periods would throw him into depression. A wizard at selecting the right rhythms for his music, he was far less sagacious in finding a steady syncopation to measure the movement of his life. Gaye was caught somewhere between too fast and too slow.

While Holland-Dozier-Holland concentrated their efforts on the Supremes and Tops, Smokey turned his attention to Marvin. In 1965, Gaye had two hits written and produced by Robinson: "I'll Be Doggone" and "Ain't That Peculiar." Both gems, the songs reflect the friends' easy rapport and mutual respect. Smokey understood Marvin's light side and love for the fanciful phrase. Gaye and Robinson's friendship, though, was not without problems. Some years later, when Marvin's relationship with Anna broke down completely, he worried that Berry had turned against him. Since Gaye considered Smokey Berry's closest friend, he began suspecting Robinson's loyalty. Yet the admiration that Marvin felt for Smokey was deep enough to last a lifetime.

"Smokey wrote something in 'I'll Be Doggone' that knocked me out," said Gaye. "He said that a woman ought to be whatever a man wants. I believe that, though it's a thought that's caused me powerful grief. But I can't blame that on Smokey.

"Some of my greatest times in Detroit were playing golf with Smokey at Palmer Park. We fell in love with the game around the same time. Berry, too. Seemed like it was the leisure sport we'd won the right to play. I liked the outfits—the shoes and the pants and the little golfing hats. Nothing frantic, no pushing or shoving, though I was still real competitive. I proved to be a good golfer, and I know with practice I would have been a champion."

Suburban lifestyle was the goal. Gordy was getting there, not only on the golf links but in the media as well. From the beginning, Berry understood how TV could sell records. On December 27,

1964, the Supremes appeared on *The Ed Sullivan Show* for the first of many times, along with the Serendipity Singers, Leslie Uggams, Frank Gorshin, and the Iceland National Basketball Team. In the spirit of the Pepsodent commercial that had run during the program, "for people who like to smile . . . white, white, white," the Supremes led the way. Soon the Four Tops, the Temptations, Smokey, Little Stevie, and Marvin were appearing on national television. Gordy flooded the airwaves, always careful that his wholesome acts appeared on wholesome shows. (Ironically, two decades later, MTV, the powerful musical cable station, would be selling white rock and roll with exactly the opposite technique—showing outrageously rebellious bands, anti–middle class to the hilt.)

Back in the sixties, with his Perry Como manner and boyish charm, Gaye appeared on *Shindig* and *Hullabaloo*, wooing his white audience, establishing what would become a very classy dancing style, smoothly swaying with a minimum of movements.

"We were all moving in the same direction," Marvin said. "We knew it was jive, but we wanted the money and the fame, so we went along with Berry's program. Some of the shit was outrageous. I think the Temps had to dress us up as riverboat gamblers for one of their Copa shows and the Supremes had these top hats and canes. They started taking my picture at plush country clubs, as though I'd always played golf and sailed yachts. Actually, it took me longer— two years longer—to get to the Copa than some of the other acts. That disturbed me, since I'd been the cat wanting to croon. The truth is that from the mid-sixties on, the Supremes and Four Tops 'were Motown's only real pop acts. The rest of us were R&B. The Supremes were the first to be big overseas. As big as the Beatles were in America, that's how big the Supremes were in England. With the right promotion, I felt I could have achieved the same success. I'd gripe, I'd walk out of the meetings, I'd miss recording sessions, I'd complain about how Berry had everything locked up— the publishing, the tours, the personal management. I'd bitch about us being slaves to the system and stir up all kinds of shit. But finally, like everyone else, I'd fall in line. Somewhere along in here—don't ask me the time or date—I lost my self-respect."

Marvin Gaye was neither destined nor suited for the sort of success the Supremes had realized. His personality just wouldn't allow him to be a packaged and produced please-the-people entertainer. During those moments when he bowed to the pressure, he was filled with remorse. He hated himself for selling out and would, years later, move to recapture an artistry he felt he had betrayed. He loathed the idea of wearing a top hat and dancing with a cane. Yet how could a twenty-six-year-old man from the projects who'd spent a lifetime dreaming of stardom, pass up an opportunity for fame and fortune in the white world of show business?

Thus Marvin made his move toward the Copacabana, his soul stirred with a mixture of confidence and contempt.

Harvey and the Moonglows. Harvey Fuqua, his arms extended, surrounded by, from left, Chester Simmons, Reese Palmer, James Nolan, Marvin Gaye, and Chuck Barksdale. 1959. (*Reese Palmer*)

Leaving for London, his first trip abroad, with, from left, Harvey Fuqua, Gwen Gordy Fuqua, Anna, Mrs. Berry Gordy, Sr., Loucye Gordy Wakefield. November 1964. (*Alan Abrams*)

Wearing an ascot and wedding ring. 1965. (*Peter Benjaminson*)

His love of caps is already apparent, along with his affinity for fancy cars. 1966. (*Peter Benjaminson*)

Berry Gordy, being interviewed by Michaela Williams in West Grand Boulevard offices. Mid-1960s. (*Alan Abrams*)

A night out at Detroit's Roostertail. From left, Motown A&R man Mickey Stevenson, Berry Gordy, Jr., Esther Gordy Edwards (on Gordy's left), Berry Gordy, Sr. (with white goatee), Diana Ross (across from Gordy Jr.), and bodyguard John Oden (on Ross's right). At the next table are Mary Wilson and, to her left, Florence Ballard. August 22, 1966. (*Alan Abrams*)

Portraits of the artist as an emerging star. Mid-1960s. (*Peter Benjaminson*)

Being interviewed at a reception at the Capitol in Washington, D.C., on Marvin Gaye Day, with Father by his side, beaming with pride. May 1, 1972. (*Dewey Hughes*)

With his arms around Father and Mother. (*Dewey Hughes*)

Janis Hunter. (*Images from Kenneth®*)

In the Motown Studios with his friend Wally Cox. Mid-1970s. (*Art Stewart*)

With Bobby Womack and Leon Ware (in center). Los Angeles, 1975. (*Art Stewart*)

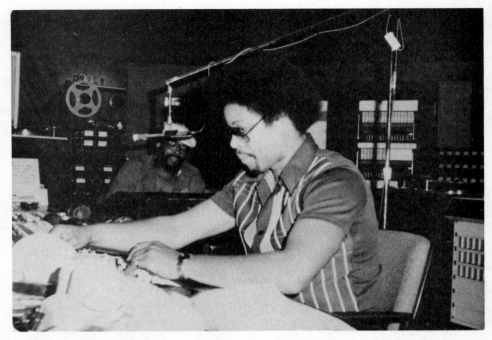

Marvin plays and producer Art Stewart engineers, Marvin Gaye Recording Studios, Hollywood. May 1978. (*Ray Baradat*)

Playing drums. Late 1970s. (*Images from Kenneth*®)

12
PAIN IN PARADISE

Marvin Gaye fought with himself all the way to the top. Even after he'd achieved his goals, his self-torturing, self-destructive design allowed for only minimal peace of mind—moments or, at the most, scattered months of calm when he sat and considered his options.

His obstinate streak, however, blinded his vision. Rather than plan, he reacted, often negatively, to the suggestions and directions of others.

"Marvin was the kind of fellow," observed Maurice King, "who liked to drive the wrong way down one-way streets."

Authority challenged something deep within him. Not to swim against the current was to admit cowardice. Doing it the easy way was fool's work. Bored by routine methods of succeeding, Gaye required the stimulus of adversity. If there were two roads leading to the mountaintop, one paved and wide, the other narrow and treacherous, Marvin wouldn't dream of taking the safe route. He'd laugh and tell you that he had to live life close to the edge. He felt compelled to create problems—both for the attention and the drama— if none were readily available.

Refusing the paved path, though, was also a matter of self-punishment.

"Watching Marvin," said Gil Askey, "I got the feeling that he was this incredibly talented man who just didn't like himself."

Yet for all Gaye's brutal self-criticism, he was also a man of rare integrity. Among the Motown pioneers, he alone had the courage to fight the system, recognizing the dark side of the glitter and glamour.

"I didn't like Motown's public relations bullshit," Marvin told me. "We were being molded into something we weren't. We were so anxious to please, we started making ourselves sick. Sometimes I felt like the shuffle-and-jive niggers of old, steppin' and fetchin' for the white folk."

Accompanying Gaye's defiance, though, was a fierce determination to succeed.

"If you were in show business, you'd have to be crazy to turn down a shot on *Sullivan* or a week at the Latin Quarter," Marvin said. "We were all racing around the track as fast as our legs would carry us. The only thing that made us stop and consider our own mortality was Loucye's death. That was a cold and ugly shock."

On July 29, 1965, the same day the Supremes opened at the Copa, Loucye Gordy Wakefield, Marvin's sister-in-law, was buried in Detroit. Marvin sang at her funeral and later recorded "His Eye Is on the Sparrow," issued on the album *In Loving Memory* which included musical tributes to Loucye by other Motown artists.

"Sparrow" remains one of Gaye's most inspired performances. Like Mahalia Jackson, Marvin cried through the lyrics, soaring far beyond this world, his voice reaching its crescendo in the arms of God.

"Earlier in the year, another death got to me," Marvin recalled. "Malcolm X. I loved Malcolm's strength and truth-telling. When they cut him down, I felt the loss inside my soul, and I knew that an age of terrible violence and suffering had just begun. I knew what my people were feeling—all the pent-up rage and anger. I felt it, too. I loved Dr. King for his idealism and courage. He did it the way Jesus would have done it, without sticks, guns, or bombs. But I also knew what happened to Jesus would happen to Dr. King. Maybe that's why I stayed away from the area of direct involvement. I wasn't ready to sacrifice my life for a cause. I'd rather give some money and sing some benefits. Berry also contributed. He even issued some of Dr. King's speeches as records, but, like the man says, the show must go on.

"I remember I was listening to a tune of mine playing on the radio, 'Pretty Little Baby,' when the announcer interrupted with news about the Watts riot. My stomach got real tight and my heart started beating like crazy. I wanted to throw the radio down and burn all the bullshit songs I'd been singing and get out there and kick ass with the rest of the brothers. I knew they were going about it wrong, I knew they weren't thinking, but I understood anger that builds up over years—shit, over centuries—and I felt myself exploding. Why didn't our music have anything to do with this? Wasn't music supposed to express feelings? No, according to BG, music's supposed to sell. That's his trip. And it was mine.

"Funny, but of all the acts back then, I thought Martha and the Vandellas came closest to really saying something. It wasn't a conscious thing, but when they sang numbers like 'Quicksand' or 'Wild One' or 'Nowhere to Run' or 'Dancing in the Street' they captured a spirit that felt political to me. I liked that. I wondered to myself, With the world exploding around me, how am I supposed to keep singing love songs?"

Rather than resolving his paradoxes, however, Gaye enlarged them. He hated show business yet pursued a show business career with singular tenacity. He believed in the passivism of Jesus while identifying with Malcolm X's explosive anger. He advocated political involvement yet, reluctant to alienate any part of his audience, wasn't especially active himself. As an artist arguing against the notion of entertainment, he nonetheless did everything he could to win a mainstream middle-class audience, crooning the ballads he thought white music lovers wanted to hear.

"If I want to sing a ballad," Marvin told the *Washington Evening Star* in 1965, "I'd like the public to listen and be attentive." That year he released no less than two albums directed at the white market: *A Tribute to the Great Nat King Cole*, who had just died, and *Hello Broadway*, with Gene Page arrangements highly influenced by Nelson Riddle, the man who wrote for Sinatra. The records were interesting, artistically uneven, and not big sellers. The Cole album, coproduced by Harvey Fuqua, included silly-sounding material like "Ramblin' Rose" and "Calypso Blues." Hearing himself sing "Hello Dolly" or "My Way" from *Hello Broadway* reinforced his yearning, in spite of his reservations, to join his colleagues on the posh supper-club circuit. For all of the big-band charts, though, Marvin wasn't convincing in his Frank Sinatra, up-tempo frame of mind. Emotionally, he distanced himself from these songs; his performance lacked the impassioned sincerity of his soul hits. He became a cold observer, studying rather than feeling the music. His intention, he told me, was to interpret the tunes "correctly"—"the way a Peggy Lee or Vic Damone might do them." Singing straight was as difficult for Marvin as it would have been for Billie Holiday. The results were stilted.

Not one to give up easily, a few months later he tried again. *Moods of Marvin Gaye* had him mixing his rhythm-and-blues releases with Willie Nelson's "Nightlife," Stevie Wonder's "You're the One for Me," and an especially effective down-and-depressed reading of "One for the Road." The album was far more satisfying than his previous pop efforts, the material bluesier, with Marvin more willing to gamble on his own funky style.

Gaye's next gamble was an appearance in New York that he considered the most important of his career—a run at the Copacabana. There, in spite of his reservations about pandering to Milquetoast tastes, he could test his prowess as a balladeer and pop performer. When I questioned him about the engagement, though, he was unusually reticent. "It didn't go well," was all he said.

The August 16, 1966, issue of *Variety* reviewed his Copa opening. Maurice King was conducting the orchestra; the minimum was $6.50. "Four pretty Negro models, with three complete changes of costume," wrote the critic, "pranced behind him [Gaye]. It was a whiff of the old days of the Cotton Club.

"He's just converting to adult life and getting away from the kinderspeil," the reviewer went on. "It's a difficult period of transition. However, the most grave cut came from his immediate family.

"His infant son was passed down to a ringsider for the entire audience to behold. Gaye's initially averted glance indicated that it was a mistake. The most competent performer can be upstaged by an infant. For a long time nobody paid attention to the headliner. It was a most unfortunate intrusion."

The incident not only embarrassed Gaye but placed him at odds with his infant son, who'd stolen the spotlight, reminding Marvin of the intensely competitive, push-and-shove relationship he faced with his own father.

Public tensions in Anna and Marvin Gaye's family soon became more pronounced. The couple were quick to voice their displeasure with one another and didn't seem to care who heard.

"Anna and I had some famous fights," Marvin said. "Seems like we liked to battle in public. Especially in nightclubs. Ask the people back in Detroit. I think it was at the Twenty Grand where we wound up screaming at each other. At home, we'd throw things. We came to blows on more than one occasion, and I'm going to tell you something: Anna could hold her own.

"I wasn't happy 'cause the Supremes and the Tops were touring all over the world. I was excluded from those big Motown shows going over to England. They said my English following didn't amount to anything. That hurt. Of all the countries where I wanted to be loved, England headed the list. I loved them and felt hurt that the love wasn't returned. In Great Britain, compared to Diana and Levi, I was nothing. For a while I blamed myself. Maybe I shouldn't have played hooky from the Motown charm school, where they taught us how not to act like niggers. But that wasn't it. The real reason was that groups were in and solo acts were lagging behind. That's why I didn't hesitate to keep the duet thing alive."

Marvin made his last record with Mary Wells in 1964, his first with Kim Weston in 1966.

"Kim's a great gal and we became very close friends," Marvin remembered. "Anna didn't appreciate the relationship. Just as she was jealous of me and Mary Wilson, she grew jealous of me and Kim.

"Actually, I had a right to be jealous myself. You see, Anna and I had a strange sense of when we were being untrue to each other. We always knew. One night, for example, I found myself getting in the car and driving to a motel, walking up to a certain room and knocking on the door. All by instinct. How could I be so sure that Anna was in there with another man? I had no way of knowing the motel and the room number. Some force led me on. I think that's the same force that transforms my happiness to misery."

What did he do to his wife and her lover?

"Nothing, really. I don't even remember. I think I laughed. I might have cried. But certainly there was some enjoyment in finding them. It was definitely an adventure. I suppose I've always been obsessed with the notion of another man making love to my woman. In my fantasy, that man is always more powerful than me. He alone can satisfy her, while I can only watch."

In this sexual obsession lies the root of Gaye's masochism, the physical pleasure he derived from painful self-denial. In his second marriage, the complex would grow to even larger proportions, with pleasure and pain more intricately confused. As he grew older, he'd try to cover over these feelings with his playboy image, the debonair gentleman sampling beautiful women as he might sample fine wine.

Always a reluctant worker, much like his father, Gaye was none-theless prolific by the mid-sixties, averaging two albums a year, cutting nearly thirty songs every twelve months. "It was the heat of competition," he said, "and Berry's insistence. When I wouldn't want to record—just flat-out refuse—Berry would get mad, his voice would get real high, he'd lose his cool. I'd feel bad and finally get my ass back in the studio."

Marvin continued working with Smokey in 1966, scoring with two hits—"One More Heartache" and "Take This Heart of Mine"—which seemed minor in comparison to the success of the Supremes, Four Tops, and Temptations. This was the period of "You Can't Hurry Love," "Reach Out and I'll Be There" and "Ain't Too Proud to Beg." Holland-Dozier-Holland produced Marvin's "Little Dar-ling, I Need You," a Top Ten rhythm-and-blues tune that failed to cross over. Gaye was still looking for his first Number One pop record.

He did, however, enjoy a degree of duo success with Kim Wes-ton, whose exceptionally soft, sultry voice reminded Marvin of his mother's. Their album *Take Two* was released in the same 1966–1967 period that produced smashes by Donovan, the Monkees, and Aretha Franklin, while Herb Fame, Marvin's contemporary from Washington, D.C., formed Peaches and Herb and hit with "Let's Fall in Love," "Close Your Eyes," and "Two Little Kids."

Such romantic mood music—Peaches and Herb, Marvin and Kim—was an attempt to catch the elusive but powerful pull of puppy love. It required a very special touch. Listeners had to believe in the sincerity of the singers, who were symbols of sweet infat-uation. Even more than Peaches and Herb, Tammi Terrell and Marvin Gaye became that symbol—the Jeanette MacDonald and Nelson Eddy of the sixties.

"I knew I needed something different. That's why I threw myself into the duets," Marvin explained. "It was acting. It was an escape for me. I could imagine with Kim, for instance, that we were innocent young lovers. The thing with Anna was the opposite of that. A year or two before, our thing had slowly started to sour. We'd polluted pure love and were suffering from the fallout. The difference in our ages seemed more pronounced. I had women screaming for me everywhere I went. But I was trapped. I had trapped myself—too early, too soon. It'd take Superman to satisfy so many women. But when I sang those duets, I could simplify things. I could sing to a real-life woman in the studio. I remembered how pure love might have been. I'd trained myself for the part with Mary Wells and Kim. When Tammi came along in 1967, I had the role mastered."

Tammi Terrell had been Tammy Montgomery when she was discovered, still in her teens, by James Brown. Brown produced her first record, "I Cried," and featured her, along with the Famous Flames and Yvonne Fair, in his Mr. Dynamite Review. Publicity shots from the period presented her as a coquettish woman-child. Kim Weston described Tammi as a "free spirit—wild, raw, and beautiful."

"Tammi was the kind of chick who couldn't be controlled by men," said Marvin. "That can drive a man crazy—trying to deal with a woman who won't be dominated by anyone. I loved that about Tammi. I knew we could be friends, but never lovers. Independent women hold no romantic interest for me. James Brown and David Ruffin both had stormy relationships with Tammi, but mine was completely creative. Because she was fun and funny and totally unpredictable, I loved her. Her singing style was also perfectly suited to mine. What we chiefly accomplished, though, was to create two characters—two lovers that might have been taken from a play or a novel—and let them sing to each other. That's how the Marvin-and-Tammi characters were born. While we were singing, we *were* in love. The vibe was incredible. The emotions were heartfelt and real. But when the music ended, we kissed each other on the cheek and said good-bye."

There was magic between Marvin and Tammi in the studio. His fluid tenor and her slightly salty soprano were marvelous contrasts in vocal textures. Their voices wound around one another like arms and legs. Even covering Frank and Nancy Sinatra's banal "Something Stupid," their harmony was irresistible.

"Ain't No Mountain High Enough," their initial 1967 hit, was written by Nick Ashford and Valerie Simpson, extremely talented writers who later turned into a Marvin-and-Tammi style duo themselves. Valerie's church-rooted sense of composition proved to be the perfect vehicle, just as Johnny Bristol and Harvey Fuqua were the right producers.

Harvey held a number of high-ranking jobs at Motown before leaving the company and his wife Gwen in the late sixties. Marvin was happy to be produced by his old mentor and brother-in-law who musically understood him so well. An experienced duet singer himself—first with Betty and Dupree, then Harvey and Ann—Fuqua understood better than anyone how to elicit the most romantic side of Marvin's moody musical character. The tone harked back to the days of the Moonglows, when romance was viewed as fresh and unspoiled.

"I stopped greasing and conking my hair," said Marvin. "I told myself I'd never put crap in my hair again. I wanted another look. A more natural look. That's when I was wearing lots of cardigan sweaters and crew necks—the college boy image. I also told myself that I'd start wearing glasses. It gave me a studious touch. I've always needed glasses but have been too vain to wear them in public. I tried for a while. My attitude was, who cares, this is me. But I guess I did care because I didn't like the way they looked and stopped wearing them. I also told myself that as soon as I got the confidence, I'd drop the 'e' from my name."

He never did.

In 1967, Berry Gordy moved from his home on Outer Drive to an Italian Renaissance mansion on Boston Boulevard. Built in the twenties, the three-story edifice looked like a museum or library, authentically European down to the marble floor and columns in its ballroom. There was a billiard room, screening room, gym, English pub, two-lane bowling alley, gold frescoes, fancy filigrees, and Greek statues in the yard.

"When Berry moved in," Marvin remembered, "he gave me, Anna, and little Marvin his old house. We'd been living in a home of our own, not far away. Now his old place was cool—very cool—right out there in a woodsy, suburban part of town. It was luxurious and roomy and the nicest crib I'd ever had. There was this sunken living room with a gold grand piano—that's where I'd sit and work—and a nice yard. Anna did it up nice, with gold carpets and fancy drapes. It was so soft and comfortable I never wanted to leave. But it wasn't anything like Berry's mansion. I couldn't turn it down, but I couldn't help but resent it a little. After all, the king was living in his castle while the poor relatives got the hand-me-downs."

As late as 1967, Marvin still hadn't achieved the sort of financial independence he'd sought. He felt tied to the fortunes of his brother-in-law and certainly didn't consider himself rich. That wouldn't happen until the seventies. According to Gaye, no Motown artist, with the possible exception of Smokey, emerged from the sixties with real wealth. "The Emancipation Proclamation for us singers," he said, "was still a ways off."

"If you look at what happened in Detroit, common sense will tell you that Berry got the money, damn near all the money," said Clarence Paul whose plain-spoken stances endeared him to Marvin.

"There was a point when BG stopped giving anyone any real money," Beans Bowles claimed. "That's when a lot of folk fell away from him."

Nonetheless, Esther Gordy Edwards contended in a speech I heard her deliver in Detroit that many individuals working at Motown became millionaires on their own. The press-shy Gordys, though, have never elaborated on this point. One wonders whether that's due to Berry Gordy's generally paranoiac view of the press—he has yet to grant a single in-depth interview—or because facts would prove that Motown's true wealth never trickled down to the writers and performers.

"The whole reason Holland-Dozier-Holland walked out in '67 had to do with money," Marvin said. "Given their contribution to the corporation, they didn't feel as though they were sharing in its real wealth. Lots of us felt exactly the same way, and an exodus began."

"Mickey Stevenson and I got out in 1968," Clarence Paul remembered. "Naturally Mickey took Kim Weston with him. Gladys Knight and the Pips left—Motown never did right by them—and so did a whole lot of other acts like the Isleys, the Spinners, and the Tops."

"Down deep," Marvin felt, "I'm a fiercely loyal man. Maybe if Motown hadn't been a black business I'd have left. For all my bitching, though, I believed in the company and what Berry was fighting for in the white man's world. Besides, Motown was all I knew. Motown made me. Anna and Berry kept me together, at least as far as business. When I didn't want to record, they knew how to get me in the studio."

"They'd send me over," said Clarence Paul. "There was only one sure-fire way to get Marvin Gaye to record—go over to his house, throw his ass out of bed, and take him down to the studio.

That's what I'd do. In the car we might have a toot of coke and go off and work for God knows how many straight hours. Once Marvin was in the studio, he was cool. It was the one place, maybe the only place in the world, where he could really relax. Marvin was a master in the studio—creative, happy, loose, funny. And once Marvin got anywhere, he wouldn't want to leave. That was doubly true of the studio. He wasn't a performer. He'd never perform if it hadn't been for the money. In the truest sense, Marvin Gaye was a recording artist."

In the period I watched Marvin record, I never saw him sing when he wasn't high. Had it always been that way?

"For the most part, yes," Gaye said.

"There were lots of drugs around Motown in the early sixties," said Clarence, "just like there were lots of drugs around any black neighborhood. Marvin and I did our fair share of cocaine beginning in the early sixties. We were into it early on. Other artists, like Little Stevie, hated the stuff."

"I've been tooting," Marvin told me, referring to cocaine, "for a good twenty-five years." That was an exaggeration. He made the statement in 1982 in Europe after I'd witnessed him castigate his coke dealer for selling him impure stuff. "I consider myself a connoisseur. I'm passionate about good cocaine," said Gaye who had never experimented with the drug in the fifties.

"Marvin's nasal membranes were funny," Clarence remembered, "and he couldn't snort as much blow as some of us. He'd get a freeze by rubbing it over his gums, and then he'd eat it. I'm telling you the truth."

"The most deadly thing about cocaine," Quincy Jones told me, "is that it separates you from your soul."

"I like the feeling," Marvin admitted. "No one will ever tell me it's not a good feeling. A clean, fresh high, 'specially early in the morning, will set you free—at least for a minute. There are times when blow got to me, and sometimes I know it built up bad vibes inside my brain. I saw coke, though, as an elitist item, a gourmet drug, and maybe that was one of its attractions. Was I corrupting myself? Slowly, very slowly."

Corruption and material success were very much mixed up in Marvin Gaye's mind. "Like Jesus," he told me, "we should keep nothing for ourselves. Possessions are burdens, and the less I have, the happier I'll be."

That was the altruistic Gaye speaking, the man who admired Saint Francis and felt that he, too, could communicate with the birds and bees. But as long as Marvin kept his distance from Jesus, he knew that he couldn't be a happy man. His original joy, his most authentic musical ecstasy, was intermingled with the blood of the lamb. Only with the Lord's love could Marvin be fulfilled. As he himself testified, he had heard the command to spread the gospel at a very young age. The longer he avoided his musical ministry, the more painful his separation from God.

Meanwhile, though, the worldly Marvin marched on. He had set his sights on stardom; he'd been playing the circuit now for eight long years and was ready to strike it rich. Not one to deny himself pleasures, Gaye began to give himself all the drugs, all the highs, all the women he wanted. No longer a babe in the woods, he'd seen the world for what it was. In the slow decay of his own marriage, he began to think that he'd lost his adolescent view of true love. As the next phase of his recording career would reveal, though, that vision, in spite of everything he'd seen and would see, remained pure as a dove, a sweet symbol of God's perfect peace.

13

AN END TO INNOCENCE

The starry-eyed, younger-than-springtime Tammi-and-Marvin musical affair continued, the essence of what innocence remained for a country caught up in a bloody and bitter war in Vietnam. Beginning in 1967, and for two years to follow, the duo released three albums and sent nine songs racing up the charts. In an era when "The Ballad of the Green Berets" became a Number One hit, when Clarence Paul and Stevie Wonder's duet of Bob Dylan's "Blowin' in the Wind" went Top Ten, Marvin and Tammi's themes tenaciously clung to the heart: "Your Unchanging Love," "Your Precious Love," "If I Could Build My Whole World Around You."

If these songs created fairy-tale fantasies of lovers living happily ever after, the story turned tragic on the stage of Virginia's Hampton-Sydney College in the summer of 1967. In the midst of performing, Tammi collapsed in Marvin's arms. Gaye carried her off into the wings and was never quite the same man again. Mystery shrouded Tammi's physical problems. Some said it was a brain tumor; others said she'd been beaten in the head by jealous boyfriends.

"No one really knew," Marvin told me. "Not even the doctors. Either way, I couldn't help but see Tammi as a victim of love. She was in her very early twenties, but she had been out there for a long time. I knew that she was an experienced, worldly woman. In the songs we sang, though, she became something else, some-

117

thing very warm and special and hopeful. Couples would say to us, 'You're singing our song,' and we were. When I learned just how sick she was, I cried. Love seemed cruel to me. Love was a lie. Tammi was the victim of the violent side of love—at least that's how it felt. I have no first-hand knowledge of what really killed her, but it was a deep vibe, as though she was dying for everyone who couldn't find love. My heart was broken. My own marriage to Anna had proven to be a lie. In my heart, I could no longer pretend to sing love songs for people. I couldn't perform. When Tammi became ill, I refused to sing in public."

After a number of operations spanning three years, Tammi Terrell died in 1970. The process was agonizing for Marvin, and ironic because their songs, recorded before her illness, continued to ride a crest of national popularity. Their first album, *United*, was released in 1967; the second, *You're All I Need*, a year later; and the third, *Easy*, in 1969.

"Was the last album recorded before or after Tammi became ill?" I asked Marvin one night in Belgium.

"Tammi didn't do most of that last album with me," he said. "She wasn't able to sing then."

"I don't understand. Who sang the female part?"

Gaye looked away from me and remained silent. Seconds ticked by before he sighed and asked me, "Do you have a copy of that album?"

I did. We began listening to the duets.

"Listen carefully," he urged. "Listen to the quality of the female voice. It's close, but it's not Tammi."

"Who is it?"

"Care to guess?"

Not fond of guessing games, I pressed him to reveal the singer.

"She's a wonderful musician who also wrote most of these songs. Now do you know?"

Listening again, it became clear that Valerie Simpson was doing a remarkably skillful imitation of Tammi Terrell. Only a slight nasal exaggeration of Tammi's style provided a clue.

"At first I refused to go along with the plan," Marvin expanded. "I saw it as another money-making scheme on BG's part. I said it was cynical and wrong. I didn't want to deceive the public like that. Then Motown convinced me that it'd be a way for Tammi's family to have additional income. Valerie had sung many of the demo tapes to teach Tammi her songs, so she was a natural choice. She's a wonderful singer herself and amazed me with how faithfully she captured Tammi. No matter how good the music was, though, I felt strange singing to Valerie. I suppose I felt guilty."

Marvin claimed that both hit songs from the album, "What You Gave Me" and "The Onion Song," were done with Valerie. So close were the voices that he was uncertain about one track, "I Can't Believe You Love Me," which, he said, might have been recorded with Tammi.

"That was such a bizarre time in my life, I hardly knew what I was doing. The world was coming down around me. Dr. King's death confirmed my instincts about this country. America couldn't deal with someone that good and just. Suddenly everyone was going nuts. The riots in Detroit hit close to home. We could smell the smoke and hear the gunfire on West Grand. Berry freaked. He moved the offices to a building on Woodward. We were hardly there at all when he decided to get the hell out and move to California. That was 1969. His thing with Diana had gotten heavy. Holland-Dozier-Holland had quit and sued him and for a while the Supremes couldn't hit the side of a barn. Everyone was mixed up, I think, because the era was changing the music. Gut-bucket soul—like Aretha and Wilson Pickett and Otis Redding—had gotten popular. Did you know, by the way, that Berry passed on Wilson when he was with the Falcons? Anyway, the white kids wanted a different kind of music. They wanted to hear about something besides love. They were smoking weed and dropping acid and I went along with them. I loved the hippies. They were rebels, like me, and they did this country a world of good. They finally stopped a terribly unjust war. They looked at the status quo and called it bullshit and they were right. They also had the right idea about the power of love. Who else was offering hope? For a while, when Bobby Kennedy was shot and the cops ran over the kids at the Democratic Convention in Chicago, it looked hopeless. I felt despair. I felt misunderstood and very unloved. Anna and I had lost each other. The only bright spot in my life was when the Tigers came back to beat the Cards in the 1968 World Series. I sang the national anthem at one of the games—a life-long dream come true."

Gaye's relationship with Anna had grown ugly and violent. At the lowest point in the marriage, torn by the pressures of his career and personal demons, Marvin did something crazy.

"I got a gun and holed myself up in an apartment," Gaye told me, "threatening to kill myself or whoever walked through the door. I didn't know what I was doing or saying. I was angry at Anna for being unfaithful, angry at myself because I had been just as wild, angry at love for turning to hate. The only person who could have saved me, did. That was Pops Gordy.

"Oh, how I loved the man! He was more a father than a father-in-law, and he knew how to deal with me. He'd tell Anna, 'Marvin's a little mixed up, but the boy's going to be all right.' Somehow, when Pops said it, I believed him. Anyway, when everyone was scared of getting near me, Pops walked right through that apartment door. I was sitting with a loaded gun in my hand and he came over and said, 'Now Marvin, why do you want to go acting the fool like this? Give me that gun, boy, before you hurt yourself.' And I did. No questions asked. Pops Gordy saved my life."

This was the first of what would become a series of near-suicides for Marvin. Typically, he'd draw attention to the incidents by pulling in friends or family members, wanting to see their reaction as he threatened to destroy himself. It wasn't that the episodes were fake or staged. Marvin's despair was real. His tendency, though, was to dramatize his depressions with distinctive theatrical flourishes. Never, though, would he be able to pull the trigger.

"If you die by your own hand, it's next to impossible to inherit eternal life," the Reverend S. P. Rawlings, head of the House of God, told me.

"I do believe suicide is a mortal sin," Marvin himself had said, "as serious as murdering someone else."

Still, Gaye's reveries of self-destruction would remain. His reminded me of Keats, the poet in "Ode to a Nightingale" who fell "half in love with easeful Death." Like the English romantic, Gaye began to look upon death with wishful lyricism, seeking to escape from a world where, as Keats wrote, "but to think is to be full of sorrow/ and leaden-eyed despairs." Marvin's supersensitivity didn't stand a chance against this world's rough reality. While the poet in "Nightingale" saw escape through magical wine—"that I might drink, and leave the world unseen"—Gaye's method was drugs.

"Not herb," he said. "Herb wasn't about nothing more than a

quick giggle. But coke was a different deal. Blow is what really let me fly. There were moments when I really thought I was gone. I'm talking about times—really down times—when I snorted up so much toot I was convinced I'd be dead within minutes. I rather liked the idea of there being nothing left of me but my music."

Marvin yearned to disappear into the sweetest side of his nature, pure melody, just as Keats longed to join the bird and "fade away into the forest dim."

No matter how poetic the expression, though, Gaye's heart overflowed with pain. His polarities tore at him unmercifully. "The voice of an angel," I jotted down one night after he spoke to me of his traumatic childhood, "trapped in the body of a man."

It was music—and only music—that drew Gaye out of these periods of abject depression. In the late sixties Marvin opened an impassioned new musical chapter, startling in its intensity and remarkable for its commercial success. He recorded a string of hits, different in approach to anything he'd done before. He put the bright-eyed bliss of his Tammi duets behind him. His love songs to Anna were long gone. Now his voice revealed disappointment and anger. He openly expressed the turbulence of his personal life in his singing. Though the songs of this period were written by others, Marvin infused them with his own anguish. The single compelling theme might well have been taken from his daily life: infidelity.

The first of these songs, "You," from the winter of 1968, introduced his obsession with forbidden love. It was the story of tormented lovers meeting "in shadows," and a "secret rendezvous."

By late summer another solo release, "Chained," hit the charts, even while his previously recorded Tammi duets continued to soar. "Chained," like "You," bristled with troubled energy. (Michael Jackson would also sing the song on his family's first album—*Diana Ross Presents the Jackson Five*—released in 1969.) Gaye's voice was aflame, hot with frustration. "I tremble!" he sang, his searing falsetto igniting sparks of rage.

"I felt chained," Marvin told me. "I saw no way out. I couldn't control the cheating—mine or Anna's. Every day we found new ways to needle each other. Yet we needed each other. She knew I was afraid of what would happen to my career if I left her, and I knew she couldn't do without the status of being married to me.

My family accused me of making myself miserable, and maybe they were right."

"Marvin loved misery," said his sister Jeanne. "As time went on, he wallowed in it. If misery wasn't there, he'd find a way to invent it."

Norman Whitfield best exploited this emotionally heightened moment in Marvin's life. In doing so, Whitfield co-wrote (with Barrett Strong) and produced the most popular song in Motown history.

"Heard It Through the Grapevine" had already been a huge hit for Motown by Gladys Knight and the Pips. Released in the fall of 1967, it reached Number One on the soul chart and Number Two on the pop listing. Though Gaye's version was recorded before Gladys', it was issued afterward, in October 1968. Phenomenally, only a year after Knight's salty rendition, the same song, this time sung by Marvin, sold nearly four million copies. Fifteen years later over the opening credits of the film *The Big Chill*, it played as an anthem for a whole generation.

"Bearing down on every word," wrote critic Dave Marsh, "making each syllable count, Gaye explored 'Grapevine' as if the song were a lost continent of music and emotion, as if the plotters in the song were his true and personal demons, had in fact scorched his identity all but out of existence. . . . In those three and a quarter minutes, Marvin Gaye earned his independence from the Motown mill."

"When I heard 'Grapevine' for the first time," Marvin said Little Richard told him, "I jumped up and down three times and screamed 'Hallelujah!' "

Now Gaye couldn't help but realize that he rendered his most powerful performances when he sang directly from life.

"I believed every word of the song," he told me. "It *was* happening to me. The doubting, the friends whispering in my ear, the suspicions. I was surprised, I mean completely shocked, that the tune took off. I had no idea it would mean anything to anyone else, especially since Gladys had done such a great job with it."

Billboard magazine, for the week ending December 26, 1968, showed Motown with three of the top five pop hits and five of the top ten. Marvin's "Grapevine" was Number One across the boards, his first ever.

A few months later, in April of 1969, during a phone interview from Detroit with *Melody Maker* in London, he commented on "Grapevine's" enormous success in England. "I can't see why it should be such a big hit in Britain," he said. Apparently, he also had thoughts about ending his self-imposed ban on performing. He spoke of plans for British concerts in late spring or summer: "I love the English people very much and I even like your weather." He didn't go, though, for another seven years, establishing a perverse pattern he would follow for the rest of his career—arbitrarily canceling concerts and tours at the last minute.

The London article was headlined, "With the Solo Success Comes a Little Sadness," referring to Tammi Terrell. "Tammi is still very ill," Marvin told the paper. "She had to have brain surgery. And both Mary and Kim left the company after we'd done duets together. We did duets because we thought they'd be a novelty, but after a while they became a necessity. I don't anticipate doing any more in the near future. . . . I don't think I'm very lucky for whoever I'm doing duets with."

Marvin's sensitivity was apparent. So was the severity with which he judged himself. Just as he sometimes acted as an initiator of good, other times he felt like Satan's pawn. The twin gods within him—the female artist and the male aggressor, the loving Jesus and the backbiting devil—would never make peace.

He tried. He sought to heal himself by making amends with his father. In 1968, he bought Gay Sr. a Cadillac.

"Was he grateful?" I asked.

"Not especially," Marvin answered. "I wanted to ask him to visit me, but I didn't. I really didn't want him around. He knew that, and that made him angrier. It was a vicious cycle."

The cycle's spin would turn at higher speeds as Marvin's success multiplied—the father growing proud and jealous while the son, afraid of the heights to which he was ascending, needed the father's hand to steady his balance. That hand was not extended, though the son proved strong enough to make it on his own.

And make it big. *In the Groove*, the album containing "Grapevine," "You," and "Chained," was released in 1968. Tough-talking Norman Whitfield, the man Gaye considered his nemesis, was producing Marvin's hits.

"Norman used to bang the tambourines for Popcorn Wylie and the Mohawks," Billie Jean Brown remembered. "There was an arrogance about Norman which put some people off. He was a pool shark. That's how he supported his family before he started in music. When 'Grapevine' hit, he wound up buying a manor."

"Whitfield was tremendously important to the development of the company," Ralph Seltzer, a high-ranking Motown executive in the late sixties, told me. "Norman should have been given his own label. Unfortunately, granting that sort of autonomy was not Berry's style."

Whitfield captured the raw soulfulness of the Stax-Volt/Atlantic school—Sam and Dave, Solomon Burke, Johnny Taylor—as well as incorporating a psychedelic-sounding flavor into the arrangements, giving Motown the modern edge it needed. The centerpiece of Whitfield's music, though, was a traditionally brawny male vocal. His association with the Temptations began in 1968 with the heartrending "I Wish It Would Rain." Later that year, when Dennis Edwards replaced David Ruffin as lead singer, Whitfield produced a series of scorching soul sermons: "Cloud Nine," "Psychedelic Shack," "Run Away Child, Running Wild."

Marvin was deeply influenced by Ruffin and Edwards, church shouters of the first order. "I'd have to call myself a Dennis Edwards and David Ruffin fan," Marvin admitted.

The brand of macho soul which Whitfield concocted was an integral part of the producer's professional personality.

"Norman and I came within a fraction of an inch of fighting," said Gaye. "He thought I was a prick because I wasn't about to be intimidated by him. We clashed. He made me sing in keys much higher than I was used to. He had me reaching for notes that caused my throat veins to bulge."

Yet Whitfield and Gaye made brilliant music together. One way or the other, Norman brought out another side of Marvin—toughminded, aggressive, angry. The great Whitfield-Gaye matchup, *MPG*, came in 1969. The cover was a radical departure from the pretty-boy pictures of the past. A stoic, tight-lipped, mezzo-tinted Marvin stared from an austere black-and-white photo. Gaye's gaze was steely-eyed, intense. In the lower right-hand corner, written in his own hand, Marvin's initials formed the album's title.

Here Whitfield's songs mirrored Gaye's tortured resignation to the collapse of his marriage. (Amazingly, Marvin and Anna wouldn't actually get divorced until 1977.) "The End of Our Road," for example, was filled with accusations Marvin might have made to Anna—that she'd been "reckless" with his heart, that she'd been "running around" with other men. In the end, he had to get away. Fed up with her stuff, he sang, "enough is enough."

In "Memories," Marvin mourned that their love had become nothing but "lies and schemes." He saw it as an "empty shell."

Other tunes—"It's a Bitter Pill to Swallow," "More Than a Heart Can Stand"—expressed the same sentiments, with Marvin singing as though his life depended upon ventilating these frustrations. ("Too Busy Thinking About My Baby," from this same album, was an exception, and also a huge hit on both the black and the white charts. The innocence of its lyrics harked back to Sam Cooke's 1960 "Wonderful World.")

In "Only a Lonely Man Would Know" Marvin uttered an incantation which would reverberate in his mind, a strange and sullen prophecy of his life to come. He foresaw only loneliness and tears for himself, his world coming to an end, "black's closing in."

The last of the Gaye-Whitfield projects, *That's the Way Love Is*, produced two hits in 1969–1970, the title song and "How Can I Forget." The highlight of the album, though, was Marvin's version of Lennon-McCartney's "Yesterday." Now he was finally in full command of what he'd developed as three distinct voices—a smooth midrange, an explosive rasp (in the Ruffin-Edwards style) and a silky falsetto (inspired by the great Motown high-pitched tenors— Smokey, Eddie Kendricks, and Ronald Isley). Sliding from voice to voice, Marvin transformed "Yesterday" into a lament of his own broken marriage, his voice crooning, cracking, crying with pain.

In spite of his success with Whitfield's material, Marvin retreated into loneliness, the condition of his childhood. He still refused to tour behind his recent hits. His inclination toward self-pity and his pattern of beating back boredom with disasters of his own making only intensified.

"Even after Pops took that pistol away from me, I toyed with suicide several more times," he told me. "I'd go off and hide for weeks without telling anyone. Sometimes I'd go to a lady friend to take care of me. Not so much for wild sex, but just peace of mind. But mostly I just needed to be alone."

Why at this stage? I asked him. When "Grapevine" had earned him a mass market, why was he so despondent?

"My success didn't seem real. I didn't deserve it. I knew I could have done more. I felt like a puppet—Berry's puppet, Anna's puppet. I had a mind of my own and I wasn't using it. I'd seen how the business was destroying many of my friends and colleagues. I was afraid the same thing would happen to me, so I backed off. There had to be a limit to commercialism. At some point, every true artist realizes that. I'd made some compromises, but at least I hadn't gone all the way. I remember there was a brand of 'Supremes' white bread. The company had some tie-in deal and the girls were actually photographed holding the stuff. I couldn't believe that shit. If it wasn't so funny, it'd be sad. I had lots of chances to endorse products, but I refused. I wasn't about to do any commercials."

Records from the Zimmer, Keller and Calvert Advertising Agency of Detroit show that Marvin did, however, make a commercial. In November 1965, on local Detroit radio, he sang a jingle for the *Detroit Free Press*. He also read the copy: "Hi, I'm Marvin Gaye. You know, the *Free Press* swings pretty good with Teen Beat. That's a special page that covers the record beat, the what's happening beat, the I-got-a-problem beat. . . ."

Gaye tended to exaggerate his purity.

In 1967, Florence Ballard, one of the original Supremes, was fired by Berry Gordy. Nine years later, at 32, she died of a heart attack. She'd been living on welfare. Her dismissal from the Supremes is one of the most controversial chapters in Motown history. In a long series of unpublished interviews with Peter Benjaminson, Ballard expressed deep bitterness toward Berry Gordy, whom, she felt, was prejudiced against her. She also saw Diana Ross, at least in part, as cold and calculating, a position that Mary Wilson has also taken.

Marvin had his own view of Ballard's problems.

"We called Florence 'Blondie,' " Marvin told me. "She was a beautiful person—loving, warm, and a hell of a singer, probably the strongest of the three girls. She was down-to-earth and she loved to laugh and everyone dug her. Lots of people think that by getting next to Berry, Diana did Blondie in. Not true. It was just a matter of temperament. Some people can deal with the business, some can't. As the Supremes got bigger, so did the pressures. Berry nearly worked those girls to death. You either ride that wave or you go under. Believe me, I was dealing with the same thing. That's why I had to cut loose. Sure, Diana was pushy, and Flo resented being shoved to the side. Who wouldn't? But Diana deserved her glory. She earned it. She had the ability to entertain a football stadium filled with people. Fate dealt Blondie a dirty blow. I know she suffered. So did Paul Williams."

Paul Williams was one of the original Temptations. Owing $80,000 in back taxes, he died of a self-inflicted gun wound in 1973. "His problem," said Beans Bowles, who knew Paul well, "was booze."

"These people were victims, just like Tammi," Marvin explained. "The business turned them inside out. They couldn't cope. It's unfair to blame their downfalls on others. For all the happiness and joy it offers the world, the music business is nasty and dirty. Don't ask me how I've lasted this long. God has protected me. God has given me the strength to be a man. Without God, I'd have gone the same way as Flo and Paul. God knows, I've come close."

In 1969, Diana Ross sang "Someday We'll Be Together," her final hit with the Supremes, and left the group to go solo. Marvin attended the Supremes' final performance, at the Frontier Hotel in Las Vegas on January 14, 1970, recorded live and recently reissued by Motown.

During a version of *Hair*'s "Let the Sunshine In," then a big record by the Fifth Dimension, Diana traveled through the audience, addressing the Gordy girls—Anna, Gwen, and Esther—as her "sisters" and then briefly turning the mike over to Marvin. The gospel fire he ignited in a few fleeting seconds electrified the house. The fans screamed for more, but Gaye coolly deferred to Diana.

Just as Gordy had served as personal manager of the Supremes, he would concentrate on Diana's solo career with similar single-mindedness.

"I knew I'd lost BG a long time ago," Marvin said. "Diana dazzled him, just like she would dazzle the world. She meant everything to him—Vegas, Broadway shows, movies. In my heart, I knew I could do the same. But I needed time to regain my strength. I needed a game plan."

Meanwhile, Gordy developed a game plan of his own, one which gave considerable power to his tough-minded lieutenants. Many of those executives, like Ralph Seltzer, were white. In order to develop Diana's solo career, Berry turned to others to run the company on a day-to-day basis.

Barney Ales, another white, had taken over collections after Loucye died. He ran the sales department during Motown's mid-sixties boom.

"Ales," said Beans Bowles, "organized one of the most effective selling operations in the country. He had as much to do with Berry's success as anyone."

"By 1970," wrote Motown historian Peter Benjaminson, "four of Motown's eight vice presidents were white. By 1977, whites held four-fifths of the positions of real power. In addition, Gordy had long-lasting relationships with white lawyers and white accountants."

Clarence Paul felt that Seltzer was prejudiced, and said so at a Motown meeting before leaving the company in 1968. "He hated issuing those big checks," Paul said, "especially to people who, unlike him, hadn't finished high school, much less college."

"Motown was filled with petty thieves," Seltzer told me during a four-hour interview in Detroit. "Lots of little people were involved in larceny. Berry could trust only three executives—George Schiffer, Suzanne dePasse, and me. BG always suffered with organizational problems. Administration wasn't his strength. Berry was a deal cutter. He also knew how to deal with the white community. He looked good, smelled pretty, spoke well, and displayed fine manners. He was acceptable. But he was also a reckless gambler. On any given day, he could lose $50 to $100,000—on a whim. Yet for all his risk taking, he understood how to control his artists. In those years, he'd never allow an artist to produce himself, not even Marvin. Smokey was the only exception. Berry created a caste system, but he also established a community with great creative cooperation. Most of the problems you hear the artists bitch about were caused by themselves. They just didn't pay their taxes."

Clarence Paul corroborated this view. "Marvin and I spent lots of money on drugs," Paul freely admitted. "When it was time to figure out taxes, we'd be surprised by just how much we owed. You drop a check for $50,000 in the lap of someone like me—a guy who'd been working in the Chrysler plant before I started in the music business—and it'd be gone before long. We had a hard time putting money away for taxes. So we fell behind. Some of us—I know it's true of me and Marvin—never did catch up."

"I hate the government," Marvin told me when he first started discussing his tax problems. "Especially back then during the war.

They wanted *me* to pay for the guns and the bombs with my hard-earned money? I felt like Muhammad Ali. No North Vietnamese had done nothing to me. I still hadn't forgotten what happened to me in the Air Force. I resented like hell having to give Uncle Sam a dime. I knew I could never beat the mothers, and I knew that attitude would get me in trouble, but I didn't give a shit.

"Not that I was any hero. Other people went to jail and I didn't. I was privileged. I saw what was happening in this country, and I wasn't doing a damn thing about it. All I could do was admit how much I hated show business. Show business is shit—the pressures and the hypocrisy, the endless hustle and the ass kissing. That wasn't me. Neither was performing. I was tired of going out and getting the women to scream. I had to be more than a sex symbol. I had to be an artist, and artists work in the privacy of their own imaginations. I hated being on stage, so I told myself I'd never go on stage again. I was only performing for the money anyway, and with 'Grapevine' that was no longer necessary. Berry was off on his Diana trip. His head was in Hollywood, and we were all supposed to follow after him like little puppy dogs. Let the others go. Let them chase after the bright lights. Not me. I was cool in Detroit. I stayed out and wasn't about to move until I got damn well ready."

Gaye's ambivalence about his female fans—needing their adoration and resenting their demands—only worsened. Shaken by Tammi's demise, distracted by Diana's drive, Marvin preferred to lie low. For the past decade, things had been moving with such rapidity he no longer felt in control. His temperament required that he regain that control. Gaye needed time to consider what he had seen: the spectacular success of some of his friends—Stevie, Smokey, the Supremes, Tops, and Temps—and the pitiful fall of others—Tammi Terrell, Florence Ballard, and Paul Williams.

Having turned thirty, Marvin remained a man who was incapable of enjoying his own success, even as he sought greater success, and searched for a peace which, he knew, would only come outside a limelight he could never resist.

14

GAMES

As the sixties came to an end, Gaye decided to play games—mind games with Motown, career games, athletic games—while he bided his time and waited for his creative well to refill. Marvin's self-created amusements, however, often took the form of emotional dilemmas.

On the major issues of his life—whether to divorce Anna or abandon his driving ambition—he remained divided.

"We are schizophrenic," Gaye once announced from the stage, "but we are not lost." In public, he liked using the kingly "we." To Marvin, not being "lost" meant maintaining sanity.

"I looked up the word 'schizophrenic' when I went into my withdrawal period in Detroit," Gaye told me. "Someone said the term applied to me, so I thought I better see what the books say about it. Schizophrenia is fascinating. It's not just having a split personality. It's a sickness that scrambles your feelings until you lose all emotional balance. That balance, especially in my case, is very delicate. I found myself uncertain of whether I could carry on. I needed rest."

Did he see a therapist?

"Are you kidding?" he answered with a laugh. "What am I going to tell a stranger? And what's a stranger going to tell me? *Never!* Besides, the cure is already inside us. All we have to do is bring it out. All answers are contained within. God is within each of us.

If we stop long enough to listen to the rhythm of our heartbeat, that's the rhythm of God's voice. After leaving Washington, I've never regularly attended church, but neither did I ever leave the church. The church never left my heart. I had religion, so why did I need head doctors? No, I didn't need to go to cocktail parties and talk about my psychoanalysis; I didn't need no shrink. It was just a matter of changing styles."

At the conclusion of the sixties, Marvin Gaye did alter his style, just as consciously, say, as Michael Jackson altered his in the early eighties. The difference is that Marvin's new style, unlike Michael's, was anti-glamour. At least for the time being.

"I was through wearing ties," Marvin said. "I promised myself I'd never wear a tie again. I'd always liked comfortable clothes, and from then on I wore only loose sweat pants, sweat shirts, gym shorts, and tennis shoes. If you look back, you may see that I started something of a trend. I didn't do it intentionally, but suddenly I looked around and saw all the cats wearing jogging suits just like mine."

Though Marvin was changing styles, he lost none of his self-centeredness. He did fashion sociocultural changes and wasn't hesitant to brag about it.

"I also grew a beard, which, back then, was not all that common for black men. Black men weren't supposed to look overtly masculine. I'd spent my entire career looking harmless, and the look no longer fit. I wasn't harmless. I was pissed at America. I didn't want to shave every morning, and so I didn't. I was interested in taking as much pressure off myself as possible. You might even say I became a recluse. That scared me because for the past ten years, Father had been leading exactly that kind of life. I couldn't help it, though. I wanted to get out, but I couldn't. I spent days never leaving my bedroom—never wanting to—depressed enough to call it quits. Little Marvin was growing up and we were taking care of other kids in Anna's family, but even the laughter of children couldn't pull me out of it. More than anything else, it was probably just walking over to the park and playing ball which saved my ass."

Marvin's battles with reclusiveness worsened as the years went on. There were periods when he was able to move about freely, but he'd inevitably find himself, like Father, retreating back to his bedroom where he might remain for months, seeking relief from the world's temptations and confusions. He was going through just such a depression at his death. His running buddies—Dave Simmons and Cecil Jenkins among them—begged him to get out of the house and play ball, knowing that physical activity was Marvin's best therapy. By then, though, it was too late.

Dave Simmons had met Marvin in 1970 and remained one of his most trusted friends through the very end.

"We got to know each other during a celebrity golf tournament," Simmons said. "He was surrounded by athletes like Bob Lanier, Lem Barney, and Dave Bing. He was crazy about sports—all sports—but that's not what really impressed me about Marvin. He had such a relaxed and breezy sense of humor that you'd think he didn't have a care in the world. Then the next day he might start telling you about his problems, and it seemed he was carrying the world on his shoulders."

"I was always a sports fan," Marvin said, "but I was determined to play for real. I knew I could. When I was a kid, I was scared to compete. Father wouldn't let me. Preachers' sons weren't supposed to be football players. Well, I decided to change all that. I trained with the Detroit Lions and was convinced I could start at offensive end. You see, I had this fantasy. I was in the Super Bowl, with millions of people watching me on TV all over the world, as I made a spectacular leaping catch and sprinted for the winning touchdown."

Gaye was a good athlete, but not of professional quality. His football playing, just like his basketball playing (where he loved to hog the ball and shoot), were further examples of his delusions of grandeur.

In 1970, Marvin began hanging out with Mel Farr and Lem Barney, both all-pro starters for the Lions. The three men became close friends.

"It was a very strange time in Marvin's life," said Mel Farr, who owns a Ford dealership in Oak Park, Michigan. "Marvin was depressed. He'd been holed up in his house for a long time. We convinced him to get out and play ball. Marvin was a guy who needed exercise. It lifted his spirits and made him feel better about himself. At first it was simply fun, but then Marvin got very serious. He went from 170 to 195 pounds, ran six miles a day, worked with weights and became convinced he was actually going to make the team. He could catch the football, he learned all the pass patterns and had great stamina. He also worked out with the East Michigan

University squad. He devoted his life to this goal—quit cigarettes, didn't do any drugs, just kept on training. I don't know whether he would have made it but it never got that far. Management nixed the idea. Coach Schmidt worried that Marvin would get hurt and the team would be sued. The attitude was that Marvin Gaye was a great musical talent who should be protected, not endangered. Lem and I had to break the news to him, and I've never seen anyone so disappointed in my life.

"Marvin was intent on proving he could do something other than sing. If you told him something was impossible, that's all he needed to hear. Playing golf, he'd bet you $500 on some ridiculous shot, just 'cause you said he couldn't make it. I never had the feeling Marvin cared about money or material things. He was adventuresome."

In a concert program from the late seventies produced under Marvin's scrupulous supervision, pages of color pictures show him playing ball and riding a dirt bike. His swimming style is compared to that of Mark Spitz. The blurb reads, "Marvin Gaye is a brilliant, all-around athlete. He could have been outstanding as a swimmer, sprinter, high jumper, baseball player, football player or basketball player. He competes on a regular basis against name performers in all these sports. Football-great turned actor, Jim Brown, after a grueling three-on-three basketball game, recently remarked, 'Marvin would have been a super jock.' "

"I tried to tell Marvin," said Beans Bowles, "that you just couldn't train for six months and then make the team. The guys out there had been playing—seriously playing—since junior high. Marvin had never played. And that's what was bothering him. He was crushed when they told him he couldn't play, but he would have been crushed *for real* if he had played."

Marvin wasn't the only member of the Motown family to watch professional sports longingly. "Gaye and Gordy's sister Esther Edwards," Peter Benjaminson reported, "were two of the thirty-three announced owners of the Detroit Wheels, the city's entry in the World Football League. Gaye had once expressed an interest in buying a WFL franchise for Memphis, Tennessee, so he could coach, play in the backfield, and sing the national anthem before games."

"I also played baseball with Willie Horton of the Tigers," Marvin told me. "I twisted my ankle skating with Gordy Howe of the Red Wings, so that didn't go too far.

"I've been called a black George Plimpton, and I resent that. George is cool, but I didn't play ball to gather material for a book. I played because I had every intention of becoming a superstar athlete. I played for keeps. I liked hanging around athletes because I respected their courage. It takes courage, day in and day out, to put your body on the line. I used to laugh when the jocks told me it took guts to get up and sing. They were right, because that was more frightening to me than catching a football in a crowded stadium. Ever try singing to 20,000 women, all of them screaming and grabbing for a piece of your hide? Getting popped by some defensive end is mild in comparison."

Did he really view women as opponents?

"Let me put it this way," he said. "I felt their demands upon me, and I hate demands. Once a person tells me what I must do, my first reaction is to refuse. I realized that women buy records in far greater numbers than men. I also believe that women feel music much more deeply than men. Women are rooted in the earth and in the spirit. They're more sensitive than we are. I appreciate that, because that means women appreciate me. But every man knows that a woman can tire him out, and, believe me, I was pooped."

The cover of his *Super Hits* album released in the fall of 1970 was the perfect artistic expression of Marvin's mystique at that point of his career—Gaye as an established sex symbol. Carl Owens' cartoon-styled illustration depicted Marvin as Superman, his muscles bulging. He flew through the air, with a buxom, scantily garbed black woman grabbing at his waist and neck for dear life, as he catches the falling, cracked sky-high antenna from radio station WHIT.

Since "Stubborn Kind of Fellow" in 1962, he'd sung over thirty hits, which spanned an emotional range from sweet innocence to sour frustration. He'd proven himself as perhaps the most dependable money-maker on the Motown roster. He'd survived a decade marked by volatile musical changes. Yet the one thing he wanted most—to become a ballad singer—still eluded him.

"I hadn't given up. In the late sixties, when I was trying to figure things out, I had Bobby Scott, the jazz pianist, write arrangements on a group of pop songs like 'The Shadow of Your Smile.' Now string orchestrations are something I understand. Right about then,

I myself was writing a two-movement symphony. But when Bobby played me his charts, I had to put away my own work. His arrangements were absolute genius. There were four ballads and two jazzy big-band numbers, and never before had I been so excited about music. Strange, though, because when I went in to record, I couldn't pull it off. It was as though the arrangements were too deep for me. Maybe I froze up thinking that the ballads would flop like all the ballads I'd sung before. Later I learned that it wasn't really a block. I couldn't sing the songs because I wasn't old enough. I didn't know enough. I had more suffering to do before I could get to the feelings."

Marvin's inclination was to revel in his own misery. "Artists suffer," said Gaye, "so you don't have to." His psyche demanded it. His art demanded it. By design, his suffering soul became his most powerful source of artistic inspiration. Closely identifying with Jesus, Gaye saw himself as a martyr, a man whose pain could be converted into artistic statements of real worth. In that sense, he triumphed. Where he failed, though—where he so desperately wanted to succeed—was in creating a happy family. Unable to realize this goal or to break from Anna, he prolonged his domestic misery. Marvin was less frightened of stale heartaches than fresh loneliness.

"I suppose most people as unhappy as I would have gotten divorced in a year," he said. "It took me fourteen. Maybe that's because when I sing, I have to be singing to one particular woman. For a long time, that particular woman was Anna."

His recording career divided in two equal parts: in the sixties— aside from his duets—he sang to Anna; in the seventies and eighties, he sang to Janis, his second wife. By personalizing his music, Marvin was able to express exactly what he was feeling. Consequently the experience—for him and his audience—was charged with real emotions.

Between Anna and Janis, however, he passed through another period, pausing in 1970 to create a socioreligious work of astounding originality, a bridge over the troubled waters of two turbulent marriages, a suite concerned not with romance but with soul and salvation: *What's Going On*.

Before starting *What's Going On*, however, Gaye put himself through a period of both hibernation and preparation. In the late sixties, he psychologically insulated himself from the pressures of show business by refusing to perform. Musically, though, he continued to experiment and grow. In fact, while he wanted to give the world the impression that he had retreated, he was, in fact, stepping out: For the first time in his career, he decided to produce.

Rather than begin with himself, Marvin, always somewhat cautious, practiced on a Motown group called the Originals. His first effort for them, "Baby, I'm for Real," hit Number One on the soul chart and Number Fourteen on the pop listing in late 1969.

Deeply derivative, the Originals' misty, wistful romanticism brought the Moonglows to mind.

"In trying to figure out what to do in the future," Marvin said, "I felt the need to examine my past. When I heard the group, I was excited by their possibilities. I loved the idea of writing for four different voices."

Oddly enough, Marvin wrote "Baby, I'm for Real" with Anna. If their marriage was rocky, how did they manage to work together?

"You have to understand me," Marvin explained. "One day I'd be throwing bottles at Anna, and the next day I'd be loving her like we'd just met. Fighting stimulated us. Besides, Anna was always good for my music. She'd give me ideas and push me any way she could. I'm the sort of artist who can always use a push. My moods can get a little heavy."

"The Bells," which Marvin co-wrote and produced for the Originals, was also a commercial success. The song even included an old-fashioned spoken recitative, similar in style to the opening lines of "Twelve Months of the Year" that Gaye had done eleven years earlier with the Moonglows. By championing and training the young group, by weaving their harmonies and contrasting their vocal textures, Marvin stepped into the role Harvey Fuqua had played for him. He was now a teacher.

"I was also writing—really writing—for the first time in years," said Marvin, who suffered from creative blocks. "I could feel my juices flowing again and began realizing that there was really only one person who could design my music—me."

A third Originals number, also written and produced by Marvin, "We Can Make It Baby," appeared on the soul chart in 1970.

Marvin's relationship with the group was marginal and lasted only a few years. He was unable to divert attention from himself to produce anyone else for very long. But eventually, as he listened to the Originals, he began hearing his own voices. By rehearsing and recording the group, he realized that he himself could—and would—sing all four parts. Through the Originals, he was able to merge past and present, to withdraw from what he viewed as the crass demands of the marketplace while at the same time expanding his current music to wider harmonic horizons. As recording technology in the early seventies radically improved, so did the possibilities of vocal experimentation. In *What's Going On*, which came out in early 1971, Marvin Gaye was among the first to take advantage of additional tracks by filling them with variations of his own voice.

As a suite, *What's Going On* was slow to develop. Both its musical and literary origins came from outside sources, men close to Marvin.

"I'd been stumbling around for an idea," Marvin explained. "I couldn't hear myself singing the Originals material, and I wasn't in the frame of mind for love songs. Tammi had just died."

Gwen McClendon was at Tammi Terrell's funeral in March of 1970. "The service was at night, in Cherry Hills, New Jersey," she said. "I never saw anyone as distracted and distraught as Marvin Gaye. I remember that he talked to Tammi as though she were still alive. He was devastated."

Gaye projected his own death upon Tammi's. "I felt that I had somehow died with her," he told me. In his imagination, she'd come to symbolize the hope of romantic love. With such hopes dashed, Marvin despaired not just for Tammi but for his own future, even as he stood on the brink of the most monumental creative breakthrough of his career.

In the same year, while Sly Stone was broadening the boundaries of soul music, influencing everyone from Marvin to Miles Davis, the Beatles had split up and John and Yoko were singing about "Instant Karma." The Carpenters were hot; so were Simon and Garfunkel. Al Green, a funky young soul singer, had his first R&B hit covering Norman Whitfield's "Can't Get Next to You." Meanwhile, at Motown, Whitfield found another macho voice in Edwin Starr whose "War" went Number One on the pop chart. Message songs were selling. Diana Ross successfully kicked off her solo career with Ashford and Simpson's "Reach Out and Touch Somebody's Hand" and "Ain't No Mountain High Enough," the same song which had worked wonders for Marvin and Tammi.

By then Diana and Berry were living out in Hollywood. I asked Gaye whether there was anything to the rumor that Gordy was pushed out of Detroit by the Mafia.

"That's utter bullshit," Marvin told me in a conversational style marked by a combination of candor and blarney. "All the time I was at Motown—over twenty years—I never heard or saw a single thing involving the Mafia. Berry was probably the most independent record man out there. The only time I came up against anything resembling the mob was at the Apollo. Some guys came into my dressing room saying they wanted to manage me and mentioning something about an ice pick. I treated it like a joke, told them to get out and never heard from them again.

"Berry left Detroit to make Diana a Hollywood movie star. BG was no different than anyone else. He needed to prove himself by making it outside his hometown. He worked like a demon. He personally produced her nightclub acts, spent unbelievable sums of money on costumes and scenery and lighting. He booked her into the swankiest joints in the country, and they were getting ready to jump into the movies. Berry was betting the bank on Diana. Even when Bobby Taylor had found the Jackson Five, BG sold them to the press as Diana's discovery, though everyone at Motown knew that was bullshit."

Between November 1969 and September 1970, America's first response to Michael Jackson's eleven-year-old voice was spectacular. The group's first four releases were successive Number One pop hits: "I Want You Back," "ABC," "The Love You Save," and "I'll Be There." Michael was deeply influenced not only by Marvin, but by Diana and Smokey. Fourteen years later, he would realize Berry Gordy's wildest dream: a graduate of the Motown school of song and dance became the most popular entertainer in the world. By then, though, Michael was recording for CBS.

"It was Frankie Lymon all over again," Marvin said. "Only this kid had mastered James Brown's moves. Michael was like Stevie. From the very beginning, he worried me."

In every period of his life—active or inactive, happy or depressed—Gaye studied popular music with detached sobriety. His reaction to new stars and trends was always cautious. Rather than jump on the bandwagon, Gaye would wait an extra year, analyzing the situation while developing his own strategy. The result would often be a startlingly original synthesis, a trendsetting form in itself. This reflective process was especially true in the period preceding *What's Going On*.

"There were so many musical changes floating in the air, it was hard to find a handle. That's why for a long time I did nothing. Actually, I found some comfort in singers like James Taylor. James' voice has a soothing, mellow quality which came at just the right time, like a lull in the middle of the storm. Later when he did 'How Sweet It Is,' I felt gratified.

"Meanwhile, Motown was looking for me to hit Vegas and play the big hotels in Miami. They kept screaming—'Why aren't you in the studio? Where's your record? When are you going to give us product?' Well, I couldn't look at my music as product."

By now Marvin's political consciousness could no longer be suppressed.

"My phone would ring, and it'd be Motown wanting me to start working and I'd say, 'Have you seen the paper today? Have you read about these kids who were killed at Kent State?' The murders at Kent State made me sick. I couldn't sleep, couldn't stop crying. The notion of singing three-minute songs about the moon and June didn't interest me. Neither did instant-message songs."

Gaye was also feeling the influence of the alternative culture of the times.

"Someone had slipped me a copy of *The Teachings of Don Juan* by Carlos Castaneda, and at first I wasn't real interested. I'm a slow reader and don't read more than a book a year. But I opened it up and saw this quote on the first page from Don Juan that said, 'For me there is only the traveling on paths that have heart . . . the only worthwhile challenge is to traverse its full length.' I studied that book and treasured its wisdom. I looked at what was happening at Woodstock and thought to myself, Here's a whole generation of people about to travel a new path. I understood that musically I'd have to go on a path of my own. The Motown corporate attitude didn't give me much room to breathe, but I was starting to feel strong enough to start down my own path. When my brother Frankie came home from Vietnam and began telling me stories, my blood started to boil. I knew I had something—an anger, an energy, an artistic point of view. It was time to stop playing games."

Finally, Marvin was ready to go to work. An artist of brilliant intuitive timing, he had waited just long enough. By allowing time for reflection, even his writing blocks had worked to his advantage. Gaye had refilled his creative cup. For the first time in his career, he felt capable of moving beyond the personal to the universal. Although the first song would be written by a collaborator—giving Marvin his usual initial push—the scope of the suite itself came from Gaye's spiritual examination of the ways of the world.

He turned his thesis—which, like Gaye himself, was a mixture of faith and despair—into a simple question. Looking at a crazed America at the start of the seventies, he asked, "What's going on?", convinced that he had the answer.

PART
TWO

15

SERMON FROM THE STUDIO

One theory of the life of Marvin Gaye could view his personal history as a carefully predetermined work—a play, a novel, a suite of songs—consciously constructed by the singer himself. Marvin liked to give the impression that he was calling the shots, creating wild twists and turns in order to keep himself amused. He possessed a highly developed sense of drama which, to some degree, shaped the very events of his existence. Gaye made himself into the author and principal actor in an incredible adventure which took him to the very top, then threw him to the bottom, only to have him rise again even higher, so that in the end his final fall would be his most spectacular.

The deeper truth, though, is that Marvin was only partially in control. His script had been written long before he appeared on the planet in Sophocles' play *Oedipus Rex*, produced four hundred years before the birth of Christ. The murderous relationship between father and son was a theme known to both the soul singer and the Greek playwright, and this classical sense of tragic inevitability hung over Gaye's life like a dark cloud. Guilty of another tragic failing, that of hubris—wanting too much, reaching too far, confusing himself for a god—Marvin fought his fate in vain.

The fundamentalist Christian view of Marvin Gaye would see him as a fallen preacher. Born with the sacred power to transmit Jesus' love through heavenly song, his religious responsibility was, at least in Marvin's own mind, clear. According to his own testimony, he'd felt the calling as a small child. But Marvin's electricity, like Al Green's, generated two sorts of reactions, sexual and spiritual, depending upon which switch Gaye chose to pull. "When Marvin defied God," a member of the House of God told me, "he understood the terrible price he'd have to pay."

The proof of his ability to preach is found in *What's Going On*. Along with Gaye's *In Our Lifetime*, written a decade later, *What's Going On*, like Ellington's sacred work, has the unmistakable sound of divine inspiration. But even more than Ellington, Gaye's gift was to reach out to millions on Top Ten radio, to wrap his holy messages in irresistible swathings of richly colored musical cloth.

What's Going On was the quiet moment in the raging storm that swept through so much of Marvin's life. In searching for subject matter, Gaye wisely chose to write about someone he knew—his brother. He made Frankie the main character of his work, looking back at America through the soul of his sibling.

With his sloped eyes, soft speaking voice, and lilting intonation, Frankie bears a striking resemblance to his brother. He also shares Marvin's acute sensitivity.

"The death and destruction I saw in Vietnam sickened me," Frankie told me. "The war seemed useless, wrong, and unjust. I relayed all this to Marvin and forgave him for never writing to me while I was over there. That had hurt, because he was a big star and none of my buddies believed he was my brother. 'Wait,' I told them, 'he's going to write me back and prove it to you.' He never did."

The tenuous relationship between the brothers would continue through the seventies, with Frankie gently pushing Marvin to let him sing while Marvin gently pushed Frankie into the background. For a short while, Frankie became one of Marvin's background vocalists. His contribution to *What's Going On*, though, was one of inspiration, not participation. Frankie's religious disposition set the record's tone. Far less troubled than his brother and father, Frankie was the perfect persona, adopted by Marvin, to express the sorrows and offer the solutions to what was ailing a war-torn America.

"I know this sounds strange," Frankie told me, "but I think that Marvin was always envious of my war experience. He saw it as a manly act that he had avoided. It's even stranger because while Marvin was always my hero, I was also his hero. I really believe he wanted to be me."

To some degree, there were musical precedents for *What's Going On*. Curtis Mayfield had long been intrigued by social themes, incorporating Christianity into "People Get Ready," a pop hit in 1965. Isaac Hayes, whose *Hot Buttered Soul* profoundly influenced Marvin, was voicing strings and writing his quasi-symphonic score for *Shaft* at about the same time Gaye was composing *What's Going On*.

As with almost all Marvin's major projects, he himself didn't initiate the musical action. He needed help to get past his inertia. The title song, "What's Going On," was composed by Renaldo "Obie" Benson of the Four Tops and Al Cleveland, though there are somewhat conflicting explanations of its specific origins.

"We argued over the credits," Obie told me. "Marvin was funny when it came to credit, but basically it went down like this: I gave Marvin one-third of the song to sing and produce it. Naturally he put his own touches on it, being the master that he is. But all the music was already there."

"One day after Lem, Marvin, and I played golf," Mel Farr remembered, "we went back over Marvin's house on Outer Drive. We'd hit the ball especially good that day and we were all feeling good, sitting around and kibitzing, when I said, 'Hey, what's going on?' Marvin said, 'You know, that'd be a hip title for a song. I think I'll write it for the Originals.' He started fooling at the piano and when we dropped by to see him the next day he was still fooling with it. 'That's not for the Originals, Marvin,' we told him. 'That's for you.' "

Marvin wrote most of the songs in conjunction with others. Though he never stopped worrying that he wouldn't receive enough credit, Gaye still preferred company in the early creative stages. The major work, however, was essentially his.

"From Jump Street, Motown fought *What's Going On*," Marvin claimed. "They didn't like it, didn't understand it, and didn't trust it. Management said the songs were too long, too formless, and would get lost on a public looking for easy three-minute stories. For months they wouldn't release it. My attitude had to be firm.

Basically I said, 'Put it out or I'll never record for you again.' That was my ace in the hole, and I had to play it."

The ploy worked. Marvin won, and the winnings were bigger than even he had imagined. His first self-produced, self-written album altered not only his career but his very life. From now on, he'd be perceived—by the white community as well as by the black, in Europe and in America—as a complex and serious artist.

Everything about the album was different. The back cover showed a bearded, distraught Marvin standing in the rain, wearing a tie he had sworn never to wear. For the first time on one of his records, lyrics were listed and musicians credited. In spite of the fact that, according to his sister Jeanne, he had long ignored his family in Washington, D.C., he dedicated the work to his parents, among others—"thanks to the Rev. & Mrs. Marvin P. Gay Sr. for conceiving, having and loving me"—his sisters, brothers, wife, son, and friends, Clarence Paul and Harvey Fuqua among them. Berry Gordy was not mentioned, nor would Marvin ever thank him on the back of an album.

Vince Aletti spoke for a number of critics when, reviewing the record for *Rolling Stone*, he admitted that he had underestimated Marvin Gaye. *Time* magazine wrote a two-column review of the work: "After listening to . . . *What's Going On*, the Rev. Jesse Jackson informed its creator, Soul Crooner Marvin Gaye, that he was as much a minister as any man in any pulpit." The article quotes Marvin: "God and I travel together with righteousness and goodness. If people want to follow along, they can."

The *Time* reviewer went on: "The LP laments war, pollution, heroin and the miseries of ghetto life. It also praises God and Jesus, blesses peace, love, children and the poor. Musically it is a far cry from the gospel or blues a black singer-composer might normally apply to such subjects. Instead Gaye weaves a vast, melodically deft symphonic pop suite in which Latin beats, soft soul and white pop, and occasionally scat and Hollywood schmaltz, yield effortlessly to each other. The overall style . . . is so lush and becalming that the words—which in themselves are often merely simplistic—come at the listener like dots from a Seurat landscape."

From the opening alto riffs of the title song, the listener was ushered into new musical territory. The establishment of a groove—lightly swinging, sweetly mellow, deeply relaxed—became Gaye's hallmark. For all the emotional and literary complexity, the effect was easy listening. Marvin sang to please the ear.

His multitracked voices were startling. He'd become a one-man Moonglows, a one-man Originals, singing duets and trios with himself, juxtaposing his silky falsetto and sandpapery midrange, weaving the fabric of his voices into a tapestry of contrasting shapes and colors.

"I felt like I'd finally learned how to sing," Marvin told me. "I'd been studying the microphone for a dozen years, and suddenly I saw what I'd been doing wrong. I'd been singing too loud, especially on those Whitfield songs. It was all so easy. One night I was listening to a record by Lester Young, the horn player, and it came to me. Relax, just relax. It's all going to be all right.

"I also saw that I wanted to treat the album as an album, not as a string of small songs. So I found a theme, and I tried to explore it from several different angles. At first, I was afraid, because I didn't know whether this had ever been done before, but when I got started I actually found that the process came naturally. It was easy. Don Juan was right: I was traveling down a path of the heart."

Marvin's instincts were to write from his immediate experience. Thus *What's Going On* was set in America's black urban neighborhoods, the territory of his childhood. The title song began with party sounds. Marvin's friends—Lem Barney, Mel Farr, Bobby Rodgers of Smokey's Miracles, and Elgie Stover—created an intimate atmosphere in which Marvin felt most comfortable. They were family.

"Later on," Mel Farr told me, "Motown convinced Marvin to re-record the tune with a group of professional backup singers. But it didn't sound as natural as the original, and Marvin stuck to his guns."

The first two songs set the scene and stated the sermon's thesis, combining an urgent 1971 political plea with a personal note to his own father. He cried out to his mother, to his brother, to all the brothers dying in the war, and finally pleaded with Father, singing that there's no need to "escalate."

"If I was arguing for peace," Marvin said, "I knew I'd have to find peace in my own heart. All the time since I'd been in Detroit, Father and I had little to say to each other. It was still hard for me to even look at him, even though I knew that he'd been collecting articles on me for the last ten years. He kept everything—more for his ego than mine. He might have been proud, but he was more jealous than anything else. Secretly I was wishing Mother would throw him out and divorce him, but I knew that could never happen. I didn't want him living off me, but how could I stop him when I had to support Mother? Basically, I was supporting the whole family. I resented that. But now was the time to put those resentments behind me. Jesus said forgive, and I needed to forgive, and be forgiven. Love should be unconditional. To be truly righteous, you offer love with a pure heart, without regard for what you'll get in return. I had myself in that frame of mind. People were confused and needed reassurance. God was offering that reassurance through his music. I was privileged to be the instrument."

In "What's Happening, Brother," Marvin spoke through brother Frankie, just back from Vietnam, facing a divided country and an uncertain future. The central character admitted confusion, not understanding what was happening "across this land."

Uncertainty led to escape. Drugs—its pains and pleasures—were the subject of the eerily seductive "Flyin' High (in the Friendly Sky)." Containing the seed of *Trouble Man*, Gaye's next major work, the song not only lamented the spread of dope in the ghetto, but echoed Gaye's concern with his own growing cocaine habit, calling it "self-destruction" and admitting he was "hooked."

The despair expanded to the horror of a nuclear holocaust. "Save the Children" became the album's most poignant piece, as Marvin asked a series of questions in a speaking voice filled with melancholy: Will all the flowers fade? Can the world be saved? Is humanity destined to die? Are our children fated to suffer? Do we care enough to save ourselves?

Based on Revelations and the state of the world, Gaye was convinced that the end was imminent. As time passed and his own fortunes fell, those convictions deepened. Now, though, after his doomsday vision, his depression was suddenly assuaged: Affirmation arrived in perhaps the single most emotional moment he ever reached on record. He spoke the words, "Let's save all the children," and then answered himself in song, pleading, "Save the babies, save the babies!" In the transition between the plainly spoken word "children" and the impassioned cry of "babies," Gaye's clarion call was clear as the light of day.

With lifted spirits, the suite continued seamlessly. The rhythm quickened. Hope was offered. "God is love." Marvin mentioned Jesus, whose only demand was that we "give each other love."

"I respect the Eastern religions," said Gaye. "Their philosophies are beautiful and wise. They've taught me to root myself in the present. I also believe in reincarnation. We're destined to return to repeat our mistakes if we don't grow toward God in this form. I respect Islam, though I worry that the Koran makes it too easy to kill. I respect all the great religions. But my own beliefs come down to two simple points. One, believe in Jesus, and two, expand love. Both points, you see, are really the same."

I said that I was surprised, given how he had rebelled against his father, that he had never rebelled against his father's Christianity.

"I could see the truth," Marvin explained, "not in Father's example, but in the words he preached."

Even at the bottom of his bluest funks, Gaye was clear about the lessons of Jesus. At some point Marvin lost the way—he himself said he didn't deserve to be called a practicing Christian—but God was always the light toward which he longed to travel.

"One of the reasons I love my father," said Marvin in one of his preaching moods, "is because he offered me Jesus. He made Jesus come alive for me, and that's reason enough to be grateful to him for the rest of my life. It's not about this church or that church. Almost all churches are corrupt. My church lives within my own heart. Jesus is there when you call him, whether you're strolling through a garden or caught in a storm at sea. He's a lifeline. He's a healer. His name is magic. His example is eternal. His hope is a beacon of light, and with him there is no fear, no death. When we don't follow his example and turn to exploitation and greed, we destroy ourselves. That's what 'Mercy Mercy Me' is about."

The song catalogued the ecological nightmares plaguing the world —mercury in our fish, oil spills, radiation, endangered species. How much more, he asked, can this "overcrowded" nation endure?

But in "Right On," Marvin turned away from the world—at least for a moment—to describe his own condition with characteristic candor. He admitted to a life of privilege, money, and "good fortune." And yet with so much wealth surrounding him, he saw himself as a man who "drowned in the sea of happiness." Such was the story of his life.

If he was to be spared, only love could save him, a unity of spirit expressed in the song "Wholly Holy."

Moving full circle, the suite ended where it began, back in the neighborhood, describing the plight of the poor through an ancient black blues—"Inner City Blues"—measured by the cadence of an urban bongo beat. The burden of taxes was a theme that ran through Marvin's work, just as it ran through Marvin's life. He viewed the obligation with adamancy and anger: Why pay taxes to buy moon rockets when we can't feed our poor? Why are we sending innocent sons off to die in wars that make no sense? Why have the cops gone "trigger happy?" Why has the world gone mad?

What's Going On concluded by repeating a small section of the title song in which Gaye expressed his sympathy with the rebellious youth of the early seventies, arguing against the injustice of judging people by the length of their hair.

Despite what Marvin called Motown's skepticism, the response in the marketplace was immediate and overwhelming. The album was the most successful in Gaye's recorded history. Between February and October of 1971, three of the songs—"What's Going On," "Mercy Mercy Me," and "Inner City Blues"—hit the Top Ten on the soul and pop charts.

It's easy to forget how radical the work was by 1971 standards. Structurally, the songs were not typical Top Ten fare. They owed as much to jazz as to soul or pop. "Wild Bill" Moore's raging tenor, for instance, was mixed under many of the tracks, an ongoing jazz counterpoint to the rest of the musical action. Song lengths were unconventional. "Inner City Blues" was over five minutes. Commercially, the notion of a black bitterly criticizing America was thought to be risky. For instance, James Brown's message songs, like "I Don't Want Nobody to Give Me Nothing (Open the Door, I'll Get It Myself)," had a conservative bent. Brown was basically patriotic; Gaye was not. There was also the old adage that, lyrically at least, gospel and pop never mix. Jesus simply wasn't mentioned in secular songs, not if you were aiming for a pop market.

In one fell swoop, Marvin disproved these theories. He revolutionized soul music by expanding its boundaries. He changed the direction of Motown by showing the sales potential of thought-provoking inner monologues. In winning the fight for his own integrity, others—equally talented and capable of creating their own art—benefited: Stevie Wonder, who since age ten had been studying Marvin, and now another Motown pre-teen, Michael Jackson, who would eventually follow Gaye's artistic lead as a singer, writer, and producer.

"When I was struggling for the right of the Motown artist to express himself," Marvin told me, "Stevie knew I was also struggling for him. He gained from that fight, and the world gains from his genius. Don't get me wrong—Stevie would have made it big without me. His talent is cosmic. But as it turned out, Stevie's really a preacher like the rest of us. I like to think I helped show him the light. Now every time I hear him, in between my twinges of jealousy I thank God for Stevie's gift and the privilege of feeling his energy at such close range.

"The biggest result of *What's Going On*, though, had to do with my own freedom. I'd earned it, and no one could take it away from me. Now I could do whatever I wanted. For most people that would be a blessing. But for me—with all my hot little games— the thought was heavy. They said I'd reach the top, and that scared me 'cause Mother used to say, 'first ripe, first rotten.' When you're at the top there's nowhere to go but down. No, I needed to keep going up—raising my consciousness—or I'd fall back on my behind.

"When would the war stop? that's what I wanted to know . . . the war inside my soul."

Even with his creative breakthrough accomplished, Marvin's soul remained split. His ego demanded that he return to center stage, but his insecurities made him want to hide. As a result, Gaye alternated between two extremes, seeking love and rejecting love, realizing success and throwing it away, assuming the attitude of a prince while living with the fears of a pauper.

16

THE LURE OF ADORATION

Marvin turned to his fans, to the very women whose love he both resented and required, to regain his strength. He needed to be adored.

Such was also the situation after making *What's Going On* in 1971. In spite of his fears of going public again, Marvin hungered for attention and gradually emerged from his cocoon to accept the praise for what was being called his masterpiece.

The NAACP gave Marvin their fifth annual Image Award, naming him the "nation's most socially significant entertainer," as well as the year's best singer and producer. He was *Cashbox*'s Male Vocalist of the Year and won *Billboard*'s Trendsetter Award. Little by little, as he slowly emerged from feelings of despair brought on by his doomed marriage and Tammi Terrell's tragic death, he accepted a few prizes in person but still refused to perform.

"Strange," he told me, "but these two fears I have—flying in airplanes and singing on stage—have something in common.

"If I toured, that involved flying, though sometimes I'd travel by train or bus. Usually, though, I kept changing my mind till the last minute—would I cancel or wouldn't I?—so if I wanted the money, there was just enough time left to fly to the gig.

"The longer I didn't perform or fly, the worse the fears. Once I started and got into the groove, I could mellow out and handle the situation. It was just a matter of starting up again—that was the trick. It was nearly four years since I'd sung in public. Had I lost it? I didn't want to know. I still wasn't prepared to dash out on stage. Being inaccessible has never hurt an artist. An artist must guard his time. Besides, when they can't see you, fans start missing you. I wanted to be missed. I had to trust my sense of timing, and that sense said, Stay away."

He didn't stay away, however, from the 1971 Super Bowl in Miami, where he had his picture taken with Gale Sayers. He also suited up for a Grambling State–Fullerton College football game in Los Angeles, where he did warm-up exercises with the players.

In the aftermath of *What's Going On*, the white press rushed to interview this enigmatic figure who had suddenly emerged as a genuine artist. Marvin was ready for them. No one knew better than Gaye how to play the press. Finally free of Motown's restraints, free to develop his own image, he spoke at length and in depth, delighted to talk about himself with a heady brew of candor and caution.

"The more you get to know me," he said the first time we met, demonstrating his charm and confidence as an interviewee, "the more you'll want to get to know."

In early 1972, Ben Fong-Torres did *Rolling Stone*'s first major piece on Marvin, who was still living on Outer Drive in Detroit. By then, most of the Motown gang had long settled in Los Angeles.

Marvin offered Fong-Torres a joint, then announced that he'd given up hopes of becoming a football star and had decided to box instead. He painted an idealized picture of his childhood, a version which he thought would be acceptable to a white audience, the pop market which he had worked so long to sell. Gaye wasn't prepared, not in front of these new fans, to wash his dirty laundry. As though he were trying to convince himself that his childhood was really not a nightmare, he glossed over his pre-adolescent conflicts. Ray Charles had played the same trick on Whitney Balliet in *The New Yorker*. But even in ignoring the pain of his past, Gaye revealed a great deal.

"I've been competitive all my life," he told Fong-Torres. "I've never had a chance to exercise my competitiveness through athletics, of course, because my father loved, I imagine he overloved me, if that's possible. . . .

"I just wanted to say that I bested you at a physical game or a mental contest, football or chess. Just for the thrill of it. If I beat you playing pool I enjoy it. But what I enjoyed was controlling myself when I was behind. And I think, 'Now am I going to be a chicken and just fall away or am I gonna muster myself together, swallow my spit and really get down and win?' If I come up from behind and win like that, it's a fantastic feeling. I get chills all over. If I lose, I feel like a faggot."

He also discussed his ego, describing how he conceived "every bit of the music" for *What's Going On*. Because Dave Van DePitte did the actual scoring, though, he was afraid Van DePitte would claim credit. "But I'm gonna learn to write music," Marvin promised. "Why? Because I want all the credit."

Gaye never did learn to read or write music. The two-part symphony he claimed to have composed was a series of melodies sung on a tape recorder. Nothing was notated. He did, however, prepare an album for Sammy Davis, Jr., who had just signed with Motown. Marvin's tracks, though, which he claimed cost $45,000 of his own money, were rejected by the label and never played for Sammy.

When asked how he conceived a complex work such as *What's Going On*, Marvin was defensive. "What you're trying to find out is am I really a genius or a fake. And I think I'm a fake." In the next breath, though, he called the album divinely inspired.

The highlight of the interview took place in a gym. This was how Marvin wanted his public to view him—at the King Solomon Baptist Church gym down in the ghetto.

While Fong-Torres watched, Gaye worked with his trainer, punching the bag and showing off Tommy Hanna, the first of three professional prize fighters he would own in the next seven years.

"I think I can make him the next middleweight champion," Marvin claimed.

When asked about the morality of boxing, Gaye was ambivalent. Later he clearly articulated his distaste for the emerging women's liberation movement, even arguing for the superiority of men.

Somewhere in the course of the interview Marvin's ebullience faded. He grew depressed. He'd fought with Anna. He also learned that *What's Going On* hadn't been nominated for a single Grammy. Ten years later he would still be angry.

Gaye yearned for the approval of his peers. But in a year dominated by Carole King's *Tapestry*, *What's Going On* failed to make a dent. In the category Marvin expected to dominate—best rhythm-and-blues male vocal performance—Lou Rawls won.

"Lou had gotten it before, and I never had—not in the eleven years I'd been making records," Marvin told me. "I knew it was my time. But it wasn't. I was deeply hurt by the whole affair. I felt like I was swindled. I was mad at Lou. I didn't like the way he handled it and, if I hadn't watched myself, I could have wound up fighting him. That's how pissed I was. I thought I'd turned out a great work, and the Grammys didn't even give me the time of day. Politics, that's what it was. Hollywood games. I refused to play those games, and I suffered.

"I also started wondering whether I shouldn't really be out there in Hollywood with everyone else. The stubborn side of me said, 'Stay, hold your ground.' But Detroit was starting to look like a ghost town, and I was feeling stranded. Anna's sister Gwen had this beautiful house in Beverly Hills and we were spending more and more time there. Naturally Berry had an even bigger house. The first one was up on Curson Terrace in the Hollywood Hills. He'd bought it from one of the Smothers Brothers. Then he got this super mansion in Bel Air from Red Skelton. That was *the* house. He'd finally become King of the Hill, not in little old Detroit, but big-time L.A.

"Anna and I hadn't been a couple for a long time. Now that I had hit it big, I suppose my ego was even more swollen. Maybe I didn't handle it well. I was angry because, for all my hits, I still couldn't call myself sure-enough rich. Motown had it set up funny. But that was changing. I was getting more control, and I was determined to be rich—richer than Berry himself. That's always been a goal of mine. It's hard to describe how competitive I felt toward Berry Gordy.

"At the same time, I didn't fool myself. I knew I still needed Berry, and Anna, too. I knew the Gordys had the Hollywood connections. Without Anna, how could I reach my next plateau? With Anna, though, how could I ever be a happy man?

"I kept having dreams about another woman. In my dream, I'd be off in the shadows, and this young girl would be dancing in front of me. She didn't know I was there, but I could see everything. Other men—football players, boxers, weight lifters—would take her and whirl her around. Everyone was naked except me. She'd go from man to man, coming close to me, moving away from me. She couldn't get enough sex, she was a freak, and I was the only man who could please her. It was a fantasy.

"I was still recovering from the excitement of the sixties, the mobs of women, and I preferred fantasy to reality. A whore now and then might be an interesting diversion, but nothing heavy. I was mainly into my music. Stevie gave me a Moog, which had just come out, and I was like a little kid with a new toy. Music, not sex, got me aroused. I still didn't want to be disturbed by audiences."

Soul magazine reported that Marvin planned to return to the stage by performing in Atlanta for the first annual Martin Luther King Birthday Commemoration. Later, furious with the magazine, he denied ever saying such a thing and refused to appear. The public clamor to see him perform, though, didn't die.

"I felt the heat," Marvin said, "and found myself doing this tug-of-war with my fans. My attitude was, I'd given them a good record. Wasn't that enough?"

To a degree, he enjoyed this cat-and-mouse game. He viewed the act of public singing as a kind of collective sexual intercourse, an attitude which became especially pronounced toward the end of his life. He was never able to lose the adolescent fantasy—and frustrations—of being faced with the impossible task of satisfying his dream girl's nymphomaniacal needs. Because he was never confident about his sexual performance, he transferred the fear to stage performance.

"Frankly, I enjoy the teasing part more than the sex," he once said. "After you've had as much as I've had, the thrill is more in the mind than the body." He saw the ritual of cancelling concerts—of being begged to sing—as a form of sexual foreplay, reasoning that it made his female fans want him that much more. His fear of performing, however, was very real, and only one person had the power to persuade him to sing in public—Mother.

The coming-out concert was arranged by Marvin's childhood companion Dewey Hughes, the same friend with whom he'd gone to junior high school. Then a broadcasting executive in Washington, Hughes convinced the District to declare Marvin Gaye Day on May 1, 1972. There'd be honors at Cardoza, his former high school, a motorcade, a congressional reception, and a benefit concert for Pride Inc., a black self-help group, at the Kennedy Center. But even that wasn't enough to guarantee Marvin's appearance.

"First he agreed to do it," Hughes told me, "then he changed his mind. We recruited his mother to convince him. That was the only way he finally came."

"I was still mad at Washington. What had they ever given me?" Marvin asked. "Why should they all of a sudden love me, now that I'd sold a few records? Where were they when I needed them? For years I'd considered Detroit, not Washington, my home. I resented the whole thing and I desperately didn't want to do it. Until the last few minutes, I wasn't going to go. You see, I'd just turned thirty-three. That was the age that Jesus died. I had a strong fear that I'd never live longer than Jesus, and I wasn't interested in exposing myself any more than necessary. Getting through that year—worrying about airplane crashes or dying of cancer—wasn't easy."

A *Washington Post* reporter went to Detroit and wrote a feature on Gaye which appeared the weekend before the concert. Like Ben Fong-Torres of *Rolling Stone,* he was whisked to the King Solomon Baptist Church gym to watch Marvin spar in the ring. Back at home, on Outer Drive, Marvin told the *Post,* "I didn't really want to do this concert . . . but . . . my mother kept calling and asking me if I'd do it for her. Mothers are like that."

On May 1, 1972, Marvin Pentz Gaye, Jr., came home again. In spite of his trepidations, the event was triumphant.

"I got through it, but I was a wreck," Marvin remembered. "I hardly remember what happened. I must have blocked it out, because I was nervous enough to piss in my pants."

"I've never seen anyone so relaxed and charming," Dewey Hughes reported. "Marvin Gaye was the absolute epitome of dignity and graciousness that day. Everyone—absolutely everyone—loved him. He was as suave as any diplomat in the District."

At 10 A.M., in the auditorium of the high school from which he never graduated, thirteen hundred students gave him a tumultuous welcome. He sang "What's Going On" with the Cardoza band, signed autographs, and gave a brief speech.

"They wanted me to say something about drug abuse," Marvin told me. "I went along, but I really can't remember what I said. I'm sure I was a little stoned."

He was dressed in a white suit and black shirt open at the throat, its collar cut extra-long in the mod style of the day. He also wore a pair of large-framed scholarly looking glasses, highly unusual attire for Marvin. He, his father—dressed enigmatically in dark glasses, dark suit, white shirt, and flowery tie—and his mother rode in an open-car motorcade, led by marching bands. At the district building, Mayor Walter Washington reminisced about being director of the projects where the Gays once lived and presented Marvin with a key to the city.

Standing between his parents, towering over them both, Marvin accepted the key, remarking, "I've often wondered what you do with a key to the city. . . . I wonder if it'll do any good if I get stopped by a police officer. . . ." Then he sang "What's Going On" again, this time accompanied by the Howard University band.

Mrs. Gay was also asked to speak. "I was terribly afraid," she told me. "I'd never spoken in public before, so I prayed to Jesus for the courage and the right words. God gave me a beautiful speech to say. I told the people how proud I was of my son, and how I appreciated the way they loved him."

At 6 P.M., prior to the concert, Gaye was honored at a VIP reception in the Rayburn Building. Continually wedged between his parents, Marvin worked the crowd with aplomb, displaying his boyish charm, granting TV and radio interviews, greeting congressmen, and putting his arm around his father as photographers popped pictures.

"The whole family was there for the celebration," Jeanne Gay said. "I've never seen Marvin happier. It was a very warm and wonderful day."

A little past 11 P.M.—after an opening act, an intermission, and numerous delays—Marvin made his long-awaited return to the stage. Before he sang, a congratulatory telegram from Mrs. Coretta King was read to the audience.

"I wish you could have been at the Kennedy Center that night," said Maurice King, who conducted the orchestra. "The people—his people—oh, how they had been waiting for him! In all my years in this business, I've never seen such an outpouring of love and affection. They went crazy for that boy. People were crying just to see him, just to hear him. Marvin had to realize how foolish he'd been cooping himself up all those years."

Supported by ten Motown studio musicians and a twenty-piece brass-and-string ensemble, Gaye sang a medley of his early hits followed by a rendition of the complete *What's Going On*.

"I want to thank you for being here at my attempt to return to a live performance," he announced afterward. "We hoped to perform the album exactly as you can hear it in your home . . . but I'm a perfectionist and I wasn't completely happy with the way things sounded, so if there's anything we did that you'd like to hear again, we'll try to do it."

The nearly all-black crowd screamed for "What's Going On," and Marvin sang the song for the fourth time that day.

"I understood that I'd been punishing myself by staying away so long," Marvin thought back. "I'd been denying myself love, and that's one of the most foolish things a man can do. It was certainly the biggest day of my parents' life. Here they came to Washington in the thirties without a penny, and their son was being honored by the mayor as some sort of hero. At least on this one day I felt like I made Father proud."

Nineteen seventy-two was an election year—Nixon and Agnew would win by a landslide in November—and in April, just before his Washington concert, Marvin released a highly political single, convinced that, after the success of *What's Going On*, his socially conscious songs would sell. He was wrong.

"You're the Man" (Part I) became a Top Ten soul hit but never crossed over. It was a disappointment to Marvin and Motown and, aside from being released in his 1974 three-LP anthology, was never included on an album. More importantly, it gave Gaye serious doubts about the direction of his career. He worried that he could no longer count on social issues for sales.

The percussive, spicy, Latin-tinged number was a perceptive musical profile of a politician, seen through Marvin's skeptical eyes and sung in Marvin's many voices. Aside from the matter of busing, the song anticipated the single theme which would dominate black political thought for the next dozen years: economics. The lyrics were not only specific—arguing for higher employment and lower inflation—but pointedly angry: if the candidate didn't have a plan to help improve the lot of the poor, to hell with him.

At the same time, Marvin began answering Hollywood's calls. He started commuting between Detroit and a small apartment on Cattaraugus Avenue on the west side of Los Angeles, where he found himself immersed in his one and only serious film project, the score to *Trouble Man*.

In the early seventies it looked like Hollywood was finally opening its doors to black films. This proved to be an illusion, though at the time some black urban-action stories were proving profitable. Producers were churning out low-cost movies and big-name musicians were providing the scores. Isaac Hayes's *Shaft* set the precedent. Curtis Mayfield's *Superfly* came out in 1972, the same year as *Trouble Man*.

The musical scores were far more interesting than the silly cops-and-robber films they accompanied. *Trouble Man* was no exception. Gaye viewed it as a large canvas on which he painted his newly discovered Moog figures. He'd always wanted to do a jazz instrumental album, and *Trouble Man* became just that. A large part of the score was a sultry duet between Marvin's blues-based keyboards and Trevor Lawrence's hard-biting sax, augmented by lush, big-band charts by arrangers like jazz trombonist J. J. Johnson.

Trouble Man was one of only two albums where Gaye wrote every song alone. He lost himself in the mood of the movie, a mood corresponding to the dark side of his own soul. Marvin himself was fascinated by the underworld and, from time to time, surrounded himself with real-life gangsters.

"Just being in a room with them, you can feel their power," Gaye observed. "They keep me from being bored. Besides, who isn't fascinated by evil?"

The transition from the lofty spirituality of *What's Going On* to the bleak pessimism of *Trouble Man* was astounding, though no more astounding than the contradictions in Marvin's personality.

There was very little singing on the album, which was celebrated by European avant-garde artists as an innovative work. The one vocal, the title tune "Trouble Man," became a major hit—pop and soul—and a permanent part of Gaye's repertoire. In it he identified with the hero-victim, bringing to the suite a distinctively, frighteningly autobiographical voice. Like Marvin, "Trouble Man" didn't make it "playing by rules." Gaye could well have been speaking of himself when he sang that only three things in this life are certain— "taxes, death, and trouble."

Strangely enough, the lyrics didn't appear on the sleeve, as they had on *What's Going On*. In fact, it wasn't until 1982, when he left Motown to join CBS, that Marvin reprinted lyrics on his album. Why?

"I respect poetry," Gaye answered, "and I try to write subtly, but lyrics really aren't poems. Printing them like poems can make them seem silly. Besides, I like the idea of everyone guessing at what I'm singing. I like mystery."

The type style on the album cover showed Marvin Gaye's name shot through with bullets, and the final musical figure in the suite, after Marvin repeated the word "trouble" over and again, was the sudden sound of a pistol shot, a chilling prophecy of his own death.

"This is probably my favorite work," Marvin told me, though he said the same thing about *I Want You.* "I was listening to a great deal of Gershwin at the time, and I really wanted to do something great. I was amazed at my concentration. It had never been this intense before. Working with the film images added to my inspiration. I consider Mr. Moog an absolute genius and felt grateful to him all the while I was working. For years afterward, I wanted to do another score, but no one offered me one. I kept telling my managers to get me movie scores, but I also told them not to tell me if producers weren't interested in me. Rejection is something I don't handle well, and I'd rather not know about it. That's how I protect myself."

Trouble Man was released in the last half of 1972 and sold well. In late September, Marvin flew to Chicago where he performed two songs from *What's Going On* for a benefit Operation Push concert arranged by his friend the Reverend Jesse Jackson to celebrate the opening of Black Expo. The program, "Save the Children," which included a slew of other soul stars, was filmed and released as a soundtrack album by Motown.

In October, Hollywood caught Marvin's attention again: *Lady Sings the Blues* opened big, and suddenly Diana Ross was a movie star.

"Diana showed me that *I* could be a movie star," Marvin said. "Not that she wasn't good. She was great. She deserved her raves. By putting her heart into the role, she showed everyone that she's a natural. It was a bullshit plot, but her singing was right on. Give me a male musical role that juicy, though, and I'll accomplish the same thing. Diana was the princess, but I was still the prince. I'd done nothing to hurt my public image and was convinced that by waiting as long as I did, my timing was perfect.

"Naturally I could have used a Berry Gordy. Berry had been with Diana every step of the way, practically directing the movie himself. He understood her, just as he understood me. In my opinion, he proved to be as good at movies as music. There's no denying Berry's genius. He molded Diana. She became his living, breathing brainchild. He made millions off her and she made a few dollars off him.

"With all his great accomplishments, though, people forget Berry had his share of flops. At one point, he signed Sammy Davis, Tony Martin, Barbara McNair, Connie Haines, and Billy Eckstine, and never did figure out how to sell records on any of them. For every hit, Berry must have had three duds, but that's okay. His lifetime batting average was still an all-time high. When he believed in something, he went all the way. When he heard the Jackson Five in Detroit, for instance, he scooped them up, threw 'em in a plane, and flew 'em to Hollywood and got his production teams cranking out songs for 'em—all in a matter of days. Berry could smell money.

"I'm not saying Berry didn't love me. But what good was he doing me by spending all his time selling Diana as a black Barbra Streisand to a white market? Not that I ever let him know my attitude. My attitude was, I don't need anyone. In fact, I had something that Diana and Berry lacked. I was sure I could write screenplays and decided to do one based on a character in *What's Going On*, a black man returning from Vietnam. I'd star in the movie. Maybe I'd even direct it. I wasn't completely confident, but I felt myself moving in the right direction."

Screenwriting and acting would exist only as unrealized fantasies imagined by a man determined to ignore what he considered sad reality.

"I remained hopeful," Marvin said. "I left Detroit convinced that I had everything going for me. It's hard for me to make a move— moving involves so much work—but when I do move, it seems like the stars and the moon and the will of God are bending me in one direction."

Marvin would not move, however, without taking Mother with him, especially since Anna was of such little comfort.

"Ever since the celebration in Washington, things had been a little more peaceful," Marvin remembered. "It had been so many years since I'd lived in the same city as Mother, I thought that maybe it was the one thing that could make me happy. My family and I could all start a new life together in L.A., maybe even live under the same roof again. It was a beautiful dream while it lasted. But then I'd think about Father, and the old nightmares returned."

It's not unreasonable to assume that in 1972 Marvin might have found a degree of serenity in his life. Trying to put the games behind him, he nearly gained an equilibrium between his life and art. He came close but missed the chance, just as he'd miss so many chances, to heal himself. Destiny's demands were too great. His heart hungered for peace while his mind drew him into wars he knew he could never win.

17

HOLLYWOOD HUSTLES

Gaye cut the cord with Detroit and made the move in 1973. For a while, he, Anna, and Marvin III, then eight years old, lived with Gwen Gordy in her Benedict Canyon home in Beverly Hills.

Marvin maintained several different residences, as he would for the rest of his life, changing homes according to his moods, hiding from whatever pressures seemed too great to bear. He and Anna purchased a house on Outpost Drive, an exclusive section of the Hollywood Hills. He maintained his small apartment on Cattaraugus in west Los Angeles and later in the year bought his parents the sprawling lime-green, Tudor-styled home, built in the thirties, on Gramercy Place in the Crenshaw district, the black middle-class low-rent business-and-residential neighborhood which spread over the smoggy center of L.A. The house was large enough to accommodate Marvin's mother, father, sisters, brother Frankie, and assorted nieces and nephews.

The good feeling from Marvin Gaye Day in Washington, D.C., lingered on. Marvin hoped his family would help assuage the fears he felt in moving to Los Angeles. The Gramercy Place home became his refuge, the place where he claimed to feel safest, the same place where he'd meet his death.

"The early seventies in Hollywood," Marvin said, "was an especially heady time for black music. We were being given movie scores, our records were selling, and it looked like the sky was the

167

limit. Artists were finally getting their dues, with bigger royalty rates. A lot of the biggest record producers were seriously into cocaine. We figured that we all deserved the treat. And we had the bread to buy it."

The next couple of years would be an especially chaotic time for Marvin's business interests. Not only would he be hustling himself—trying hard, in his own way, to make it big in Hollywood—but he would be hustled by others convincing him to invest in a wide range of speculations and schemes.

For a long while he was close to Ewart Abner, the first man Berry Gordy appointed, other than himself, as president of Motown. A highly respected black record executive and presently Stevie Wonder's manager, Abner was the man who originally signed and promoted the Beatles on Vee Jay Records in the early sixties.

"Marvin had a falling out with Abner," said Jeanne Gay. More and more, Marvin began depending on his sister to oversee his business affairs. "But then again, Marvin was never able to maintain a relationship with any manager or record executive. He turned them all into glorified secretaries. Me included."

"I'll be unmanageable till the day I die," Marvin told me.

Yet in spite of this self-knowledge, his search for a manager continued, almost as though he were looking for something more than a manager—a guide like Fuqua, a father or big brother like Berry, even though he had never completely trusted either man.

"Berry always made it a point to stay out of the squabbles between Anna and me," said Gaye. "He didn't even want to hear about them. But I knew how close they were. I knew she was telling him everything."

Marvin was afraid of losing Berry's love.

In 1973, Gordy did something else which deeply affected Marvin: He married off his daughter Hazel Joy to Jermaine Jackson of the Jackson Five.

BG gave a wedding party which, according to Peter Benjaminson's *Story of Motown*, cost $200,000. It included 175 doves and 7000 white camellias, a guest list of international luminaries and a closed-circuit TV hookup. Why would such an event disturb Gaye?

"Because I saw myself being replaced. Jermaine was a singer marrying into the family, just the way I had, and just when I was being moved out. It was all part of Berry's plan to get himself a new, younger Marvin Gaye."

Gordy had, in fact, launched Jermaine's solo career earlier that year with an updated "Daddy's Home," a doo-wop tune decidedly reminiscent of Marvin's earliest work. The song became Jermaine's first hit. For the next several years, Berry developed his son-in-law's career, either producing him himself or calling in his finest producers—Stevie Wonder and Smokey Robinson. For all Gordy's efforts, though, Jermaine—an unusually gifted singer-composer—never reached superstardom under Gordy's tutelage. The irony is that both Jermaine and Berry revered Marvin as Motown's greatest talent, and the notion of replacing Gaye or hurting him was furthest from their minds. Besides, Gordy still stood to make money on Marvin.

"My idol was Marvin Gaye," Jermaine wrote on the sleeve of his 1984 album, his first after leaving his father-in-law's company, "and I loved him as much as you did. Being that his spirit will live on forever, I am going to sing about the influence he has had on me and the world through my music. I love you, Marvin, I really do."

Jermaine's highest achievements—"You Like Me, Don't You," "I'm Just Too Shy," "Still Undone"—reflect Gaye's rhythmic and emotional influence. There were no public tiffs between the singers; Marvin liked Jermaine, though he continued to be concerned that Jackson, like all young male soul singers, was after his throne.

In spite of the fact that Gordy would attempt to help him for years to come, Gaye no longer viewed Berry as someone in his corner. Yet for all Gordy's shortcomings, he still understood better than anyone how to deal with his brother-in-law. He not only pampered Marvin but worked around his artistic temperament with singular skill. It was clear to everyone except Marvin that Berry loved him. Gaye wasn't capable of accepting that love.

"When we moved to Los Angeles, my husband became even more withdrawn," Marvin's mother told me. "He'd never change. He'd never give Marvin any affection. He treated me the same way. After we moved from Washington, we had no sex—ever. Also, for the first time, he started using profanity. That made me very unhappy."

"I tried not to think about Father," said Marvin. "Thinking of him would keep me in the dumps for days. So I did my best to keep working and try to stay happy. I even built up my nerve and flew to Jamaica." He performed there in January 1973, in Kingston, at a benefit for the Boys Club of Trenchtown, the poorest slum on the island. Gaye's new manager, Stephen Hill, an aristocratic-speaking Jamaican, arranged the concert, which also featured Bob Marley. According to Marvin, though, he never met Marley that night, not even to shake hands. Gaye also bought land in Jamaica, where he planned to build a home—another unfulfilled dream.

Back in Hollywood, Marvin carefully considered his alternatives. As a result of signing with the William Morris Agency, he'd done bit parts in a couple of movies—*The Ballad of Andy Crocker*, with Lee Majors, and a motorcycle flick, *Chrome and Hot Leather*, which, according to Gaye, "never amounted to anything." The relationship with William Morris didn't last a year. "The place was too big for me," Marvin said. "With all the stars they represented, I never felt important enough. I required far more attention than they were willing to give."

In this same period, when he was trying to find his bearings, he agreed to record a duet album with Diana Ross.

"At first I refused," he told me. "After Tammi, I'd promised there'd be no more duets. But the notion intrigued me. You see, Diana did well in *Lady Sings the Blues*—the film made a fortune for Berry—but at that point her recording career was starting to suffer. They were also pissed that Liza Minnelli beat Diana for the Academy Award. Some people thought BG tried to buy her the Best Actress Oscar by putting so many ads in the trades. His campaign might have backfired. Anyway, with the success of *What's Going On*, Berry saw this as an opportunity for me to help Diana. The prince was in a little stronger position than the princess. I told him I'd do it, but only if I got half the producer royalties and the guarantee that my name went above hers. I lost on both counts, but I agreed to the concept anyway. I saw how it could help me. I actually returned to the old Motown way of doing things. As executive producer, Berry picked the songs—Hal Davis did most of the work—and I just went in and sang."

Typically inconsistent, Marvin turned around after winning his hard-fought artistic freedom from Motown and consented to a sixties-styled company-produced album. The decision showed how he could be a calculating careerist at times.

"The chemistry was all wrong," said Art Stewart, then a Motown staff engineer who worked all the Marvin-and-Diana sessions. "It was extremely tense. Marv would wander in, sipping wine and smoking a joint, ready to sing, while Diana was much more formal. Then, adding insult to injury, he sang circles around her. She just couldn't keep up with him, and finally they wound up recording their parts separately."

Marvin's attitude toward Diana was nearly as ambivalent as his feelings for Gordy.

"Diana Ross," he contended, "is a fine singer. All you have to do is listen to her Billie Holiday stuff. It's marvelous. But during this album, she was on pins and needles. A couple of years before she'd gone off and married a white man. That made Berry a little crazy. Now she was already very pregnant with her second child and her marriage seemed shaky. Professionally, she and BG were still together for the same reasons that Anna and I were hanging on. Fear and money. So there I was in the middle of the whole thing between Diana and Berry. I'm not sure I handled the situation very well. Musically, I may have overplayed my hand. I was too cavalier. I should have done everything in the world to make Diana comfortable. After all, she was making movies, recording two or three albums a year, starring in her own TV specials, and about to have a baby. I could have been a little more understanding. But I'm afraid I went the other way. It's hard for me to deal with other prima donnas. We were like two spoiled kids screaming for the same cookie. It was definitely *not* a duet made in heaven."

Given the fact that Motown's two most popular artists had joined forces, the album was a disappointment. "You're a Special Part of Me," the biggest single, never cracked the pop Top Ten. Marvin's duet days were over. Musically, he had moved far beyond the simple boy-girl format. He required greater depth from his material and found it impossible to convincingly cast himself in that light-hearted frame of mind.

The songs themselves were hardly challenging, although he still managed to put on an impressive display of his several singing styles. There were some passages of high emotion—especially his powerful rendering of the first chorus of "Pledging My Love." The problem, though, was that Gaye sang against Diana rather than with her. There was nothing of the effortless romantic rapport he shared with Tammi, Mary, or Kim. The spirited moments—"Love Twins," "My Mistake"—weren't great enough to relieve the tension between the two competing stars.

A decade later, explaining the difficult circumstances under which the record was made, Marvin was still preoccupied with his relationship with Diana. "In spite of everything," he told me during a moment of unrestrained egotism, "she loves me. Listen to 'Love Twins.' She actually says the words, 'I love you, Marvin.' That's proof, isn't it?"

Diana was very much on his mind as he sat for a long interview with Paul Bernstein and Bob Eisner of *Crawdaddy* magazine in the first half of 1973. They met in Tommy Tucker's Playroom on Washington Boulevard in L.A., a bar not far from his parents' home on Gramercy Place.

He tried to hype the album, but his candor got in the way. He admitted that his real reason for working with Diana was to boost his career.

"I think it's gonna be a good album—Motown duet music. . . . I imagine they'll do a big promotional thing. I might even be talked into coming on and doing a duet number in one of her shows. I'd like that. . . . I think I can act. It would be nice to do a love story with her. I think I have the sensitivity to pull that off. . . . I'd like to do anything with her, quite frankly. . . . I could be a good actor if I can get rid of all these feelings of being not for real with myself."

As far as cultivating Diana, Marvin worked against himself. Rather than demonstrate to her the rapport they might enjoy on records or in movies, he was defiant and aloof.

For the rest of the *Crawdaddy* interview, he waxed philosophical, his mind racing in a half-dozen different directions. He spoke of inventing new instruments, even a new musical scale. "There's another music that we hear all the time that's all around us and we hear it but we don't hear it. We hear it subconsciously and I'd like to bring it to a conscious state."

He confessed that money was still a problem. He mentioned property he wanted to buy in Arizona but couldn't afford. "I'll do some jobs because I need the money. . . . and that's the way to get it. It's hypocritical . . . but my back's against the wall."

He boasted. "I don't compare myself to Beethoven. I must make that clear. I just think that I'm capable of all he was capable of. I think the only thing between me and Beethoven is time. Beethoven had it from the beginning. I'm acquiring it. It's gonna take me time because I don't have formal training."

He touted his church training and described his ongoing metaphysical crisis. "I have constant battles with the flesh. I don't think my spiritual thing is as stable as it should be."

He also worried about his need for perfection. "I think we'll become so acute with our senses of nature, and our thought processes will become so acute, after a point there'll be no place to go. We'll just have to become gods. The world'll be like it started. Maybe God will know himself. Perhaps He's using us to help him learn who He is."

His main concern, though, was his next album. Because of the high praise for *What's Going On*, he worried about an encore. He felt drained of ideas. "All I can do is expound on what I said before," he said. "There have really been no changes to write about."

It's revealing that, in spite of his musical metamorphoses, Marvin still clung to his original, childhood dream—to become a pop crooner. He mentioned the Bobby Scott ballad arrangements which he hoped to sing, though, in truth, wouldn't record for another six years. "I hope that eventually I make it to the plateau where I'm able to sing romantic songs and torch songs and songs of love. . . ."

With all the changes, nothing had changed. In vain, Gaye was still trying to reconcile the warring factions raging within him— the independent artistic integrity of *What's Going On* versus the Motown-produced Diana duets.

"I decided again not to do any more concerts," he said. "I needed to figure out my next musical move. There were moments when I was still convinced that I could and would change the world. I kept thinking of the Pied Piper. The fact that this one cat, with the pure power of musical notes, chased the rats away—man, that should be an inspiration, perhaps *the* inspiration for all musicians. But by taking all the kids with him, you see the extent of his power. There's no doubt music can lead. I know music can heal. On the other hand, music means money. It had been over two years since I had a record of my own on the charts, and I was starting to worry."

Gaye's vision was sometimes startlingly clear, other times clouded. Because he lived his life high, it's difficult to tell the extent to which dope exacerbated his problems. He himself admitted in 1979 that being stoned didn't help solve his problems. On the other hand, using the age-old rationalization of all addicts, he claimed he could stop smoking and coking at will.

* * *

In 1973, Marvin was arrested on Sunset Strip for pot possession. Motown lawyers got him out in a matter of hours. He was also the star attraction at a Motown company picnic, where he played softball against Gordy's team. To Marvin's enormous satisfaction, he tagged out his boss at home plate.

Gaye was still trying to score in Hollywood—either literally score another movie or land a meaty acting role. Rather than go begging to the studios, though, Marvin insisted that the studios come to him. He never fulfilled his film fantasy because he never really tried. His fear of failure finally immobilized him, and he was left with the maddening freedom won by virtue of his success with *What's Going On.*

"No doubt I could have been a Hollywood star," said Gaye, "but it was something I consciously rejected. Not that I didn't want it. I most certainly did. I just didn't have the fortitude to play the Hollywood game and put my ass out there like a piece of meat.

"Years back, when we were still in Detroit, Berry saw my acting potential, even before he started pushing Diana. He wanted to do the Sam Cooke story and have me play the lead. This was in 1964 when Sam had just died. I told Berry the idea was morbid. I got chills thinking about it. There was no way I'd even consider the role. It made me extremely nervous to even think about a soul singer who gets shot to death."

As Gaye spoke the words, he shuddered and quickly changed subjects.

While Marvin's movie career never happened, his value as a recording artist continued to rise. In 1973 he began negotiating a new contract with Motown that would give him the kind of royalty percentages which, for the first time in his career, might make him a fortune. Like all matters with Marvin, the deliberation would drag on for months. Just as he considered divorcing Anna, he also considered divorcing her brother. He sought freedom—from his mother and father figures—that he had never tasted. In both instances, though, his fear of the unknown kept him close to his Motown home.

Over and again he asked himself the question, what could he record next which would please his public, please him, and still move him up, far above his present plateau of material comfort, to the realm of the really rich?

But those concerns would suddenly be diminished by a fresh new obsession, one which would last until he died, an obsession so deeply sexual and wildly romantic that Marvin would never recover from its impact. The obsession would possess him totally, changing his music, altering his life, making all other matters mundane. The obsession was a sixteen-year-old woman-child who walked into the Motown studio while Gaye was recording the song, "Let's Get It On."

18

GETTING IT ON

"She seemed not to be the daughter of a mortal man, but of God," Dante quoted Homer when he wrote *La Vita Nuova* in 1292.

"I saw her as more than a real girl," Gaye said of the woman who would become his second wife. "She suddenly appeared as a gift of God."

Dante was speaking of Beatrice, the lady who stood in the center of his poetry, an erotic figure whom he'd later transform into his holy guide.

Marvin was speaking of Janis Hunter, the girl he would sing to and about for the rest of his days, the woman who would inspire, enrage, and preoccupy him in a manner bordering on madness.

"She was the figure in my fantasy come to life," Marvin told me, "the one I watched dancing round and round in my imagination, whirling from man to man. I'd never encountered a more beautiful creature in my life. I had to have her."

Janis was the daughter of close friends of Ed Townsend, the man with whom Gaye was collaborating on "Let's Get It On." Through Townsend, Jan's mother Barbara brought her daughter to the Motown studio to meet Marvin. Janis's father was Slim Gaillard, the legendary jazz entertainer of "Flat Foot Floogie" fame. With a white mother and black father, Janis had the light, red-boned complexion of the dream girls of Marvin's youth. With long, lustrous black hair, a wide, sensuous mouth, dark, radiant eyes, a slender, slightly

freckled nose, and a fine figure, she appeared as a stunning appa-
rition of unspoiled beauty. Her shy, soft-spoken personality touched
Gaye's heart.

"I was a gentleman about it," he said. "That first night I treated
her and her mother with absolute respect."

"Marvin has been accused of giving only eighty percent of his
effort when he sings," commented Curtis Shaw, the man who
would become Marvin's attorney. "His talent allows him to get
away with that. Marvin wasn't a singer who liked to exert himself.
But that night, with Jan listening, he gave a hundred percent. Listen
to 'Let's Get It On' and you'll hear what I'm talking about."

"When the session was over," reported Art Stewart, who was
there as Marvin's chief engineer, "all of us walked Barbara and Jan
to their car. As they drove away, Marvin turned to Ed and me and
said, 'That's the finest woman I've ever seen.' "

"My greatest concern," Gaye said, "was her age. Sixteen is very,
very young, especially when you consider the fact that, at the time,
I was a thirty-three-year-old man married to a fifty-year-old woman.
Wasn't that something? My wife was seventeen years older than I
was and this girl was seventeen years younger. I worried how
everyone would react—my family, my friends, my fans. I worried
about the law, although Jan's mother, who's a wonderful woman,
encouraged the relationship."

Meeting Janis at the moment he created *Let's Get It On* consummated another major marriage of life and art.

Trouble Man and the Diana duets were side trips for Marvin. He'd
yet to come out with a follow-up album to *What's Going On*. Finally,
then, in 1973 he made his statement in the form of a complex
autobiographical work, a serious inner monologue on matters philosophical and spiritual, although the title of the suite—*Let's Get It
On*—misled his fans and critics into thinking the subject was strictly
sexual.

"An unabashed paean to fucking," critic Jim Feldman called it.

"A carnal feast," wrote Vernon Gibbs in *Crawdaddy*.

"A brilliant celebration of the joys of sex," said Tim Cahill in
Rolling Stone.

The liner notes, though, gave the first clue to Gaye's cross-
purposes. Written by Marvin himself, they revealed his struggle to
get past the sex-only-for-procreation concept of his father's church.

"I can't see anything wrong with sex between consenting any-
bodies," he wrote. "I think we make far too much of it. . . . SEX
IS SEX and LOVE IS LOVE. When combined, they work well
together, if two people are of about the same mind. But, they are
really two discrete needs and should be treated as such. . . . I don't
believe in overly moralistic philosophies. Have your sex, it can be
very exciting, if you're lucky.

"I hope the music that I present here makes you lucky."

Then a quote from T. S. Eliot stating that the essentials were
nothing more than "birth and copulation and death."

This was Marvin in his *Playboy* magazine frame of mind, a publication with which he strongly identified. (One of the things Gaye
admired most about Berry Gordy's L.A. lifestyle was that BG hung
out at Hugh Hefner's mansion.) "I've been jerking off to these
pictures for twenty-five years," Marvin told me in 1982 while
thumbing through a French edition of *Playboy*. Still a heavy masturbator as an adult, he saw the activity as relief from the pressures
of real women. It was easier for Gaye to deal with females as
fantasies. "Please don't procrastinate," he whispered into the microphone at the end of "Sexual Healing" in 1982, "if you do, I'll
have to masturbate."

In addition to its adolescent sense of horny-boy sexuality and
presentation of females panting for the pleasure of every male reader,
Playboy represented a side of himself Marvin liked to project—the
cool playboy, the cocksman connoisseur. The photos on the album—
studio shots of Gaye in his knit cap and jean jacket—reflected his
casual stance. Yet the laissez-faire attitude Marvin adopted about
sex was not only shallow, but, once the music began, quickly took
on a new and deeper meaning. For Gaye, songs were methods of
search and discovery. No matter what predetermined ideas might
be floating around his head, Marvin's artistic instincts led him toward the exposure of his most sincere feelings.

In 1979, Gaye and I were discussing the title song, "Let's Get
It On," when I read him part of Andrew Marvell's poem *To His
Coy Mistress:*

> Now let us sport us while we may;
> And now, like am'rous birds of prey . . .
> Let us roll all our Strength, and all

> Our sweetness, up into one Ball:
> And tear our Pleasures with rough strife,
> Through the Iron gates of Life . . .

Marvin smiled and wanted to know when the poem was written. "The seventeenth century," I told him.

"It was the same even back then," he smiled. "Cats begging for it."

"Let's Get It On" fit squarely in the metaphysical convention of lulling women—through extravagant imagery, sweet language, and philosophical logic—into sexual submission. From the start, Gaye made it clear that all humans are "sensitive people" and that sex musn't be abused. Sex isn't wrong, he sang, "if the love is true." He promised his lover—Jan was the woman whom he saw in his mind's eye—that he wouldn't grab, wouldn't push, but, in the name of love, pleaded for a taste of paradise.

Marvin was arguing with his Pentecostal upbringing, even arguing with his own liner notes. The song concerned the union of love and sex, not their separation. In spite of his chauvinistic posturing, his art elicited a powerful desire to wed feeling and flesh.

As a child, he told me, he'd always heard the love act called "the nasty." Now he sought to replace that image with gentler emotions. Sensitivity was seen as a vital adjunct to sexual intercourse. The movement wasn't toward mere physical satisfaction, but spiritual fulfillment. There's no good sex, said this song, without real love. His growling and groaning, his shouts and whispers, were cries for understanding, not mere satiation. And it was inevitable that Marvin introduced holy images of God, just as clearly as his brother poets used the same device three hundred years earlier. In *A Rapture*, Thomas Carew wrote:

> Bathe me in juice of kisses, whose perfume
> Like a religious incense shall consume

Conversely, John Donne used the imagery of rough sex to convey God's love in his *Holy Sonnets*, written around 1610.

> Batter my heart, three person'd God . . .
> Take me to you, imprison me, for I

Except you enthrall me, never shall be free,
Nor ever chaste, except you ravish me.

At the end of "Let's Get It On," Marvin did much the same, heightening the physical by calling on the spiritual, asking his lover whether she understood what it meant to be "sanctified." The "spirit" to which he referred was holy as well as sexual. Making certain his point was clear, Gaye repeated the word "sanctified," specifically comparing bodily and religious ecstasy.

Even in the final year of his life, Marvin was still trying to close the gap between spirit and flesh. After acknowledging his mother's presence at the Greek Theater in Los Angeles in the summer of 1983, he told the audience about a conversation in which he'd informed her that the follow-up release to "Sexual Healing" was entitled "Sanctified Pussy." Mother was horrified by the idea, he said, and wouldn't hear of it.

Having visited Marvin in the last week of his life, Clarence Paul told me, "He kept on talking about that 'Sanctified Pussy' business."

Friends took it as a joke. It wasn't. It was Marvin's attempt to merge the profane with the profound, to integrate his two strongest sources of emotional enthusiasm—God and sex. He knew it was the only way he could ever be happy. During the period in which he wrote *Let's Get It On*, he struggled to reconcile these battling forces which kept him at war in his home life and at the studio.

Gaye's methods of composing were largely subconscious. Watching him record, I noticed that usually no lyrics were written before he started singing.

"That's always been his way," said his long-time engineer Art Stewart. "Once we worked out a way for Marvin to do the vocal from the console, he never even bothered to go on the other side of the glass to sing. For the most part, he sang sitting down, right there at the controls."

"I mumble things into the microphone," Marvin told me. "I don't even know what I'm saying, and I don't even try to figure it out. If I try, it doesn't work. If I relax, those mumbles will finally turn into words. It's a slow, evolving process, something like the way a flower grows."

The process, a variation of W. B. Yeats' automatic writing, was especially clear on *Let's Get It On*, where the title song opened and closed side A. The second time around, though, it was called "Keep

Gettin' It On"—same melody, only different words. Marvin picked up where he left off, at the vamp, the final section of the song.

Suddenly the message evolved. The come-to-bed conceit was gone. Rather than address a woman, Marvin started preaching.

He contrasted making love to making war, recommending the former, finally calling out the name of Jesus, explaining that this was an attempt to "tell the people"; we must "get it on" in the name of Jesus.

The meanings had changed. To "get it on" now carried the significance of loving fully, and had the blessing—indeed the mandate—of the Lord of Love himself.

A thin line separates the sensualist and the spiritualist, a tightrope upon which Marvin Gaye tenuously traveled. (One thinks again of John Donne or Little Richard or Al Green, love poets who turned to Jesus.)

The first side of *Let's Get It On* was a self-contained suite. Like *What's Going On*, Gaye required the initial inspiration of a colleague, Ed Townsend, who, along with Marvin, coproduced the side and cowrote its four songs.

The second side was another mind-set entirely. According to Gaye, he wrote the first two tunes for the Originals and then decided to record them himself. "Come Get to This" and "Distant Lover" carried the same theme: separation and sexual frustration. The first song, recorded at a bouncy jazz tempo, would later be slowed down and inserted into Gaye's live show as a quasi-burlesque routine. He'd grind his hips and thrust his pelvis forward at the very instant he'd shout out, "Come get to this!"

"Distant Lover," written with his sister-in-law Gwen and Sondra Greene, was far more elegiac. The ballad would become a Marvin Gaye standard and permanent part of his show, even to the point of Marvin crying real tears and falling to his knees like one of his boyhood stage models, Johnnie Ray. The theme, a Gaye favorite, was traditional for blues singers and balladeers—pleading with a woman for forgiveness. The lyric was drenched in longing and frustration, a throwback to the Church of Holy Doo-Wop, invoking heaven's help, even asking his lover to pray for him. There was also the suggestion of unrequited love, a painful notion which excited Marvin's artistry by tapping the wellspring of his deepest desire and fear—sexual, romantic cruelty.

The last two songs were harbingers of Marvin's next major music projects.

"You Sure Love to Ball" was easy-over R-rated soul, lushly orchestrated and seamlessly sung, Marvin's voices accompanied by the sound of a soft-moaning woman simulating sex. The attitude was frankly voyeuristic, Gaye taking pleasure in watching and listening to a female enjoying intercourse. In this same musical genre, Barry White was experimenting with similar sounds. His "I'm Gonna Love You Just a Little More, Baby" hit the charts two months before "Let's Get It On." (White's co-arranger, Gene Page, also co-orchestrated Marvin's "Come Get to This.") Two years later, Donna Summer would popularize the horny, slightly porny style even more with "Love to Love You, Baby." And Gaye himself would return to the genre in 1976 with *I Want You,* his most sensuous production.

"Just to Keep You Satisfied" was the final cut on *Let's Get It On,* co-written by Marvin, Anna, and Elgie Stover. It should be viewed as the preface to *Here, My Dear,* the album from 1978 in which Marvin revealed the bloody details of his divorce from Anna. A painfully slow ballad, "Satisfied" was the open expression of Gaye's relationship to his wife in the early seventies. Though they receive no credit, Marvin told me that the Originals accompanied him, providing rich backdrop to a short story in which Gaye exposed the hopelessness of his marriage.

"Farewell, my darling," he sang in a formal cadence reminiscent of seventeenth-century poet John Dryden. "Once more, hail and farewell," wrote Dryden. Thus with the fiery beauty of his piercing falsetto, Marvin kissed Anna goodbye.

"We hadn't been a couple in years," Marvin said, "and all we were doing was improving our methods of hurting each other. Jan only made things worse. But even if Anna hadn't been in the picture, Jan would have captured my heart. Remember the old song, 'Have you ever seen a dream walking?' That was Jan."

This was fresh fuel for Marvin's madonna-whore complex, his feeling that a woman was an object of either sanctity or scorn, either all-good or all-bad, always fantasy and never human. The fact that Gaye couldn't relate to women as equals—as flesh-and-blood mortals—made it impossible for him to enjoy a single long-term romantic relationship.

Walking on the beach at Malibu one day, I told Marvin the story of *The Divine Comedy*, of how Dante turned Beatrice, the woman who'd once excited his lust, into a spiritual guide, leading the poet to heaven and a holy vision of moral purity.

The notion fascinated Gaye. "I understand," he said, "that he needed to sing to the same lady. But wanting to be free of sin, he turned her into a saint. That way he kept her inspiration."

Hoping Marvin would do the same thing, I asked him whether the concept could be applied to his own work.

"The only place any woman will ever lead me," Gaye scoffed, "is to hell."

As the years went by, Marvin's anger at women only increased, making him far more interested in seeking pain—sexual and romantic pain—than pleasure.

When released in the summer of 1973, the commercial response to *Let's Get It On* was immediate. It was the biggest hit of Gaye's career, leaping to Number One on all charts and earning him the wealth he'd long sought.

"We'd never seen anything like it before," said Tom Noonan, who was a Motown executive at the time. "One initial reorder on the single, 'Let's Get it On,' was 350,000. It was phenomenal. The thing must have sold over four million copies.

"Just about this time, we completed the negotiations on Marvin's contract, which naturally was very juicy—a multimillion-dollar deal. But Marvin being Marvin, he had one crazy demand—that Berry Gordy personally sign a check made out to him for $1 million. No one else's signature would do. I agreed, figuring that Berry wouldn't care. I called Berry's house, but they explained it wasn't possible because Berry was about to fly off to Europe. I *had* to get that check signed. I was afraid that Marvin might change his mind and call off the deal. I drove to the airport, like a New York cabby, in fifteen minutes, got Berry's signature just before he stepped on the plane, blew up the check a hundred times its size, and presented it to Marvin. You've never seen such a happy man."

The incident reveals the intensity of Gaye's feelings—positive and negative—for Berry. Like a son wanting a father to sign an A+ report card, Marvin needed Gordy's approval.

The stunning success of *Let's Get It On* vindicated the two years it took Marvin to produce the new work. At Motown, where major acts were sometimes expected to record an album every six months, Marvin's singular timetable was viewed with skepticism.

"I tried to tell those folks," Marvin said in his sly-fox slur, "that I'm always right on time. Management was worried to death I'd deliver a lame product. So when I delivered the goods, and when the goods shot to the top, I couldn't help but smile. It proved *What's Going On* was no fluke. I still knew something about selling records, and I was sure that this time I had a Grammy in the bag."

Seemingly, Marvin had reached another high point in his career. "Let's Get It On," with its seductively smooth groove, was the record sensation of a year marked by other smashes—Stevie Wonder's "Superstition," the Rolling Stones' "Angie," Gladys Knight and the Pips' "Midnight Train to Georgia," Tony Orlando and Dawn's "Tie a Yellow Ribbon 'Round the Ole Oak Tree." His Diana duets, recorded earlier but released after *Let's Get It On*, also began selling. Gaye's stock was on the rise.

"I knew things were getting better," he said, "when Agnew got the axe. I think I enjoyed his downfall more than my hit records."

In spite of so much success—or perhaps because of it—the pressures mounted. The old demands, fears, and conflicts returned. His public was calling him to the stage. Promoters were waving money at him. Having already made millions on *Let's Get It On*, he stood to make millions more on the concert circuit.

"I didn't want to. I *desperately* didn't want to," he claimed. "But it was my destiny. The same thing had happened to me ten years earlier with 'Stubborn Kind of Fellow.' I won my audience with the hot stuff. And now they were making me jump back out there and shake my booty, just like a teenage kid all over again. I hated it, and I was determined not to succumb. Besides, I was in love with Jan. All I wanted was to be alone with her, shut off from the rest of the world forever and ever."

Marvin never made anything easy for himself. Inevitably, he would turn happiness to sorrow, blessings to burdens. This next period of his life would be no different. With a new Number One record and a new woman, he'd find new ways to restimulate old fears.

19

THE HOUSE IN HEAVEN

Instead of embracing his material success, Marvin Gaye ran from it, hiding from the very thing he'd once sought—the glamour of the movie capital of the world. In a modest, small mountain-top house outside Los Angeles, he continued the process of self-searching, planting the seeds for what would become his next bitter crop.

Being an artist whose work grew richer and more complex with time, Gaye's troubles would grow, along with his music, into new and daring areas. If they had not, that part of his psyche stimulated by trauma and self-created crises would be left unsatisfied. Marvin had no tolerance for emotional boredom.

Another part of Gaye's soul, though—a simpler side—still yearned for old-fashioned domestic happiness, away from the distractions of Hollywood's hustle and hype. Marvin loved the country, the ocean, the clear skies and free-flying birds. He reasoned that here he could escape with his new woman and seek peace of mind.

Depending upon traffic, Topanga Canyon is forty-five to ninety minutes from Los Angeles, up U.S. 1 toward Malibu, across the road from the Pacific Ocean. Part of the Santa Monica mountain range, the land is dramatically rugged, steep and picturesque. The feeling is rustic, far removed from "sin city," as Gaye called Los

Angeles. In the sixties, the area was inhabited by colonies of hippies
and artists—Charles Manson's family among them—and in the
early seventies, when Marvin moved to his mountaintop retreat
with his girlfriend Janis Hunter, the atmosphere was still slightly
Bohemian.

"It wasn't fancy or very big," Marvin said, describing his house,
"but it was the most wonderful place I'd ever seen. Old wood, the
scent of pine, and completely cut off, so no one could find me. If
I wanted company, I'd have to meet them at a gas station on the
highway and lead them up the hill around all these twisty unpaved
roads. The air was clear and the clean smell of the country was
everywhere. I had two Great Danes to protect me from intruders,
a little phonograph, an old piano, a wood-burning stove, and a
righteous woman. What more did I need?"

Two walls of the living room were enormous plate-glass windows
affording a spectacular view of the ocean and distant city.

"For weeks I'd just sit and stare into space," Marvin remembered.
"I'd never tire of gazing at the water. With enough time, I was sure
this was the place where I could create my masterpiece. I'd wake
up in the morning, smoke a little herb, and listen to the songs of
the birds, the sound of the wind, the rustle of the leaves. A million
musical ideas came to mind, a suite of natural noises, each one more
enchanting than the other.

"Isn't the artist's real job to learn from nature? Instead of churning
out pop hits, shouldn't the truly talented among us be listening to
the flutter of a butterfly's wing? Oh, if I could only reproduce the
delicacy of that sound! For a moment, or an hour, or even a day,
I'd set my sights on such tasks, convinced that this was my contribution to the world of serenity and peace.

"I was a man very deeply in love, thrilled that this woman had
said that she loved me with all her heart. I wanted to live with her
and didn't care what the world thought. I felt above the world.
Our happiness was all that counted. I knew people were pissed at
me. Motown was pissed and Anna was pissed and here were these
movie scripts to read and songs to write and money to be made,
but screw it all—that was my attitude. When I looked at Jan, I
didn't want to go anywhere, I didn't want to leave our little house."

Was he hiding her?

"I wasn't ready to expose our relationship—that part is true. I
wanted to keep her for myself. Even though I knew I couldn't do

it forever, I didn't want to share Jan with the world. I wanted her to have my children.

"Not long after we met, when she was seventeen, she became pregnant and we were both happy. But she lost the baby. She was young to go through something like that. Up in Topanga, I think I was trying to shelter her from all the pain of the real world. I saw Topanga as our little house in heaven."

With a wine-colored Cadillac and two jeeps at his disposal, Marvin drove through the countryside, finding inspiration wherever he looked.

"The phone ringing usually meant good news. *Let's Get It On* was selling up a storm. Since 1971, they said I'd sold five million albums. They kept asking me to perform, and the more I refused, the fatter the offers. I tried to stick to my guns and refuse, but I felt myself weakening. After all, I had a big family to support—my mother, father, a wife, son, and now a girlfriend."

Marvin's reluctance to work involved more than just his usual indolence. He feared that anything he made now would eventually be taken by Anna. Never having really managed his money in the past, he felt trapped. The more he made, the more she'd get to keep, especially since Berry, in Marvin's mind, could juggle the books any way he—or Anna—saw fit. He saw that leaving her had been a huge financial mistake, and yet going back was impossible.

The idea of performing still left a sour taste in his mouth. Why go out there and do the very thing—live concerts—which he hated? The answer was always money. No matter how much Anna might get, he needed to keep earning, especially since he kept talking about retiring to a ranch in Arizona that he longed to buy. More than just an actual plot of land, the ranch represented Marvin's dream of total escape from nagging reality.

For all Gaye's ambivalence, it took Wally Cox, a close friend, to convince him to do a date in the Bay area in November of 1973. Like Ed Townsend, Cox had a finely honed sense of humor. He was one of Marvin's party partners and could always make the singer laugh. Yet even with tickets printed and ads published, Marvin's nerve failed him; he bailed out at the last minute. Toward the end of the year, though, he changed his mind again, agreeing to appear at the Oakland Coliseum on January 4, 1974.

"I knew I had to come down the mountainside for somebody, so it might as well be for Wally."

Visiting Marvin in Topanga Canyon for a major *Rolling Stone* piece, Tim Cahill reported that "it wasn't a week before the show that Marvin finally gave the final go-ahead. Now he was terrified."

Still, he performed. Motown recorded the concert and released it later in 1974 as *Marvin Gaye Live!* His outfit, photographed on the album jacket, was a symbol of his current divided self. He wore work clothes—a denim shirt and rolled-up blue jeans—representative of his semi-rugged rural existence in Topanga. The shirt collar and cuffs, though, were bejeweled with sparkling beads, his plain red-knit cap adorned with glittering silver thread, and on his feet a pair of silver-glo rock-and-roll platform shoes—high-topped, red-laced, super-bad. Though later in life he'd dispense with almost all jewelry, he now wore an earring in his left lobe.

"I love earrings," he said. "I also adore lace collars and silky kimonos. Were it not for Father, I might even permit myself to wear such outrages in public."

The style that emerged in Oakland was uniquely Marvin, a combination of casual, country, and show-biz pizzazz.

Gaye put out the word that this was his first concert in five years. That wasn't true. He'd performed in Jamaica only a year earlier and in Washington, D.C., seven months before that. Exaggerating the length of his hibernations was a device Marvin used for the rest of his career, convinced that it added to his mystique.

"Five years this man has been absent," said Wally Cox, promoter and one of Gaye's background singers that night, to a sold-out crowd of fourteen thousand who'd just heard Ashford and Simpson open the show, "a man who's become a legend in his own time."

With few alterations, the concert presented in Oakland would become a model for all Marvin Gaye shows to follow. As time went on, he'd add dancers and change costume styles, but the aim would remain the same: drive the women wild. That's how Marvin viewed his theatrical obligation. He was convinced that it was only sex the women wanted from him, the sexual longing they heard in his voice. Through the years, as his insecurity grew he'd stress this aspect of his showmanship until, on his final tour in 1983, he did a literal striptease, dropping his pants while the band played "Sexual Healing."

A completely spontaneous singer, he approached dancing from the opposite viewpoint. He learned certain dramatic gestures and positions—buttocks pumping, arms raised to the sky, head cocked to the side—and used them at specific intervals in the songs. All this was worked out ahead of time. When it came to dancing, Marvin left nothing to chance.

One night in 1979, I went with Marvin and several of his friends to a San Francisco disco. They were playing Michael Jackson's newly released *Off the Wall*, and, as much as Marvin admired the production, he refused to dance. Instead, he coolly stood at the bar, greeting fans. Suddenly "Got to Give It Up," Gaye's disco hit from 1977, came on, and everybody dragged Marvin to the dance floor. A group of five of us danced together. Watching Marvin move, I could feel the pain of his self-consciousness. Naturally graceful, he felt awkward as he barely lifted his arms and feet. It was particularly strange watching him mouth the words of the song which is the story—Gaye's story—of a wallflower.

That night in Oakland in 1974 he was nervous as well, afraid of being out of shape. The situation surrounding the concert was uncertain, even to the last minute. Tim Cahill reported that "by 8:30 P.M. showtime it was one of the most chaotic backstage scenes I have ever seen."

Gene Page, who wrote the arrangements and, along with Leslie Drayton, conducted the orchestra that night, told me that Marvin asked him to string all the songs together, without interruption, so there'd be no pauses. "Marvin was so afraid that no one would applaud," said Page, "that he wanted to cover the silences with music."

"The show began in a strange way," Page remembered. "Marvin had his brother Frankie, who greatly resembles him, come out first. Naturally everyone thought Frankie was Marvin—that was Marvin's intention—and they hollered and applauded like mad. Then when Marvin appeared a minute later, it was as though his prophecy had come true. People were confused—who were these two Marvins?—so the reception for the real Marvin was very quiet."

The incident is a microcosm of the apprehension Gaye had about his brother. By allowing Frankie to go on stage, Marvin was afraid his sibling just might steal his thunder. By directing him to do so, Marvin forced himself to live through the trauma. Over the next few years, he kept trying to buy Frankie a gas station or bowling alley—anything to keep him out of show business.

When Gaye finally started singing in Oakland, the ovation was tremendous. At the very start, his voice sounded rusty. The orchestra—Marvin never liked to perform live with anything less than fourteen pieces—helped hide his initial uncertainty, but in the show-opening "Trouble Man" he hadn't yet found his confidence. (The band included Ray Parker, Jr., on guitar, Ernie Watts on sax, and Jamie Jamerson, the great Motown bassist. Joe Sample was on keyboard, who, along with fellow Crusader Wilton Felder, had played on *Let's Get It On*.)

On "Inner City Blues," Gaye, still stumbling, invoked the sanctity of his father's church—just as years before he'd called upon Ray Charles' muse—to fortify his soul. "A long time ago," Marvin sang, "my daddy told me, he said, 'son, feel it . . . feel it' . . . said, 'shout!' . . . said, 'shout!' " Only through the Holy Spirit—the strength of his country-church roots—did Marvin find the strength to fight his fears.

The opening strands of "Distant Lover" ignited a thunderstorm of shrieks. As the powerful pain in his voice brought down the house, he knew he'd won over the women.

From Oakland on, Marvin's shows would consist only of his own hits. He had more than enough to fill up an evening of entertainment. The practice would never change: no one else's material, no old ballads, just Marvin Gaye hits.

"All they want me to sing are the records they've been hearing at home. Why even try anything else?" he asked.

Didn't he get tired of singing the same stuff?

"Yes," he answered, "which is another reason I didn't like performing. But I wasn't about to change. It took all I had to sing these songs, though I knew them like the back of my hand. Sometimes I'd throw up before getting out there—that's how scared I was. Imagine what would happen to me if I sang other artists' songs! Besides, why should I plug someone else?"

That night in Oakland, though, he made a rare exception and sang something new. Self-assured after his heartrending reading of "Distant Lover," he told the audience, "Here's a new song I wrote . . . a song about a little girl, who's really a beautiful, beautiful young girl. She asked me to write this. I promised her I would. It goes like this . . ."

The song, called "Jan," was a tribute to his new woman in which Marvin prophesied that without her his life would be "tragic." The meandering ballad was never released as a single or included on another album. It was simply sung this one time in acknowledgment of his new love. Not atypically, Marvin introduced the song by ungraciously revealing that it was Janis who asked him to write it. On *Trouble Man*, he did the same thing. After failing to list the musicians, he wrote, "A special credit . . . to Trevor Lawrence for solo work on alto, tenor and baritone sax (thanks for the reminder, Trev)."

Although he sang to her in Oakland, Marvin was careful not to present her to the press when, after the concert, he returned to Topanga to consider his next move.

Tim Cahill, whose *Rolling Stone* interview covered this period in Gaye's life, wrote, "For all the activity going on around him, Marvin seems a remarkably unfocused man. . . . He wants to do movies. He wants to produce a Marvin Gaye television special. He is thinking of marketing 'some device' that will help us know ourselves better."

Cahill ended his article with Marvin taking him to a prize fight in San Diego, where they watched Gaye's fighter, Lee Mandingo, get decked by Duane Bobick in the second round.

Back on the mountaintop, fears came and went. A storm had blown off his second-story balcony. "With those Santa Ana winds and brushfires," Gaye remembered, "I was feeling uneasy. It'd only take the tiniest spark for my paradise to go up in flames."

When Walter Burrell of *Soul* magazine came up the canyon, he found Gaye in a reflective mood.

"I have a profound ego that's very active and live," Marvin told the reporter, "I try to keep it in harness."

He eschewed any political opinion. "My political thoughts are my own. Nobody should follow me in anything."

He also dispelled rumors about leaving Motown, expressing anger that white people were still making most of the money from black music. "I can't even think of myself with a white company," he claimed, though nine years later he actually signed with a white company.

The reporter concluded the article by observing that Gaye was "truly a nice human being." Meanwhile, Janis was nowhere to be found.

"I was uneasy about how to present Jan to my public," said Marvin. "There's the fact that she looks white, and I certainly didn't want to offend my black female fans. They're my bread and butter, the women who made me. Also, how far could I go with this thing? Did I want headlines reading, 'Marvin Gaye living with high school girl!'? No, I had to be very careful, very cool. I knew only one thing—this lady had worked some sure-enough magic on my soul. She danced through my dreams. The girl was in my blood."

By the beginning of March, Jan became pregnant again.

"My first feeling was of joy and happiness," Marvin remembered, "especially after we'd lost the first child. I wanted us to have a family. Naturally, still being married to Anna, things were a little complicated. But I've learned over the years that sometimes complications are best handled when they're ignored. Simplicity is the key to life. Myself, my woman, my children, a little house in the country—that's all I needed. Why should I climb back down my mountain?"

The answer could be found in the blow-up of the $1 million check which Marvin had hung over his mantel in the Topanga Canyon house. He wanted money. He was driven by an incessant need to grow rich, though at the same time money slipped through his fingers like water. According to Gaye, by 1982 he'd made three separate fortunes and three times threw the fortunes away. At the time of his death, he was heavily in debt. Time and again, he used the concert circuit to bail himself out.

In 1974, afraid of the consequences to his career and finances, he still wouldn't sue for divorce. By openly living with Jan, and now starting a family, he was testing the boundaries of his marital distress. He was also dealing another blow to Anna by having a child with another woman.

Rather than make a firm decision, Marvin played out his options, agonizing over whether to continue his hibernation or hit the road. He bought a motor home so that he could camp anywhere for a day or a week—in front of a friend's home or deep in the backwoods. He took a $1500-a-month apartment in a high-rise on La Cienega near Sunset where, from time to time, he'd entertain himself with a bit of Hollywood high life. One way or the other, he prolonged his deliberations, running from the country to the city, from Janis to Mother, from Mother to Anna, who had charge over the son whom he loved so dearly.

"The rainy season came," he recalled, "and that made me edgy. I kept seeing everything sliding down—rocks and trees and houses. Topanga wasn't as friendly as it used to be. Someone slit the throats of my Great Danes. That scared the shit out of me. I had nightmares for weeks. I knew there were bad people out there after me, and living where I did—so high up and isolated—I was extremely vulnerable. In comparison, being on stage didn't seem so terrible. It was time. I had to come down from my mountain."

The edges of his paranoia, which would only sharpen as time went by, had begun cutting into his heart.

"I decided to tour, to do the whole blasted thing, to come out smoking, coast to coast, with the biggest, baddest show ever. Everyone was talking about new funk groups like the Commodores, Earth, Wind & Fire, and Kool and the Gang. Well, Kool was cool, but I could be just as funky as the funkiest dude in the neighborhood. Man, I was ready to kick ass."

Gaye would go off and tour the country, this time at the height of his popularity, reacquainting himself with his fans, who were increasingly fascinated by the energy and complexity of his music. He had the recognition of a real artist. In Marvin's mind, though, he was simply turning another trick, selling sex, singing on demand. To the world, the tour would seem triumphant; to Gaye, it was another form of self-exploitation.

20

OUT THERE

With a troop of dancers bopping around him, a stunning four-woman backup group called Ladies' Choice, and a twenty-piece orchestra, Marvin finally hit the road in 1974. He also required the company and comfort of a large entourage, which included his mother.

"If Mother hadn't traveled with me," Gaye said, "I'd never have the nerve to do live performances again."

The jovial company of friend Wally Cox, one of the few people who could make Marvin work, helped the singer enormously.

Scheduled to go out in April, Gaye finally made it in August, doing twenty dates in twenty cities.

"I couldn't leave till the Watergate hearings were over," he explained. "It'd be like watching a cowboy movie without seeing the bad guy punched out. I had to see Tricky Dick go down, down, all the way down."

At a time when Elton John was setting the standards, Marvin's new show was by far his most extravagant. "Having dancers meant I didn't have to work so hard," he said, "and a full orchestra could cover me over if I messed up."

He kept a grand piano on stage—from now on a fixture at Gaye's concerts—in order to play a solo, usually during "Inner City Blues." Marvin's piano playing was fluid and artful, though largely restricted to extravagant variations of simple gospel or blues. Unlike Ray Charles, he was unable to improvise complex jazz.

According to *Variety*'s review of Gaye's New York Radio City date, "He returned to live performing after an eight-year hiatus." In fact, it had been only eight months since he'd played Oakland.

For the most part, he stayed with his beaded-jeans routine, occasionally substituting an all-white suit or, in place of his knit beanie, a richly embroidered skullcap. Never, though, would he perform bareheaded.

"I was starting to get a bald spot," he laughed, "and I was very self-conscious about it. Anyway, those caps were becoming my trademark. I'd see dudes wearing them wherever I performed."

According to *Ebony* magazine, he grossed over $1.5 million in August alone, playing ballparks like Braves Stadium in Atlanta.

"They said it was the biggest tour since the Beatles," Marvin remarked with his usual brand of exaggeration. "Everyone was loving it except me. Jan was about to have a baby and I was about to have a fit. Touring always tears at my gut. I do enough drugs in my normal life, but on the road the quantities triple. I'm always looking for extra energy, another little kick in the booty. So there am I, smoking and snorting up a storm, suffering with a nervous stomach from all these airplanes I gotta take, staying up all night and trying to sleep, trying to relax, the phone ringing and the promoters screaming, 'Is he going to do it? Is he going to fink out or sing?' Then I get out there and try to act like every woman's lost lover so she'll go out and buy three more copies of my latest record. Be serious. Is this me? How in the name of a just God did I ever turn myself into a sex god? And why?"

Perhaps no man is suited to be a pop idol, but certainly Marvin Gaye was less suited than most. Introverted, sexually unsure of himself, essentially private, he kept seeking solace in the form of cocaine or, ironically enough, prostitutes.

"Sometimes when I was on the road—not in '74, but other times," Marvin said, "those were the ladies who gave me the most relief. They were the least demanding. I could talk to them, and if I wanted to get a little freaky, hey, no big deal. It was reassuring to hear them tell me that they'd been with a lot freakier freaks than me."

It's hard to believe that one of the most desired men in America, someone with legions of women seeking his bed, would be comforted by whores. But it's easy to understand. The business arrangement set boundaries, allowing Marvin to retain control. In general, Gaye himself would never approach women directly but speak to them through his aides. Thus, if he was rejected, Marvin's frail ego was spared a painful blow. That was another reason he was drawn to prostitutes: prostitutes usually don't reject paying customers. Marvin not only sympathized with ladies of the night, but given his attitude about sexy music—in his heart, he always felt he should be singing holy hymns—Gaye closely identified with prostitutes.

In September, Jan gave birth to a girl, Nona Aisha, nicknamed Pie.

"Seeing her for the first time," Marvin said, "just the tiny size of her head, the sweetness of her nose . . . oh, at that moment it all seemed all right. I just wanted to stay with my baby. I wanted to cancel the rest of my tour, but they told me that the lawsuits would land me in debtor's prison. Somehow I dragged myself back out there and faced the music."

Ebony's story from November 1974 covered the tour and portrayed Marvin as "a man of stark contrasts and seeming contradictions. . . . What really marks Marvin Gaye is his own bemused recognition of those contradictions."

For the first time in print Jan was mentioned and shown at a Gaye family reunion on Varnum Avenue in Washington, D.C. Marvin III, who accompanied his father on part of the tour, was also there.

"I feel safest and most secure in my parents' home," Marvin commented. "I never really feel secure anywhere else."

He discussed his insecurities—fear of flying and fear of peaking too early in his career with nowhere to go but down. "I'm a little afraid of living," he told the reporter. "Most fears stem from sin. To limit one's sins must assuredly limit one's fear, thereby bringing· more peace to one's spirit."

He admitted to *Ebony* that his entourage indulged him. "My people serve me genuinely—though I don't demand it and I sometimes may be guilty of not treating them with proper respect. It's easy to get off into that holier-than-thou trip. I don't deserve treatment as God yet. But I hope my spiritual level will progress one day to the point when I do."

"People want to believe that I'm this raging sinner," Marvin told me. "I feed that image of myself only because the public demands it. Every woman wants to believe that I'm secretly lusting for her. Meanwhile on that '74 tour I was pure as Ivory Soap. I spent a lot of the time reading a novel which was written all about me."

He was referring to a book published that year, Elaine Jesmer's *Number One with a Bullet*, a thinly disguised fiction about Motown. Gaye was the model for the main character, soul singer Daniel Stone, whose brother-in-law—the Berry Gordy character, named Bob Vale—owned Finest Records. Included were sketches, most of them unflattering, of the major Motown people.

Marvin was ambivalent about the book. He was angry at being portrayed as sexually passive but flattered by the attention. He called the story "half true." He loved being the hero of a novel, even a trashy one. He was also intrigued with seeing himself in semi-pornographic settings, something he himself would soon create in his own music. In fact, when there was talk of a film based on the book, Marvin called his friend Clarence Paul to help him write the theme song, "Number One with a Bullet."

"The project didn't last long," said Paul, "because the movie deal was nixed. Rumors were that Berry Gordy had bought up the rights and stopped the film. People said he was afraid of what the movie would show."

Either way, the novel never found a market and was soon forgotten.

A far more revealing publication during this same year—1974—was the color brochure accompanying the three-LP Marvin Gaye anthology from Motown. Among shots from the sixties, he was photographed in his Topanga Canyon hideaway, a skullcapped, shirtless thirty-five-year-old man, slightly thick around the middle, gazing into the light of day.

"I couldn't wait for the '74 tour to end," said Marvin, who could just as well have been describing his 1983 tour. "A lot of people thought I'd bail out before the end, so naturally I had to prove them wrong. Without that challenge, I wouldn't have made it through. I figured that if Muhammad Ali bounced back and beat George Foreman—probably the greatest comeback of all times—I could slug it out with young cats like this boy Teddy Pendergrass, who sang with Harold Melvin and the Blue Notes. It wasn't anything personal, but everyone wanted to claim my title. The young cats will do it to you every time. I know. I did the same things to the singers who came before me. You either keep steppin' or get stomped."

When the tour finally wound down at the end of the year, Gaye moved out of Topanga permanently, gave up his place on La Cienega, and rented a spacious apartment for himself, Jan, and their infant in a high-rise on Barrington Avenue in Brentwood, a well-to-do suburb west of Los Angeles.

"I needed time to recover from the tour," he said. "A long time. I still hadn't pursued my movie career, and there were a million and one things I needed to do. I had these notions of building an empire. If Berry did it, why couldn't I?"

Gordy was having problems of his own. Between 1974 and 1975 he was still deeply involved in Diana Ross' career as the moving force behind her second film, *Mahogany*. Having fired the director, Tony Richardson, Berry took the plunge and decided to direct the film himself—a huge gamble. While shooting in Rome, where Gordy lived at the Villa Angelino, the palatial love nest customized for Elizabeth Taylor and Richard Burton, Diana and Berry's relationship reached the boiling point.

Like Marvin and Stevie before her, Diana had grown increasingly independent. She was about to turn thirty and was tired of being directed. Besides, she missed her children and wanted to go home. According to Rob Cohen, the producer, when Gordy reprimanded Ross on the set in front of the crew, she slapped him across his face, breaking his sunglasses. "I hate you! I hate you!" she screamed, and with that, left the set, two days before completing the picture, and flew back to L.A.

"The seventies were rough for Berry," Gaye said with some sympathy, "because the artist's time had arrived. The old days, when the producer ran the show, was over. People like me and Stevie knew that. And Diana was learning. There was no more Motown sound in the seventies, just a string of separate singers doing their own thing. It wasn't easy for Berry because Berry's actually a very creative cat. He's always lived through his artists, and now all of a sudden his artists were running their own careers. He felt left out, and he got nervous. Well, we were nervous, too. He wasn't there to take care of us like he used to. We all expected our careers to take these big turns, but when? And where? The movies scared us 'cause the movies were big-time. At least Berry had the guts to tackle Hollywood. Me, I was still laying low, thinking about it."

At this very point, when Marvin's career might have taken an important new direction, something else happened which allowed him to postpone permanently his plans for becoming a movie star: Anna filed for divorce in early 1975, and Marvin realized that a new game had begun, a new chapter of his life that would pose a death threat to the very core of his psychological and financial well-being.

21
SUFFERING IN STYLE

To understand Marvin Gaye is to understand human inconsistency. He was many men. Trapped in a single body, his various minds and sensibilities fought for expression, even as they competed against themselves. As an employer or friend, he could be cruel and jealous. He himself admitted that he was spoiled, not only by Mother but by Motown as well. His whims were indulged. He used his sway over people to enforce his own will. But there was also something so extraordinarily sweet about Marvin, a kindness, an empathy of such sincerity that, despite his fears to the contrary, he was virtually without enemies. The people he hurt most—his brother Frankie, his wives, his long string of managers—were those who forgave him fastest.

Even during his darkest days there were moments when he radiated a light, a distinct divinity that had people serving him worshipfully. It was more than his surface cool or noble demeanor. You could feel Marvin's loving kindness. His capacity for love was matched only by his need to suffer. And in 1975, his real suffering had begun.

His adult life was divided between two women, both of whom he adored, both of whom he felt had betrayed him. Betrayal would be a key theme—perhaps *the* key—to the final nine years of his life. However, the real betrayal came not from his wives but from himself, his fleeing from his own spiritual nature. Ultimately convinced that all experiences and choices could be reduced to a simple decision between good and evil—the philosophy of Father's House of God—Marvin saw himself, with increasing despair, choosing the dark side of his soul. The more blatant his disregard for old-fashioned morality, the harsher his judgments of himself, until, at the end, his mind grew sick and openly yearned to leave his human form.

It's a pity that Gaye's philosophy wouldn't allow him to view his secular work—he called them "dirty songs"—as liberating modes of artistic expression, as part of a necessary journey to free himself of old fears. Critic Leslie Fiedler points to Freud, who in *The Interpretation of Dreams* quotes Virgil, Dante's adopted guide through hell: "If I cannot sway the high gods, I will move the power of Hades."

"In light of this," Fiedler writes in *What Was Literature?* "it is possible to think of the release of the repressed . . . as a way of 'giving the Devil his due,' or even, in the words of the title of a Rolling Stone song, as expressing 'sympathy with the Devil.' But the point is not evil worship for its own sake à la Mick Jagger, but a recourse to the dark powers in quest of salvation: a way out of the secular limbo we inhabit—the world of getting and spending, and of a least-common denominator consensus reality enforced in the name of sanity and virtue."

Even at his raunchiest, Marvin always sought a "way out of the secular limbo," always looking to leap into the lap of the Jesus he felt he had betrayed.

Gaye saw betrayal wherever he looked. One after another, his relationships crumbled, not through lack of love but through lack of trust on Marvin's part. He burned his bridges behind him like a general—a metaphor he himself adopted—wearily trudging from battle to battle. As his heart grew heavier, his wars grew bloodier. And as time went on, his behavior turned more bizarre.

For example, Gaye had told conductor-arranger Gene Page that he'd like to meet an older woman—someone, in Marvin's words, "stylish and smart."

"But Marvin," Page retorted, "you're already going with this seventeen-year-old girl."

"I like older women, too," Gaye replied.

Page introduced him to Jewel Price, a black woman with whom Marvin would become extremely close.

Nearly twenty years Gaye's senior, Mrs. Price was a real estate agent. Marvin found her effusive, energetic personality both earthy and charming. A woman with connections to millionaires throughout southern California, she'd sold homes to stars such as Nat Cole, Art Tatum, and Earl Bostic. An Auntie Mame, a passionate music lover, Jewel had an almost mystical power of persuasion over Gaye.

"Mrs. Price," Marvin's mother told me, "could get him to do things other people—even I—couldn't. Get her to tell you about Marvin."

"I loved him," Jewel explained enthusiastically as we sat in her spacious Los Angeles home, "and he loved me. He said he'd never met anyone like me before. I treated Marvin like a king, because that's what he was. I'd send him flowers, buy him candy—that kind of thing. He appreciated my thoughtfulness and would return the favors."

Was the relationship sexual?

"Honey, *please!* Once he playfully suggested something, but I said to him, I said, 'Marvin, I'm a Christian lady with Christian morals. We're friends and nothing more.' No, Marvin was always a perfect gentleman with me.

"He trusted me. In fact, he had me take Anna and her sister Gwen around looking for homes. That was fun for a few hours, but I couldn't keep up with those ladies. They never stopped partying. Marvin also had me looking for houses for him. He never bought one, though I did find him a three-acre place to rent in Palm Springs for a while. He took me down there all the time. Meanwhile, I'd take him up to Malibu where we'd visit my rich friends, sit by the beach, and look at the ocean. With me, Marvin could relax and be himself. When he needed something done, I'd find a way to do it.

"I was forceful with Marvin. I told him when he was doing something wrong, and I wasn't afraid to scold him. He respected that. In fact, he put me on a pedestal. He treated me like a queen. I love Mrs. Gay, but she was never firm or frank enough with Marvin. He was so good to her, she was afraid of angering him.

"Marvin confided in me when he started having problems with Jan, and that broke my heart. You see, he loved that girl heavily and strongly. But she had a very strange and powerful effect on him. She controlled him. After talking to Jan on the phone, he might spend the next three hours staring into space, looking so lost and sad. I'd say, 'Marvin, what is it?' and he wouldn't even reply. His moods changed minute to minute, and Jan could change him quicker than anyone. The more he loved her, the more mixed up he got. He was such a beautiful man, but so unstable."

Two things happened in early 1975 which added to Marvin's instability: Jan became pregnant again and Anna filed for divorce. It would take two years for the proceedings to finalize, at the end of which—in 1977—Gaye married Jan. Those two years were filled with a long series of strategic battles—psychological and legal— which, one by one, gnawed at Marvin's mind. Even as he bought a new home and built a private recording studio for the future, his past and his present were colliding. The result was chaos.

He took Anna's suit, just as he took all adversity, as a challenge to his manhood. He became intransigent, stopped sending her money, and invited all-out war. Though deeply afraid, he'd show her that he wasn't. "I knew she possessed the power to take every penny I was making," Gaye said, "but I was honor-bound to be strong."

"Marvin hired me to represent him in the matter of his divorce," said Curtis Shaw, who served as Gaye's lawyer until late 1982. "He became much more than a client, though. Marvin and I were close friends. I advised him on many matters, personal and professional."

A native of Marshall, Texas, Shaw's down-to-earth, unpretentious personality was much to Marvin's liking.

"Now one of the first things I had to learn about Marvin," said Shaw, "was that contracts don't really mean anything to him. He saw them as pieces of paper and nothing more. He was a genius— there's no doubt—and a man capable of tremendous acts of charity, but, oh Lord, Marvin didn't know the meaning of the word responsibility!

"He was certain that Motown was helping Anna with her divorce, but that was nonsense. Motown treated him like a prince. They wanted nothing more than his continued success. Why would they work against one of their biggest earners? But Marvin was certain that Berry had it in for him, even though Berry kept himself completely out of the divorce. As a result of his own paranoia, Marvin refused to record.

"Now sometime during this period, Dionne Warwick wanted Marvin to produce her. Great idea! Marvin agreed and wrote some things, picked out some songs, and we set up a meeting. Over at the studio, Dionne was telling Marvin which songs she liked and which she didn't when Marvin excused himself and called me into the next room.

" 'She's too picky,' he told me. " 'Too aggressive. I don't want to work with her.'

" 'Marvin,' I said, 'we've already signed contracts. The deal's done.'

" 'Then undo it, 'cause I'm gone.'

"And he was. He just walked out the back door, and left me to explain. That was Marvin. He had a talent for doing exactly what he wanted and avoiding everything else."

In 1975, as if to spite Anna's legal threat, Gaye bought an estate for Janis, Nona, and their soon-to-be-born infant. He found a sprawling, Spanish ranch-style home on five acres on Long Valley Road in suburban Hidden Hills, an hour west of Hollywood in the San Fernando Valley. He added a pool, spas, hot tubs, a regulation-size basketball court, and a stable. There were horses and riding paths and frequent basketball games between Marvin and his cronies.

"Marvin had at least fourteen cars," Curtis Shaw remembered, "a Rolls, a vintage '56 Mercedes, a '75 Eldorado convertible, and assorted vans and jeeps. I'm telling you, at any given moment, Marvin didn't even know where half those cars were."

He invested his money according to his moods. Still seeking the vicarious thrill of the boxing ring, he was one of the backers of George Foreman's heavyweight exhibition against five contenders in April 1975.

His devotion to sports and sports figures remained keen. In the same year, he'd promised Cookie Gilchrist, the powerful Buffalo Bills fullback who in the sixties set AFL rushing records, that he'd appear at a benefit in Toronto for retired athletes fallen on hard times. Shortly before the concert, Gaye had a benign but painful growth removed from his foot. A few days later his mother-in-law, family matriarch Bertha Gordy, passed away and Marvin flew to Detroit for the funeral. Gilchrist's benefit was the next night, and Gaye performed a full ninety minutes in Maple Leaf Garden, in spite of barely being able to walk. Marvin was famous for showing up when you'd expect him to cancel and canceling when you'd expect him to show.

On October 12, 1975, he also fulfilled a promise by playing a UNESCO benefit concert at New York's Radio City Music Hall. The next day he was commended at the United Nations by Shirley Temple Black, then ambassador to Ghana, and secretary-general Kurt Waldheim.

Though this wasn't a period when he was recording, he decided to build himself a professional recording studio—not at home but in the heart of Hollywood, a location which attracted him for several reasons.

The Marvin Gaye Recording Studio, as he named it, was on Sunset Boulevard, just a few blocks down the street from the Motown building at Sunset and Vine. He was close enough to be comforted and far enough away to feel detached. Even more intriguing to Gaye, though, was the fact that the studio was situated on a street populated by dozens of prostitutes outlandishly displaying their wares. This was the neighborhood that Donna Summer, a woman who fascinated Marvin, sang about in "Bad Girls" and "Sunset People."

Gaye found the atmosphere exciting. A sense of sexual decadence and danger stimulated him, even as his relationship with Janis worsened.

Why? What had gone wrong?

After having met Jan—or even before, during his hibernation periods in Detroit—it seemed as though Marvin, like John Lennon, had the cool objectivity to understand the pitfalls of stardom and immerse himself in domestic life, at least long enough to regain his balance. But unlike Lennon, Gaye was not only incapable of sharing household duties and responsibilities, he inevitably found ways of undermining his mate.

"It wasn't Janis, it was me," Marvin confessed. "I had no discipline. I went on with my wild and wicked ways. It was my responsibility to lead her, and I blew it. I was older, I should have known better. Not only did I indulge myself, but I pulled Jan into the web. She turned me on so much that I used her in a bad way. I taught her—I forced her—to torture me. It began beautifully, but then it quickly became brutal."

How quickly?

"Time runs together. There were months, maybe years, which were relatively calm. But I couldn't stop picking on the relationship, bending it, twisting it, perverting it. The more I lived with Jan, the more I loved her, the more I made her miserable. It was a vicious cycle, and I knew, as hard as I tried, that it could never stop. I was afraid of the thought, but here was another woman, aside from Anna, destined to destroy me."

One of the issues which quickly created tension between them was Jan's ambitions. She wanted to sing and Marvin hated the idea.

"Marvin told me about the fights," Jewel Price said. "He said that Jan was dying to be a singer.

" 'Well, Marvin,' I said to him, 'can the girl really sing?'

" 'Yes, Jewel,' he answered. 'She has a fine voice.' "

" 'Then let her sing, Marvin,' I said. 'You must let her be a person, too.'

"Then he'd just look at me with that faraway stare in his eyes," Mrs. Price concluded, "and I knew what I said hadn't made a bit of difference."

"I'm the last of the great chauvinists," Marvin told me after I'd try to argue that sexism was inconsistent with his high-minded spirituality. "I'll never change. I like to see women serve me—and that's that. In Jan's case, serving me meant feeding my fantasies— my evil fantasies."

Specifically, what were they?

"That she'd betray me."

"And did she?"

"I made her. I begged her."

The only resolution to the psychological chaos in which Gaye lived was found in his music. Here the conflict was given form. Running back and forth from his mother to Jan to fights with Anna, Marvin finally took it all into the recording studio.

Nothing depicts this period better than the music he recorded while he was living through these heartaches. The album he created in 1975 was *I Want You*, a wonder, I believe, of sensuous sound and sexual confusion, another startlingly personal statement in which we learn exactly what Marvin Gaye was feeling and fearing.

22
WANTING

As with his other major albums, the idea for Marvin Gaye's major mid-seventies project was initiated by someone else. In fact, the majority of songs for *I Want You* were written before Gaye ever heard them.

A superb singer, composer, and arranger, Leon Ware had known Marvin since their early days in Detroit. Diana Ross had asked Ware to work with her brother Arthur "T-Boy." Subsequently Leon and T-Boy wrote "I Wanna Be Where You Are," one of Michael Jackson's first solo hits in 1972. In 1974, Ware co-composed "Body Heat" and "If I Ever Lose This Heaven," singing them both on Quincy Jones' *Body Heat* album. Leon's silky, seductive voice is similar to Marvin's in its impassioned subtlety, and when Berry Gordy heard a suite of songs Leon had written with T-Boy, he was certain he'd found a way of luring Marvin back into the studio.

Gordy was having a tough year himself. *Mahogany* was released to savage reviews. "Berry panicked after reading the first line of the *Time* magazine critique," said Rob Cohen, the film's producer. "It indicted him for the mismanagement of one of America's greatest resources, Diana Ross. Berry was like a raging bull. He was crazed. He wanted to re-edit the film, but I talked him out of it. This wasn't a movie where critics made any difference. And in fact, the film was a smash hit, even though the ugly reviews kept Berry from directing again. I think he was waiting for Hollywood to treat him as a real director and offer him scripts. They never did. Hollywood was interested in Berry financing movies, not directing them. It's a shame, because I think he showed tremendous talent."

Gordy's obsession with Diana and his interest in film took its toll on the record empire he had built. "Since the early seventies," wrote soul scholar Nelson George, "the magic of Motown was dead, and it was now just another record company."

After their initial storm of hits, the Jackson Five had cooled off, and there was even talk of their desertion. Like Marvin and Stevie before them, they felt ready to write and produce their own material. Joe Jackson, the boys' father, made it clear that he, and not Berry, was running their career.

Gordy's corporate position was increasingly defensive as he pulled back into the privacy of his Bel Air mansion. He still considered Marvin, whom he always held in esteem as a brilliant artist, a vital profit center. To convince Gaye that he really wasn't interested in interfering in his divorce—that he viewed him as an important artist and wanted him to work—Berry brought him Ware's music, hoping to crack Marvin's creative block.

It had been over two years since Gaye had recorded *Let's Get It On*, and Marvin's absence was considered negligent. Gaye enjoyed the negative attention. As he had taught Stevie Wonder, he believed that artists are entitled to create their own schedules. As always, he'd been searching for the right subject matter, avoiding the studio until he knew just what he wanted to sing. An updated *What's Going On* seemed unlikely, since he viewed two of the major political movements of the seventies—women's liberation and gay liberation—with special antagonism. He felt absolutely no sympathy for either cause. For now, politics couldn't provide his music with much lyrical content.

In Ware's work, however, not only did he hear his own voice, but the subject matter—like Norman Whitfield's material eight years earlier—was perfectly in tune with his current state of emotional affairs.

I Want You, in essence, was an invitation for Marvin to enter a world of uninhibited sexual fantasy. With overtones of Barry White, the suite offered Marvin just what he wanted—escape into pure eroticism. Gaye loved White's brand of schmaltz and sugar-coated strings, viewing such arrangements as appropriate vehicles for expressing physical passion.

"Berry played 'I Want You' for Marvin, just the one song," Ware told me, "and the next day Marvin was ready to do the album. Actually I'd written it as a vocal album for myself, but I was pleased to have Marvin sing my songs. It was rare for Marvin to let anyone produce him, so naturally I was honored. I thought we could do it all in a matter of weeks. It actually took thirteen months—just to lay down Marvin's vocals."

There's a close correlation between the content of the record and the atmosphere in which it was recorded. To a large extent, Gaye lived out his fantasies, even as he sang about them. Cocaine was consumed in extravagant quantities, creating—like Samuel Coleridge's poem "Kubla Khan" from 1797—a drug-induced state of euphoric imagery, much of it sexual.

"It was an amazing period," said Leon. "There was definitely something godly about Marvin. He had this incredible magnetism. We all felt that, and we knew that to work for him meant serving him at his pleasure."

At the beginning of the sessions, T-Boy Ross took his role as co-producer seriously, giving Gaye strong suggestions about how to interpret the work. That didn't go over well with Marvin. For the remainder of the project, T-Boy wasn't invited back to the studio.

"Marvin has a big kid inside him," said Ware. "I'm the same way. But Marvin usually let that kid have his way. For example, in the middle of the session he might just stop and say, 'Let's go play basketball.' Well, that'd be it for the day. We'd go play basketball. I'd never met anyone who could say 'fuck it' as quickly as Marvin.

"He was also going through a heavy push-and-pull domestic thing. You never knew where he was. Even though we might be waiting three hours for him to show up at the studio, we were prepared to wait three hours more. That was Marvin. He figured out a long time ago that he could have it his way, and so he did. He took advantage of his charm.

"Marvin loved brainy conversations, and once he said to me something I'll never forget. 'You escape from people too often,' he said, 'and you wind up escaping from yourself.' In other words,

the same stuff he pulled on us—not showing up, messing around—
he pulled on himself. It's like that song, 'I've Never Been to Me.'

"For all the delays, though, he took my material and turned it
into his own thing by adding a few lyrics and phrases and, of course,
working his vocal magic. That was a thrill to see—how he person-
alized everything."

The album was recorded partly at the Motown Studios, then
completed at the end of the year at Marvin's new studios. The move
to his own recording environment affected him profoundly and, to
some degree, brought out a certain adolescence within him.

The studio, on Sunset near Hudson, was a free-standing building, one-and-a-half stories high, with plain brick façade and no
identification other than the street address. There were no windows, only a front and back door. It had been built according to
Marvin's design. The security was tight, the decoration slick, with
earth-tone carpets, dramatic wooden walls, and plush furniture. In
addition to a spacious control room and a studio large enough to
contain Marvin's eighteen-piece band during rehearsals, there were
two reception areas, and upstairs, accessible only through a single
heavily locked door, a loft bedroom with a one-way window looking
into the studio below. Gaye's mini-apartment had a small refrig-
erator, stove, large closet, bath, and shower. The centerpieces were
Marvin's custom-made king-size waterbed and Jacuzzi big enough
to accommodate a dozen consenting adults.

The decor had strong overtones of *Playboy*—the carefree bachelor
recording at leisure with all the amenities a man could want. Marvin
continued to speak about the friendship Berry Gordy had struck
up with Hugh Hefner, and how Berry, Wilt Chamberlain, and
Hugh loved to party together at the Playboy mansion. Gaye was
clearly envious, and rather than try to crowd into Gordy's circle—
an unthinkable move for Marvin—he consoled himself with a play-
pen of his own.

In the control room several oil paintings of Marvin were prom-
inently hung on the walls. In general, the images idealized him,
showing him, Christ-like, speaking with children and holding doves.

The first time we had a long discussion in the studio, I asked
him whether such reverential portraits were incompatible with the
notion he was touting—that egotism was a roadblock to God?

"Perhaps," he answered candidly, "but no more so than that

poster." He pointed to a hot photo of Jane Fonda stretched out in a leotard.

"Sexy" is the word Marvin liked to use in describing his studio, and sexy was his mood when he began working there. From the day it opened in late 1975 to the day a bankruptcy court shut it down four years later, the studio was a magnet for Marvin's family and friends, consultants and conspirators, parasites and partners, a steady stream of people looking for an audience with the prince— a job, an interview, investment capital, or the simple pleasure of his company.

His sister Jeanne was in charge of operations, though as she herself admitted, her power was limited. It was a question of anticipating Marvin's whims. Still ambivalent about his family—willing to help them to some degree, but angry about their dependence upon him—Gaye both resented and relished the fact that he, and not Father, was responsible for everyone's welfare.

Of all the siblings, baby sister Zeola "Sweetsie" enjoyed the least strained relationship with Marvin. She was the only family member to follow his lead and change her name from Gay to Gaye, thus expressing her loyalty. Like Mother, she saw her role as subservient and was willing to cater to her brother's needs and moods. Soon he'd take her on the road as a dancer and, for much of the time, keep her close to him as confidante and friend.

Jan also became a fixture at the studio, although Gaye soon began resenting her presence. When she was there, he was reminded of her desire to sing.

"I tried to make it clear," he told me, "that there was room for only one singer in our family."

In a sense, the studio became a refuge, a place to fulfill his schoolboy fantasies. Marvin saw it, in the words of "Kubla Khan," as a "pleasure dome."

While he was finishing the album in his studio, Gaye halted production several times for what he described as "serious parties." These parties—along with his music, his sexual reveries, his obsession with Janis, and his attraction to prostitutes—were all ideas which came to play on his new record.

If the suite was shocking, it also stood as a testimony to the changes Marvin was going through. As he admitted, Jan's impact on his sexuality was both liberating and shattering, finally throwing him out of control. The album was a further step into chaos, a revelation of his heart's wildest confusions.

The cover was from a magnificent Ernie Barnes oil painting—later to hang in Marvin's Hidden Hills home—of blacks at a neighborhood dance hall, caught in the motion of music, their bodies provocatively curled around invisible notes as a vocalist and band drove them to physical frenzy. (The men in the painting, by the way, were almost all completely bald, a cue Marvin himself would pick up when, the night before his November 29, 1975, benefit concert in San Francisco for the Reverend Cecil Williams' Glide Church, he shaved off all his hair.)

Marvin stated the story line, corresponding to Barnes' painting, in "Since I Had You," reciting the tale of two former lovers who meet at a neighborhood dance and renew their desire for one another.

Gaye's passion, in spite of the oversexed aura, was for fidelity, something which he simultaneously sought and destroyed. Like *Let's Get It On*, the album wasn't what it appeared to be. It wasn't an argument for free sex, but rather another expression of Gaye's deep-seated desire for domestic bliss. It was, in fact, a long love poem to Janis, whose actual name he cried out twice in the course of singing, and the candid story not only of their courtship but of Marvin's preoccupation with her physical and spiritual being.

In "After the Dance" he openly described her as the woman of his dreams—the lover he had always known—the dancing girl he'd envisioned in his archetypal fantasy, whirling away from him, naked, into the arms of others. "What a freak!" he softly exclaimed in the mike.

"Come Live with Me, Angel" had Gaye poignantly describing the kind of life he offered Jan, even as he was moving her into his dream home in Hidden Hills. He sang of "comfort" and "freakish pleasures."

"I Want You" expressed his most basic fear—being unloved. All he felt from his woman was "half a love," and it wasn't enough. Confirming his long-held commitment—ever since his lonely doo-wop days—to romantic love, the relationship was viewed as something to "cherish" forever.

"Feel All My Love Inside" was, in one sense, a musical impression of sexual intercourse. But even on this, the most overtly physical song on the album, Marvin was unable to tolerate sex for its own sake; he was compelled to elevate physical love, necessarily incorporating it into the holy act of matrimony.

On the album, there was talk of aphrodisiacs, with Gaye mentioning wine and weed. He sounded bold by whispering, "Let's get naked." Then the sounds of love began, but only as background, as mood music for the most serious of statements—that he wanted her for his wife.

"I proposed to Jan on that record," Marvin told me. "A lot of people didn't hear it, but it's there. Of course I couldn't marry her then, and I changed my mind a million times before I finally did, but I wanted to, I needed to, I had to. With all the freakery I did during those sessions, all the crazy parties, Janis never left my mind."

His mind was filled with fantasies of Jan with other men, fantasies that he not only wished upon her, but, according to Gaye, insisted that she realize.

"Marvin just didn't ask Jan to fool around," Jeanne Gay told me, "but he'd become angry at her when she refused to obey and wouldn't tell him the stories of the affairs he wanted her to have."

"He wanted Jan to go with other men," Marvin's mother said. "Then he'd suffer with the consequences. He wanted to suffer."

With Marvin's madonna-whore mind-set, he wouldn't be happy until Jan fell from her pedestal. He pushed her off and cried over the broken pieces.

In "All the Way Around" he sang of this vision—the unfaithful female to whom he's eternally bonded, calling the woman "promiscuous" but forgiving her because she was "still the greatest lay."

Jan unleashed in Gaye a flood of feelings—wanting to protect and worship her, wanting to lose himself in her beauty. Through her, he encountered the sort of uninhibited sexuality that overpowered and frightened him. Finally, he couldn't accept it, and rather than embrace the love, he invented torturous ways of destroying it.

"I loved Anna very much," he told me, "and sometimes our sex life was exciting, but it was part of another generation. Janis was born at a different time. She was young and free, and I found myself doing things with her—beautiful things—I never dreamed I'd do with any woman."

"Soon I'll Be Leaving You," from *I Want You*, explained what Marvin meant. He sang of how he believed in "dreams and fantasies" and then mentioned there was something he'd never done before. It was going to be his "first time." You could feel him struggling for the courage to say it, to do it. Finally, the words came: He was going to give her "head," oral sex. He convinced himself he could "handle" her, though in mentioning the act, as if to "sanctify" it, he quickly suggested marriage and even pregnancy, singing that he was going to "knock up" this woman.

This is one of the moments in which he actually called out her name—"Oh, Janis!"—exploding with an anguished shriek, a cry of limitless pleasure and pain.

Like a little boy afraid of jumping off the diving board, Marvin built up his courage—"soon," he repeated, "soon"—trying to convince himself that he was man enough to do the job. He viewed oral copulation as a complete commitment of his affection. For Gaye, the act was the highest expression of his love since, as he told me several times, it was something he didn't enjoy. It's no accident that "giving head" was joined to the notion of conception and pregnancy, further validating his feelings of sacred romance and familial sanctity. In fact, in November of 1975, Janis did give birth to her second child, Frankie Christian "Bubby," born a day after his namesake, Marvin's brother.

Mother took a different view of her son's sexual relationship with his wives. It's interesting that, throughout his adult life, Marvin had long and intimate conversations with his mother about sex.

"Anna taught Marvin certain tricks," Alberta Gay told me, "tricks with her body, sex tricks, that Marvin taught Jan.

"I liked Anna. She always loved Marvin, and she begged him to come back to her. She said she'd take care of his two babies by Jan. And she would have. Anna loves children.

"Now Janis wasn't ready for Marvin. She was too young. And he took advantage of that. She meant well, but Marvin didn't. What he really needed—and never got—was a wife who wouldn't do any drugs with him. He needed someone sober and strong."

The search for sexual strength was the heart of the matter. *I Want You* perspired with that theme. Gaye worked overtime to please the women in his life and dreams, another theme of his troubled existence—the effort he exerted to seduce women. The seduction, though, was public, not private. He desperately needed the all-night-lover image.

Still, the final statement from *I Want You* came in the abbreviated version of Michael Jackson's hit, "I Wanna Be Where You Are" (which, oddly enough, along with Bill Green's gritty tenor work, wasn't listed on the credits). As the song faded away, Marvin leaned into the microphone, letting emotion pour from his heart. This was the passage I read on the phone to Marvin III, then eighteen, in 1984, a few months after his father had been killed. It came at the very end of the song when Marvin spoke to his children, naming each of them—Frankie, Nona, little Marvin—and wishing them goodnight. He tenderly told them how he loved them, just as he told Janis how he'd always love her. "Oh, my children," he cried, leaving the lyrics of the song to sing from his soul, "I'll always be where you are."

"All Marvin ever wanted," Curtis Shaw said, "was to have a little cottage by the sea and live happily ever after with his wife and children by his side."

Such was the anguish behind the record—the knowledge that simple happiness would never be his.

The public loved *I Want You*—the album sold over a million copies—but the critics weren't impressed.

"With Barry White on the wane," wrote Vince Aletti in *Rolling Stone*, "Marvin Gaye seems determined to take over as soul's master philosopher in the bedroom, a position that requires little but an affectation of constant, rather jaded horniness."

"Slush for disco dancers," wrote *Down Beat*, ". . . the bogus over-blown manner of Barry White."

The sentimental quasi-symphonic school of soul has generally met with critical disfavor. While it's true that Gaye was an experimental artist—he expanded the pop song, successfully toyed with new keyboards and percussive combinations, and was an unconventional lyricist—he also loved fully orchestrated, wildly romantic music. Leon Ware's lush production of *I Want You* inspired him to sing with remarkable intensity. By now he had mastered multitrack vocalizing, the art of playing with his voices, a skill perfectly suited for an album so rooted in masturbatory imagery. The use of moaning women in the background sounded childish, but sexual noise was an integral part of the little-boy fantasy which lay at the heart of what seems to me a work of rare beauty.

Generally, as Marvin's records became less obvious, critics lost patience. They missed the subtleties and evolution of his personal art. In these last seven years of his life—with the notable exception of his final album—Gaye's musical and literary growth was inspiring. He took his old-time rhythm and blues, his new-fangled funk, and his romantic laments and fit them all into forms—personal confessions and philosophical dialogues—which broadened the range of popular music without betraying its basic ear-pleasing personality. While he was never able to put the pieces of his private life together, he successfully fashioned those same pieces—same emotions, same frustrations—into suites of lasting value, placing his compositions, I believe, in a category with Duke Ellington and Stevie Wonder.

It was Wonder, by the way, who, in the mid-seventies, won the bulk of the Grammys which Marvin had been counting on. Stevie's *Fulfillingness' First Finale* in 1974 and *Songs in the Key of Life* in 1976 walked off with the prizes. It wasn't until 1983 and "Sexual Healing" that Gaye won his first Grammy.

"Of course I was jealous of Stevie," Marvin admitted. "How could I not be? He won Grammys the way Disney used to win Oscars—by the truckload. But Stevie deserved them. He'd become a great artist, and even though I'd been there as an influence for him and maybe even an inspiration, his songwriting was in a class by itself. I was envious but, believe me, I was also very proud. I didn't even mind when Paul Simon won in '75. I also considered his *Still Crazy After All These Years* the story of my life. Lou Rawls, though, was another matter. When he won again in '77 I knew I was going to punch him out on national television. God intervened on Rawls' behalf and kept me in my seat."

After the adulation he received in the earlier part of the decade, he was feeling increasingly neglected. "In the same week," he said, "I saw that this new rock singer, Bruce Springsteen, was on the cover of *Time* and *Newsweek*. That was a little too much. Nothing against Springsteen, but cats like me and Smokey who've been rocking and rolling from Jump Street are still waiting to be on the cover of a national news magazine."

Released in the first half of 1976, *I Want You* was a point of particular pride with Marvin. He considered it among his best work. Usually Gaye procrastinated before releasing an album. He might hold it back for months, even years, afraid that it wasn't perfect or wouldn't sell. This was a fear he shared with Stevie. But *I Want*

You was a different story; he had unusually strong confidence in the record.

"Marvin and I waltzed it into Berry's office," Leon Ware said, "happy as we could be."

Having honestly confessed his heart's desire—his love for Jan and his children—having once again tried to reconcile sex and romance, what would be his next theme? What would be his next move—musical and otherwise? The answer would come from Anna. She'd punch and Marvin would counterpunch as their divorce became more brutal. The war was heating up and Gaye's inclination, as always, was ambivalent. Part of him said stay and fight; part of him said run. As his actions in 1976 would reveal, he'd wind up doing both.

Marvin P. Gaye III at 14. February 1979. (*Images from Kenneth®*)

At his fortieth birthday party, singing with Stevie Wonder. Hollywood, April 1979. (*Images from Kenneth*®)

At his fortieth birthday, with Smokey Robinson. (*Images from Kenneth*®)

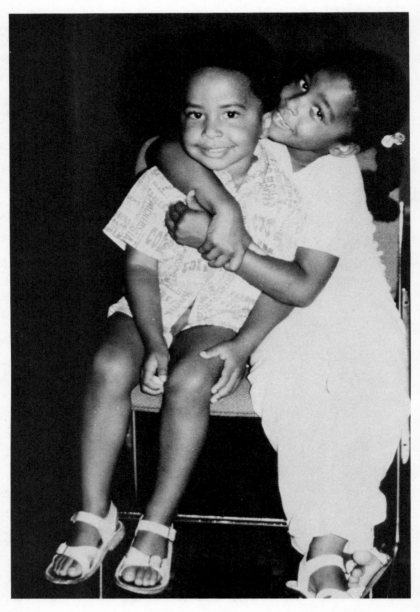

Marvin and Jan's children in 1979: Nona "Pie" and Frankie "Bubby."
(*Images from Kenneth®*)

Greeting Mrs. Curtis Shaw at his fortieth birthday party, with a smiling Curtis Shaw looking on. (*Images from Kenneth*®)

ON TOUR

(*Images from Kenneth®*)

(*Images from Kenneth®*)

(*Images from Kenneth®*)

(*Images from Kenneth®*)

With dancer Jocelyn Lufton at the Circle Star Theater. San Carlos, California, 1979. (*Images from Kenneth*®)

The finale to "Distant Lover," in concert. 1979. (*Images from Kenneth*®)

In Diana Ross's dressing room, after her Caesar's Palace show, September 27, 1979, the night before the Price-Leonard fight. From left, Berry Gordy, Diana Ross, Marvin, Dave Simmons, and Vilma Simmons. (*Images from Kenneth*®)

During the same evening: Gordy and Gaye. (*Images from Kenneth*®)

With Michael Jackson after Marvin's performance at the Black Radio Exclusive conference, Los Angeles, 1979. From left, Randy Jackson, Michael, and their father, Joe Jackson. (*Images from Kenneth*®)

23

GIVING IT UP

During 1976, even as *I Want You* worked its way up the record charts, the tide started turning against Marvin Gaye.

Marvin admitted to doing everything he could to antagonize Anna, thus raising the stakes in a divorce suit which could only take more of his money. It was pure self-punishment.

"There were times," he said, "when I could have been nice. Times when I might have acted the part of the gentleman. But, you see, I was also scared. I'd put myself in this public position of having two children with my girlfriend. In my mind, that put me outside the law. An outlaw! That's how I began thinking of myself. So I got this place in Arizona where I'd hide out. I was a cowboy on the open range. I would have liked to be one of those dudes in the old John Wayne movies, gun strapped to my thigh, taking shit off no one. I wasn't about to let no woman tell me what to do."

Just as he'd never lose his preoccupation with Janis, Marvin would remain attached to Anna for the rest of his life. Both women were permanently connected to his psyche, figments of his imagination, mothers and madonnas, heroines and harlots. He tried to purge them through his music, and with Anna he finally did earn a measure of peace. But Janis haunted him until the end.

In 1976 he felt compelled to win the war against Anna, thus earning his stripes and proving himself man enough, in his phrase, to "handle" Jan.

*   *   *

"Marvin Gaye faces two consecutive five-day terms in L.A. County Jail for contempt of court in an alimony and child support case if authorities catch up with him," reported *Variety* on August 18, 1976. "But attorneys . . . who represent Gaye's estranged wife, Anna, admit they have been stumped in their efforts to find the singer."

A week later, *Variety* wrote that "soul singer Marvin Gaye couldn't go on in Buffalo's Memorial Auditorium (Saturday, August 14) and 9,000 ticket holders stood three hours in the rain for the doors to be unlocked in a dispute over advance rental fees.

"Everybody went home, a few rocks were tossed through the auditorium windows, Gaye sang gratis for an NAACP convention in his Buffalo hotel and the next day one of the promoters was arrested on a charge of making off with ticket refund money."

As Marvin's helter-skelter life became more fragmented, he was unable to stay still long enough to work out solutions.

"I was running," said Marvin. "I needed money, so we went out on tour. It was that simple. I wasn't going to sit around L.A. with all those folks taking potshots at me. There was too much heat. At some point, the road looked good. From afar, I'd have an easier time dealing with these things—Anna, taxes, my own production company."

Right On Productions was the name of the firm Marvin had incorporated to run his studio and scattered interests. His plan was to rent out his facilities to other artists, though he refused to let Motown use it for their overflow work, a headstrong stand that cost him money. In addition to the high overhead of the studio, his home in Hidden Hills, and his fleet of cars, he also had made a slew of unprofitable investments—$100,000 in the New Orleans Jazz basketball team, for example, which he never recovered, as well as highly speculative oil deals that came up dry.

"In that mid-seventies period when Marvin's earnings were so high," Jeanne Gay said, "his only sound investment was with Wally Amos."

Amos had been a show business agent with William Morris. In fact, he had booked the Supremes on the Dick Clark tour that resulted in their first hit in 1964. One of America's great salesmen, Wally persuaded Marvin to invest $10,000 for thirteen percent of his Famous Amos Cookies venture.

Money was the root of Marvin's material problems—his need to feed his extravagant lifestyle and supply himself with high-priced cocaine.

"How much have I spent on toot over the years?" he laughed when I posed the question in 1982. "I don't even want to think about it. To be truthful, I've been careful never to keep track. I don't want to know. My attitude has always been, whenever good blow is around, buy it, regardless of price. It's cost me hundreds of thousands of dollars. Maybe more. Enough to certify me as a fool. You'd have to call me a drug addict and a sex freak. Didn't you write the same thing about Ray Charles? Wasn't that his story? Well, if it's good enough for Uncle Ray, it's good enough for me," he laughed.

"Ray gave up hard drugs," I said.

"I don't want to hear about it," Gaye replied, half joking, half serious.

Marvin's steady use of cocaine was taking its toll. His fears increased as he envisioned plots of friends and colleagues to confiscate his money. As usual, the only real plots were ones he had invented to work against himself.

"The bad guys who hung around my brother," Jeanne Gay told me, "were people who Marvin brought in. If they took his money— and they did—it was at his invitation."

Back out on the road with Jan and their two babies, Marvin made a stop in Lexington, Kentucky.

Bishop Simon Peter Rawlings' wife, Mary, remembered the trip: "Marvin came to our house to visit us and then spent a lot of time in the park, playing ball with the children. He also came by the church and sang. Kids were following him everywhere."

"I went to Lexington several times," Gaye told me. "I liked talking to Bishop Rawlings. I felt drawn to the place, like I was looking for something I'd once lost."

The ghosts of Father's past and present never vacated Marvin's mind. Even as Gay Sr. spent year after year secluded in his bedroom on Gramercy Place, Marvin never felt free of his influence.

"Marvin used to ask his father to go on tour with him," Jewel Price told me. "He even wanted to take him to Europe. But Mr. Gay always refused."

"So many times," Marvin's mother said, "my son would call me and say, 'If only Father could throw his arms around me and squeeze me and hold me and tell me he loves me!'

" 'I understand what you're saying, darlin',' I'd answer him, 'but it ain't going to happen. So just put it out of your mind and think of all the people who do love you.'

"Marvin didn't believe me. My son didn't really believe that anyone loved him."

In September 1976, for the first time in ten years, the Marvin Gaye Show traveled to London, where he recorded a live album. Because of his fear of flying over the ocean and the overall anxiety running through his mind, he canceled out at the last minute but was finally convinced by his manager, Stephen Hill, to go.

Gaye went over with his sister Zeola, his friend Wally Cox, and an orchestra conducted by Leslie Drayton which included musicians who, for several years to come, would be permanent members of Marvin's band—trumpeter Nolan Smith, drummer Bugsy Wilcox, percussionist Melvin Webb, vibist Elmira Amos—in spite of his chauvinism, Gaye loved the idea of a female vibist—and saxists Fernando Harkness and David I.

The concert, recorded on the two-LP set *Live at the London Palladium*, issued in 1977, revealed the changes in Marvin's show. The days of his glitter denims were over. Now Gaye was more inclined toward dark suits offset by sun-yellow vests, hot-yellow shirts, and yellow-checked bow ties.

Since his 1974 tour he had spiced up his act considerably. There was more stress on sex than in earlier performances. Continually addressing the audience as "baby"—speaking to all the women as one—he began with fresh interpretations of his recently recorded "All the Way Around" and "Since I Had You" from *I Want You*. The background voices were actually Marvin's. In fact, he later re-recorded most of the vocals. A perfectionist, Gaye wasn't at all satisfied with his live performance.

He came on as a wolf. He offered the women "Come Get to This" as pure prick-tease, and "Let's Get It On" was little more than a long, drawn-out seduction sequence during which Marvin slowly stripped off his coat and removed his tie, all the while promising "baby" the night of her life.

The sex syndrome, the sacrifice Gaye felt he had to make for womankind, grew more blatant with each show. "I'm going to work hard for you, baby," was something he liked to tell his audience. He'd still wipe his sweaty brow with silk handkerchiefs and casually fling them into the audience, then watch the ladies fight over them, a gimmick, he told me, that he found degrading, but also thrilling.

The English press liked the show. *Melody Maker* wrote that "hopefully we shall not have to wait another twelve years to see him again."

Geoffrey Wansell in the *London Times* was more expansive. Reviewing the Albert Hall concert, he reported, "Marvin Gaye swayed, immaculate in electric blue suit and red velvet waistcoat and bow tie, like the Cary Grant of soul, and just as relaxed. . . . It was an entirely young audience of both white and black, whose enthusiasm almost threatened to stop the show at at least one point."

Marvin was elated to be so appreciated in Britain. He never ceased to be surprised by a display of love on his behalf.

"I had suffered ever since Berry wouldn't let me tour there in the sixties," Gaye said, for the moment forgetting his fear of live performing and long plane rides. "And now I saw that the English did understand me, and I understood them. They're wilder than they let on. And they appreciate sexual nuances. I said I'd be back and I kept my promise. It still seemed to be a place where I could live out my days with dignity—another fantasy which I'd make come true—stealing away to secret orgies with duchesses and countesses."

London appealed to Marvin's sense of nobility, and he toyed with remaining, thus avoiding the nightmares awaiting him at home. It was impossible, though. He couldn't think of abandoning his children or his mother. Also, according to Gaye, Jan wasn't willing to leave her parents in Los Angeles and live in Europe. He was forced to go back and face the music.

The hot-selling music of the mid-seventies was disco, a trend that Marvin bucked. It wasn't the instrumentation or rhythm that bothered him. In fact, he had high regard for the work Giorgio Moroder and Pete Bellotte were doing with Donna Summer. He also respected Van McCoy, a fellow Washingtonian and disco pioneer. McCoy, who died in 1979, wrote "The Hustle," a Number One song from 1975, as well as producing David Ruffin's exquisite "Walk Away from Love." Gaye was equally as impressed by the dance songs by Harold Melvin and the Blue Notes. Their lead singer, Teddy Pendergrass, was someone about whom Marvin had great ambivalence.

"I loved 'Don't Leave Me This Way,' " said Gaye. "I recognized Teddy's strength early on. But I could see that Gamble-Huff in Philly were planning the same thing for Teddy that Berry was planning for Jermaine. Teddy even grew a beard like mine."

Pendergrass' powerful style, modeled upon Marvin Junior of the Dells, was a special threat to Gaye. Teddy possessed the sort of operatic voice which excited Marvin's feelings of smallness and inadequacy.

Disco, though, was really nothing more than a new name for souped-up soul sung to soaring violins, a super-busy bass, and jet-propelled percussion. What Marvin objected to was the pressure of having to write in the disco mold. As always, he didn't want to be told what to do.

"Motown was screaming disco at me," Gaye remembered, "disco disco disco disco! I couldn't be bothered. But I also had this problem. The live-London thing took up three sides and we needed something to fill side four. Perfect for a long disco song, they insisted. Round out the record with disco. I stuck my nose in the air and said, 'fuck it,' but don't you know that in the end I did what they wanted—my way."

Credit must go to Gaye's engineer Art Stewart, who conceived and produced "Got to Give It Up," the eleven-minute forty-eight-second dance song which comprised side four of *Live at the London Palladium*, though it was neither live nor recorded in London. Instead it was simply Marvin playing around with his friends in the studio, Marvin in his casual light-hearted party mood, which Stewart was astute enough to capture on tape.

By then, Art had been with Gaye four years and had a good grasp of the man's mercurial manner. Whenever Marvin toyed at the piano, Stewart found inconspicuous ways to mike and record his improvisations. He encouraged his boss to noodle, understanding these jams to be the essence of Gaye's genius.

"Marv used to fool with this thing called 'Life's Opera,' " Art told me. "Absolutely brilliant reflections on his life. Genius stuff. He'd do it in between his other projects. I'd urge him to keep working on it, but he'd say, 'Oh Art, that thing ain't about nothing.' He said the same about 'Got to Give It Up,' only I was more insistent on that one.

"He had this riff that seemed very danceable. He was doing crazy things like banging on a half-filled grapefruit juice bottle for rhythm. Well, I kept stuff like that on the track. Also people talking in the studio—that loose feeling. At one point, Don Cornelius from *Soul Train* comes in and Marvin shouts out, 'Say, Don.' I left that in. Marvin wasn't sure of what I was doing, but he left me alone to piece the song together. On Christmas Day, 1976, after working on it for months, I ran it over to his house in Hidden Hills. He liked it but still wasn't sure—a typical Marvin reaction. Soon *everyone* was liking it. And when it came out in '77, it shot to Number One—soul and pop."

Stewart said the original title was "Dancing Lady," a title, Marvin explained, which referred back to his dream. In the course of his improvisations he altered the lyrics, keeping that image but also introducing his own fears of dancing. The new title, "Got to Give It Up," referred to giving up his inhibitions, becoming free with his body, whether on the dance floor or in bed. His days as a wallflower, he sang, were over.

In the lyric, Marvin turned the tune's focus from himself to the image of a dancing woman, urging her to keep on moving, to shout, to get down, to get "funky." Earlier in 1976, Johnnie Taylor's "Disco Lady" was a huge hit, considerably influencing Gaye. "I love the way Johnnie sings, and I thought it was a fabulous song," Gaye said. "As good as disco ever got. I appreciated the picture of the super-sexy woman on the dance floor, though in my version, I tried to give it a little twist."

Because of its relevance to his performance hang-up, Marvin immediately began using the song as the opening number of his live shows while trying to sing through his shyness.

That Marvin was able to create an autobiographical disco tune is testimony to the perennially personal nature of his art. And that Stewart, in his subtle production, was able to capture the very essence of Gaye's studio personality is an indication of how well the engineer-producer understood the singer.

With his light gourmet touch, Marvin created a kind of *nouvelle disco*, lean and cool, free of thick, heavy sauces. It shows his mastery of controlled excitement—the single element which, more than any other Marvin Gaye trait, helped mold Michael Jackson.

Because during this phase of his life Marvin was unable to concentrate for long periods of time, "Got to Give It Up" is the true record of his musical and social distractions.

The fact that Janis and brother Frankie sang background on the song was especially significant. With the help of Ed Townsend and Frankie, Jan had been recording some tracks of her own, yet on the issue of her singing career Marvin remained intransigent.

"I wanted her to be a housewife," he said, "and hearing her talk about being a star annoyed the hell out of me."

After "Got to Give It Up" he never allowed her to record with him again.

As for Frankie, he, too, was waiting for Marvin either to record him or help get him a deal. But Gaye, still afraid of his brother's talent, was determined to keep Frankie dependent upon him.

"We sounded so much alike," Frankie told me, "that Marvin worried about my voice being out there. He was still trying to convince me to open some sort of boutique. I didn't want to do that, but I didn't want to upset him. I suppose you could say that I loved Marvin so much that I stayed out of show business rather than compete."

During this same year, while passing over his brother, Gaye was instrumental in launching the career of another young singer. Ironically, his name was also Frankie—Frankie Beverly and his group Maze. Marvin not only worked with Maze for months, he found them money and booked the band as an opening act on his own show. Within a year, Beverly's superb funk group had a gold record.

Generous one day, withdrawn the next, Marvin kept running around, out to Arizona with his half-brother Michael Cooper for a few weeks, over to the place on Gramercy, back to Hidden Hills with Jan and his two babies, all the while cutting himself into small pieces.

The war with Anna raged on—hearings, depositions, demands. The divorce got nastier, and the financial threat to Marvin's unsteady empire grew more ominous with each new legal maneuver.

"I tried to reason with him," said Curtis Shaw. " 'Marvin,' I'd say, 'let's just get this thing settled.' But Marvin had to go all the way, to see how much he—or she—could take."

Then, in a sudden surprise, Shaw suggested a solution which ultimately settled the matter in a manner which stimulated Marvin's creative imagination. "Pay her off in music," was the lawyer's plan.

Though uncertain at first, Gaye bought the strategy, loving the literary concept of turning his divorce—and all his feelings for Anna—into the next major musical chapter of his life.

24

INSPIRED DIVORCE

The legal end of the marriage between Anna Ruby Gordy Gaye and Marvin came in March of 1977. The most revealing document of that dispute isn't to be found in courtroom records, though, but in record stores. It's the album, *Here, My Dear*, recorded in 1977 but not released until 1978, that best details the struggle—at least from Gaye's defensive point of view.

Since the days of "Pride and Joy," Anna had always inspired her husband's best work, and the pattern proved no different, even as their relationship turned rancorous. Gaye never before or after created a suite large enough to cover two LPs. *Here, My Dear* was an explosion of feeling, a composition unique in the annals of American pop in which Marvin used the medium of music—just as Ingmar Bergman used film in *Scenes from a Marriage*—to explore the dark side of a male-female conflict. On a personal level, it was a work every bit as powerful as *What's Going On*, and proof of Gaye's artistic courage. Without consideration for the mood of the marketplace, without the slightest nod to current fashion, Marvin used his art as an outlet for his feelings in an attempt to heal his own heart.

In another one of those literary twists which typify Gaye's atypical career, the album was released according to his final divorce decree. Curtis Shaw explained the concept:

"Anna was asking for $1 million to settle. Now Marvin didn't have that kind of money, so I proposed he pay her $600,000. Since coming up with even that much cash would be a problem, I suggested that we give her the advance due to Marvin for his next album—$305,000—and pay her the other $295,000 from the earnings on that same album. Anna liked the idea. I got Marvin to agree, the judge wrote up the order, and that was that."

"At first," Marvin said, "I figured I'd just do a quickie record—nothing heavy, nothing even good. Why should I break my neck when Anna was going to wind up with the money anyway? But the more I lived with the notion, the more it fascinated me. Besides, I owed the public my best effort. Finally, I did the record out of deep passion. It became an obsession. I had to free myself of Anna, and I saw this as the way. All those depositions and hearings, all those accusations and lies—I knew I'd explode if I didn't get all that junk out of me. So I had Art open up the mikes and I just sang and sang until I'd drained myself of everything I'd lived through. That took me three months, but then I held back the album for over a year. I was afraid to let it go.

"You see, the divorce had cleaned me out. I'd really messed up my taxes, and a lot of the people I'd counted on were no longer there. In fact, they were suing me. I owed Stephen Hill, my ex-manager, $2 million and a cat named Patrick Cavanaugh, who ran my business for a while, claimed I owed him a fortune, but meanwhile I said—wait a minute, y'all. No one's getting any money—and that includes the feds—'cause I don't have any. Then Motown was giving me all kinds of crap, and I was worried about how they'd ever promote an album that talks about me divorcing the Chairman's sister."

In the seventies, Berry Gordy was no longer BG. Now that Motown was a sophisticated corporation, his employees called him the Chairman. Like Gaye, Gordy's enigma expanded. He sometimes traveled under fake names, even wearing disguises. The more remote a figure he became, the more Marvin longed for his love and approval. In Gaye's mind, it was Anna and Berry who had made him, and Anna and Berry who would destroy him.

In spite of such fears, Marvin moved ahead with his divorce statement, focusing on the matter as though nothing else existed.

"When I was doing *Here, My Dear*," Marvin remembered, "the only politics that interested me were the politics of my divorce. I felt out of touch with the world. To me, the presidents passing through—Ford and Carter—were non-people. At least Nixon was someone to hate. Aside from sports, I didn't read a newspaper or look at TV news for a year. I was generating my own news show every night. It was one disaster after another."

Gaye's fear of folding without Anna by his side was one of the suite's recurring themes. To counteract his anxiety, he tried to play the part of the brave warrior, all the while frightened by the thought of losing everything. As with so many divorces, money played a prominent part in the proceedings—and in the punishment.

The cover illustration shows a bearded, toga-clad Marvin in a neo-Roman setting. His demeanor was especially noble, his hand raised like Marcus Aurelius. On the back cover, the holy temple of matrimony was collapsing around a mock-Rodin statue of a couple in passionate embrace. Fire leapt from the man's crotch. The album folded out to an illustration of a Monopoly board on which the word "judgment" was written. A male hand offered an outstretched female hand a miniature record. On the board were miniature pianos, tape recorders, a rose, a house, a Mercedes, Monopoly money, dice, a skull and crossbones. The scales of justice sat above a mantel, as, from a window, hundreds of faces peered inside, watching the game.

Marvin loved symbolism. The idea of his divorce seen as a game—his favorite metaphor for life—was especially appropriate.

Before getting into the brutal details, though, Marvin set the stage in the opening song, "Here, My Dear," by dedicating the album to Anna and launching into his most serious accusation, the one charge with which he hoped to win his audience's sympathy. He claimed Anna kept him from seeing his son.

"When things got rough between me and Anna," Marvin told me, "she wouldn't let me see little Marvin for weeks. That hurt. Of course I did things worse than that to her, but the point of this record was to tell my story, not hers."

The self-serving, self-justifying, self-pitying nature of the work is disconcerting at first. But soon it becomes clear that the singer was concerned with more than this divorce; his struggle was to keep himself from going mad. Singing was his only way of saving himself. If the emotions weren't expressed, they'd strangle him.

Marvin wrote most of the songs alone, though Ed Townsend,

his music and party partner from *Let's Get It On* days, co-wrote three tunes. Later, Gaye's musicians would claim co-authorship of some of the numbers and threaten to sue.

"I Met a Little Girl" began at the beginning of Marvin's music and marriage. In old-fashioned doo-wop style, he described his abject loneliness in the early sixties, his melancholy and subsequent gratitude for having found Anna.

In the same song, he musically duplicated his wedding vows before declaring his own independence and the end of the dream, all the while maintaining a hallelujah, high-church tone and finally declaring his freedom from the same woman he once viewed as his savior.

The dense harmonies sound like ghosts from his Moonglow past.

"When Marvin created his harmonies," Art Stewart told me, "he'd close his eyes and say, 'Now Chuck's note would be down here,' and then do the part that Chuck Barksdale of the Moonglows used to sing."

The suite's recurrent theme, in words and music, was "When Did You Stop Loving Me, When Did I Stop Loving You," in which Marvin bitterly complained that Anna turned him over to the cops, a reference to a restraining order issued against him.

As Gaye's rage boiled, though, he realized that he was destroying himself. Filled with remorse, he addressed the issue head-on in a funky, hot-blooded song called "Anger," in which he preached one of his wiser sermons. In the name of Jesus, Marvin prayed for patience. Anger, he argued, leads only to misery and shame.

Gaye tried to put out his own fire, to turn his anger to understanding. He declared "Everybody Needs Love," citing his mother, and, even more poignantly, his own father as people who require affection.

"Time to Get It Together" was pure confession, its recitation section highly derivative of Stevie Wonder's "As" from *Songs in the Key of Life*. Openly mentioning his cocaine habit and taste for prostitutes, Marvin saw his life slipping away and, alarmed, vowed to reform.

Gaye's heart was frozen by moments of creative impotence. In supplication, he invoked his muse, symbolized in the song "Sparrow," the bird who, like the poet and singer, suffers for all humanity.

As Marvin and I listened to this tune one night, I read him the

Shelley poem "To a Skylark." "Teach me half the gladness/That thy brain must know," wrote Shelley. Gaye's lyrics were remarkably similar, though he himself had never read a line of the English poet.

"Anna's Song" brought Marvin back to the matter at hand. The scorching ballad painted exquisite pictures of an opulent, indulgent sex life. For an instant, he reflected on how she had built his career. Then suddenly all thoughts stopped. A radiant image, clear as day, came to light, a quiet afternoon in Detroit—back in the sixties—when his domestic life was not yet in shambles, a rare moment of graceful peace in which Marvin felt genuinely satiated, the sound of playing children offering him comfort.

Just as suddenly, the singer screamed with bloodcurdling anguish. "Anna!" he cried. "Anna! *Anna!*"

There was no real escape from the woman—that's the point of "A Funky Space Reincarnation." Set far in the future—2084—Marvin wrote of a time when music will transcend race. On another planet, in another lifetime, he envisioned meeting Anna at a party. He offered her a joint, space dope from Venus. They got stoned and, in a scene reminiscent of Woody Allen's *Sleeper*, made love in a space machine. Afterward, Marvin directed the other party-goers to an orgy, while he stole away with his futuristic Anna.

With allusions to *Star Wars*, the song was welcome comic relief. There were shades of George Clinton's far-out funk with Parliament and Funkadelic, though Marvin was subtler, especially in his judicious use of softly synthesized rhythms.

Gaye's good humor didn't last. Try as he might, he couldn't stop reliving the past, couldn't get Anna's threat out of his mind: "You Can Leave, But It's Gonna Cost You." He remembered a day at his sister-in-law's home when he announced that he was leaving for good—the precise moment when Anna explicitly warned him that Jan, "that young girl," would cost him his fortune.

The final song, "Falling in Love Again," belonged to Jan. For all his melancholy, Marvin concluded on a happy note, though in truth his relationship with Janis was already troubled.

Gaye hoped, however, that by putting Anna behind him, he could finally make peace with his new woman. In fact, Jan was often around the studio when he recorded *Here, My Dear*.

"When he was through and wanted Anna to hear the record," engineer Art Stewart told me, "he asked me to play it for her. She listened to it in the control room. All the time Marvin was upstairs in his loft, but he never came down. Anna just sat there and listened, didn't say much, and left."

When the record was released, *People* magazine reported she was contemplating a $5 million invasion-of-privacy suit. "I think he did it deliberately for the joy of seeing how hurt I could become," said Anna.

"Does this album invade her privacy?" Marvin replied to *People*. "I'll have to give it another listen . . . but all's fair in love and war."

The skirmishes and maneuvers involving love and money—twin causes of Marvin's misery—would escalate dramatically as time went on. Dissolving the relationship with Anna didn't help. If anything, it threw Gaye into deeper despair, even as he prepared to marry Jan, a woman whose intense beauty—whose feminine force—drove Marvin to the brink of madness and beyond.

25

DISHEARTENED
VOWS

Desperate for money, in the late summer of 1977 Gaye turned to his usual means of quick cash—a national tour. Opening in September in New York with Average White Band and Luther Vandross, Marvin had fashioned a new look for himself. According to *Billboard*, he wore "a loose diaphanous white outfit that made him look like an effeminate karate expert."

"I'd always wanted to dress up in something frilly," Marvin said, "but lacked the guts. Finally, I did what I wanted."

He also hired a new group of dancers, led by Cecil Jenkins, to augment the show. Jenkins took some of the pressure off Marvin.

"Cecil was my dancing alter ego," Gaye told me. "He did what I couldn't."

Later in October in New Orleans, after four years together and two children, Marvin Gaye married Janis Hunter.

"He had great ambivalence about it," said Curtis Shaw. "He really didn't want to marry her, not after what he went through with Anna, but he was afraid that if he didn't marry her, she'd make good on her threat to never let him see his kids. He couldn't handle that. Marvin Gaye was a man who loved his children. He had me write out a pre-nuptial agreement protecting his property, but he was afraid to show it to Jan, so he never did."

"Once we got married," Marvin remembered, "things only got worse. I saw that I'd trapped myself again, but I couldn't help it.

Jan fascinated me. I know you think I'm crazy, but go around asking other men what they'd do if their fantasy suddenly turned up as a flesh-and-blood woman. You want to play with the fantasy all the time, in a hundred ways."

He used this fantasy to keep him increasingly away from reality, and with good reason. His reality was harsh, and he made it even harsher by ignoring all warnings—from his sister, lawyer, and mother—to put his financial house in order. His back-tax bills mounted, while he spent most of his concert money on drugs, cars, and investments that tickled his fancy. He began working with a new prizefighter, Andy "Hawk" Price, whom Gaye viewed as a contender to Sugar Ray Leonard's welterweight throne.

In December, *Variety* reported that a Los Angeles superior court awarded $196,800 to four of Marvin's musicians who claimed not to have been paid for a year. Patrick Cavanaugh, once a close friend and now a former executive with Right On Productions, told the newspaper that "Gaye had failed to pay, either partially or completely, at least thirty musicians since 1973."

Marvin was usually broke in small ways as well as large. "For all the years I knew him, he never had any money on him," said Dave Simmons, his running buddy from Michigan who had moved to Los Angeles and renewed their friendship in the late seventies. "I remember once he called me to pick him up in Santa Monica because his Rolls had run out of gas and he didn't have a cent. He didn't even have a wallet with a credit card. That was Marvin. He meant no harm by it, but he naturally presumed—and he was right—that other people would pick up the tab. You wanted to help him in any way you could."

During 1978, Gaye didn't have a hit. Ironically, in this same period, the Bee Gees's *Saturday Night Fever*—heavily influenced by Gaye's feline falsetto and slick rhythms—was an international sensation, giving the music business its final surge before the great slump of the late seventies and early eighties.

Gaye's reaction was to ignore the trend and, instead, return to his earliest passion—the love ballad.

"The mistakes I made with Jan became clearer and clearer. But there was no going back. I was on the wrong road. I had dragged this poor girl along with me. I tried to get off, but I couldn't. I couldn't live with her, I couldn't live without her, so what else was there to do?"

Sing about it.

In late 1978 and early 1979, Gaye finally sang the Bobby Scott pop orchestrations he'd been saving and studying for nearly a decade.

"Suddenly," Marvin said to me, "in the midst of one of my worst depressions over Jan, I went into my studio and recorded them. I had the tracks for years, but it took me only a single night to sing all those songs . . . and a lifetime of pain to gain the wisdom."

The results are, I believe, Marvin Gaye's most moving vocal performances. In singing achingly slow ballads—"Why Did I Choose You?", "She Needs Me," "I Wish I Didn't Love You So," and "I Won't Cry No More"—he achieved the mastery of Sinatra's *Wee Small Hours* or Billie Holiday's *Lady in Satin*. Going a step further than the jazz and pop singers before him, he applied his multi-tracking technique, accompanying himself with three distinct voices, the icy beauty of which fires the soul. To hear him interpret "The Shadow of Your Smile"—altering, improving the already exquisite melody, honing harmonies in the stratosphere—is an emotional experience of gentle grandeur. His versions of "Funny" and "This Will Make You Laugh," sung with a big band, revalidated his jazz credentials.

Sadly, just when Marvin appeared to have achieved his original goal of becoming one of the great pop singers of his day, his efforts were in vain. The album was never released.

"Berry wouldn't put it out," Gaye told me, "because he didn't think it was commercial. At least that's what he said."

Given Gordy's fine ear, this is hard to believe. When it came to Marvin's relationship with Motown, you couldn't take Gaye at his word. He played an endless series of hide-and-seek, push-pull games with the company. If anything, Gordy endorsed Gaye's creative independence by releasing *Here, My Dear* at the end of 1978. If he had been interested in censorship, that would have been the record to stop.

What were Berry's feelings about these ballads? Why weren't they released? I wish I could report his side of the story, but he refused my many requests for an interview. The dispute aside, I pray that the powers that be release the album. It's a crime that the public, for whatever reasons, has been deprived of these examples of Gaye's most sensitive artistry.

Jan was the subject matter of these songs, just as she would be the woman to whom he'd sing for the rest of his life—even after they separated, even after they divorced, even after he'd sworn, for the fiftieth or five-hundredth time, that he was through with her for good. He used her to inflict pain upon himself—the more profound his suffering, the more soulful his singing.

In the midst of this melodrama, though, Marvin paused for an afternoon to sing to someone else for whom he had boundless love. In celebration of Pops Gordy's ninetieth birthday, Gaye, Stevie Wonder, Smokey Robinson, and Diana Ross formed a spirited quartet and recorded the infectious "Pops, We Love You." Released first as a single, the song was part of an album issued in 1979 after Pops had died. (The same album includes "I'll Keep My Light in the Window," a Marvin Gaye–Diana Ross duet not included in their 1973 release.)

"If Pops had been my father instead of Berry's," said Marvin, who often blamed Gay Sr. for his own failings, "maybe I could have achieved as much as Berry."

Yet for all his suspicions about Gordy, it was Berry who time and time again bailed Marvin out of trouble. At the start of 1978, for example, while Marvin was at the Super Bowl in New Orleans, marshals broke into the Marvin Gaye Recording Studios on Sunset Boulevard, leaving the doors on the sidewalk and shutting down the place because of $175,000 of unpaid back franchise taxes. According to Curtis Shaw, Gordy ordered Motown to pay the bill, thus saving the studio.

On September 20, 1978, Gaye signed a lucrative seven-year contract with the company he mistrusted, the label with which he'd been fighting for seventeen years. Marvin had earlier demanded a million-dollar bonus in cash to be put in a suitcase which he wanted to show his father. Gaye told Shaw that he planned to tell Father, "See that? That's $1 million. I just want you to know how successful I am." Motown refused. Instead they offered him $600,000 per album for his next two releases, then a cool $1 million per album after that. He took the deal, though a year and a half later he'd be looking to break the contract.

"Look," said Curtis Shaw, who negotiated these agreements,

"whatever you say about Marvin, you must remember that deep down he loved Motown. He cursed them and taunted them and drove them crazy, but he was also very, very loyal. They indulged him and spoiled him. He was like a baby who'd never been out of the crib. Motown was Marvin's crib."

On October 7, 1978, *Billboard* ran a story on two Marvin Gaye bankruptcy pleadings filed earlier in the year. His unsecured debts were estimated at nearly $7 million. He showed monthly income at $40,000 against $34,860 of monthly expenses, with $1.27 million in assets against $1.8 million in liabilities.

"My attitude toward reforming my spending sprees isn't any different from my approach to giving up blow," Marvin explained. "I'll try every once in a while. I'll even go a few days without. But after a week or so, I find myself slipping back into the old skin— maybe 'cause it's comfortable, maybe 'cause that's me."

In the midst of his money madness, there were surprisingly good times, weeks when, if you didn't know better, you'd think Marvin Gaye was the most relaxed, trouble-free man in southern California.

Dave Simmons described such a time:

"He and I were alone down in Palm Springs when the phone rang.

" 'That was Jane Fonda,' Marvin said in that smooth, easygoing voice of his. 'She wants me to model in some charity fashion show she's putting on in Beverly Hills.'

"So we drive to L.A. in my 450 SL, but when we get there, Marvin's forgotten to ask Jane where the show's supposed to be. We try the Bel Air Hotel. No show. Finally I suggest the Beverly Wilshire and sure enough, that's where it's at. It turns out Jane Fonda and Jon Voight, who've just done *Coming Home*, are hosting this thing together. We're rushed to a big dressing room filled with sissies in charge of bringing all the male stars, like Robin Williams, outfits to model.

"Well, Marvin's supposed to be getting into a suit, but he won't drop his pants. 'Not with all these fags around,' he whispers to me. 'Besides, I don't have any underwear on. Dave, go out and buy me some shorts.' So I run out and buy him a pair of jockey shorts and finally he goes off in a corner and changes.

"We head toward the stage and there's Jack Nicholson in the

wings passing around a joint and Jane introduces Marvin and every-one goes nuts. Marvin was a great model. He comes off and sud-denly there's Margaret Trudeau throwing herself at him, talkin' 'bout how she's always loved him and, oh God, is it really you, the real Marvin Gaye? This was when she was heavy into her jet-set thing. We walk out of the hotel with Margaret draped all over Marvin, and suddenly an army of photographers start popping flashlights while Marvin's smiling and, with that certain cool of his, he whispers in my ear, 'Don't look now, Dave, but we've gone international.' "

Gaye's attitude about Hollywood was still ambivalent. He com-plained about the crassness of publicity-hungry Hollywood, but, from time to time, he'd contradict himself, even appearing on game shows like *Hollywood Squares*. Generally, though, Marvin was re-luctant to do television, an attitude which hurt his career. He com-plained that the bright lights distracted him and that talk shows were interested only in superficial chatter. The same went for glam-orous, high-profile parties.

"I like to stay away from the 'in crowd,' " he told me, "because when I finally do decide to appear, I'm something of a novelty. They don't take me for granted. Never, never have I given the beautiful people the idea that I need them."

There were exceptions—Barbra Streisand being one.

In this same period, he dined with Barbra and her then boyfriend and producer Jon Peters.

"It was a most cordial evening," Marvin told me. "And, in my own way, I made it clear that I'd like to sing with her. I've always considered her voice a gorgeous instrument. Besides, she could deliver me that pop ballad market.

"She was extremely charming and complimentary, most willing to do a duet. Peters asked that my lawyer, Curtis Shaw, call him the next day around noon. Well, Curtis called at two o'clock, and Peters blew his top. 'How can you treat Miss Streisand with such disrespect?' he wanted to know. Naturally that sort of attitude didn't go over well with me. I figure *I'm* the one who should be treated with respect. Besides, she was more interested in sending flowers to Neil Diamond, which is how I really got shot out of the saddle."

Marvin expressed a similar interest in singing duets with Aretha

Franklin. "That," he explained, "would be strictly for historical purposes." Unfortunately, nothing ever came out of his wish. Like so many of Marvin's designs, the plan was lost in the chaos of his daily life.

"Marvin was a traditional star," Curtis Shaw said, "in his need to get top billing. For example, in 1978 I had an idea for him to do a live concert from Havana broadcast on international TV. Given his attitude about the U.S. government, I knew he'd like the idea, and he did. If I could arrange the whole thing, he told me, he'd give me a percentage of the gross. So I flew to Washington and met with Castro's brother. After long negotiations, it turned out we could put on a show, but it'd have to include people like Diana Ross, Donna Summer, Quincy Jones, and the Brothers Johnson. To make it plausible, they'd have to share the billing. When Marvin heard that, he called the whole thing off. 'It's either Marvin Gaye Live from Cuba,' he said, 'or nothing.' So it was nothing."

For all his surface cool and confidence, though, Gaye grew more anxious as 1978 came to a disastrous end.

"I no longer had any choice about performing," he said. "All my other money was so funny that the only real bread I could count on was cash being handed me by promoters."

He hit the road in the fall, playing to less-than-capacity crowds. It'd been a year and a half since his last hit, "Got to Give It Up," and he found himself struggling for the strength to carry on. In November, he collapsed on stage in Chattanooga, Tennessee, and was hospitalized for a few days. The usual reason—"physical exhaustion"—was given. Was it drugs?

"Whenever I completely crash," Marvin told me, "it's always a combination of things. You can't blame it on drugs alone. Drugs are as much a part of my day as the weather, so you might as well blame it on the weather. It usually involves some fight I just had with Jan. I'm always half-hoping she'll feel sorry for me and rush to my bedside. I don't like crashing 'cause I hate hospitals. For me to wind up in a hospital is bad—it means there's no other place I can find any rest."

At the end of the year he was back in Los Angeles, just in time for the release of *Here, My Dear*.

"I tried to keep a happy face," he said, "but it was impossible. Jan had filed for divorce, though I talked her out of it time and again. We'd come together only to break apart, and each time it was more painful. We were making each other sick, but I guess I needed that sickness."

Marvin's life would continue its downhill slide. Gaye was a man who tested the depths, wanting to see how far down he could go, needing the challenge to rise. But that was only a partial explanation. Another side of Marvin—the masochistic side—was simply out of control. As his mother told me, "My boy couldn't take care of himself. He needed someone to take care of him."

Gaye's stubbornness, though, forced him to direct his own destiny. He couldn't listen to anyone else, at least not for long. Unable to tolerate independent opinion, he surrounded himself with yes men. He was a prince who required the constant reassurance of his court.

A day off for basketball with the boys. An afternoon at the beach with his kids. A weekend in Palm Springs. There were times when he recovered his equilibrium, when his rare charm was as radiant as a California sunset. But the pressure of his past kept his present filled with fear. And his future—ominous and dark—was locked in the tight embrace of unyielding fate.

PART
THREE

26
CLOSING IN

The final five years of Marvin Gaye's life were tumultuous. Trying to avoid his own traps, even while he was setting new ones, he soon became a man without a home, without a woman, and finally without a country. Having lost everything—his family and fortune—he found a way back, only to turn his miraculous recovery into the final, tragic confirmation of his worst fear: that he was doomed from the start. But before the day he was devoured by his demon, Gaye would raise some hell of his own.

The first ten months of 1979 were Marvin Gaye's last period in America before he fled the country for three years. The action leading up to his flight was fast and furious, a wicked combination of money hassles, romantic heartaches, and recording dilemmas. Disaster was closing in.

Marvin and Jan were getting along no better, even though she accompanied him to his fortieth birthday party, an especially happy occasion. Gaye was gratified that Smokey Robinson, Berry Gordy, and Stevie Wonder attended. Yet he began his fifth decade with great longing.

"I'd always thought," he said, "that at forty I would have pulled off the Sinatra bit and been able to call my own shots. But there I was, miserable as hell, with everyone telling me that my new record was a total downer."

After equivocating for nearly a year, Gaye had finally released *Here, My Dear* at the end of 1978. His worst fears came true: the reviews were hostile, and, even worse, sales were poor.

"Pretentious is too good a word for this clutter," said *The Village Voice*.

"A soap opera set to music," wrote *Stereo Review*, "but with limited action based on a predictable plot."

The most vicious attack was Vivien Goldman's from *Melody Maker* in London. She called the work "banal meanderings" and then, interviewing Gaye on the phone in Los Angeles, wrote that "there's something about Marvin I don't trust."

She also asked him why he didn't credit the musicians on the record.

"I didn't cut the album under normal union procedures," Gaye answered, "and I'll have union problems enough without listing them (the players) on the sleeve. It's mostly the musicians who played with me in London and on the road . . . like Bugsy Wilcox and Fernando Harkness. That's enough names, isn't it? The musicians are all really pissed with me that they're not on the credits. . . . In fact, one of them's suing me. He says I stole his ideas for "Anger" and "A Funky Space Reincarnation." But he *volunteered* his chords. I didn't *steal* them," Marvin claimed as he often did when, in other such cases, his sole authorship was questioned.

The one bright spot surrounding the album was Robert Palmer's review in *The New York Times*. "*Here, My Dear* may not be a commercial blockbuster," Palmer wrote, "but only because it is too rich, too demanding. At its best it is something much more valuable than potential platinum. It is an inventory of the whole expressive range of black popular music at the end of the seventies, a testing of limits, and an affirmation of musical values. It is Mr. Gaye's personal statement . . . of his own musical possibilities. It is flawed, but much of it is simply brilliant."

Palmer, however, represented a slim minority. Dennis Hunt expressed the majority view in the *Los Angeles Times*, writing that "the album should be a potent, cohesive statement about the trials of romance but it just fizzles."

Hunt's review motivated me to write an angry defense, in January 1979, which the paper published. Marvin saw the letter and we met shortly afterward.

At his Sunset studio, minutes after we were introduced, Gaye asked engineer Art Stewart and me to join hands with him in meditation. "Think on God's infinite love, God's infinite love," Marvin whispered, "just that one thought and that one thought only." A few minutes later he added, "We should do this every day with our loved ones, our wives, parents, and children. Stop whatever you're doing in the middle of the day and sit and be silent. Meditate on God's infinite love."

There was no order to his life. Like a jazz improvisation, he made it up as he went along, hour by hour—where to go, what to do. There was no discipline, no telling what his mood might be. Ebullient, warm, withdrawn, or witty, Marvin was either a perfectly relaxed host or a bundle of frazzled nerves. His need to talk was excessive, and he continually sought sympathy and friendship. The next five years would see him increasingly dislocated and confused.

He began a new record. The title changed day by day, but finally he settled on *Love Man*. The critics of *Here, My Dear* and the album's poor commercial showing had convinced him it was time to make money again. He worried that the great soul stars of the sixties, his own cronies—Wilson Pickett, James Brown, Aretha Franklin— were struggling in the seventies. Some of them were without record deals. Others were disillusioned and bitter. Gradually, Gaye's hotly competitive nature was driving him back to work.

"I'm tired of watching Teddy and Peabo and Michael Henderson get all the glory," he said. "Then there's this new cat that people in the industry are talking about. Prince. Doesn't he know *I'm* supposed to be the only prince? They say he's sexy and has a high voice that sounds like mine. All these boys are romancing my fans, and I don't like it. I'm getting my fans back. I'm doing a straight-ahead make-out party album."

The music he created, though, was anything but straight-ahead. Stronger than his competitiveness, stronger than his concern for falling out of fashion, was his preoccupation with Janis. In the first months of 1979, they went through a series of nasty fights. Jan had left him again and his songs revolved around getting her back. One was simply called "Come Back, Baby." He argued, in lyrics never released, that if God could forgive him, so could she. "Life's a Game of Give and Take" was another one of those unpublished songs in which he described his mistakes and inability to live without her.

Janis came back, but only to be sent off again—by Marvin himself, who continued encouraging her romances, thus creating the pain he felt he deserved.

"It's ego," he told me, "that destroys us all." And with that, he wrote the extraordinary "Ego Tripping Out," actually released as a single in 1979 but soon withdrawn from the market. Motown claimed neither the disc jockeys nor the public liked it. Unfortunately, it never appeared on an album and is now out of print. The song expressed some of Marvin's most poignant wisdom, dramatizing his struggle with his self-centeredness, his reliance on "toot" and "smoke," and his enormous desire to go only "one way," the way of God.

Yet his fears overwhelmed his faith. When, for instance, money demands again forced him back on the road in 1979, he avoided flying by buying himself a bus.

John Henry Cammon took a 1966 MC 5 Challenger Motor Home and converted it into a customized luxury cruiser. The bus seated fourteen, slept seven, with a galley, kitchenette, shower, and separate bedroom for Marvin. Big John, a large, gregarious gentleman, was hired as driver and confidante. The rest of the congenial crew included Ken Grant, Gaye's personal photographer, and George Odell, better known as Gorgeous George, emcee, clothes designer, tailor, and on-the-road cook. Invited to travel with the group, I was amazed by what I saw.

The bus was filled with dozens of cassette tapes filled with songs written by Gaye—tapes scattered on the floor, left on the window sills, thrown into a big pouch. Some of the tapes were labeled: "Ditty for Miles Davis," "Song for Peggy Lee." One was called "Oh Lord, Why Can't All Niggers Sing like Charley Pride?" with Marvin wailing in a mock country accent. Another was a funk groove for James Brown.

Disturbed by his lack of organization, I asked Marvin whether he wanted to put the songs in some kind of order. No, he wasn't interested. Well, did he at least plan to get them to the artists for whom they were written?

"No," Gaye answered. "If one day I meet Miles and he happens to say, 'Hey, Marv, you don't have a tune for me, do you, man?' I'll be able to say, 'Matter of fact, Miles, I wrote something for you the other day, baby.' But I'd never try to hustle the songs. For someone like me, that'd be degrading."

But what about the worth of these songs? Wasn't he interested, like Stevie, in building his catalogue?

"I've always been so broke that I've had to sell my publishing up front for the cash," Gaye explained. "Berry owns my tunes. I get my writer's share, but I hardly own any copyrights. Stevie's been a lot smarter about that than me."

"Kiss my ass, Teddy Pendergrass!" screamed an excited woman seated in the front row as Gaye, in the midst of his show, smiled at her. "I love you, Marvin! I love only you!"

This was still 1979, at the Circle Star Theater in San Carlos, California, where he performed for impresario Don Jo, the man who became one of Gaye's major backers during the final eighteen months of his life.

That night, introducing Marvin on stage, Gorgeous George, whose handlebar moustache had him looking like General Custer, grabbed the mike and screamed, *I want everyone to stand up! Stand up! Time to introduce a young man that needs no introduction! This young man is one of the most creative entertainers in the world! This young man doesn't even know how many records he's sold!*"

"I love when George says that," Marvin told me later, "because it's so true."

Marvin's stage movements were mannered. He was clearly dependent upon the presence of Cecil Jenkins, who swirled, swung, and swished about him.

After the beat subsided, Gaye sighed and said, "In my heart, I feel like dancing; right now, I feel like dancing. Is there anyone out there who would dance with me?"

Marvin took the woman Gorgeous George had found among the many screaming women and held her, slow-danced with her, whispering in her ear, dipping her back into her dreams, releasing her to the sounds of even shriller shrieks.

For all its sexiness, though, the show was shopworn. Just as he hadn't scored in 1978, Marvin had no current hits in 1979. Bravely, he sang a medley from *Here, My Dear* to lackluster response. He threw his sweaty silk handkerchiefs to the audience as dozens of women scrambled for them. In the past, the women would have numbered in the thousands.

"Without a hit in this business," Marvin said later, "you're flying at half-mast. Sinatra can live on his legend. He doesn't need hits. But I still do. After all these years, I'm still out here on the rhythm-and-blues circuit."

The show was a sad echo of the vitality of Gaye's former self.

"You should have been on the rest of the tour," Big John told me, referring to Marvin's last cross-country excursion before leaving America behind.

"We drove to Denver and Milwaukee and New York and Chicago—all over," said Cammon. "Marvin could relax on the bus. It was his method of getting away. One time, I remember, he got on the CB and started talking, telling people that he was Marvin Gaye. When they asked him to prove it, he started singing. Well, they sure-enough believed him then, and soon we were leading a caravan of thirty cars and trucks. This went on for a hundred miles. Finally he had me pull over at a truck stop, and everyone stopped along with us. He broke open a half-dozen bottles of champagne, and we had a beautiful party.

"Another time Marvin was driving. Sometimes I'd make him drive, just 'cause it cooled him out. He was speeding and a cop stopped us. Marvin being Marvin, he had no license or identification. He told the cop who he was, but the cop wanted proof. 'Don't you have your name on something?' the cop asked. Marvin told me to reach in the glove compartment. 'Not that,' I whispered to Marvin, realizing that he wanted me to show the cop another speeding ticket he'd gotten. 'See there,' Marvin said, handing the ticket to the cop, 'that's me. Marvin Gaye.' The cop looked at the ticket and laughed. 'You'd have to be Marvin Gaye to pull something like this. Just sign an autograph for my wife and go on.' "

The long months spent on the road—out of touch, with no phone—was the perfect escape from Hollywood, from a world about to close in on him.

"There would be days, even whole weeks," said Ken Grant, who was there for the entire trip, "when he'd never even check in with L.A. He didn't want to know what was happening. If he didn't feel like performing, he'd just tell John to drive on. He must have missed a dozen engagements on that tour. If we were on the highway for a long while and he wanted to party, he'd have John pull into the next city. We'd drive to a disco, tell them who was in the bus, and the owner would usually empty out the club except for a handful of people. Marvin enjoyed some women on that tour, but not many."

When he returned to Los Angeles, he labored on his album, trying to please Motown, who reminded him that they needed his "product" immediately. He still hadn't paid his federal taxes and was months behind in his alimony and child support payments to Anna and Janis. Jan had moved out of their Hidden Hills home and taken the kids to her mother's in Hermosa Beach.

He went down there to visit them but wound up at Midway Hospital in Los Angeles.

What had happened?

"Cops beat me up. Beat me up bad."

In his hospital room, half a dozen young nurses surrounded his bed. Marvin amused them with show business stories. Later, he told me that Jan was afraid he was going to kidnap their kids, so she called the cops. The police asked him to leave, and he wouldn't. A fight ensued. His left eye was blackened and his cheek bruised.

"I'm proud of these wounds," he said. "I took my blows like a man."

An hour later, his mother came to take him home.

A week later, his new album was still in disarray. Gaye had chosen a cover shot taken by Ken Grant. The photo showed Marvin in the midst of a frantic dance move. When I pointed out that Otis Redding had used the same title—*Love Man*—for an LP issued ten years ago, Marvin was annoyed. "He was one love man," he said, "I'm another. The title stays."

The theme of the music, though, was not the party motif Marvin had promised, but rather further lamentations about Jan. One song, "Life Is Now in Session," openly confessed that for the rest of his life he would fantasize about her making love to other men. He still couldn't get her off his mind.

Gaye was convinced that Jan was in love with Rick James, a rising Motown star. Slick Rick hung around Gaye's studio a great deal and called his idol Uncle Marvin.

"I hate being referred to like that," said Gaye. "It makes me sound ancient." Marvin was also jealous that James' music was scoring with the young market, and Marvin's wasn't.

Furthermore, for his early successes Rick had borrowed Gaye's funk spirit, and his right-hand man as well. Art Stewart co-produced James' first hit records, such as "You and I," which burst on the scene during the very period Marvin desperately needed a hit of his own. Gaye's current songs were sounding too diffuse, too cerebral, too personal for the Motown people. Making slight alterations, he invited a few of the corporate executives over to his studio to hear his efforts during the summer of 1979.

Gaye kept them waiting an hour before he arrived, his face coated with a thick, white substance. He said nothing about it as he played the most current version of *Love Man*. The response was tepid, but he insisted that they sit through a full session of his love ballads. Comments were favorable but there were no commitments. When the executives left I asked him why, in the name of reason, was he in white face? Was it just to upset the execs?

"No. I'm going to the Donna Summer concert in a few hours," he said. "When I have an important date, I keep this crap on my face all day. When I take it off, my skin glows. I literally shine. It's really quite effective. I expect Donna to fall for me tonight. Wouldn't we make a wonderful couple?"

Marvin's dreams of being kept by a rich woman were never more than that. Even after the emotional debacle of their duets, Gaye claimed that he and Diana Ross would marry—the princess and prince uniting their power. (Actually, that might not have been a total delusion. On Ross's 1984 *Swept Away* album, released six months after Marvin's death, she sings the Lionel Richie–written "Missing You," "dedicated to my beloved Marvin Gaye," with enough fervor to convince you of her love.)

These, though, were fairy-tale loves, fabricated relationships in which Marvin envisioned himself being bailed out by a wealthy woman. Here, in his wildest fantasies, he became the ultimate prostitute, saving his life by turning a trick. But he was still too proud, too shy, and too afraid of rejection to actually make a play. He saved his real-life passions for hopeless situations—Anna and Jan. Toy as he might with promiscuity, Gaye's relationships were anything but superficial. With his wives, managers, family, and friends, the emotional bonds were deep, though in the end he'd find a way to hurt those he loved most.

Meanwhile, he was scrambling—for a hit record, a way to escape this love dream of Janis, now six years old, which had turned into a nightmare. He saw himself slipping and, even worse, realized that he still had a long way to go before reaching bottom.

"I was hanging onto the ropes," said Gaye, describing his last months in America. "I was punch-drunk. How many blows can a man take? I didn't know how to react anymore. I kept telling myself that good news was around the corner, but there wasn't anything around the corner except some big IRS dude ready to mug me. I was tired of getting beat up."

Marvin liked feeling sorry for himself; he confused love and pain so hopelessly that a part of his psyche still sought the beatings his father had inflicted upon him as a boy. As the eighties began, he pushed himself into a prolonged period of severe self-pity, extending his problems, credit, and credibility until, at least in his mind, only one option remained—escape.

In the studio, I watched him try to complete *Love Man*, but it wasn't to be. "This letter is to your heart," he sang in one of his unreleased songs. "Jan," he whispered into the mike, "I'm going to be loving you as long as there's breath in my body." Like a character in a novel, he was fixated on a woman who was real and unreal at the same time.

One night I mentioned Somerset Maugham's novel *Of Human Bondage* and the central character's inability to stay away from a woman who makes him miserable. Marvin wanted to hear the plot in detail. He was engrossed until I described the happy ending. "I don't believe it," he said. "A man who lived that miserably would die the same way."

In the first half of 1979, despite his self-imposed personal suffering, he remained a dedicated writer, devoting himself to his art, genuinely trying to make musical sense out of his scattered life. Watching him at the studio, his recording technique was a wonder to behold.

He executed all his vocals seated at the console, modulating his voice with extreme subtlety, singing effortlessly. "I have this theory that anyone can sing. If you can talk, you can sing."

Marvin's voice could almost be seen as a thin stream of light between his mouth and the mike. With remarkably little exertion, he could sound loud, gruff, pained or powerful. He could sing on his back. Often he sang reclining on a couch, his favorite piece of furniture. "If I could," he said, "I'd spread myself out on a couch, have them wheel the couch on stage, and sing like that."

Because he was a perfectionist, recording his vocals was a laborious process. He'd sing a phrase, listen to it, and reject all but a tiny section. "Punching in" is what musicians call it—a taping technique which allows you to build your performance note by note, stopping as often as you like to redo whatever strikes you as wrong. Ray Charles, Marvin's idol, records in exactly the same manner. Every grunt and groan, which sound so natural to the listener, is selected scrupulously, like a painter mixing colors.

Gaye's trademark self-harmonies were created with the naturalness of a simple sigh. He wove his voices, one upon another, with the skill of a medieval craftsman. His tapestry of sound, his musical universe, was born of an aural vision of extraordinary sweep.

He heard himself objectively, which made him his own best producer, a rarity among singers. To some extent, he still had some objectivity about his emotional battles, an objectivity which allowed him to laugh at himself in the midst of murderous pressure.

He often sought relief in pornography—video tapes, magazines, even old-fashioned picture postcards. He also created musical pornography of his own. His dirty songs were usually funny. "Dem Niggers Are Savage in the Sack," recorded in 1979, was a comical investigation of the cultural myths of blacks' potent sexuality, a song expressing Marvin's own fear of being unable to live up to the legend. Naturally the tune was never released, though he loved to shock studio guests by playing it.

Gaye always saw himself split in half, a picture he would soon realize on the cover of an album which, in 1979, he hadn't yet conceived—the good Marvin and the bad Marvin, the angel and the devil, the masochist and the messiah. For Gaye, it was all or nothing.

By fall, trying to finalize his new record, trying to make money on the road, he was exhausted. He had honored none of his major financial commitments and was growing increasingly hostile and paranoid about Motown, the federal government, Anna, and Jan— the four forces he saw as aggressive enemies.

"The bankruptcy court was going crazy," Curtis Shaw said, "and I couldn't get Marvin to pay anyone anything. I couldn't even get him to hire an accountant. They were about to close down the works—his studio, his estate, every last asset he had."

In an effort to reason with Marvin, Shaw made several trips in 1979 to catch him on tour.

"Houston was a good example of what Marvin was going through," the lawyer said, "and the way he needed to be treated. He was booked into the Kool Jazz Festival at the Astrodome and still getting $50,000 a night. Well, when I arrived in town everyone was excited. 'Marvin's depressed,' they started telling me, 'and he won't sing tonight.' I went to his hotel room where he'd just fought with Jan on the phone. 'I'm not singing tonight,' he said. He was wiped out. Knowing Marvin, I didn't argue. Instead, I went to my room and called a local disc jockey I knew. I asked if he could get a basketball team together to challenge Gaye's team, which was made up of Marvin and the cats in the band. My man loved the idea and said he'd do it. I went back to Marvin's room where he was still moping and I turned on the radio. Sure enough my friend was on the air, saying how he'd heard that Marvin Gaye wasn't much of a round-ball player. 'Hey Marvin,' I said, 'this cat's talking about you.' Marvin's ears perked up. He loved the dare and the next thing I knew he was down at some gym playing in front of five thousand kids. He had a ball. I never saw him so energized. On the way back he stopped at the NAACP convention, which happened to be in town, and sang a few songs for free. On stage that night, he was sensational."

During the same tour, he shared the bill with the Temptations, his colleagues from early Motown days. One story revealed how Marvin often distanced himself from his cronies.

"Before the show," remembered Glenn Leonard, then a relatively new member of the Temptations, "word came down that Marvin wanted to see the Temps. I was excited because he's one of my favorites. But when we got to his hotel room, we were asked to wait in the hallway. It was very much like waiting for a prince. I didn't mind at first, but after a long, long while, we just got up and left."

Just as Gaye could be inconsiderate, he was capable of great generosity. According to Curtis Shaw, he once gave a man he'd just met $10,000 to keep the guy from committing suicide. "Suicide," Gaye often said, "is a terrible waste of precious life." That was the good Marvin speaking. But the bad Marvin was undermining every move, ignoring reality, ingesting larger and larger quantities of cocaine, turning love into hate, purity into perversion, trust into jealousy.

In spite of it all, he held out hope. "Once my man wins the crown," said Gaye, "everything's going to be all right."

He was referring to his fighter, Andy Price, who, on September

28, 1979, in front of a national ABC TV audience, took on welterweight champ Sugar Ray Leonard.

Marvin had Big John drive Mother, Marvin III, and him to Las
Vegas on the bus. Diana Ross was headlining at Caesar's Palace,
the same locale as the fight. Berry Gordy flew in for the festivities.
Gaye viewed the proceedings as a moment of personal triumph;
this was his comeback.

"I'd trained two other fighters," the singer said, his left eye still
puffy from the cop's punch on the beach, "and they both got whipped
bad. Each time I'd put my heart into them—they were really *me*
up there fighting—but now I was sure that with Andy I'd found
a winner."

The night before the bout, Marvin and Mother attended Diana's
show, which was taped for a TV special. Ross introduced Marvin
and Mrs. Gay and, during the audience sing-along section of "Reach
Out and Touch," Diana asked Marvin to croon a couple of lines.
He did so reluctantly. "Actually," he told me later, "I was dying
for her to ask me on stage and do a duet on 'All for One,' my all-
time favorite Ashford and Simpson song. But Diana's funny about
sharing the spotlight, especially with me."

Considering the trouble they had recording duets, Diana had
good reason to be cautious with Marvin.

Minutes before the fight the next night, Howard Cosell told a
nationwide audience that expectations for Marvin Gaye's fighter
were high. This could be the surprise upset of Sugar Ray's otherwise remarkable career. Marvin was feeling anxious, confident
but concerned about sitting in the front row next to Berry, an ex-
boxer who had proven himself in the ring, and Diana, a fight fan
herself—they, the very people who needed to know that Marvin
Gaye was still a champ.

Beyond ego, it was also a question of money.

"If Price could win," said Gaye, "I was looking at millions of
dollars in future revenues. With one blow, I could win the world's
respect and clean up my whole financial mess. People said I couldn't
do it; well, that night I was going to show them I could. This was
going to be my knock-out punch."

The punch came, but from Sugar Ray, not Price.

"Andy was lost out there," said Dave Simmons, who as Marvin's
guest, sat next to Price's mother during the fight. "All the lights
and glitter and glamour of Vegas got to him. He was in shock.

Sugar came out there and hit him and hit him and hit him and kept hitting him until he crumbled."

Leonard made it look easy, knocking out Price in two minutes and fifty-four seconds in the first round.

Marvin absorbed every last punishing punch. He was devastated, depressed beyond hope. The $40,000 purse for Price—as opposed to Sugar Ray's $300,000—didn't come close to solving Marvin's financial problems. It was hardly compensation for the blow to his ego. In the midst of this mood, he had to perform. He had promised to sing before the main event—the Ernie Shavers–Larry Holmes heavyweight championship fight—which followed Leonard-Price. On national television, his dress shirt open at the collar, his tie pulled down, his sloped eyes half-closed and filled with disappointment and hurt, he delivered a soul-searching rendition of the national anthem, turning a hymn of hope into a cry of despair.

Cosell complimented Marvin's pipes, but no praise could mitigate Gaye's blues. His best bet had been beaten down. This was to be the turning point, the miracle. Instead, in Marvin's mind he had experienced the most visible and spectacular fiasco of his public life. How much more, he asked himself, could a man take?

The final blow, though, didn't come from a boxer, but from a singer. It happened shortly after Marvin sang at the Black Radio Exclusive concert in Los Angeles, where Michael Jackson patiently waited outside Gaye's dressing room for an opportunity to shake his hand.

"Jan ran off with Teddy Pendergrass," Marvin told me. "I set myself up for it, just like I set myself up for getting beat by Sugar Ray. But I didn't realize what it would do to me. I couldn't take it. I became sick, seriously sick. This was supposed to be the end of a long, bad period, but it was just the beginning."

27

TROPICAL NIGHTMARE

From the winter of 1979 until the summer of 1980, Marvin Gaye lived in Hawaii—mysteriously, reclusively, caught in a state of chronic depression. There he tried to kill himself with a cocaine overdose and also came close to murdering Jan.

"Death was much on my mind," he said. "It seemed the only way out. But forcing death upon yourself is a sin against God. I tried, but I couldn't go all the way. God had other work for me to do."

Gaye initially went over on tour for the Norby Walters Agency. There were a few concerts in Hawaii in early November, then three weeks' worth of dates in Tokyo and Osaka, where Marvin took Mother and brother Frankie along for moral support.

"His spirits seemed good in Japan," said Cecil Jenkins, who worked the tour as Gaye's lead dancer. "He was so relaxed in Tokyo he lit a joint right on the street. Our Japanese guides went crazy. Man, you just don't do that over there. They'll haul you in. But you know Marvin. He just smiled and took another toke."

Back in Los Angeles, billboards advertised a Marvin Gaye New Year's Eve show at $100 a head. But Marvin never made the date. After Japan, he returned to Hawaii, this time going to Maui where he met Jan, who was no longer traveling with Teddy Pendergrass, and Nona and Bubby.

He couldn't face Los Angeles and the forces moving against him.

His Hidden Hills home and studio were shut down, while his family scrambled to save the furniture and recording equipment. Federal agents put everything else under lock and key. Gaye's entire empire collapsed. Depending upon his mood when you asked him, Marvin described the loss at somewhere between four and eight million dollars. All gone.

"Norby Walters wanted to book Marvin over in Europe," Curtis Shaw said, "but it turned out that Jeffrey Kruger from England had an option on Marvin's next European tour that had been arranged back in '76 by Stephen Hill. That's something I didn't even know. Marvin never told me."

Kruger had flown to Honolulu on November 8, where, with Shaw present, he made plans for Marvin to work Europe in early 1980. Later Gaye canceled. "It was apparent when I visited him again in January," Kruger told me, "that Marvin was in no shape to go anywhere. He was very, very ill."

"I felt like I was in a cowboy movie," said Gaye. "The sheriff and all his deputies were after me with their big guns, and I had to get out of Dodge.

"I wanted Jan to stay with me in Hawaii, I wanted her gone. Here I was, on an island paradise in the most beautiful spot in the world, with no one around, no one to be jealous of, and all the time we needed to work the thing out. But her thing with Teddy was still fresh on my mind and all we did was fight and scream and scratch at each other. The island paradise turned out to be hell. I had a knife so close to her heart that I thought I was dreaming. Oh, it was so close! I wanted to kill her. I almost did. I wanted to kill myself, but I didn't have the guts."

When Jan returned to America, she took only her daughter Nona with her. She and Marvin decided that four-year-old Bubby would remain in Hawaii with his father.

Still, Gaye was even more depressed and lonely.

"In one hour I snorted up a full ounce of pure coke and knew I was dead. I called Mother to tell her. But God wasn't ready to take me. I was saved that day, only to suffer the next."

In the early part of 1980, Gaye sent for his mother to help him care for Bubby.

"Marvin asked me to bring two diamonds he had given me," Mrs. Gay told me. "That's how broke he was. I did as he asked. The diamonds were worth $6000, but I don't think this pawnbroker gave Marvin more than $2000 or $3000. Anyway, we used that money to get an apartment and live. Marvin had tried to borrow money from some of his celebrity friends like Smokey, Little Stevie, and Famous Amos. But they turned him down. Motown wouldn't give him anything because he hadn't finished his record. Some members of his fan club and a few women who used to work for him were sweet enough to send checks for $200 or $300. But it was still a sad, sad time."

"I'd given up," Gaye said. "The problems were too big for me. I just wanted to be left alone to blow my brains away with high-octane toot. It would be a slow but relatively pleasant death, certainly less messy than a gun."

After a six-week visit, Mrs. Gay returned to Los Angeles in March. In April, when Ken Grant, Gaye's photographer, arrived, Marvin hadn't snapped out of it yet.

"When I arrived in Maui," Grant told me, "I wasn't sure how I'd go about finding Marvin. We'd been arguing over money for a tour book I'd prepared for him, and he wanted me to come over and discuss it, but I had no address. Soon as I got off the plane, though, these three pretty girls spotted my Marvin Gaye T-shirt and asked me whether I wanted to see Marvin. 'Sure,' I said, and they took me right to him. He and Bubby and Fleecy, Marvin's man, were living in a bread van parked by the edge of a cliff overlooking the ocean, not far from this luxury hotel. I heard it was a bus or a motor home, but man, it was nothing but a funky old bread van! We all slept inside."

It was a testimony to Marvin's princely nature that even in his most impoverished condition, he managed to employ an aide—his slick sidekick Fleecy Joe James from the L.A. Sunset-studio days—to run errands and help care for Bubby.

"I was basically staying on the beach," Marvin remembered. "You can do that in Hawaii. The weather's perfect, and you can just live off the land. Those tropical breezes kept me sane. The fresh smell of the sea, ripe pineapples, all kinds of exotic fruits, morning dips in the warm ocean—if you're going to be a bum, Maui's the place. I needed to get away from the world to regain my strength. This was as good an escape as any."

"Marvin could never escape," said Grant. "Women came through the bushes looking for him. Banker's wives were inviting him to luaus. But he didn't want any part of them. He was withdrawing from everyone. Far as sex goes, he didn't seem at all interested. The wildest thing he did was go around in this robe with a dildo apparatus strapped to his waist."

Impotence continued to plague him. "Cocaine," Marvin told me, "is said to stimulate sex. It can. But if you get into another groove, if you get hung up about getting hard, the more coke you snort, the longer you stay soft. It's a vicious cycle that can drive you crazy."

"Marvin's routine over there," Ken recalled, "was really something. Just after getting up in the morning, he'd take a good shot of this stomp-down gut-rot whiskey, then smoke a fat joint, then snort some coke. And that's just how he *began* the day. In the afternoon he'd be with Bubby. He loved that boy. They'd swim or walk along the beach, picking shells, napping under trees. One day Marvin and I went over to Haleakala, this incredible volcano, where we picked wild psilocybin mushrooms. We tripped for hours, just wandering over the island, looking out over the water.

"By the time I was there a week, we still hadn't resolved our money dispute. Marvin liked people to think he was broke, but I knew better. Right in that bread van, with my own eyes I saw a letter from a Hawaiian bank offering him $100,000 whenever he needed it. Marvin Gaye had access to big money until the day he died. The man was always in control. It amused him to make people think otherwise, but don't be fooled. Marvin was brilliant. He was always pulling the strings."

Marvin needed money for more than himself, Anna, Jan, and his children. He was still supporting Mother, the single responsibility he embraced with more conscientiousness than any other. "Since the day he left Washington, D.C., as a young man," Mrs. Gay told me, "two weeks never passed when Marvin didn't call. A month never passed when he didn't send money."

"You'd think," Gaye said, "that when I was so sick Father might figure out a way to help. No chance. The man who thought I'd grow up to become a bum was still living off this bum's royalties."

For years Marvin had played around the edges of a bum fantasy which he was finally realizing in Hawaii—no jobs, no demands, no responsibilities. Later he'd romanticize this period of his life and view it as bold experimentation with the limits of experience, describing himself as a "gypsy with allegiances to no country. To avoid boredom, I'm open to different lifestyles."

In more candid moments, though, Gaye described his Hawaiian exile more accurately as "one long nervous breakdown." In truth, he barely stumbled through each day. He took his assortment of nerve-racking fears and gathered them into one metaphor which he called the "end of everything"—the end of his world, the end of all humanity.

"Revelations," he said, "is the book in the bible Father stresses most. It's the book I've studied most carefully. It contains the one script we'll never be able to undo—the final showdown, the day when it all comes down. With that kind of knowledge up in your face, it's hard not to go crazy."

Marvin came close, but didn't go completely crazy in Hawaii. In fact, he still proved resourceful as a fighter against his own self-destructiveness. He survived his attempt at suicide. He stopped himself from murdering Jan. He managed to do some major work, at least in its preliminary stages.

Slowly trying to put himself together, Gaye sent for some of his musicians and moved with them over to the northern end of the island of Oahu to a two-bedroom apartment in Kuilima. There they started recording and rehearsing the upcoming European tour in June that Gaye had promised Jeffrey Kruger. Marvin described his mood as "still filthy and foul."

"I had to do something for money," Marvin said, "but I also had a deeper obligation—to the truth. Motown wasn't giving me a cent 'cause they were yelling how they'd spent a fortune on the *Love Man* cover and here I was holed up in Hawaii telling them that the love man was dead. He was. The love man was me and I needed to stop that shit. No matter how much money Motown would give me to release *Love Man*, I couldn't do it. I needed to get my mind off Janis and all the agony we were putting each other through. So I started working on something else—a new album with a new concept—and suddenly I saw how silly I'd been. Who needed another record moanin' and bitchin' 'bout some woman? Why did I have to regain my throne as the sex king? Who cared about competing with Michael Jackson and Cecil Jenkins? Look what was happening in the world. I had a message to spread. I had my theme."

At the end of the seventies, Marvin Gaye returned to the political consciousness he had abandoned during the decade following *What's Going On*. The issue, which had been mentioned in that suite, had suddenly moved to the center of Marvin's music. The threat of nuclear destruction became his burning concern.

"I had to give a warning," said Gaye. "I had to write about it, sing it, prophesy. I saw it coming—I'd seen it coming for twenty years—but now it was staring me in the face."

Slowly over the next year, Marvin took the basic tracks from *Love Man* and reshaped them into a work of startlingly different dimensions. The more troubled he grew, the more entangled his personal problems, the more philosophical his music. Again, he used his songs to save himself, this time turning his attention from an obsession which threatened to destroy him—the woman he couldn't control—to an obsession which threatened to destroy the earth—nuclear power.

Gaye twisted his suffering into song. Symbolically, he was excited by the sight of his own blood. He still viewed himself as a Jesus figure, someone whose sacrifice carried heroic significance. He saw sorrow as necessary to creative expression. In Hawaii, he used that belief to regain his senses. Because he had suffered, he now had fresh material.

His fight for sanity led him back to work, his only real sanctuary from a world of rancorous hassles and hurt. "I tried to make Motown understand," he said, "that I was working as quickly as I could. And I was. But this new concept was enormous, and it would take time. Meanwhile, though, they cut off my money. They left me with nothing. Like a beggar, I was reduced to borrowing from friends."

"His friends never gave up on him," Curtis Shaw said, "and neither did Motown. Smokey Robinson, who's a vice president with the company as well as an artist, flew over to Hawaii to give Marvin money. Even though Marvin had canceled the January tour, Kruger still gave him money. But this was a period when Marvin was cutting off his nose to spite his face. He turned against a lot of people. He insulted me to the point where I had to walk away from him, at least for a few months."

As winter turned to spring, Marvin drifted in and out of Seawest Recording Studios in Honolulu, working sporadically, finding concentration more difficult than ever. He tried, but still couldn't disentangle himself from Jan any more than he could detach himself from his own father. He kept calling her, fighting, threatening, and begging, even as divorce proceedings moved forward.

In fact, Janis returned to Hawaii in the spring to pick up her son. Marvin tried again to make amends, and again he failed miserably.

"The more I loved her," he said, "the more I hated her. And the more she loved me, the more I harmed myself."

Another artist might have viewed the June tour as a godsend. After all, Gaye would soon be getting an infusion of cash, paid to him in England, thus avoiding the U.S. government. It was also a much-needed change of climate and a chance to regain his footing.

But Marvin, alarmed at the prospect of a long airplane flight and weeks of live performances, was afraid. At the last minute he refused to go, in spite of an ironclad contract and the fact that advertisements were printed and tickets sold. Kruger flew from London to Hawaii and threatened him with a lawsuit. Gaye remained unmoved.

"Isn't there anyone who can convince you?" asked the promoter.

"No one," Marvin answered.

"Is there no one you trust to give you advice? Absolutely no one?"

Marvin paused, and after a few seconds, mentioned the name of Mrs. Jewel Price.

Kruger called her from Hawaii and asked her to intervene on his behalf. He flew to Los Angeles and, in her home, continued his argument. "It's not just good for me," said Kruger, "it's absolutely necessary for Marvin. If he doesn't start working, he's through."

"Mr. Kruger said that he had mortgaged his own house," Jewel Price told me, "and was about to lose tens of thousands of dollars of deposits he had already paid. He begged me to help him. I thought he was a gentleman, and I agreed to do what I could."

Jewel Price was the woman who persuaded Gaye to leave Hawaii. How?

"Marvin was an extremely sensitive artist," she explained, "and you had to carefully tip-toe around his feelings. He appreciated little things that I did for him, like wiring him flowers. He'd always respond graciously. I remember how I'd take him to very elegant restaurants in Palm Springs, and, if I asked him nicely enough, he might go to the piano and sing a song for everyone. I asked him to tour in much the same way. I was forceful—'Marvin,' I said, 'you owe this to yourself and your family'—but never pushy. He knew I was sincere and only wanted the best for him."

As reward, Kruger paid for Mrs. Price to join the tour. In an attempt to stabilize Marvin, he also invited Mother Gay and her sister, Tolie May, as his guests. Sister Sweetsie also came, along with her husband, guitarist Gordon Banks, who had replaced trumpeter Nolan Smith as Gaye's musical director.

Kruger had prepared an itinerary the size of a small book. Every last detail had been nailed down. Press coverage was to be extensive. Gaye's time was accounted for, hour by hour. For the tour to work, Kruger was determined to keep Marvin on a very short leash.

At the end of May, though, two weeks before Gaye was scheduled to fly to England, plans were almost unhinged because of further domestic complications.

Bubby had been visiting his Grandmother Gay at the Gramercy Place home. According to Mrs. Gay, Marvin called from Hawaii one day and learned that Jan was two days late in picking up his son.

"That does it," Marvin said to Mother. "Just tell Sweetsie to get on a plane—right now—and bring Bubby to me."

His sister and mother did exactly as ordered. Sister Zeola brought him his son. Later Marvin told *People* magazine that "my wife went nearly crazy. I let her suffer for a week before I told her I had him."

Jan claimed that Bubby had been kidnapped by Marvin and was furious with his family, especially Mother Gay, for having participated in the abduction.

The complications, though, were not yet over.

Marvin, Fleecy, and Bubby were to meet Mrs. Gay, Aunt Tolie May, and Jewel Price at the San Francisco Airport, then fly off to England. Gaye was nervous about stepping back on the mainland—even for a few hours. He was afraid of being apprehended by federal agents on tax charges. "Uncle Sam," he said, "claimed I owed him over $2 million."

Gaye was also anxious because he didn't have a passport for Bubby. When the authorities discovered the boy lacked proper documents, they wouldn't allow him to leave the country. Marvin kept envisioning Jan running through the airport with a dozen police to arrest him, but he still refused to go to England without his son.

"I called Kruger, I called Motown, I called everyone," Mrs. Price told me. "Finally I got the president of TWA on the phone. After hours and hours, they gave permission, and we were gone."

"Mrs. Price," Mother Gay told me, "can get anything done."

As the plane took off from San Francisco, another intense period of Gaye's life came roaring to a close. In spite of his growing problems—his struggles with impotence and paranoia, his fear of performance and lack of funds—awaiting him were prospects for a bright new beginning, an enormous audience raised on his music, devoted fans in Great Britain and Europe, areas where he'd visited only twice in twenty years. This could be the renewal he needed. His Hawaiian exile had ended. But what no one—not even Marvin—knew was that his English exile had just begun, another ten-month span of personal pain, professional chaos, and brilliant composition.

28

ROYAL SHAFTS

Just as Gaye's final concert tour in America in the summer of 1983 anticipated—even brought on—a period of abject depression, so did his tour of England and Europe in the summer of 1981. He hated the pressure of performing and the discipline of rehearsals. He resented running from city to city and rebelled by fighting the promoters and feeding himself alarming quantities of drugs. At the end of these grueling periods, he'd fall apart.

Marvin and Kruger, for example, were on a collision course. As he'd done with Harvey Fuqua, Berry Gordy, Stephen Hill, and scores of others, Gaye responded to the older man's authority with a vengeance, all the while maintaining his cool and cagily obstinate style.

Starting on Friday, the thirteenth of June—the tour's opening date in London—the nasty tug-of-war between the two men escalated until it reached a scandalous climax at the final engagement, July 8.

"Marvin and I had a love-hate relationship," Kruger told me in his proper British manner. "I loved him when he was performing, but the rest of the time he was quite trying."

Kruger did what he could to make Gaye comfortable, giving Bubby and him a luxurious suite at the Britannia Hotel on Grosvenor Square next to the U.S. Embassy. Mother, Aunt Tolie May, Mrs. Price, and Fleecy had nearby rooms on the same floor.

Following only a day of rehearsals, the tour, which included soul singer Edwin Starr, kicked off at the Royal Albert Theatre. Suddenly Gaye's transformation from beachcomber back to superstar was complete. Seated in plush limos whisking him through bustling London, Marvin took an ironic view of it all.

"I didn't think I was ready to come back out," he told me. "But as long as I could do it in style, I couldn't complain. My initial idea was to appear in beach clothes—swimming trunks and sandals. That would have been cute, and also an honest representation of my wardrobe at that point."

"He really had no clothes to speak of," Mrs. Price remembered. "So I went down the street and found a tailor. I brought the man to Marvin's suite and had him take measurements. We selected a beautiful wardrobe—very dignified, very English. Honey, you should have seen Marvin in those tailored clothes!"

"Clad in woolly hat and conservative black suit," wrote *Melody Maker* in reviewing opening night, "Marvin was in inspired voice . . . eager to please, seemingly unscarred by his tribulations of recent times . . . eulogizing English tea, threatening to remove his trousers."

This was the first hint of a gesture he'd actually realize in 1983. In England, though, he hadn't reached that point of desperation.

Not all the opening concert reviews were favorable. "Unfortunately," wrote Peter Hepple, "not a great deal of musical excellence was evident. Having gone through his various stages, he now seems to have happily settled for the role of sex symbol, encouraged in this by his London audience, mainly late-teens and early-twenties girls to whom the albums from the beginning of the seventies, notably *Let's Get It On*, were obviously influential at the pubescent stage of their emotional development."

Throughout the grueling tour, from England to Geneva to Amsterdam to Montreux back to London, Marvin was sexually distracted.

"I'd found my powers again," he said, "and I suppose I overdid it."

"All these white women were throwing themselves at him," Mrs. Price told me. "They followed him back to London from Holland. They came from everywhere. They were in the hallways of the hotels. They just wouldn't let him out of their sight. He liked having them with him, but there was hardly room. Once he asked me if one of his women could stay in my room. 'Marvin!' I said, 'you shouldn't even be asking me something like that.' He had little Bubby with him, and I think he let the boy see far too much. It was so hard to control Marvin.

"One night he came into my room looking to borrow $1000. I knew it had to be for either drugs or women, so I said no. He begged and begged and finally I gave him $500. 'Marvin,' I said, 'you should be giving *me* money.' But I knew how Marvin was with money, and I made sure Kruger paid me back the $500 out of Marvin's next paycheck."

Verbal fights between Gaye and Kruger flared up as the tour wore on.

"Mr. Kruger worked Marvin too hard," said Mrs. Price. "Marvin wasn't used to being pushed. He resented it. Kruger didn't understand Marvin's personality. He was demanding, and that's not the way to handle Marvin. Marvin was looking for ways to pay Kruger back. For instance, Marvin embarrassed Kruger by skipping out of a press conference. He snuck out of the airport, and no one knew where he was."

To avoid going to Manchester, Gaye slipped into the men's room and climbed out a back window.

"Kruger thought he had me," Marvin said, "but I was determined to prove otherwise. I appreciated his position. I had canceled the tour once, I had this reputation for being flaky, and he was right to worry. But I'd given him my word that I'd perform, and I was performing. Jeffrey didn't trust me, though. That's what got to me. And because he didn't trust me, he always tried to keep the upper hand. Controlling the purse and knowing how desperate I was for money, he thought he had me over a barrel. But ah, that's where he was wrong."

The showdown began on the morning of Tuesday, July 8. The evening before Gaye had played the International Festival at Montreux, Switzerland. That next night the tour's grand finale was to unfold at the Royal Gala Charity Show, at Lakeside Country Club, Surrey, a half-hour outside London. Elaborate programs had been prepared: Marvin graced the cover, and inside was a full-page photograph of Her Royal Highness the Princess Margaret, Countess of Snowden.

Gaye was to join the princess for dinner at 8:15 P.M., then perform ninety minutes later. *Variety* reported that "850 people had paid between $235 and $1000 for the charity . . . for deserving children of the Docklands Settlement."

At 8:15 P.M. Marvin wasn't anywhere near the country club. Where was he?

"Stretched out in my hotel bed, naked as the day I was born," he told me, smiling as he related the incident. "Kruger had me catch a 6 A.M. plane that morning out of Switzerland. I hated getting up in the middle of the night, especially after having just performed a few hours before. But Kruger swore that was the only flight to London. So I took it. Later I learned there was an afternoon flight."

"I didn't tell Marvin about the later flight," Kruger said, "because I was certain he'd miss it. This way, if he didn't catch the morning flight, at least we had a backup. I told the people at the airport not to say a word to Marvin about that afternoon flight, but one of his musicians found out and told him."

"If that's the kind of game Kruger wanted to play," Gaye continued, "fine. If he wanted to treat me like a child, then I could damn sure act like a child. Presenting me to the princess was *his* great moment, not mine. I was tired of being manipulated. I was just plain tired. Jeffrey had pushed me one time too many. So I stayed right where I was, laid up in bed, cool as a cucumber while everyone else went nuts. I was interested to see how everyone would react."

"I begged Marvin," Kruger said, "I pleaded with him not to do this to himself or his people."

"I didn't buy the argument that I was disgracing black people," Marvin explained. "First of all, I wasn't anyone's chosen representative, and even if I was, what has the high crown of England done for us poor folk lately? No, bowing before royalty doesn't thrill me. I held my ground. I was proving a point. Let the show go on without me."

At this point Mrs. Jewel Price intervened. "If you get me a car to take me back to London," Mrs. Price told Kruger, "I think I can talk Marvin into it."

"Kruger said it was impossible," Mrs. Price remembered, "but I knew Marvin, and I was willing to try. Mr. Peter Prince, vice president of Motown in Europe and a most distinguished gentleman, accompanied me back to the Britannia Hotel with a police escort. Marvin wouldn't even speak to Mr. Prince, much less let him up to his room. I went up and said, 'Oh Marvin, why do you want to cause such a scene? Princess Margaret's people say they'll do anything—absolutely anything—to get you over there to sing.' "

"I had Berry Gordy call from California," Kruger remembered, "thinking that might help."

"Kruger made one wrong move after another," Marvin said. "Having Gordy call made things worse. Who'd he think Berry was—my father? Berry couldn't make me do a thing."

"I explained to Marvin," recalled Mrs. Price, "that Princess Margaret loved him. She was a Marvin Gaye groupy."

"Ever since I'd arrived in England," Marvin said, "people had been telling me that the princess liked to party. She was supposed to be very hip and into my music. Naturally I found that flattering."

"There must be something, Marvin," Jewel pleaded, "that will make you sing."

"Tell Kruger," Marvin instructed Mrs. Price, "that I'll appear for an extra $20,000."

Kruger immediately agreed to pay the money, but seconds later Gaye changed his mind.

"It's not about the money," Marvin said, who, according to Mrs. Price, was now so furious that he'd been charging up and down the hotel hallway in his shorts. "Tell Kruger *he* can sing."

Meanwhile, Princess Margaret's lady-in-waiting had called the hotel, telling Mrs. Price that Her Highness wanted to know what it would take to get Marvin there.

"Look, Marvin," Jewel chastized. "You've already gone back on your word. Now once and for all make up your mind what it will take to get you there, and tell this woman."

"Finally I got an idea," Marvin remembered. "I informed the lady-in-waiting that if Jeffrey Kruger and his entire party—that must have been thirty-five people—were bodily removed from the auditorium, I'd come. But I would not appear if he, his wife, or any of his employees or guests were present."

"Marvin and I were convinced that Kruger was going to be knighted that evening," Mrs. Price explained. "And Marvin wanted to prevent that. He also had told me that Kruger had physically threatened him, warning him that not to show up for a concert would mean bodily harm. Marvin was proving that he wasn't afraid.

"Anyway, the lady-in-waiting agreed to put out Kruger and his crew. She immediately detached a police escort to take us to the concert. Marvin wouldn't permit Mr. Prince from Motown to ride with us. I wouldn't permit Marvin's man Fleecy to go with us either. So it was just Marvin, Marvin's mother, and myself. Wouldn't you know it—it was raining that night, and the English bobbys got lost. The trip took forty minutes longer than it should have. We didn't get there till a little before midnight."

"When we finally arrived," Marvin said, "I saw the princess' limo pulling out. We passed each other like ships in the night. I suppose she got tired of waiting. I don't think she saw me, but I still waved weakly in her direction, just to let her know that it wasn't anything personal. I went in and started my show. But the stagehands were so pissed at me for insulting their princess that after I'd been singing only twenty minutes they brought down the curtain right in the middle of my act. I guess that was as good a way as any to end a fascinating evening."

The next morning the London press was full of it—"Soul Singer Snubs Royalty!"—as the story went worldwide. Nonchalantly, Marvin refused to apologize. "Why should a prince," he asked, "have to apologize to a princess?" His mother and aunt merely told the press that he'd been "exhausted."

Months later, when an *Ebony* interviewer asked him about the incident, he still wasn't contrite. In fact, he was angry at the press, which, through the final half of the tour, had been critical of his uneven shows.

"One reporter wrote that I did shabby shows," Marvin said, "that I snub royalty and that I'm . . . a real shithead. . . . The unpleasant thing is that he has the right to misuse his power, and that's unfair because I don't have much recourse. The fact is that nobody was snubbed, but because of threats and pressures put upon me, I could not go out there and sing. I refused to do it until certain people who were social-climbing were removed."

Whatever Gaye's reasons, it was clear, at the end of his tour, that he was again finding ways to hurt himself; he was re-entering another period of decline and depression.

On July 9, he missed his plane back to America. He couldn't face the music—the tax troubles, the alimony, and the angry women. His need for escape had not abated. His exile wasn't even close to conclusion. He would wander through England and Europe, a poet in search of his soul, for another two and a half years before being drawn home by Mother.

For the time being he insisted that Mother stay on in London after Mrs. Price and Aunt Tolie May returned to the United States. He found a flat of quiet elegance in London's West End, on a block, as one interviewer wrote, "of no small opulence." He also found Eugenie Vis, a tall, fair-skinned coed from Holland. Of the dozens of women surrounding Marvin during his tour, Eugenie became his only permanent girlfriend. She served as nursemaid to Bubby, and also, in Belgium, to Gaye himself. A sweet woman of unusual beauty, she would periodically cradle and comfort Marvin for the next two years, though never, in his fevered imagination, would she replace Jan.

She was not his only lady. "There were so many women around," Mrs. Gay told me, "that I didn't even know who they were. They'd just appear at the apartment with their suitcases. I was afraid that there wouldn't be a place for me. As it was, I was sleeping on a mattress on the floor. I didn't complain, because I was a lot more comfortable than the twelve musicians who were living with us then. You see, Mr. Kruger was so mad after the charity concert that he canceled their plane tickets home. No one had any money, so they came to live with Marvin. They slept on quilts on the floor—in the living room, in the hallway, everywhere—and I did all the cooking the whole time I was there for two or three weeks. I made eggs for breakfast and fried chicken, greens, and biscuits for dinner and, believe me, they ate every single thing I cooked. By the time I left, they'd all managed to find a way home. And before I left, Marvin also put Fleecy out."

According to Curtis Shaw, it was Motown who sent the musicians plane tickets. Gaye was blamed for stranding them, though Kruger claimed that it was someone in Gaye's organization, not Marvin himself, who frittered away the musicians' money.

Gaye took the responsibility, though; as late as 1982, he was still promising to pay them the back wages they were denied.

After Marvin's extended stay in Hawaii, London was disconcerting, the pace of the city faster than he'd expected.

"Not having lived there before," Gaye said, "I wasn't sure what to expect. But as far as drugs and women go, London's as wild as any city needs to be. I had access to anything I wanted, and that was part of the problem."

In late summer and early winter, though, he was able to turn his attention to his long-delayed album. Working at several studios throughout London—Air, Odyssey, and Pye (where for a short while he helped a group called The Kraze)—Marvin was still at war with Motown. He used the press, always ready to record his remarks, to criticize the company, voicing his usual complaints about artistic control and enforced commercialism.

Gaye's real anger stemmed from being broke again. On the tour he had netted $60,000, but much of that was spent on parties and drugs.

Because he still hadn't completed his album, Motown was reluctant to give him a cent. Once again Gaye found himself borrowing money from friends. He tried Smokey Robinson, but this time, according to Marvin, Smokey gave him advice but no cash. The same was true with Stevie Wonder, and for a period Gaye was angry at both of them. His old mentor and ex-brother-in-law Harvey Fuqua came through with a few thousand, but that would barely pay the rent. Curtis Shaw claimed, "Marvin was living off women."

The relationship with Motown was irreparably ruptured when they released his album *In Our Lifetime* without his consent. They had made certain changes in the mix that infuriated him. Marvin believed that a couple of his musicians snuck the master tapes out of London and brought them to Los Angeles. It hardly mattered. The record was shipped to stores throughout the world, and Gaye vowed never to work with Motown again.

He made good on his promise, and though he renounced the record, it remains a glowing tribute to the vitality of his musical and spiritual soul. His life in London grew wild and untamed— he was to repeat his flirtation with death—but his art grew stronger, defying even his own instincts toward disintegration and despair.

"Motown shafted me," Marvin said, discussing his album released in early 1981. "The first thing they did wrong was screw up the title. They left out the question mark. That was the whole point. The question was, Is the world coming to an end *in our lifetime?*"

Gaye's other major complaint concerned the first tune on side B, "Far Cry." "I hadn't completed it," he told me. "The song was in its most primitive stage. All I had was this jive vocal track, and they put it out as a finished fact. How could they embarrass me like that? I was humiliated. They also added guitar licks and bass lines. How dare they second guess my artistic decisions! Can you imagine saying to an artist, say Picasso, 'Okay, Pablo, you've been fooling with this picture long enough. We'll take your unfinished canvas and add a leg here, an arm there. You might be the artist, but you're behind schedule, so we'll finish up this painting for you. If you don't like the results, Pablo, baby, that's tough!' I was heartbroken. I was deeply hurt. Motown went behind my back. That's something I'll never forgive or forget."

Marvin's attitude was understandable. He felt betrayed. For their part, Motown had been waiting nearly three years for a major Marvin Gaye studio album. The company concluded that, given his state of mind, Gaye was only hurting himself. It had been four years since his last hit—"Got to Give It Up" in 1977—with sales slumping steadily ever since.

Releasing *In Our Lifetime* did nothing, however, to improve that situation. The album sold poorly. There were several appreciative reviews in England and America, but for the most part the record was viewed, along with *Here, My Dear*, as eccentric and inaccessible. Again, I believe that the critics missed a major work.

Even allowing for Gaye's complaints, I feel grateful that Motown released the album. At least it's out there; Marvin might have locked it up forever. "Far Cry," for all its crudeness, does exist as an example of one of Marvin's methods of composing—mumbling lyrics until the words take form. The rest of the record is brilliant. Together with *Trouble Man*, it's only his second album, out of more than two dozen, where he alone composed every song. This time the inspiration came not from someone else but straight from his own heart.

Try as he did, Gaye wasn't able to forget Jan. It is she—or the archetypal woman she represents—who inspired the work, who fired his passion and provoked his art. This is all the more remarkable when you consider his theme: the nuclear holocaust.

The album featured a remarkable cover illustration. According to Gordon Banks, it was conceived by Marvin as he sat in Trafalgar Square one night, relaying to the artist Neil Breeden his precise vision:

Dual Marvins face each other as they sit upon thrones above the clouds, above the world—an expression of Gaye's illusion of grandeur—while nuclear explosions rip America apart and communist troops and tanks, bearing red flags, invade the mainland. One Marvin has wings, a halo, and a dove; the second Marvin has horns and wears the cloak of Satan. The divided self is playing a game of checkers, while on the table a globe is cut equally in half. On the back, a large color photograph of Gaye, with his customary pocket handkerchief, has him looking disturbed and afraid.

In Our Lifetime, like Marvin's other masterpieces, reflected his mood at the moment of creation. He was haunted by the same sexual image, the dancing woman moving toward him, whirling away. Her presence excited his poetry, blessing it with a spiritual sensuality that turned his dark mood bright.

The first song, "Praise," did just that—praised God with the spirit and joy of his father's church. Yet even in the midst of this opening prayer, in the center of the song, he envisioned Jan dancing in a circle of light over Nolan Smith's exquisite trumpet solo as Marvin saw her "shining."

The miracle was that Marvin's musical mood was ebullient—as long as he gave praise and preached the necessity of ever-expanding love.

In "Life Is for Learning," Marvin saw himself as Jesus suffering for the world's sins, though he didn't invoke the actual name of Christ. He warned his listeners, even as he warned himself, that songs are either good or evil, comparing his thirst for God with his thirst for the Woman, for pure love, for, as he would later say, "sanctified pussy."

"Love Party" introduced the warning. There's little time left; the end is near, and what the world needs is not a nuclear explosion but, instead, a love explosion.

"Funk Me," the only lyric to survive the original *Love Man* concept, had Marvin returning to the mode of "Let's Get It On" and "I Want You," begging for satisfaction, seeking salvation through spiritual sex. The song should be counted among Gaye's most precious eroticism.

"The message of the album," Marvin told me, "is contained in 'Love Me Now or Love Me Later.' " Set against a fat, funky bass line, Gaye retold, in his own jazz-infused fashion, the myth of creation. Dialoguing with the devil, Marvin viewed existence just as he viewed his own life—in terms of warring polarities.

"Heavy Love Affair," bringing him back to Janis, was a soaring description of his ferociously ambivalent feelings for her, admitting to his obsession and confessing to his masochism, singing that he loves pleasure, but loves pain "as deeply."

The climax came with the title song, in which the words themselves, "in our lifetime," were spoken only once, at the album's very conclusion. Like Claudia Cardinale running through Fellini's *8½*, Marvin's dream girl returned. Is it true, he asked her, what people say? Is the world coming to an end . . . in our lifetime? What difference does it make? Let's just make love, he urged, leaving us hanging upon a rhapsodic limb, upon a melody of uneasy harmonic peace.

On one level—the crudest level—this attitude explains much of Marvin's behavior during the final years of his life. Convinced the world was coming to an end, the hedonist within him asked, Why not stay high? Why try to straighten out? Why not just enjoy what little time is left? He not only saw mankind as hopeless, but viewed himself the same way. In his mind, the fate of the world and his own life were inseparable. They were both overdue for a disaster which, at times, Marvin deeply desired and, in his own life, provoked.

On the other hand, he believed in Christ, even though Jesus, who was named in *What's Going On*, wasn't mentioned on this record. ("I was afraid that would hurt sales," Gaye told me.) Part of Marvin was too sophisticated to subscribe to the tenets of his father's Pentecostal church, but another part—a more powerful part—was never able to shake off those notions. Spiritually, *In Our Lifetime* represents the best of his old-time religion, the part of Pentecostal preaching that insists on unrelenting praise, on the expression of gratitude as a way of coping with a worrisome world.

The music is as complex as the message—bright and daring, sung at the very edge of his grief, yet filled with hope.

Once the album was issued, Gaye found himself in the strange position of denouncing and promoting it at the same time. He made himself available to the press and spoke of the work at great length, sometimes disassociating himself with it, other times praising it.

"It was Marvin's interview with *Blues and Soul* magazine," Curtis Shaw said, "that really infuriated Motown."

Upset about the bad reviews for *In Our Lifetime*, Gaye told the reporter that critics asked too much of him. "What do these people expect? That an artist should produce a classic every time? It's just not possible for anyone to do that."

He went to say that "as far as I'm concerned it is definitely my last album for Motown—even if Berry does not release me from my existing recording obligations and I am, in fact, under obligation to record for the rest of my natural life for Berry. If he refuses to release me, then you'll never hear any more music from Marvin Gaye. . . . *I'll never record again.*"

Shocked, the writer asked Marvin if he was serious about the statement.

"Deadly serious. I want out . . . I must be free. I will certainly not give Motown another album and you will never hear my voice on another Motown album that hasn't been previously prere-corded."

Before the interview was over, Gaye was asked how he'd like to be remembered.

"As one of, if not *the* greatest artist to walk the face of the earth . . . as one of the twelve music disciples."

"These articles," he told me, "were getting me upset. Everyone was running to me because they knew I gave great quotes, but the magazines never delivered what they promised. My policy was a cover story or nothing."

Ebony's interview with Gaye from early 1981 was especially disturbing to him. The cover headline read, "Exiled in London, controversial singer Marvin Gaye talks about—losing his home and fortune to the IRS; kidnapping his own son. . . ." Meanwhile, the cover photo was devoted to Sugar Ray Leonard and his son, the same Sugar Ray who had flattened Gaye's fighter in 1979. "Sugar Ray's Greatest Challenge," it read, "how to handle life as world boxing champ, multi-millionaire corporation chairman and family man at 24."

"I wanted to sue the magazine," Marvin said, "they did it intentionally to show him as a winner and me as a loser. It was clearly a well-orchestrated plot against me."

In the interview itself, Marvin was defensive, obviously concerned about the current success of Michael Jackson, whose *Off the Wall* album had sold five million copies. He also seemed to be shopping for a new record company. In discussing the commercial potential of his new album, he said, "I don't care about worrying whether it'll be a hit because Michael Jackson's flooding the market with a different sound, or Quincy Jones' sound is 'in' . . . I'm me. I'm not taking anything away from Quincy or Michael because they're brilliant and I love them, but I have to be me. I'm a pioneer. I'm a Ram and a leader and I like my role. I need a record company who knows what they have, who knows that I'm different, and I may have a miss or two. . . . Every great racehorse doesn't always run a great race, and every terrific running back has a bad day."

He then spent a great deal of time slamming music companies for their crude commercialism. "The job of the artist," Marvin liked to say, "is to fight The Man."

He was full of spite and anger for Motown, all spoken in his most petulant macho voice: "I've never been promoted as a record artist in twenty-seven years with Motown." (He'd actually been with them for twenty years.) "The strides I've made, I've made on my own; the mistakes I've made, I've made on my own. I can truly say that, when I leave the business, I did it *my* way—whatever that is. I am a man, and I intend to live as a man and die as a man, and that's that."

Obviously upset with himself, Gaye was often inconsistent between interviews. Still explaining his wild behavior during the 1980 summer tour, he told the *New Musical Express* of England that "those stories about me avoiding a press conference in Manchester by leaving Heathrow Airport through a toilet window do seem like something I'd be rather unlikely to do, don't they?" He went on to say that there wasn't even a window in the men's room.

But when *Ebony* asked the same question—"We heard you climbed out of a window in the men's room at Heathrow Airport to avoid going to Manchester. . . . Is it true?"—he answered, "Yes, it's true. I did it because I did not feel like going to Manchester. To admit such a thing would be unheard of for other artists. They'd cover it up, I'm sure. They would never leave it so unexplained, but I'm going to leave it unexplained. . . . Yes, I did it, and I'll probably do it again."

Chris Salewicz, who wrote the *New Musical Express* article, told me that "Marvin snorted copious quantities of coke during the interview. By the end of the time we were together—most of an afternoon and an entire evening—it began to have an extremely adverse effect on him. He started feeling ill and said that this was due to whatever dodgy substance the gear was cut with. Next he went through a long and ridiculous process of attempting to clean out all the impurities from the cocaine. He then snorted up the 'purified' powder, claiming this would blast out of his system the rubbish from the cut which was making him feel ill."

In the course of the interview, after forgiving Teddy Pendergrass and Jan, Marvin revealed his growing concern with the impending holocaust. Not only did he see the end as a manifestation of holy prophecy, but also a result of "axis shifting." The world was coming unglued. "The nuclear wars will then be seen to have been only a pittance," he predicted. "What is going to wipe out most of civilization is Mother Nature, once she decides to call 'Enough.' "

He went on to say that certain places will be safe, others will not be. "As it's an island, I wouldn't give too much for England's survival."

Incapable of separating the cosmic condition from his own, Marvin was ready to beat a hasty retreat. No longer did he feel safe in London.

He stayed around old friends—the Four Tops, for instance—who happened to be performing in town. Mary Wilson of the Supremes visited him, talking about the autobiography she was writing in which she intended to tell all about Berry, Diana, and Motown. Marvin said that she also told him that she was madly in love with him. Fond of her as a friend but not interested in anything else, Gaye found himself, as he told me, "running from Mary." This wasn't another Marvin delusion; Mary really wanted him. Finally, though, Marvin ran from everyone, though mostly he seemed to be running from himself.

"My drug thing got much more serious in England," he explained to me when we spoke in Belgium.

How so?

"The pipe." He paused, and then looked at me with heavy, hurting eyes. "The pipe is very, very deep. You don't want to deal with the pipe if you can at all avoid it. I lost myself by smoking cocaine. Free-basing became another way of trying to kill myself. I came close. For long periods of time I was in a fog, and wanted to stay there. I wanted the fog to close up all around me. A lot of the things I was doing in London—just going out to a soccer match, seeing friends—I could no longer do. I couldn't move. I cut myself off from everyone. I did nothing but stay in my room for months."

Jeff Wald visited Marvin in England. A powerful Hollywood agent, Wald had known Gaye since the late sixties. He and his former wife and client Helen Reddy had also visited Marvin in Hawaii.

"I'd heard he was in trouble and needed help," Wald told me. "So I went by his place when I was in London. He was stoned out of his mind and could hardly get out of bed. We spent the whole time talking in his bedroom. The apartment was filled with these dirty-dog women. Drug dealers were running through and God knows who else. Marvin's little boy was asleep in the next bedroom. I just couldn't believe this scene. Marvin said he didn't have a dime. He even had some bad checks floating around. He asked me to buy his stock in Famous Amos Cookies. Him, me, and Helen had been the original investors. 'Listen, Marvin,' I said, 'I'm going to play big shot and just give you some money. I don't want your stock. The way you're killing yourself, you're not going to have anything else to leave that kid in there. Keep the stock for him.' I honestly can't remember whether it was $7000 or $17,000, but I had a lot of cash—mainly American dollars, some pounds—and I put it in his hands. I also told him he was a fucking idiot for ruining his life. We talked for a little while longer, and he wanted me to call Berry Gordy for him—Berry's a friend of mine—and get him out of his Motown deal. But I wouldn't talk for Marvin, not as his manager, until he cleaned up. Marvin just wasn't snorting coke, he was free-basing. 'What a fucking shame,' I said to him, 'because if you'd straighten out, you're the one guy who could become the black Sinatra.'"

"I certainly felt ready to go under," Marvin confessed. "My record was out, but I hated it, and, as Berry was good enough to remind me, my stuff hadn't been selling for years. Motown and I were through. I'd burned that bridge behind me and really didn't care. BG and I had reached a point of no return."

At this same time, Gordy was still reeling from an even stronger blow. After twenty years with the label, his biggest star and brightest creation, Diana Ross, who had already moved from Los Angeles to New York, had finally cut the cord completely by signing a multimillion-dollar contract with RCA Records.

"Diana," said Marvin, "had somewhere to go. I didn't. I had nothing going for me. No record deal, no money. Anna had stripped me of my fortune. By then Jan had divorced me. I missed my mother, missed my son Marvin and my daughter Nona, but I couldn't go back. Not to a country that had just elected Ronald

Reagan. A cowboy was running America, and I was still running away. I had to keep running. If I hadn't got out of the crazy dope scene in London, I'd have been dead in a month."

In the spring of 1981, Marvin Gaye was saved by an unlikely source, a blues-loving businessman from Belgium who fished the singer out of England's shark-infested waters. The man was convinced he could get the singer back on his feet. To a large extent he succeeded, although to a larger extent, along with everyone else who tried to help Marvin, he finally failed.

29
DEALING AND HEALING

Marvin liked metaphors. The chess game was among his favorites. He saw God as playing chess with man. With gentle irony but absolute control, Marvin's God was the god he himself ascribed to be—the ultimate manipulator, the final winner, the eternal champ. Gaye scolded man, as might God, for his arrogance. Marvin was infuriated that mortals presumed so much when, in fact, their powers were so small. Ego was our downfall. Pride crippled us. Vanity made us weak.

But Gaye also believed that man's powers were limitless, that the individual God within enabled us to overcome any obstacle, to live anywhere, accomplish anything. And, in truth, his own ego or cunning or ability to extricate himself from situations that we might view as hopeless was one of his most intriguing qualities.

On one hand, he left England a broken man, a drug addict, a fallen star at age forty-two. Yet his reserve tank still contained enough cool to see him through several more phenomenal periods. His determination was a sometime thing. He often gave up, but only to come back, and as he rode the *Sealink*, the ship from Southampton to Ostend—a Belgium seaport, fishing center, and resort on the North Sea—his mind played with a new metaphor. He saw himself as a general who was intent on regrouping, planning a strategy, a campaign to regain his vanquished power. The campaign would work, but only as the triumph to set up his final fall.

289

Freddy Cousaert inspired Marvin. Also in his early forties, he resembles the boxer Ingemar Johansson—blond, stout, handsome. He took the role of a fight trainer—exactly what Gaye needed. In fact, the thing which impressed Marvin most when they met in London was Freddy's involvement with Muhammad Ali; he'd brought the boxer to Belgium on a promotional tour. Cousaert was, in fact, a small-time promoter whose love of jazz and rhythm and blues was strong and sincere. In his native Ostend he'd once owned a disco. Bored with life in Belgium, he spent a great deal of time in London listening to music and searching for talent. He told me that he'd known about the Stones, the Beatles, and the Who long before the rest of the world, and were it not for a twist of fate, he might well have been their manager.

Discovering Marvin Gaye, down and out in London, was one of the great events of Cousaert's life. He'd been a fan for twenty years, and suddenly here was the man himself in desperate need of help.

"When Marvin said to me that he loved the sea," Freddy told me, "I knew he would come home to live with us."

That's just what happened. Cousaert brought Marvin and Bubby to Ostend, a fashionable Flemish city of eighty thousand, where Freddy and his wife Lilliane owned a modest *pension* a block away from the beach. With their two daughters, the Cousaerts lived in the basement, while the rooms above were rented to tourists and visiting sports teams, often through arrangements made by Freddy. Lilliane managed the *pension*, cooked, and tended bar. Ostend was a *petite bourgeoisie* scene out of a picture book—the sedate city, the cafes lining the seawalk, the smart boutiques and quiet restaurants.

"Mostly," Marvin said, "it was the air that made me happy. It was incredibly clean, strong air. I could breathe again. I didn't realize it, but I'd been choking to death on English pollution. There was an energy about Ostend I found stimulating. The tempo was right, a little slow, but still hard-working. I fell in love with the city, and with Freddy's family."

"No doubt about it," Curtis Shaw told me. "Cousaert was the best thing to happen to Marvin in years."

Freddy's connections in Ostend—and throughout Belgium—were superb. An ex–American Express tour guide, he spoke fluent English, French, and Italian. Flemish was his native tongue. He could speak for Marvin anywhere in Europe. He was ready to manage him, and Marvin, for once in his life, seemed ready to be managed. They became partners, "brothers," as Freddy said, "for life." Cousaert immediately loaned Marvin $30,000 and got him a luxurious apartment perched above the King Albert I Promenade by the sea, a block from Freddy's *pension*. Gaye was in business again.

The first priority was a record deal. With the help of Curtis Shaw in Los Angeles, Marvin planned the strategy. First, he had to divorce Motown.

"Berry surprised me," Gaye said. "After all we'd been through, all the fussing and fighting, he acted like a gentleman. 'If you want out, and we get the right price for you, then go.' BG proved himself to me. I really believe he's a great man."

Just like that, in the early spring of 1981, Marvin ended a twenty-year relationship with Motown. At long last, he successfully fought the fright that had prevented him from making the move earlier. Free of Mama Anna and Papa Berry, he was finally on his own. The next step was finding a new label.

"I wasn't going to peddle myself like I was some new kid on the block," he explained. "I didn't want to hear about any rejections, so I went about it differently. I decided what I wanted—to be with the biggest and best record company in the world—and I made it happen. I told Curtis to put out a feeler to CBS."

Ironically, just about this time Larkin Arnold, head of black music for Columbia Records (CBS) was being touted as the new Berry Gordy. A black man about Marvin's age, a lawyer, and a former executive at Capitol, where he brought Natalie Cole to stardom, Arnold had a reputation as a tough, shrewd corporate infighter, a man who understood how to make money on music. Michael Jackson, for example, was among those in his current stable of artists.

Arnold was interested and had the backing of his bosses who ran CBS Records, Dick Asher and Walter Yetnikoff, but the word from London had been that Gaye had almost destroyed himself with cocaine. At the same time, though, Shaw and Cousaert were telling the executive that Marvin was on the mend. And he was.

Freddy's family bought him a racing bike, and Gaye took daily rides along the beach, sometimes traveling twenty-five miles up and down the windswept coast. He began jogging. His lungs were clearing. His heart was healing. His girlfriend Eugenie visited from

Holland every weekend, and the Cousaerts helped care for Bubby. Still, Arnold wanted to personally check on Marvin and made three trips to Europe to negotiate and help select material for a new album. The process took a year. Aside from paying off Motown, there were still the matters of the Federal Bankruptcy Court, the IRS, and Gaye's two wives, all of whom were pressing for payment.

Until the deal was consummated, Marvin needed quick money. He did what he usually did—agreed to tour. Along with Cousaert, he convinced Jeffrey Kruger, who owned the option for Gaye's next European dates, to release him. Cousaert himself would promote the "Heavy Love Affair" tour covering England from June 13 through July 1 of 1981. Gordon Banks led a small band, which consisted of, among others, Odell Brown on organ.

Bubby was a problem, since Marvin still didn't have his passport, but he came along anyway. Occasionally, as they crossed borders, Gaye hid his son under blankets.

"Glad to be Gaye," read the rave review from *Melody Maker* of Marvin's concert at London's Apollo Victoria: "Tackling his material with such a positive attitude, his performance was soul itself, stunning in its execution and hypnotic in variety."

Mary Harron in the *Financial Guardian* wrote that, "It has never been easy to figure out Marvin Gaye: he is sincere and manipulative, a preacher and a hustler. . . . Debonair in black tie, he played at his old role of sex symbol—moving suggestively, dancing with a girl on stage—but ironically, as if he were inviting the audience to laugh with him at his seducer's pose."

The rest of the dates were uneven. "I'm an uneven performer," Marvin admitted. "First of all, I'm lucky to get myself out there at all. When I do perform, it's strictly according to my mood that night."

The box office was disappointing, perhaps because it'd been only a year since he'd toured England last. According to one of Marvin's musicians, Cousaert's inexperience was evident.

Meanwhile, though, Freddy was proving to be an expert at public relations. Back in Belgium, he brought Marvin to national soccer games, where he was presented at half-time, looking especially dapper in his English tweeds. He also introduced Gaye to Prince Charles of Belgium, himself a jazz fan, and a photograph of the three of them—Marvin, Freddy, and the prince—hung in a place of honor in the bar of the Cousaert *pension*.

"The high point for Freddy," Marvin said, "was when he booked me at the Casino in Ostend. 'Freddy Cousaert Presents Marvin Gaye,' it said, with his name nearly as big as mine."

Later in the summer, Jan and Marvin's daughter Nona came to visit. Finally, the family was reunited, and Bubby went home with his mother and sister.

"Though we were divorced," Marvin said, "I had high hopes for reconciliation. In fact, for weeks before they arrived, I couldn't sleep. I just knew that everything would fall together. Instead it fell apart. I let her have her son back, but I almost changed my mind. That woman and I can't spend a day together without drawing blood. Why? Why? I keep asking myself why. It doesn't matter. She left me alone, utterly and completely alone. Without Bubby, I had no one."

Word was continually being sent back to America that Gaye was on the mend. To some extent he was, yet in several of the interviews arranged by Cousaert, Marvin's mood was as morose and melancholy as ever. Perhaps it was the winter weather—freezing cold and slate-gray on the Belgium coast—or perhaps it was because it was taking so long to finalize the CBS deal. In any event, though his drug intake had diminished, Marvin never stopped smoking or snorting for long.

Bert Bertrand of *Soldes*, an avant-garde magazine from Brussels, interviewed Gaye in Ostend. "He seemed so sad at the end of our interview," Bertrand wrote, "that I was afraid I'd been too aggressive, too direct.

"Marvin Gaye would love to think of himself as a warrior, as alert, solid, open and instinctive as Carlos Castaneda . . . but he seemed a man full of doubts, despair and regrets."

They discussed not music, but metaphysics.

A new note of pessimism ran through the conversation. In discussing good versus evil, Marvin said, "If somebody looks at history it would seem like evil's winning most of the time. Because it seems like certain civilizations that saw the world correctly and didn't look to destroy everything have disappeared. I don't see how anyone could say good has the upper hand. People say that compared to us, the Egyptians and Aztecs are barbarians, but, to me, we often seem like barbarians. Since we have jets and can go to the moon, we think we're so advanced, but actually we're stupid. People can't live well in a world that's so filled with paranoia, and individual ego, and obsession with fashion."

As usual, Gaye's comments concerned himself as much as the cosmos. He felt the rising tide of evil within his own soul, and he was frightened.

Referring to the 1980 election, Bertrand asked, "Don't you think that the people who voted for Reagan are motivated by religion more than those who voted for Carter?"

"Sixty percent of the people who voted for Reagan," Marvin answered, "are conservative Republicans whose only god is money. The other forty percent are paranoids who want a strong man as head of state."

Did Gaye feel in control?

"No! No! No! I'm learning and hope that someday I will. I don't know for sure if I'll be around that long."

Did the thought of death frighten him?

"It's great! It's marvelous."

Later, in chilling anticipation of his own death, Gaye said, "The only thing to achieve is the exit, the escape."

Yet for all his gloom, Marvin felt genuine nourishment from his new Belgium home. "The sea is pleasant," he told a French newspaper, "the life is simple and calm. It does me an enormous amount of good."

A visit from his brother Frankie and Frankie's Scottish wife-to-be, Irene, also helped. When Frankie left Europe, though, without calling to tell his brother good-bye, Marvin was angry about it for over a year.

Freddy kept Marvin busy, showing him the great museums of Europe and taking him to Paris to discuss terms with Larkin Arnold. Shortly after the start of 1982, the CBS deal was done—a triumph of negotiation. On March 13, 1982, *Billboard* reported some of the details, quoting Larkin Arnold: "Motown had agreed on a figure for which they'd be willing to let Marvin go. Then Curtis [Shaw] called me and asked if we'd be interested at that price. We said yes, after negotiating a little bit."

The quote infuriated Marvin. "Why should Larkin tell the world that I didn't go for top dollar?" he asked. "It makes me look bad."

"Motown wanted $2 million," Shaw told me, "but settled for $1.5 million, plus an override from CBS. Marvin would get $600,000 per album and was to deliver an album every nine months."

When I asked Marvin about the details, he said, "Just write that I was already getting $1 million an album at Motown, and CBS sweetened the deal considerably."

Billboard wrote that "Arnold says Gaye was instrumental in negotiating his own deal. 'His knowledge of the record business and recording contracts was surprising,' Arnold reports. 'He could hold his own—and did hold his own—with our attorneys. I was impressed. He told me he learned all the points the hard way.' "

Arnold further stated that the deal was "without question the most complex I've ever been involved with."

Were delivery dates for a new album written in?

"No," the executive answered, "but we don't pay any money until we get an album."

"Not true," Gaye told me later. "They paid me plenty of money up front before I delivered a thing."

Getting the album—that became the next great focus in Marvin's life. He kept brother-in-law Banks around for just that purpose. The decision of how to attempt a commercial comeback was on Marvin's mind night and day.

In spite of all his public statements about Motown's commercialism and his own artistic integrity, he knew that now he had to go for the money. "No matter what," Marvin said, "I couldn't come up with another art album. After all, CBS was digging me out of a hole, paying off the IRS, Anna, the feds—the whole works. I felt like an old vet, a seasoned ballplayer who'd been traded to another team that still had faith in him. I owed CBS something— at least a couple of grand slams."

But the idea of simply creating a group of commercial tunes wasn't a comforting thought. For all his contradictions, Marvin Gaye, by necessity, composed from the heart, not the head.

"I was afraid of manipulating myself," he told me. "I was very afraid that I no longer knew how to make a purely commercial record."

As the winter of 1982 turned to spring, Gaye had undoubtedly gone through a transformation for the better. He'd gotten what he wanted: his freedom from Motown and a juicy new contract to boot. His battle plan was laid out before him—retake America by storm. But he still needed the ammunition.

When I saw him in Ostend in April, I was shocked. He appeared as a ghost of his former self. Deep puffy bags hung beneath his dark, troubled eyes. His waist was flabby, his face thin and drawn. The traumas he'd gone through were evident in the lines of his forehead. We embraced warmly and, sensing my concern, he whispered, "Don't worry, the worst is over."

A few nights later, though, when we were dining at the local Chinese restaurant, his eyes were youthful and alert again. His boyish charm and good looks had almost magically reappeared.

"My looks and my voice," he commented, "are the two things I can count on. How else do you think I've survived in this business?"

During the course of that visit, "Sexual Healing" was written. The song was born out of our conversation concerning pornography. Gaye's apartment was filled with sadomasochistic magazines and books by Georges Pichard, a European cartoonist in whose drawings women were sexually brutalized. I suggested that Marvin needed sexual healing, a concept which broke his creative block. For months he'd been listening to a reggae-styled music track, written by one of his sidemen, Odell Brown, and now he had the lyrics to match.

When he brought the crude demonstration tape of his first version of "Sexual Healing" to Larkin Arnold in Brussels, seventy-five miles from Ostend, Marvin provoked his new supervisor by showing up eight hours late for the meeting. Arnold greeted Gaye's tardiness with anger, reprimanding and cursing his artist. Marvin responded by declaring that his deal with CBS was off. Finally, they reconciled, Arnold heard "Sexual Healing" and immediately called America, telling his home office that, in his opinion, Gaye had just delivered the goods.

During the same month, a half-hour documentary—the only serious film done on Gaye while he was alive—appeared on Belgian television: *Marvin Gaye, Transit Ostend*, written and directed by Richard Olivier of Brussels. ("One day," Gaye told me with his customary sense of self-importance, "this will be considered an important film.") Flashes of Marvin were intermingled with images of the paintings of James Ensor (1860–1949), a remarkable artist who had lived in Ostend. (Gaye's favorite Ensor work was a self-portrait in which the painter wore a flowery woman's hat.)

The high point of the documentary came with Marvin's comments on the United States: "I'm disappointed with America. I'm disappointed with governments. To govern people is a tremendous responsibility. It should be in the hands of those who are righteous, sane, and moral." He then paused dramatically and added, "But I'm disappointed in myself. Because perhaps I'm selfish, perhaps because I'm spoiled."

While in Belgium, Gaye participated in other important creative collaborations. He frequently jammed with avant-garde composer and keyboardist Donald Pylyser, producing challenging and sometimes strangely spiritual music, the song "Blessings" being the best example. Unfortunately, none of those sessions were released.

Though Marvin promised Arnold he would finish his record by May and tour America that summer, the album wouldn't come out until winter and the tour wouldn't start until the summer of the following year.

From his European hideaway, Gaye fantasized about putting on a tux and singing Gershwin while being accompanied by great symphonic orchestras. Unfortunately, that would never happen. The final tour, in the summer of 1983, would be a distorted replica of every Marvin Gaye tour that preceded it.

For the time being he turned his attention to the album CBS was pushing him to complete. He worked at Katy Recording Studio in the village of Ohaine, just outside Waterloo, a few miles from Brussels. The studio overlooked an enormous stretch of green rolling hills, the scene of Napoleon's last stand.

"Berry was fascinated by Napoleon, and so am I," Marvin said. "It's no accident that I'm recording here."

Didn't it disturb him, though, that Waterloo wasn't a victory, but Napoleon's most famous defeat.

"Yes, I worry about that. Maybe I am preparing to enter a campaign that I'll never withstand. I just have to put my faith in music, and its power to heal."

The initial track he recorded for his first and only CBS project was "I've Got My Music," in which he described his struggle to free himself from Jan by putting his faith in music. That version was never released.

In just a few months this same melody, which stood as an anthem of hope and strength, would be changed into a sad defense of his own sexual potency. On the album *Midnight Love*, "I've Got My Music" became "Turn On Some Music." Instead of healing his heart, music allowed Marvin to love a woman, as the lyrics stated, for the duration of three long-playing albums. The contrast between the versions is a graphic record of Gaye's own vacillations as he fought his fears of inadequacy.

At the same time, he tried to be optimistic. He began telling reporters that perhaps the world would last another ten or fifteen years, not the five he had predicted in London. He joked that he needed more time for his comeback.

Cousaert was convinced that Gaye's comeback could only be engineered in Europe. Freddy became jealous of anyone who grew close to Marvin and continually worried that Gaye would return to America.

Meanwhile, Marvin was as adamant about staying in Belgium as Cousaert. He was still angry at America, claiming that his country had rejected him. Not once during his three-year exile, he pointed out, did a white American magazine bother to interview him—not even *Rolling Stone*. Only *Ebony* and *Essence* reported on that period of his life.

What he didn't know, though, was that America was waiting to embrace him. He always underestimated his fans' devotion. His fans loved him more than he loved himself. They had genuinely missed him, and once he gave them another sexy song, they would give him all the honors and money he wished.

He couldn't escape America any more than he could escape his own fate. As a mild spring fell upon the Belgian countryside, though, Marvin didn't quite know that. He actually bought a new house outside Ostend, a twenty-one-room manor which had been built at the turn of the century for the Lord High Mayor. During World War II it had been used as regional Nazi headquarters. Local citizens claimed prisoners had been tortured in the basement.

Marvin would only live there, though, for a few weeks. As his last resurrection was slowly being realized, his exile was drawing to an end. He wouldn't be able to stay put; he couldn't resist a final journey into the dark night. Forces greater than his own will would soon sweep the singer away.

30

END OF EXILE

The final twenty-four months in the life of Marvin Gaye were as
erratic as the forty-three years that preceded them. The same sense
of painful irony that underscored his career grew stronger. His
comeback became his downfall; triumph turned to deadly defeat
as, in winning the battle he'd so passionately planned, he lost the
larger war, the fight to sustain sanity. He lost his loving self in a
search for simple peace and happiness. His life became even more
cluttered with wildly disparate elements. He could no longer separate the good people from the bad. The hangers-on returned in
larger numbers. And instead of lessening his lifelong fears, his
renewed success only aggravated his self-loathing.

Like unattended wounds, the old problems festered, infecting
his heart, mind, and soul. He relinquished the struggle and, as he'd
told Bert Bertrand in Ostend, sought only the exit. Like his songs,
though, his ultimate escape would fit into an unconsciously artful
scheme—the dramatic design of his tragic life—allowing himself a
last measure of control, even at the final moment of madness.

Circumstances and characters from long ago would return, appearing from nowhere, ushered in by a fate against which Gaye
felt increasingly powerless.

In May of 1982 he and Freddy went to see Diana Ross at her
Brussels concert. He arrived with fantasies of Diana proposing to

him, but wound up simply giving her advice about composing songs. "Just write from real life," he told her.

Then someone from still further in his past reappeared—Harvey Fuqua.

As spring turned to summer, Marvin grew more insecure about his new record. "If this thing fails," he told me, "I'm through. I'll never record again. I'd rather become a faceless bum than go out on an Oldies show. I couldn't stand that. If I'm not a headliner, I'm nobody."

According to Curtis Shaw, Marvin Gaye, the man who'd fought so long for creative independence, was now openly asking for a producer, so uncertain was he that his music might not hit. "Just about then Harvey Fuqua came up to see me," said Shaw. "He was looking for Marvin, both because he wanted to work with him and also because he needed money. I mentioned Fuqua as a possible producer to Larkin, but Larkin was lukewarm on the idea."

Meanwhile, Marvin grew more nervous. Forced to leave Belgium for several weeks over visa problems, he found himself working in Munich, Germany. The transition was unsettling. When he returned, he called for Gordon Banks, who joined him back in Ohaine.

Gaye was rattled; he needed reassurance; his incomplete album sounded uneven to him, formless. The further behind he fell in delivering the master tapes, the greater his fear that he'd lost the pulse of popular taste.

When he heard Harvey's name mentioned as a possible producer, he welcomed the idea. He greeted his first mentor with open arms. Fuqua had come through with money when Marvin was broke in London. It was the perfect time to repay the debt. Even more importantly, no matter what their prior disputes, Gaye had great respect for Harvey's musical ability. Fuqua had all the confidence that Marvin lacked, and he had something else—a woman named Marilyn Freeman, an acquaintance of Marvin's from his Detroit days who traveled with Harvey to Belgium in the last half of 1982 to help Gaye through his traumas and trials.

The reunion was sweet. Gaye was back with the man who first discovered him, who taught him his fundamental harmony and took him from the streets to the recording studio. There at the start, there at the finish, Fuqua's presence made a circular sense that typified much of Marvin's life in these final two years. "In my end is my beginning," was the T. S. Eliot line Gaye kept quoting, knowing how well it applied.

Thus in order to survive his crisis of uncertainty, Marvin had the comfort of his first musical father. Marilyn Freeman, older than Gaye, assertive and strong, became his Jewish mother. Like Cousaert, she had no other star clients. In fact, she told London's *New Musical Express* "how in her former job with Los Angeles school security she helped the L.A. police solve nine murder cases." That made little difference to Gaye, whose choices of managers and advisers were often unconventional.

"Marvin was the kind of guy," Larkin Arnold told me, "who hired people on the spot. He liked telling people they could be his manager. He'd tell them anything. He was capable of naming three different managers or tour promoters in the same month."

By the time his exile had ended, Marilyn Freeman became Gaye's new manager. As it seemed more and more likely that he would have to head home to promote his product, Marvin's need for Cousaert's European counsel diminished dramatically. Freddy was fine as long as Gaye planned to live permanently in Belgium. Now, though, America was looking better with each passing day. If he was going to come back, he'd have to do so literally—go on tour and work the press. Besides, he missed his mother, missed his kids. And, in spite of Eugenie's loyalty, Jan never left his mind.

In competition for Marvin's trust, Freddy didn't have a chance against Marilyn and Harvey. Harvey still knew his star student and former brother-in-law inside out.

Everything was running together. In October, "Sexual Healing" was released as a single. It hit immediately, becoming, according to *Billboard*, the fastest-rising soul single of the past five years. Soon it would cross over. Marvin had sung an especially spicy vocal, with Harvey and Gordon Banks adding lovely honey-dipped harmonies.

When the album was released later in the month, the influences upon Marvin were apparent—the reggae music he'd learned to love in London, the good-time feeling which Arnold and Fuqua felt were necessary for a hit. But for the first time in fourteen years, Marvin Gaye had turned out a studio album without a cohesive theme. He'd produced a party record. And yet, listening carefully, it was evident that the man wasn't capable of musical superficiality.

Midnight Love—the title was Marilyn Freeman's—tried hard to avoid introspection but, fortunately, failed.

When I spoke with Harvey Fuqua by phone after he'd returned from Europe but before I'd heard the album, I asked whether Marvin had continued working with the healing theme, the personal poetry he had discussed in Ostend.

"No," Fuqua said sternly. "I told him that I'm not interested in any more of that shit. And neither is anyone else. We want to sell records." I immediately remembered what Gaye had told me about Fuqua back in 1979. Harvey was interested in form, not content.

In order to complete the album, Fuqua had traveled back to America, where he supervised the horn sessions, brilliantly arranged and conducted by McKinley Jackson, the man who, six months later, would become the musical director of Marvin's final tour. Harvey also mixed the album and, according to Shaw, should have been credited as a full producer, though Marvin listed him merely as "production adviser."

For all Fuqua's influence, though, Marvin's mind was his own. The record, sometimes shallow, as Gaye himself admitted, still carried the torch for Janis. On the album's most spirited and complex song, "Rockin' after Midnight," with Marvin's multitrack vocals a miracle of invention, he told her—this same woman to whom he had sung for ten long years—that he would love her for the rest of his days. And at the very end, before singing Gordon Banks' "My Love Is Waiting" and after thanking Gordon and Harvey and Larkin and engineer Mike Butcher, he called out the name of Jesus—as he'd refused to do on *In Our Lifetime*—crying "Oh, Lordie!" and breaking into a gospel shout filled with the fire of Father's holy church. Finally, though, it was to Janis, not Jesus, whom he sang as he left Europe for America, hoping to be firm again, to love, as the song said, "like a rocket."

Although *Midnight Love* was embraced by many of the same critics who ignored his last two major works, Marvin himself was highly critical of the album.

Interviewing Gaye for *Musician* magazine in the spring of 1983, Nelson George asked him, "Is there anything on *Midnight Love* that you would consider contrived?"

"A couple of songs, yes," Marvin replied. 'Midnight Lady' is one that'll give you a good example of what I mean. You're surprised

I'm so honest. My honesty has gotten me in trouble in the past, but one can't be a true artist without it."

"Midnight Lady," with its cocaine and sex-freak references, was largely fluff. " 'Til Tomorrow" was just as vapid. He started the song speaking French, which was something, he told me, he had wanted to do since hearing Nat Cole's "Darling, Je Vous Aime Beaucoup" in 1955.

"Third World Girl" was a heartfelt though hardly profound tribute to Bob Marley. "Joy" meant a great deal to Marvin. It was an epiphany in which Gaye felt all the joy of his original religious experience, an emotional moment, as he often announced during his last tour, that he associated with Father, another brave attempt to use music to heal old wounds.

Vocally, Marvin stayed at the top of his form. "Just like Muhammad Ali was built to box," he told the press, remembering his old hero, "I was built to sing." It was something his diehard followers and fans had always known. He never lost his form.

As much as Marvin liked to spread the notion that the album was the product of his own invention and musicianship—critics were writing that he played nearly all instruments on all songs— in truth, the work was a long duet between him and guitarist-bassist-keyboardist-drummer Banks. As musical partners, Gaye and Gordon understood one another perfectly, and it's a shame that partnership ended before they could collaborate again. It was Banks' guitar work—slick, sophisticated, yet funky as a Georgia barnyard—that helped give the album an especially subtle charm.

Despite his aim to, as he said, "write at least four Top Ten smashes for the album," "Sexual Healing" was *Midnight Love's* only hit song. It was enough. It stayed Number One in the soul category for four months—an achievement matched only by Ray Charles' "I Can't Stop Loving You" in 1962—and, in *Billboard*, climbed to Number Three pop. The single sold over a million copies, the album over two million, with *People* magazine calling "Sexual Healing" "America's hottest pop culture turn-on since Olivia Newton-John suggested she wanted to get 'Physical.' "

It wasn't the success of "Sexual Healing," though, that brought Marvin back. It was the fact that Mother had grown gravely ill. She'd been hospitalized in Los Angeles with a kidney ailment. Marvin had to see her. She was being operated on—this, too, in October 1982—and doctors were calling the operation risky.

Gaye's relationship with Cousaert had already turned bad. Suspicious of Freddy's financial dealings, Marvin grew angry with his manager and partner, the man he claimed had saved him in England, and threw him over for Marilyn Freeman.

"Freddy," said Curtis Shaw, "was an honest, decent man who always treated Marvin right. The problem is that other people were whispering in Marvin's ear."

Those same people weren't saying especially nice things about Shaw himself, and that eight-year relationship was also nearing an end. Gaye was going through a period of tremendous change, and he chose to have his newly adopted substitute parents—Harvey and Marilyn—close by his side.

Leaving Belgium just as he had entered, his financial affairs in a state of contention and confusion, Gaye broke off his relationship with Freddy and headed back home. For all his jealousies, Cousaert proved to be prophetic when he had told me in Ostend that only Marvin's mother could make him leave Europe. Once Gaye was back home, the Belgian believed, he'd never find the strength to survive the onslaught.

Not only was Marvin himself unsure of surviving the homecoming, he wasn't at all sure he'd survive the plane trip.

"Marilyn and Harvey had to get him drunk before he'd get on the plane," Curtis Shaw said.

Still, in early November, 1982, he ended his nearly three-year exile, although he'd start telling reporters that he'd been gone anywhere from four to seven years. Nonetheless, Gaye was returning as he had planned—a radiant success. He had managed a series of miracles—changing labels, paying off astronomical debts, returning home without fear of being thrown in jail or taken to court. His blessings were many. Yet none of it mattered if his mother died. The night he left Belgium she was being operated on in Los Angeles.

Thus with Mother gravely sick and "Sexual Healing" setting sales records, Marvin Gaye flew home while still struggling with himself—half glad, half sad, frightened yet forging ahead into new territory fraught with old dangers.

31

REMARKABLE REENTRY

The wheels of fate were turning.

In September of 1982, a little more than a month before Marvin arrived in Los Angeles, his father moved out of the Gramercy Place home and went back to Washington for a six-month stay. Gay Sr. returned to the Varnum Street house, which he had rented out, in northwest Washington, D.C. Now the place was unoccupied and in dire need of repairs. Father's plan was to fix it up and sell it.

Meanwhile, in his absence the Gay family home in Los Angeles changed overnight. Everyone breathed sighs of relief—Mother, Jeanne, Frankie, Frankie's wife Irene (pregnant with their first child), and assorted nieces and nephews. They told me that, without Father's constant demands and fiery temper, the house seemed livable again.

The surprising fact, though, wasn't that Gay Sr. had left, but that after Mother became ill and went to the hospital, her husband never bothered to come back—not for the operation, not even for his wife's convalescence.

When Marvin arrived in Los Angeles in October, Father was still in Washington. The younger Gaye was glad, but also furious.

He landed in Los Angeles and went straight to the hospital to learn that Mother's operation had been successful. From there he moved into Marilyn Freeman's apartment in West L.A., where he lived for more than a month. Using Marilyn, just as he'd used

Freddy, as a buffer between the world and himself, he tried to protect himself from the barrage of people wanting to see him. Suddenly, amazingly, he was hot again.

Speaking on the phone a week after he arrived, Gaye told me he was pleased by his hit but furious with Father for having ignored Mother during her hour of need. Marvin had immediately fallen back into the emotions of his childhood.

"I told her," he said, "that she should have divorced the man long ago. He knows I told her that, and that's one of the reasons he hates me."

When asked what it felt like to be back in America, his tone changed. "I'm worried," he said in a voice laced with fear, "that there are people who don't want me back. I plan to stay only long enough for Mother to recover. Then I'll probably take her back with me to Europe."

Back to Belgium?

"Belgium or France. I'm not sure. At this point I could live anywhere. But there are certain people here I need to get away from."

Who were the people he feared? It seemed everyone was thrilled to have Marvin back. He had been missed.

"I can't tell you that on the phone."

For all his determination to quickly get out of the country, I had a feeling that it wouldn't be easy. Marvin had a way of staying put—for weeks, months, years—without moving. I remembered how long it had taken him to leave Detroit, how a short vacation to Hawaii had turned into a seven-month sojourn.

During those first few weeks back, he ran back and forth between Marilyn's apartment and the hospital. People sought him in both places. Smokey Robinson visited Marvin at Marilyn's, where they repaired their damaged relationship. "I forgave him," Marvin later told me, "for not loaning me money when I really needed it. Smokey's a very thrifty cat."

At the hospital, in between visits to his mother, Gaye insulted Curtis Shaw.

"He owed me a great deal of money," Shaw said, "but his only reaction was, 'Go ahead and draw up the papers and start suing me, Curtis.' He had changed. He'd grown very, very suspicious and couldn't tell the people who loved him from the people who were using him. All the parasites were crawling back, and I knew there was going to be trouble."

Having spent three years away from the American media, Marvin was hungry for attention. He invited the press over to Marilyn's, and they came running. In fact, in the next ten months—trying to sell his album and later promote his tour—he granted dozens of interviews.

Among the first was Dennis Hunt's piece in the *Los Angeles Times* on November 28. Smoking grass and eating watermelon, Marvin was effusive. "I'm a person who adores being adored," he said, explaining his expatriation. "I adore being revered. I wasn't being adored here."

"I was a wild freak before I left America," he announced, and, referring to his exile, added, "I had been celibate—well, almost, with just one exception—for three years."

Later Gaye told *Jet* magazine that while in Europe he had totally abstained from sex.

When I asked him about several ladies in Europe who might take offense at his claims of celibacy, Marvin laughed. "The press is looking to hear wild statements from me. Well, I like surprising them. They're ready to hear about orgies, and I'm telling them that I was a monk."

But what about his notion that a true artist be truthful?

"The larger truth is that, in my heart, I wasn't interested in sex," he said. "Besides, they're giving me good reviews over here and I'm reciprocating by giving them good quotes."

Hunt did give *Midnight Love* a good review, calling it "possibly his best ever" while referring to *Here, My Dear* as "a bitter, vengeful joke."

Rock writer Mikal Gilmore, also praising *Midnight Love*, wrote, "Gaye has suffered a long period of artistic malaise until . . . he nearly bottomed out with *Here, My Dear*."

According to Dave Marsh in *Rolling Stone*, Marvin's last couple of albums "committed the unpardonable sin of tedium." He viewed *Midnight Love* as the "biggest crossover hit of the singer's career" and gave it a four-star rating.

The irony of critics damning his most sincere and successful art while praising his most blatant commerce wasn't lost on Gaye. "No one," he said, "really takes the soul form seriously. Putting deep messages over a funk groove gets those folks mixed up. We ain't supposed to be sayin' nothing. Keep the lyrics simple and just keep everyone dancing—that's all they want."

He also discussed returning to Europe to film a video of "Sexual Healing." He never made the trip. In fact, he never left America again.

The performance portion of Marvin's one and only video was filmed in Los Angeles in November, at Carlos' and Charlie's, a slick Sunset Strip night spot. In attendance were friends, family, and CBS execs. The dramatic segment, with its mock-porn set-up—Gaye examined by a sexy female doctor who causes his blood to boil and temperature to rise—short-changed the song by making its message superficial and silly.

A little later, Gaye made his first major public appearance. CBS threw him a lavish party at the same club, using the occasion to present him with gold records for the single "Sexual Healing" and album *Midnight Love*. Throughout the year—the period of Marvin's final psychological decline—he was inundated with honors and awards.

He attended the CBS affair in a dark, double-breasted, pin-striped suit, looking conservatively elegant and diplomatic—his new image for the next few months. For the first time in twelve years, he'd partially shaved his beard, leaving only a moustache and goatee. Gaye was going for a neater, slimmer look.

He sang the Lord's Prayer a cappella, giving the Hollywood crowd goose bumps. He also snorted cocaine in the men's room. He was photographed with his son Marvin III and Anna, who kept appearing by his side throughout this period. She seemed happy to be back in her ex-husband's spotlight. Jan was there as well.

In the last year of his life, as if to show some things never change, Gaye became re-involved with both former wives, the same women he had so often sworn out of his life forever.

At the end of November, his popularity reached new heights. His hit-making talent was reconfirmed. He had now become a pop trendsetter in three different decades, having survived, rejected, or anticipated countless changes in musical fashion. In twenty-two years, he'd recorded twenty-six albums and enjoyed over forty hits. His own sound had proven durable. He was an American original.

"It amazes me," he said, "that I had to go to Europe to discover reggae." Yet his first reggae-flavored song, "Sexual Healing," stylistically a singular achievement, was now being celebrated, recorded, and emulated by Jamaican groups themselves.

You'd suspect he'd be on top of the world. Between the lines of his many interviews, though, his self-condemnation was still disturbingly evident.

He appeared, for example, on Frankie Crocker's nationally syndicated *Hollywood Live* radio program, answering phone-in questions for two hours. When a listener asked why all his songs were about sex, at first he denied it. He then half-jokingly added that it was because he was wicked, and besides, he added, sex sold records. Clearly, he viewed himself and his own success as sinful. The more he achieved, the worse he felt. Yet England and Hawaii had proven that he was just as miserable without creature comforts. Either way, he was trapped by his own sense of self-denial, his inability to accept himself as an imperfect human being. Marvin could forgive others, but never himself.

With Gaye's sales soaring, CBS had high hopes for another soul music project. Michael Jackson had just completed work on *Thriller*. Just before the album was released, I spoke with Jackson's producer, Quincy Jones, and asked him whether he considered Marvin competition.

"Not really," Quincy said. "I admire *Midnight Love*. Marvin's a genius, a crafty old fox. I think it's great that he's pulled off this comeback. But Michael is magic. He's the one everyone's waiting for."

Midnight Love, a profitable and solid hit, would sell over two million copies. *Thriller*, released in December 1982, would sell over thirty-five million units and single-handedly pull the record business out of one of the worst slumps in its history.

In the next sixteen months, Gaye, always the competitor, felt his popularity being eclipsed not only by Michael but by Lionel Richie as well. Richie, former lead singer of the Commodores, released his first solo album in 1982. It was a huge success, making him Motown's hottest act. In Marvin's mind, Richie was achieving the very thing that always eluded Gaye—stardom based on middle-of-the-road pop ballads. Though he admired Lionel's songwriting talent, it troubled Marvin to hear Richie referred to as a new Nat Cole, a title Gaye himself had long coveted. Doubly distressing was the fact that Richie's success was on the very label Marvin continued to claim never gave him the pop push he needed to crack the Johnny Mathis market.

Mathis' name came up during a discussion of duets Marvin was considering. Mathis also records for CBS.

"I'd like to sing with him," Gaye told me, "but I won't."

Why?

"Nothing personal. Johnny has one of the great voices. But I wouldn't want people going around saying I was sweet on him."

I asked him about recording with Miles Davis, also on CBS.

"It wouldn't work. There was once some talk of it, but we're both too egotistical to live together in the recording studio."

I mentioned that Cecil Taylor, the avant-garde jazz pianist, had been quoted as naming Gaye as one of his biggest influences.

"Now that's an interesting idea," Marvin said. "I think my first jazz album on CBS will be with Cecil Taylor."

It never happened.

A more distinct possibility was a series of duets with Natalie Cole, who had also been going through serious emotional problems. Marvin gave Larkin Arnold the go-ahead to search for material that the two of them could sing. But like every other recording project planned during the final year and a half of Gaye's life, nothing materialized.

Shortly after meeting the industry elite at Carlos' and Charlie's, Gaye took time to greet his public at Big Ben's record store on LaBrea Avenue in the middle of a densely populated black neighborhood. Three thousand fans lined up for hours to get his autograph and take his picture. Former aides and employees, unable to see Marvin until now, used the occasion to swamp him with requests. Hundreds of T-shirts were sold.

"It was a mob scene, but Marvin conducted himself with the diplomacy of a prince," reported his friend Dave Simmons who was there to help control the crowds.

The day was rewarding—Marvin reunited with his hard-core fans—except for a dispute between Gaye and Harvey Fuqua over money. After a long period of trust and fellowship, the singer grew suspicious of his mentor, and their relationship, in spite of their recent success in the studio, cooled considerably.

Neither was it all smooth sailing over at CBS. "The Marvin Gaye project," Larkin Arnold told me, "has taken at least thirty years off my life."

CBS was anxious for Gaye to tour, but Marvin kept putting off the plan. Dozens of major promoters were dying to book him. Anyone who had known Marvin for the past twenty years, though, could have predicted his attitude: frightened of going on stage, he put it off until the very last minute, when he could no longer do without the cash.

Friends reported him showing up at strange times and strange places.

"I was sitting in my office one day," remembered agent Jeff Wald, "when my secretary buzzed to say Marvin Gaye was there to see me. I didn't believe her. But there was Marvin, handing me an envelope containing every last dime of the money I'd given him in England. It couldn't have come at a better time. I was going through a terrible divorce and all my assets were frozen. Marvin was wonderfully supportive. We talked for two hours. He was sympathetic, intelligent, and kind. We renewed our dream about his being the black Sinatra, and I really thought it was going to happen. I believed in him. I told him there was no reason that, like Sinatra, he couldn't have a long and prosperous career which would get bigger year after year. Million-dollar concert deals, movies—Marvin could do it all. 'Jeff,' he said, 'I need your help, but please just work with my new people.' "

"I tried. But his people never returned my calls, and suddenly I couldn't even get in touch with Marvin. To me, his management situation sounded like amateur night in Dixie. Then he phoned one day to say he was signing a tour deal with Don Jo. They were giving him cash advances and a fancy new car. 'Marvin,' I said, 'those advances have always killed you. You go for the cash and wind up with nothing else.' But it was too late. My words went in one ear and out the other."

In spite of booming record sales, Marvin's money problems weren't over. When I saw him in mid-November at a family gathering at his sister Sweetsie's apartment on Olympic Boulevard, he was distraught from fighting with Jan.

"By the time the government gets their money," he said, complaining about his own finances, "I'll be left with shit. Nothing's changed. If I want to get straight, I have to tour. And that's the last thing in the world I need. Right now a tour will kill me."

Still, he made arrangements with Don Jo's Marquee Productions. (Marvin couldn't help but remember that the Marquees were his first doo-wop group.) Don Jo rented him a house in Bel Air in the same neighborhood as Kareem Abdul-Jabbar and Quincy Jones. He also gave him cash and a classic Clenet roadster worth over $120,000.

When Patrick Zerbib came from Paris to interview him for *Actuel* magazine, Gaye was vacationing in a rented house on Patencio Street in Palm Springs, where he'd spent Thanksgiving with Mother.

"You want to know how I came to write 'Sexual Healing'?" he said to Zerbib. "I started by kissing a woman behind the ear."

"And on the feet?" Zerbib asked.

"On the feet and all over. I think they should have locked me up for some of the outrages I've committed against modesty. . . . The other day I tied a girl to a chair. She liked it, and so did I. You see, it bores me to always do the same thing to women."

"It must be your age," Zerbib commented.

"*What!* Are you insinuating that I'm impotent?"

Obviously the reporter's remark struck a sensitive chord. Marvin's defensive reply revealed a growing concern with his sexual dysfunction. Yet Gaye wasn't prepared to ask for help of any kind. Instead, he returned to the obsessions of his past. He spent time at the Hollywood Hills home he'd bought for Anna, telling friends that he was intrigued with the notion of reigniting those old flames. At the same time, he pursued Janis even more intensely, not able to resist her painful rejection, again and again banging his head against the wall of a twisted, hopeless love.

In the same month—January 1983—something else occurred, a further twist of fate which would set the stage, sixteen months later, for the final act. Father returned from Washington.

He moved into his bedroom in the Gramercy Place home as though he'd never been gone. The atmosphere grew so tense that Jeanne, who'd been living in the house, moved out.

"I sensed the trouble," she said, "and wanted no part of it."

Because Marvin had been floating in and out of the house, it was inevitable that the two would clash. With Father gone, Marvin had felt like the head of the household. With Father back, the savage struggle reared its ugly head again. Always at stake was the love of Mother. Where had Father been, wondered Marvin, during her hour of need? And what business did he have walking back into the house as though he owned it, not bothering to explain his absence, not apologizing for his negligence?

Marvin's instincts were to throw his father out of the house. Father's instincts were to prevent Marvin from entering the house. Nothing had changed—the fierce competition, the jealousy, the head games, the hatred, four long decades of smoldering resentment.

Gaye tried to stay away. Blowing more and more money on coke, he was forced to give up the rental houses in Bel Air and Palm Springs. He spent more time at Sweetsie's apartment. And it was there, on a Saturday night, February 12, that he and Gordon Banks, working on a drum machine squeezed in a closet, developed the rhythm track for a song he'd sing the next day on national television from the Forum in Inglewood.

Dressed in a conservative dark suit, his eyes covered by aviator shades, Gaye walked into the center of the arena before the National Basketball Association's All-Star game and sang the most soulful version of the national anthem since Jose Feliciano had interpreted it for a World Series in the late sixties, the same series, incidentally, during which Gaye had also sung the song.

Marvin drove the Forum crazy. The drum pattern, vaguely reminiscent of "Sexual Healing," lent the anthem a funky finesse that only Gaye could have realized. It was a great moment in his career, both defiant of tradition and respectful of the song itself. While darkening the rhythm, he elevated the lyrics by singing, "O say does *thy* star-spangled banner," later comparing his rendition to the way Mahalia Jackson might have sung it. In the face of some criticism, he justified himself by saying that Dr. J, basketball great Julius Erving, approved.

Nothing could have pleased Marvin more than moving the performers he respected most—America's top-rated athletes—with a spectacular performance of his own.

When he sang "Sexual Healing" at the twenty-fifth annual Grammy Awards show at the Shrine Auditorium in Los Angeles on February 23, however, his timing was off. He forced the vocal—a rarity for Marvin—and this resulted, he later admitted, from being too high. It hardly mattered. The night was a personal triumph. He won the only two Grammys of his career and didn't even care that they were restricted to rhythm-and-blues categories—for Best Male Vocal and Best Instrumental Performance, both for "Sexual Healing." The idea of carrying home the little statuettes thrilled him. Earlier he had said if he didn't win at least one, he was prepared to attack Lou Rawls, his old Grammy nemesis. His acceptance speech was sweet and sincere as he acknowledged his children and his life-long desire to be recognized by his peers. He even puckered up and kissed the Grammy.

There were other happy occasions. He sang "Heard through the Grapevine" for a Dick Clark–produced Gladys Knight and the Pips TV tribute. Before the show, Gladys and Marvin had a good-natured disagreement about which version to sing—his or hers. "Mine came out first," Gladys said. "But mine sold more copies," Marvin reminded her. Gladys deferred, only to inspire Marvin to be a gentleman and insist that they sing the song *her* way. Finally, it was essentially Gaye's rendition that they sang.

Another television special, the Motown twenty-fifth anniversary concert, taped at the Pasadena Civic Auditorium on March 25, was an extraordinary event, a sentimental though tense homecoming for many of the performers who had started out together nearly a quarter of a century ago but had ended up in radically different positions.

Looking glassy-eyed and sounding drugged, Marvin meandered through an improvised bluesy rap at the piano before singing "What's Going On." He was well-received, but the emotional charges of the evening would come from others—Michael Jackson, whose ferocious version of "Billie Jean" brought down the house, and Diana Ross, who played the part of the spoiled princess by grabbing the mike from Mary Wilson and cutting off a medley with the reunited Supremes, an incident that was edited out of the tape played on national TV. Though Berry Gordy was finally coaxed on stage where the performers embraced like long-lost relatives, the irony was that his biggest stars—Jackson and Ross—were recording for rival labels. Meanwhile, one of Motown's first major stars, Marv Johnson, watched from Detroit, waiting in vain for the mere mention of his name.

The more Gaye appeared on television in the first half of 1983, the more disturbed he seemed. Interviewed by Tom Joyner for *Ebony/Jet Celebrity Showcase*, he was obviously distracted and unable to stop chewing gum, something he began doing whenever he spoke in public. Joyner, who taped the conversation while Gaye was rehearsing for the road, told me that Marvin seemed "very drugged."

The road.

Inevitably, Marvin was unable to avoid it. Once again, his end was his beginning. He felt no differently than when, in his earliest Motown days, he so desperately wanted to be a star without having to step on stage and shake his ass. For months, he'd tried to resist— CBS had been pushing him to tour now for over two years—but finally money demands forced his hand.

The pattern of his professional life was remarkably repetitious. After each of his major recording successes, his reluctance to tour finally crumbled. He went out on the road filled with resentments and fears. Plans discussed in Belgium to sing before symphony orchestras or with a simple jazz trio were no longer serious considerations. Gaye would perform as he had always performed. As he himself had stated in "Ego Tripping Out," his would be the biggest, baddest show in town.

This time he was pulling out all the stops. There was a new set of costumes, new singers and dancers, a bright new band. Yet the old guilt and anxieties not only remained but were aggravated. He felt himself being dragged back as a servant of sex. In Marvin's mind, the devil called, the devil he could never quite resist.

On April 2, 1983, preparing for his first American concert since 1979, he turned forty-four. His usual ability to step outside himself and give a slight Zen giggle was gone. He would live exactly one more year—a year of nearly constant decline and degradation. In some part of his teeming brain he realized there was no escape. He himself had created the fatal trap of success. What could he do to avoid the vicious cycle?

Death awaited him. He knew it; and soon he would envision it, day by day.

With Mother, in Palm Springs, 1979. (*Images from Kenneth®*)

At the hoop.
(*Images from Kenneth®*)

With Janis in Hawaii, 1979. (*Art Stewart*)

With Art Stewart, Janis, and sister Zeola "Sweetsie." Hawaii, 1979.
(*Art Stewart*)

After his Hawaiian concert, with Helen Reddy and his daughter Nona. 1979. (*Art Stewart*)

In Maui, playing with his son Bubby in the bread van. April 1980. (*Images from Kenneth®*)

In Arizona, summer, 1979. (*Images from Kenneth*®)

Ostend, Belgium, 1981, by the North Sea. (*Daniel Francois*)

In Japan with, from left, Cecil Jenkins and brother Frankie. 1979.
(*Art Stewart*)

In Japan with his beloved percussionist, the late Melvin Webb, and
guitarist Spencer Bean (wearing cap). 1979. (*Art Stewart*)

With Jeffrey Kruger in Ostend. 1981. (*Jeffrey Kruger*)

With author Ritz, preparing to leave Ostend for Brussels, with demo tape of "Sexual Healing." April 1982.

On the "Sexual Healing" tour, introducing guitarist and brother-in-law Gordon Banks to audience, summer, 1983. (*Images from Kenneth*®)

Singing "Sexual Healing," usually the final number during his 1983 tour. (*Images from Kenneth*®)

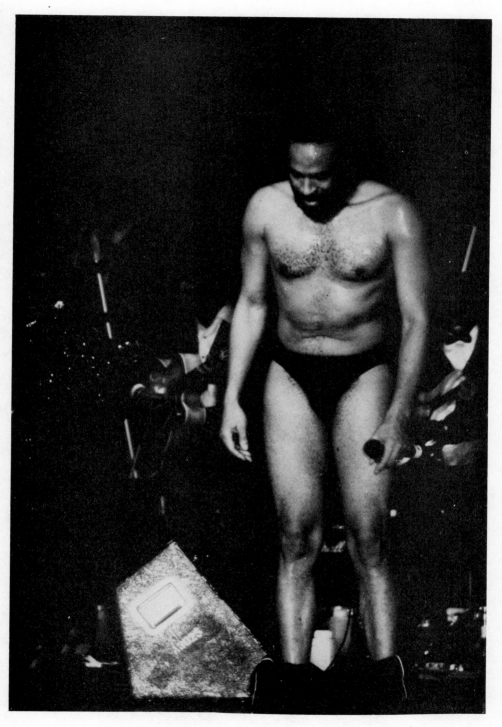

The finale to "Sexual Healing." (*Images from Kenneth*®)

The face of Father. Charged with murder, April 5, 1984. (*AP/Wide World Photos*)

32

THE LAST WALTZ

We were once discussing tragedy. I was telling Marvin what I remembered of Nietzsche's *The Birth of Tragedy*, of the struggle between Apollo, the god of individual song, and Dionysus, god of collective chaos, of how Apollo's art represents specific dreams and how Dionysus ignites uncontrolled intoxication. The two Greek gods exist, I said, as opposites, incompatible dualities. Gaye loved the metaphor.

"So my dream of becoming a ballad singer," he reflected, "is the Apollo inside me. And I can blame my crazy sex shows on Dionysus."

Like Dionysus, Marvin would be emotionally torn to pieces by the very women he felt compelled to excite. He sacrificed himself to what he viewed as their expectations. He sought to fulfill them, worried that he couldn't, and, in the end, often unable to raise an erection, felt like a fraud. Ever since he'd been a teenaged singer turning on women, he'd lived with the fear: performance anxiety. Now the nightmare had come true. With his sexual powers waning, he felt stripped of his last vestments of masculinity. "I am a man," he said, "or I am nothing."

When his final tour opened in San Diego on April 18, 1983, Robert Hilburn wrote the review for the *Los Angeles Times*:

" 'I love you, baby,' Gaye assured the crowd again and again as he prowled the stage, twisting his hips at every possible opportunity

317

and smiling at the audience with the nervousness of a negligent lover trying to overcompensate for his absence."

"It also seemed peculiar," Hilburn added, "that someone who has struggled so publicly to assert his artistic independence would surrender so completely to the most clichéd sex-symbol stereotypes."

Such was the sad truth.

Like the last books of Faulkner and Hemingway, once great stylists themselves, Gaye's final appearances across America turned into a parody of his former artistry.

His hair greased back, his freshly grown beard cut close to his face, he would be helped out of his white admiral's robe by sister Sweetsie and stand there, on stage, in radiant mock-military glitter, gold braids upon his chest, purple epaulets upon his shoulder. It was a dazzlingly decorated fashion which Michael Jackson would soon adopt as his own, the uniform of outrageous royalty, the high commander-in-chief of scorching soul.

Marvin felt pressure to give his all. In spite of obvious mental deterioration, his show energy remained high. His band, with, among others, Gordon Banks and Wah Wah Watson on guitars, Fernando Harkness on tenor, William Bryant on keyboards, and the fabulous Escovedos on percussion—was brilliant.

Before he left in April, there were predictions that he would never make it through to the tour's end of August 14. He made it, but only because of the challenge.

"It will be quite a triumph for me to have completed a grueling tour and prove a lot of people wrong," Marvin told *Jet* magazine.

"The one thing that kept him going," said Dave Simmons, "was the idea that everyone was waiting for him to crumble. The best way to get Marvin to do something was tell him he couldn't."

The early part of the tour seemed promising. On May 16, the night the Motown twenty-fifth anniversary special aired on national television, Walter Yetnikoff, head of Columbia Records, threw a bash for Marvin at Studio 54 in Manhattan. Gaye sold out Radio City Music Hall for eight consecutive shows. George Steinbrenner also arranged for him to take batting practice with the Yankees. When *The New York Times* came calling, Gaye was in a metaphorical mood, saying that he went into exile because "I was too deeply in the forest to see the trees." Straying from the truth to put on his continental airs, he claimed to currently keep a house in Belgium and an apartment in Paris.

Underneath the public facade, though, Marvin was going through hell. His divisions were as deep and bitter as ever. He kept a preacher in one room and his drug supply in another as he ran back and forth, comforting himself with scripture, crazing himself with cocaine.

Sheila Escovedo—now Sheila E., a pop star protégée of Cecil Jenkins'—described Marvin's behind-the-stage behavior to Nelson George: "On opening night he came to Radio City an hour and a half late, spaced out, and didn't even know where he was. He was yelling he couldn't stand the pressure, that he hated performing, just before the curtain went up."

"There was more coke on that tour," said another of Gaye's veteran musicians, "than on any tour in the history of entertainment. Marvin was smoking it, even eating it."

The description was reminiscent of Clarence Paul's stories of Gaye's early days at Motown.

"In my end is my beginning."

Interviewing Gaye before a concert in San Mateo for *Musician* magazine, Nelson George found him "surrounded by bodyguards and roadies," watching a fight on TV. George wanted to know why, if he was serious about his spiritual talk, he hadn't gone the way of Al Green and become a full-time preacher.

"If he wants to turn to God and become without sin and have his reputation become that, then that is what it should be. . . . I am only concerned with my mission here on earth."

"What is your mission?" George asked.

"To tell the world and the people about the upcoming holocaust and to find all of those of higher consciousness who can be saved."

When questioned why, then, *Midnight Love* concerned romance, and not God, Marvin replied, "For legitimacy I need worldwide exposure."

At the end of the conversation, Gaye expressed his career-long resentment about not making it as a pop artist. "Pop means making money," he said, "soul means exploit."

During this first phase of the tour—in Missouri, Oklahoma, Nebraska, and Ohio—paranoia plagued him night and day. Apparently there were several death threats, though nothing out of the ordinary for a major entertainer on a national tour. Marvin took the notes seriously. In truth, there was little real danger. At least no evidence of actual attacks ever materialized. Still, Gaye told his aides, his musicians, anyone who would listen, that his life was on the line. He was being stalked. Someone was out to murder him. He even knew how it would happen; he actually envisioned the way he'd be killed: shot to death with a pistol.

Gaye tried everything he had ever tried before, grasping at straws, reaching for hope, even as he ingested more of the murderous white powder. Janis came out on the road. For ten years they had been fighting, and now it was worse than ever. He used her only to torture himself and soon sent her home.

His dealings with CBS had become a carbon copy of his relationship with Motown. He told the press that he anticipated a fight with CBS over his new lyrics for "Sanctified Pussy." He described the tune as "religious" and "spiritual," arguing that if a James Bond movie could be called *Octopussy*, he could call his song "Sanctified Pussy." "It says," Marvin explained, " 'boyfriend here, girlfriend there. Herpes germs everywhere. Some girls do, some girls don't. Some girls will, some girls won't. I want a sanctified pussy.' "

He actually recorded a rough vocal of the song on a four-track machine at his sister Sweetsie's apartment, with Gordon Banks' assistance. He sang another tune as well—"Let Me Spank Your Booty ("My Masochistic Beauty"), a cruder version of an idea he had lyrically expressed as early as 1973 on "You Sure Love to Ball" from *Let's Get It On*, when he asked his woman to "please turn yourself around." In the last desperate months of his life, he sought to purge himself of what he considered his wickedness, using his customary tool—artistic candor—to free his soul. Neither his recording label nor his mother, though, would permit it, and the public was denied his final outrages.

Insecure and confused about his music, Marvin sought a producer, an indication of his weakening condition. Searching through his past, he envisioned a duplication of what he had done with Leon Ware in 1976, *I Want You*.

He called Barry White, a producer he had long admired, and asked him to write and arrange his new album. At his Sherman Oaks home, White played me one of the songs he had prepared. It would have been an intensely erotic musical marriage.

"I was flabbergasted that Marvin called," White said. "I was honored and thrilled. I started the work, but even after Marvin got off the road, he never came by, never sang a single note."

Gaye's distractions grew. In Boston he called a press conference to announce that he'd hired famed lawyer F. Lee Bailey to conduct an investigation on why he, Marvin, had recently been poisoned. "I feel as though there has been a conspiracy," Marvin told *Jet* magazine. He went on to say that were it not for Dick Gregory's formula, which counteracted the poison, he'd be dead.

Nothing ever came of the investigation—no motives, no clues, no suspects.

But that didn't help Marvin. More afraid than ever, he asked his brother Frankie to travel with him.

"Frankie called me one day from the road," Dave Simmons told me, "and said I better join them. He said that Marvin was hurting. I met them in New Haven in July and I'd never seen Marvin in such a state. He'd do a concert, be completely drained of energy, but then stay up for another eight hours, getting high, making up stories about how he was going to be murdered. It was so sad. He had developed this whole thing about how Jan was plotting to kill him. Knowing Jan as I do, I knew there wasn't a lick of truth in that, and I told Marvin just that. But he was far gone by then.

"Frankie and I tried to lighten him up, tried to get him to laugh, but he had others around him who fed his fantasies. People who were scared of getting cut off from him. Oh man, it was bad, and the worst part was all these guns showing up."

One of his aides carried a submachine gun, and there was an assortment of pistols. For the final ten months of his life, Marvin would become obsessed with guns, the classic pattern of a frightened and enraged man, countering his own impotence with the hard steel of a pistol.

Even when sick, Marvin's foxy mind worked overtime. He always viewed himself as a schemer, and part of him believed that, through deception, he could fool the devil himself. Brother Frankie and friend Dave, both bearded and approximately Marvin's height, bore a striking resemblance to him. That's why, while the band traveled by bus, Gaye had Frankie and Dave by his side, walking through airports and riding on planes, hoping that the killer might confuse them for him.

That devil, though, lurked within his own imagination. No matter how many times Marvin asked his limo driver to circle the hotel, convinced he could throw off his assassin's timing, no matter how often he avoided stepping out of elevators on certain floors, afraid of walking into a blazing pistol, the heat of terror continued to rise. He wore bulletproof chest protectors; he placed burly body-guards—Dave Simmons and Andre White—on stage during his performances; he stationed armed security men outside his hotel rooms. Still, Gaye was certain that each new city he traveled to—Rochester or Greensboro, Dallas or Atlanta—was the one where he would be gunned down.

He knew that there was an antidote for his illness. It was the Ninety-first Psalm, he told people, that supplied the answer, the very psalm which responded to his specific fear: "Thou shalt not be afraid for the terror by the night; nor for the arrow that flieth by day. .... For he shall give his angels charge over thee, to keep thee in all thy ways." Marvin so deeply wanted to believe, as the psalm said, that God would grant him "long life" and "salvation."

But death pursued him, and death even emerged—real death—after the concert at the Meadowlands in New Jersey. A member of his road crew, Eric Sharpe, hanged himself from a shower curtain rod.

"When we found out what happened," said Dave Simmons, "it was total insanity. Some of Marvin's men were running around the hotel courtyards with guns. Everyone was screaming. I was standing guard outside Marvin's room—I never carried weapons, never would—when suddenly I started thinking, 'What if someone is really after Marvin? How am I supposed to protect myself? What if it's real?' But it wasn't. At least not as far as I saw. But you couldn't tell that to Marvin. He and some of the others stayed up night after night, tooting and smoking and concocting theories of how everything really had to do with the plot to kill Marvin."

Sharpe's death was ruled a suicide by New Jersey officials.

There were lulls in the storm, poignant photographs from the road. The same night of the suicide, for example, Marvin gathered his troops together and comforted everyone with a moving prayer. The next day he decided to travel on the band bus to bring the group, which had started to unravel, closer together.

Marvin tried—he always tried—but he was simply too weak, tired, and sick.

Before his Georgia concert, he spoke backstage with James Brown, two American musical masters who had admired one another over the long span of their roller-coaster careers.

"Come on out to my country house after the concert, Marv," Brown urged.

"I'd love to, James," said Gaye, "I'll try."

From the stage, Marvin acknowledged Brown to the audience. But the two never saw one another again.

"Marvin was too afraid to go anywhere but the hotel," Simmons said. "And he was even scared to go there."

Business was hurting. Half-way through the tour, attendance fell drastically.

"Marvin had simply gone out too late after the release of the album," Curtis Shaw believed. "They begged him to leave before, but he couldn't get it together. Then when he got it together, it fell apart."

Finally, he resorted to something he'd been threatening for years. Uncertain whether he was getting through to the women, increasingly insecure about his virility, anxious to keep up the show's excitement, he felt compelled to go for the last thrill—he started dropping his pants.

The routine centered around "Sexual Healing," the concert's final song. After a show in which he introduced the song "Joy" from *Midnight Love* by mentioning Father and the joy of Father's holy-roller church, Gaye fell from grace to the final indignity. He left the stage, only to return in an extravagant robe—sometimes velvet, sometimes silk, jet black, or multicolored—then peeled off the robe to reveal pajamas underneath. The top would go next, but the bottoms always remained. Until now. Now he needed—or felt his fans needed—an extra charge. The setup was to have Paulette McWilliams, one of his background singers, sneak up and pull down his pants. Faking surprise, Marvin would stand there in modified bikini briefs, leopard skin, gold, or black.

Dionysus prevailed.

How much further could Gaye get from his dream of wearing a tux, sitting on a stool, and coolly crooning like Sinatra?

Depression fell over him like a worm-eaten blanket. He was hospitalized in Florida for exhaustion; he missed engagements in Tennessee.

In Baltimore, he was thrown a life raft, and, for a moment, it looked like he would grab it.

"Marvin revered Dick Gregory," said Dave Simmons. "He respected Dick's politics as well as his dietary wisdom. Dick had talked Marvin into accepting his help. Marvin agreed to go to Gregory's retreat in Cape Cod to cool out. In fact, Dick was waiting in his hotel room, just a couple of floors below us, to accompany Marvin there himself. I had Marvin's bags packed, and I was excited. I was sure this was going to be the turning point. At the last minute, though, Marvin called me into his bedroom. He was staring out the window, looking down into the Baltimore harbor, with his back to me. 'Tell Dick I'm sorry, but I can't go,' was all he said. There was no arguing. I went down to tell Gregory, who'd already made all the plans. Man, he was so disappointed. We both wanted to cry."

The tour limped into Los Angeles in August. The series of concerts at the Greek Theater were far from sold out. *Billboard* published a picture of an after-the-concert scene of Marvin with Magic Johnson, Stevie Wonder, Dyan Cannon, and Anna squeezed in the center.

For a year now, when photographed by the press, Gaye always wore dark aviator shades, another touch Michael Jackson hadn't failed to notice.

Behind the glasses, Marvin's eyes were half-crazed.

"When the tour was over," Mrs. Gay told me, "I never saw Marvin in such bad shape. He was exhausted. He should have checked into a hospital. Every time I mentioned it, though, he said that if anyone came to get him, he'd scream and yell and bite them. It would be prison, he said. 'No, darlin',' I told him, 'it would be help.' But Marvin was too stubborn. Oh, the boy was so stubborn! The people around him should have forced him to go, but they did whatever he wanted. That's the way it had always been."

In the end, his paranoia enflamed, Marvin ran to the only secure place left.

Home.

33

TWILIGHT

Gaye's behavior became more unpredictable, his paranoia more pronounced. He was steadily losing his grip on the last remnants of reality. Whenever he looked, he saw—and helped provoke—his own destruction.

"One day," Jeff Wald told me, "I got a call from Marvin. He told me that he'd slapped Jan around, her father had found out, and he was after him with a gun. Marvin said he also had a gun, but he was very scared. I didn't know what to tell him. We talked for a long time. I tried to calm him down. Maybe he did a little bit—I'm not sure—but that was the last time I ever heard from him."

"It wasn't Jan's father," according to Jeanne Gay, "it was Jan's stepfather, Earl Hunter, who was so furious with Marvin. That's what brought Marvin back into the house. He was sure Earl was out to kill him. That's what got him to start hiding."

"Marvin began the whole thing," said Dave Simmons. "He had slapped Jan around—I don't know how badly he'd beaten her—and Earl was justifiably very, very angry. He didn't want his stepdaughter treated like that. I was with Marvin when he and Earl spoke on the phone. Hot words were exchanged. Then Marvin mentioned guns. He said why didn't they settle it once and for all; he had his pistol so Earl better get his. It was Marvin acting out some Wild West fantasy, like the showdown in those cowboy movies he loved to watch on TV.

"By coincidence, Frankie and I went to the Golden Gloves that night and the first person we ran into was Earl. Frankie was so upset with his brother's behavior he was crying. He pleaded with Earl to settle the thing without violence, and Earl was a complete gentleman. Earl wasn't looking to hurt Marvin—just to protect Jan. He promised Frankie that he'd avoid a confrontation at all costs. I believed Earl. Neither he nor Janis were plotting against Marvin. That was only something Marvin wanted to believe."

The notion that Jan would kill him was further indication of the torturous medieval turn his mind had taken: Convinced that the woman of his dreams was really the angel of death, he equated sex with his own extinction.

In the late summer of 1983, Marvin Gaye's madness accelerated. He closed himself off in his parents' home, sleeping in his bedroom next to Mother. Next to Mother's bedroom was Father's.

"Things weren't right between my husband and myself then," said Mrs. Gay. "He had sold our house on Varnum in Washington, but he hadn't given me my half of the proceeds. All this got Marvin even more upset than usual. He always seemed to be caught in the middle.

"He also started taking more drugs. He'd even do it when I was there. I'd have tears in my eyes as I watched him, and each time he'd say, 'Mother, this is the last time. I promise. The last time.'"

With Marvin high on coke and his father, a few steps down the hallway, drunk on vodka, the atmosphere was poisoned by chemicals, memories, and mutual antagonism.

Larkin Arnold, like Berry Gordy before him, did everything he could to drag Marvin into the recording studio. In addition to Barry White's work, producer Leon Sylvers was preparing songs for Gaye. Earlier, Marvin had mentioned to friends that he wanted to update and re-release "You're the Man," his political single from 1972. He never did.

Even closer to home, brother Frankie and his friend Les Temple had written, arranged, and produced an entire album, an inspired work, which Marvin had promised to sing. The project might well have been the resolution of a lifetime of sibling rivalry. Gaye was finally going to record with his brother. Appropriately enough, the album was called *Together, You and Me*.

But Marvin was too sick to sing, too sick to leave the house. At times, he was incoherent.

He told Bobby Womack, for instance, that he'd sing a duet on Womack's new album. The next day, though, he'd forgotten the promise and denied having the conversation.

It was Womack, an old friend, who said, "Marvin had a lot of love, more than normal, for his mom."

Even Mother, his staunchest defender, couldn't deny what was happening.

"He was turning into a monster," she told me. "They kept coming by and giving him drugs. 'They won't stay away,' Marvin said. 'Just throw the drugs in the toilet, son,' I pleaded with him. But he didn't have the willpower. He just stayed in that room, looking at that gun. Guns were always on his mind."

Months went by. Fall came. A dry, warm winter saw him even more afraid.

"He was a scared little boy," Mother said. "He was pitifully scared. I kept reminding him, I kept saying, 'Darlin', a perfect love casts out all fear.' Finally I got him to throw out his gun. Then someone gave him this big submachine gun. 'Lord have mercy, Marvin, get rid of that thing!' I begged. He threw it through his closed bedroom window, smashing the glass. The gun landed in the backyard and someone ran off with it."

"Another time," Dave Simmons said, "he threw a telephone through the window."

"It wasn't the same Marvin," said Cecil Jenkins, his friend and one-time lead dancer. "I'd go over there and try to get him out of bed—to walk, jog, play ball, anything involving exercise. But he just wouldn't move, and I got scared. His bedroom looked like something out of *The Exorcist*. I had no doubt that the devil got him. All his spirit and energy was gone."

There were fights over access to Marvin, and Jenkins participated in one of them. He clashed with Gary Woodard, an aide to Marvin and boyfriend of Sweetsie who had separated from Gordon Banks nearly a year before. Jenkins and Woodard fought in the alleyway beside the Gaye family home. In the midst of the fray, Marvin came running out of the house, wearing his robe, waving the Bible in his hand. There were tears in his eyes. "Why?" he asked, crying. "Why am I causing all this?" He separated the two men and, for the moment, made peace.

"It was so crazy," Dave Simmons said. "I'd be over there and I'd think he was entirely out of his mind. But then we'd go up to his room and watch *Baseball Bloopers* on TV and he'd fall down laughing. I'd think to myself—well, that's the old Marvin.

"Then he'd do things like question Frankie's loyalty. He started thinking that Frankie was part of the conspiracy. That got to me. I grabbed him and shook him and said, 'Marvin, how could you ever think that about your own brother, the same guy who put his body between you and those bullets you thought were flying at you? How could you ever think he'd plot against you?' He just looked at me with those eyes and nodded. He said I was right. He apologized. For a moment, I thought he'd be all right."

He wasn't. Fear was paralyzing him.

A new year made no difference. Outside events seemed further and further from his mind. Even his friends making news—Al Davis' Los Angeles Raiders winning the Super Bowl, Jesse Jackson becoming a presidential contender—didn't seem to matter. Weeks went by when Marvin wouldn't see his children. A few days at Sweetsie's apartment didn't help. He was back on Gramercy Place. Father wouldn't leave. The struggle over territory, the fight over Mother, only grew nastier. Memories of beatings. Threats. Marvin's talk of suicide. Father's talk of murder. "If he touches me," Gay Sr. had informed the rest of the family, "I'll kill him."

Seeing the change of seasons in Los Angeles can be a struggle. January and February and March—more oppressive sunshine, an endless stream of cars rushing east and west on the Santa Monica Freeway, just below the Gaye family home.

There were days when, struggling with insanity and hopeless depression, Marvin managed to leave his bedroom, comb his hair, put on a clean robe, put aside his fear of being shot, and sit on the brick wall that faces the street in front of the house. There, if only for an hour or two, he regained his footing, waving at the cars driving by, greeting his fans.

"He'd get angry," observed Simmons, "if even one single person didn't recognize him. When a woman stopped her car in the middle of the street and ran over just to touch his hand, that made his whole day. That's how he'd get energized."

"I'm bored," he told photographer Ken Grant who saw him up until the end. "I've done everything and I'm bored."

Grant was the only person I interviewed who didn't think Marvin was losing his grasp on sanity. "He knew exactly what he was doing," Ken said. "He *wanted* people to think he was crazy because that amused him. He liked to provoke them, to see their reactions. That was Marvin's form of entertainment. He loved those mental games, and when there were no more games to play, he found a way to check out."

"He wanted to die," sister Jeanne said. "He couldn't take it any more."

"A man in prison can feel free in his soul," said Frankie, discussing his brother's last days, "or a free man—like Marvin—can feel locked in prison forever."

"I spent a whole night with Marvin just a week or so before he died," Clarence Paul told me. "I'd given up coke and Marvin asked how. 'Just didn't want the feeling anymore,' I told him. He acted amazed. He was also frightened to death. He had me standing guard at the window, looking for whoever was supposed to come by to kill him. 'There ain't no killer, Marvin,' I said, 'you're making this shit up. Who the hell would want to kill you?' He said he couldn't tell me. Said it was real complicated. But I didn't believe him."

There were reports that Marvin's fury in the final months was unleashed against women, that he went as far as kicking one down the staircase of the Gramercy Place home.

"Yes, there were these women around," Mother said, "who he treated terribly. An English woman and a Japanese girl. He lost control and hit them. My son, my poor son, turned into a monster."

The guns, the violence against women who still pursued him, women he could no longer please, women who only reminded him of his own impotence—Dionysus destroyed by his own furies, his duality finally dominated by the devil. His prediction had come true: Evil was winning.

In the last week of his life, he fell even lower.

"I can't describe how terrible he looked," said Irene Gay, who brought him his food every day for the final months of his life.

"He'd gone completely crazy. He couldn't even put on his clothes, and when he did, he dressed like a bum."

It was another of his fantasies—his prophecies—come true. "Ah, to be a bum!" he liked to say during his better days. "To blow off even the smallest responsibility! If only I could get away with it!"

Demanding more coke, demanding pornographic movies that he viewed on a video tape recorder in his bedroom—more decadence, more decay—hiding in his bedroom, always in his bedroom, just like Father.

The killer was loose. Father was down the hall. Beatings that lasted a decade. Revenge. Fear. Death. How and when would it come? How much longer?

Stop the fear!

Oh Jesus, stop the fear!

Today was Sunday. Tomorrow was his birthday.

Dear God, not another day.

Marvin couldn't stand it another day.

34
APRIL FOOLS' DAY

April 1, 1984, was a typical Sunday morning in Los Angeles. The weather was warm enough so that people waking up in mid-city were thinking of going to the beach for a bit of fresh air. Others considered heading over to Chavez Ravine where, in a few hours, the Dodgers would play an exhibition game with the Angels. Back in the Crenshaw district, Marvin Gay, Sr. watched from the living room window as a number of churchgoers walked by the house on Gramercy Place that his son had bought his wife and him eleven years earlier.

Mr. Gay regarded the passersby with disapproval. These people were going to church on the wrong day. The Jews were right, thought Gay. The Hebrew Bible insists that the Sabbath is Saturday, not Sunday. He turned his attention from religious matters to the mundane. A letter concerning insurance was missing. Who had taken it? Who had misplaced it? It was now nearly noon, and Father was furious that he couldn't put his fingers on the letter he'd been hunting for hours.

He was also annoyed that Marvin Jr. had been living in the house for the past six months. Their relationship, like a festering scab on an old wound, had only worsened. Their feelings for one another had turned deadly poisonous.

In Marvin's mind, he had long ago taken over as head of the

household. He, not Father, was providing for Mother. But Gay Sr. had never accepted the fact. Not then, not now, and especially not in these past few months.

Marvin had grown desperately ill. His paranoia had reached debilitating proportions. He was afraid to leave his room. He could speak of nothing except suicide and death. Frozen with fear, he waited for his killer like a trapped animal. On those few occasions when he ventured from the house—high on coke—he put his shoes on the wrong feet and wore three overcoats at once as he stumbled out onto the freeway overpasses until someone caught him and brought him back home.

"Four days before the tragedy," Jeanne Gay told me, "Marvin tried to kill himself by throwing himself out of a car going sixty miles an hour. He was only bruised, but there's no doubt he wanted to die."

Marvin was frantic, unable to accept help or to help himself. Father watched his son's friends come through the house at all hours and resented the intrusion. He knew Marvin was consuming frighteningly large quantities of cocaine, just as Marvin knew that Father was usually drunk on vodka. Like two cats fighting over territory, they each wanted the other out of the house.

The final battle, long suppressed, had been building for four decades. The smoldering acrimony had reached a boiling point. Both sick victims of different chemical addictions, both highly spiritual men who had fallen from their own set of lofty moral standards, father and son saw their own demise in one another's eyes. Their primal love for each other had turned to primal hate.

Father Gay had to find that letter.

Impatiently, he shouted to his wife, his voice carrying up the staircase of the enormous home. In one section of the second story were three bedrooms: Mother's room was flanked by her husband's and son's, a perfect symbol of the position she had long tried to maintain—keeping them from each other's throat. Marvin was in his bed, wearing a maroon robe, Mother by his side. Both whisper-quiet speakers, they spoke in sweet, delicate voices. Trying to soothe her son's troubled psyche, Alberta Gay, a deeply religious seventy-one-year-old woman, often read him the Bible, offering her usual potion of optimism and hope. But recently her energy had been depleted. It had been only eighteen months since she had nearly died of a kidney ailment. Also suffering excruciating pain in her legs, she was barely able to walk.

The voice of his screaming father cut through Marvin like a knife. He shouted back downstairs, telling Father that if he had something to say to Mother, he'd better do so in person.

Frustrated by his inability to find the letter, Gay Sr. walked up the staircase in a fury. He entered his son's bedroom where he scolded his wife. Marvin leaped to his mother's defense, ordering Gay Sr. out of the room. Father stood his ground until his son—despondent, enraged, half-crazed—shoved him out of the room into the hallway.

"Marvin hit him," Mother Gay told me. "I shouted for him to stop, but he paid no attention to me. He gave my husband some very hard licks."

"In the past Father had made it very clear," Jeanne Gay, explained to me, "that if Marvin were to strike him, he'd murder him. Father said so publicly on more than one occasion."

Later Gay Sr. would claim that his son kicked and beat him brutally.

Finally, Mrs. Gay was able to separate the men and talk her son into returning to his bedroom.

Minutes later, Father appeared at the door. He seemed composed. In his hand he held a .38 caliber revolver which Mother remembered Marvin having given her husband four months earlier. At the time, Marvin said that having several guns in the house gave him a feeling of protection.

Father aimed, then squeezed the trigger.

Flaming red heat spread over Marvin's chest; the bullet ripped through Marvin's heart, his body slumping from the bed to the floor.

Father waited, took a few steps forward, aimed the gun again, and, this time at point-blank range, fired.

Afraid of being shot next, traumatized by the murder which she'd just witnessed, Mother Gay screamed for the mercy of God.

"I could hardly walk," Mrs. Gay told me. "My legs were very, very weak, but somehow I got out of Marvin's bedroom and swung my body down the staircase, all the time begging my husband not to shoot me. 'I ain't going to shoot you,' he said, but I didn't believe him."

Father followed her downstairs, took a seat on the front porch, threw the gun on the lawn and waited for the authorities.

At 1:01 P.M. at the California Hospital Medical Center, Marvin Gaye, Jr. was pronounced dead.

The next day, April 2, the singer would have been forty-five years old.

His agonizing struggle with life was finally over.

35
NIGHT

The night was gentle. A silver moon shone brightly as a slight breeze blew over the Hollywood Hills, looming large in the backdrop. It looked like a painting—the enormous green lawn of Forest Lawn Memorial Park, the mile-long line of mourners, most of whom were black, patiently waiting to see him one last time, to say good-bye and pay their last respects.

The line led toward the white church, its steeple rising high into the cloudless sky. The wait took nearly two hours. No one seemed to mind. Before the gates closed at 9 P.M., over ten thousand people would pass by his open coffin.

Drawing closer, I felt a sense of overwhelming anticipation. I wanted to see him again.

Ushers instructed me to keep moving, and once in the church it took only a few seconds to reach the coffin.

Looking quickly, my heart beating wildly, I faced him. His skin was pale, light, glowing. His eyelids were shut. He seemed distant, cold, regal. Around his shoulders, warming his neck, was a fur shawl fashioned of fabulous white ermine. He wore one of the glittering gold-and-white military attires from his last tour.

He was buried as a prince, and his people came to honor him.

At his funeral the next day—April 5, 1984—his band came together and played his music. Bishop Simon Peter Rawlings, head of the House of God, traveled from Lexington, Kentucky, to lead the services in his robe and hat decorated with oversized Stars of David. Dick Gregory spoke from the pulpit, saying how he wished Mr. Gay Sr. were there so he could tell him that he loved him. Stevie Wonder sang Marvin a song. Smokey Robinson said farewell, his voice fluttering with grief. Larkin Arnold spoke. Marvin's friend Cecil Jenkins sang the Lord's Prayer. Anna and Marvin III, Janis and Nona and Frankie Bubby Christian with tears streaming down his cheeks, Zeola and Jeanne and Frankie and Irene and little April, Marvin's half-brother Michael Cooper and Berry Gordy and Quincy Jones—they were all there. Mother bent over his body, kissed his cheek, and wept. The coffin was closed. The next day he was cremated, and on a ship at sea, Anna and his three children threw his ashes to the wind. *Jet* magazine carried the photo.

For days afterward, crowds slowly drove by the Gramercy Place home, stopping to stare, placing flowers and wreaths, looking to catch a glimpse of the bereaved family.

"I have no doubt that this is exactly how Marvin chose to die," Jeanne told me when we spoke after the funeral. "This way he accomplished three things. He put himself out of misery. He brought relief to Mother by finally getting her husband out of her life. And he punished Father, by making certain that the rest of his life would be miserable. I do believe that Marvin was very crazed and disturbed, but, even at that point, in his own way, my brother knew just what he was doing."

Dan Rather reported Gaye's death on national television. *The New York Times* played the story on page one. Eulogies appeared in Asia, Europe, and the United States, with writers continuing to confuse the man with his masks.

Dennis Hunt, for example, still saw Gaye as a fun-loving swingle. "A noted carouser and womanizer," he wrote in the *Los Angeles Times*, "Gaye was the idol of playboys everywhere."

Newsweek wildly misinformed its readers by stating that "he was on his way back. . . . The last year of life must have been sweet for this difficult, talented man."

Berry Gordy, deeply grieved, took out full-page ads in the entertainment newspapers, calling Marvin the greatest of his time, considerable praise from a man who had worked with Stevie Wonder and Michael Jackson. Gordy broke his usual silence with the press to tell a reporter that he didn't think Gaye had any musical equals. "The closest person I can relate him to is Billie Holiday," he said, "and I even consider Marvin better."

Smokey Robinson called a press conference in his Motown office in Marvin's memory. Three singers, he said, had moved him most—Sam Cooke, Jackie Wilson, and his former drummer, Marvin Gaye.

Certain things hadn't changed. With his demise, Gaye's record sales soared while his finances were still in shambles. He left no will, and Anna was quick to have eighteen-year-old Marvin III named co-administrator of his father's estate. Marquee Enterprises, promoters of Gaye's last tour, sued Anna, who, they argued, had taken possession of the custom-made Clenet. The car, the suit said, belonged to them and had only been loaned to Marvin.

It was reported that Gaye died owing the IRS more than $1 million, the State of California $600,000, and back alimony of more than $300,000 to Anna and Janis. A woman was also suing him, claiming that he'd beaten her in late 1982 and early 1983.

Motown and CBS began fighting over Marvin's unissued recordings. Early indications were that Larkin Arnold had convinced Mother that Gaye's contract gave CBS the right to her son's unreleased masters, which she and Frankie had kept in storage. Arnold was compiling the material and planning a record for the winter of 1984. At the same time, Berry Gordy was planning a movie on Marvin's life, though the Gaye family complained that he offered them very little for the rights. Meanwhile, biographers outside the company wanting to quote from Gaye's Motown songs were refused permission.

Father pleaded not guilty and, while in jail, was interviewed once, saying that he didn't think the gun had real bullets. Only Sweetsie visited him, bringing *Jet* magazine along to take pictures. She told the magazine that there was no truth to the rumor that her parents had been separated. "She also denied," *Jet* wrote, "that her father and Marvin had a history of confrontation."

Later in April, a medical examination revealed a walnut-sized brain tumor in Father's head. The tumor was successfully removed in May and a superior court judge ruled him mentally competent to stand trial. The court-appointed psychiatrist said Gay "continued to provide a consistent story regarding the shooting of his son, which he labels as self-defense."

On June 18, after forty-nine years of marriage, Mrs. Gay sued her husband for divorce. Two days later she arranged for a $30,000 bond, allowing him to leave jail and return to the Gramercy Place home. Meanwhile, Mrs. Gay had moved in with her daughter Jeanne.

On September 20, 1984, Father pleaded no contest to a reduced charge of voluntary manslaughter. According to the *Los Angeles Times*, Judge Ronald George accepted the plea after seeing police photos taken shortly after the shooting of "massive bruises" on Gay Sr.'s body.

Relying on the lawyers' misreading of the coroner's report, the judge also noted that PCP was found in Marvin, a drug which can induce violence. Later, when told that the coroner's report said just the opposite—that no other drugs except traces of cocaine were evident in Gaye—Judge George said the PCP question hadn't been a major factor in his decision anyway.

On November 2, 1984, Gay Sr. was sentenced to five years probation, thus avoiding jail. The judge was persuaded by his argument that a drug-crazed Marvin had attacked him twice before Father shot him in self-defense.

36
DAY

Mrs. Gay sat on the couch only inches away from me. Still, I leaned toward her to hear what she was saying. Even more soft-spoken than Marvin, her voice was slight and slender as a reed.

I had spoken with her two other times since her son's death, but on this Saturday morning, with sunlight pouring through the living room window of her daughter Jeanne's Hollywood apartment, for the first time Mother Gay seemed to be on the mend. For a long while, she spoke of her husband.

"I had thought of leaving him many, many times before he shot Marvin, but I didn't have the courage. I felt sorry for him, and he also frightened me. Now I'm divorcing him because I no longer want to be called his wife. I no longer want to be told what to do. There's too much sorrow in my heart. So much sorrow. Every time he calls, I suffer for days. He always knows how to upset me. You can't tell him anything because he says he knows everything. That's how it's always been."

Why did she pay for his bail?

"I still felt sorry for him, and I no longer saw any reason for him to suffer."

Has she seen him since then?

"Once, at the house. I went back to get some things. I'll never live there again because it's nothing but a tomb to me. He doesn't feel that way. He doesn't mind staying there. He started speaking to me, but said nothing about Marvin. His eyes were dry. He wasn't apologetic or repentant. He acted like someone who had finally gotten something out of the way. Now that Marvin was out of the way, he didn't express any regrets. Since he's been home from jail, he's been drinking again—a fifth of vodka a day. He can't even find his way from the backyard into the house. I don't know how to pray for him. I don't know where to begin. I ask God for guidance every day. I try to pray for my husband. I want to. I wish I could. But I can't. Now I realize that he didn't love me any more than he loved Marvin. My love for Marvin and Marvin's love for me was so strong. My husband was jealous of that love. He was jealous of Marvin ever since Marvin was a baby. It's all in the Bible. Jealousy destroys. It destroyed Marvin, it destroyed my husband."

"Save the babies!" he cried in *What's Going On.*
"Save the babies!" was his most poignant plea.
Marvin never recovered from being an abused and battered child. His talent wasn't enough to see him through. Because he never loved himself, he always felt unloved.

Yet love broke through the barrier and infused his songs with something greater than passing pleasure: genuine joy. He had the rare courage to pour the pain of his troubled life into his art, and, as a result, his art was expanded and enriched. His creations, like prayers, were filled with a longing for love, not self-love, but a far wiser, far larger love, a love that transcends ego and turns our hearts back to the source of art itself. Marvin's music—the sexual as well as the spiritual—is God-given, God-inspired, God-blessed.

"As an artist," he said, "my purpose is to awaken the human spirit."

Triumphantly, that purpose was met.

MARVIN GAYE DISCOGRAPHY

Unfortunately, most of Marvin's pre-Motown material is out of print.

The majority of his Motown releases, though, with the exception of the early Broadway and pop albums, have been reissued.

I've also listed his unreleased ballad album from 1979 in the hope that the powers that be will put it out at once.

Greatest Hits packages are only mentioned when they include material not otherwise available.

Album titles are italicized. Dates indicate year of release.

PRE-MOTOWN

1957: With Marquees, Hey, Little School Girl/Wyatt Earp (Reese Palmer singing lead)
Okeh Records

with Marquees, singing background on Billy Stewart's Baby, You're My Only Love/Billy's Heartache
Okeh Records

1959: with Harvey and the Moonglows, singing background on Chuck Berry's Almost Grown/Back in the U.S.A.
Chess Records

with Harvey and the Moonglows, singing background on Etta James' Chained to My Rocking Chair
Chess Records

with Harvey and the Moonglows, singing lead on Mama Loochie, background on Unemployment, and opening and closing recitation on Twelve Months of the Year
Chess Records*

MOTOWN

1961: *The Soulful Moods of Marvin Gaye*
(I'm Afraid) The Masquerade Is Over/My Funny Valentine/Witchcraft/ Easy Living/How Deep Is the Ocean/Love for Sale/Always/How High the Moon/Let Your Conscience Be Your Guide/Never Let You Go (Sha-Lu-Bop)/You Don't Know What Love Is

1963: *That Stubborn Kinda Fella*
Stubborn Kind of Fellow/Pride and Joy/Hitch Hike/Get My Hands on Some Lovin'/Wherever I Lay My Hat/Soldier's Plea/It Hurt Me Too/ Taking My Time/Hello There, Angel/I'm Yours, You're Mine

Recorded Live at the Apollo, Volume 1, with other artists
What Kind of Fool Am I/Stubborn Kind of Fellow

Marvin Gaye: Live on Stage
Stubborn Kind of Fellow/One of These Days/Mojo Hanna/Days of Wine and Roses/Pride and Joy/Hitch Hike/Get My Hands on Some Lovin'/You Are My Sunshine

1964: *The Motortown Revue, Volume 2*, recorded at Fox Theatre in Detroit with other artists
Pride and Joy/Days of Wine and Roses

How Sweet It Is
You're a Wonderful One/How Sweet It Is/Try It Baby/Baby, Don't You Do It/Need Your Lovin'/One of These Days/No Good Without You/Stepping Closer to Your Heart/Need Somebody/Me and My Lonely Room/Now That You've Won Me/Forever

Together, with Mary Wells
Once Upon a Time/Deed I Do/Until I Met You/Together/(I Love You) For Sentimental Reasons/The Late Late Show/After the Lights Go Down Low/Squeeze Me/What's the Matter With You, Baby/You Came a Long Way from St. Louis

*These sides are available on the reissue *The Moonglows, Their Greatest Sides*, Chess Records. At press time, Chess was preparing another reissue of unreleased Moonglow songs with Marvin Gaye.

When I'm Alone I Cry
You've Changed/I Was Telling Her about You/I Wonder/I'll Be Around/
Because of You/I Don't Know Why/I've Grown Accustomed to Your
Face/When Your Lover Has Gone/When I'm Alone I Cry/If My Heart
Could Sing

Greatest Hits includes Can I Get a Witness/I'm Crazy 'Bout My Baby/
Sandman

1965:   *A Tribute to the Great Nat King Cole*
Nature Boy/Ramblin' Rose/Too Young/Pretend/Straighten Up and Fly
Right/Mona Lisa/Unforgettable/To the Ends of the Earth/Sweet Lor-
raine/It's Only a Paper Moon/Send for Me/Calypso Blues

Hello Broadway
Hello Broadway/People/The Party's Over/On the Street Where You
Live/What Kind of Fool Am I/Days of Wine and Roses/This Is the Life/
My Way (the Miller-Jacques song, not the more famous one by Paul
Anka)/Hello Dolly/Walk on the Wild Side

1966:   *Moods of Marvin Gaye*
I'll be Doggone/Little Darling (I Need You)/Take This Heart of Mine/
Hey Diddle Diddle/One More Heartache/Ain't That Peculiar/Night
Life/You've Been a Long Time Coming/Your Unchanging Love/You're
the One for Me/I Worry 'Bout You/One for My Baby

Take Two, with Kim Weston
It Takes Two/I Love You, Yes I Do/Baby I Need Your Loving/It's Got
to Be a Miracle (This Thing Called Love)/Baby Say Yes/What Good
Am I without You/Til There Was You/Love Fell on Me/Secret Love/I
Want You 'Round/Heaven Sent You I Know/When We're Together

From the Vaults, a Motown compilation (from 1979), includes one previously unreleased Gaye: Sweeter As the Days Go By (recorded 1966)

1967:   *United*, with Tammi Terrell
Ain't No Mountain High Enough/You Got What It Takes/If I Could
Build My World Around You/Somethin' Stupid/Your Precious Love/
Hold Me Oh My Darling/Two Can Have a Party/Little Ole Boy, Little
Ole Girl/If This World Were Mine/Sad Wedding/Give a Little Love/
Oh How I'd Miss You

1968:   *In Loving Memory*, with other artists
His Eye Is on the Sparrow

In the Groove
You/Tear It Down/Chained/I Heard It through the Grapevine/At Last
(I Found a Love)/Some Kind of Wonderful/Loving You Is Sweeter Than
Ever/Change What You Can/It's Love I Need/Every Now and Then/
You're What's Happening (in the World Today)/There Goes My Baby

You're All I Need, with Tammi Terrell
Ain't Nothing Like the Real Thing/Keep On Lovin' Me Honey/You're
All I Need to Get By/Baby Don'tcha Worry/You Ain't Livin' Till You're
Lovin'/Give In, You Just Can't Win/When Love Comes Knocking at
My Heart/Come On and See Me/I Can't Help But Love You/That's
How It Is (Since You've Been Gone)/I'll Never Stop Loving You Baby/
Memory Chest

1969:   *Easy*, with Tammi Terrell
Good Lovin' Ain't Easy to Come By/California Soul/Love Woke Me
Up This Morning/This Poor Heart of Mine/I'm Your Puppet/The Onion
Song/What You Gave Me/Baby I Need Your Loving/I Can't Believe
You Love Me/How You Gonna Keep It (After You Get It)/More, More,
More/Satisfied Feelin'

MPG
Too Busy Thinking About My Baby/This Magic Moment/That's the
Way Love Is/The End of Our Road/Seek and You Shall Find/Memories/
Only a Lonely Man Would Know/It's a Bitter Pill to Swallow/More
Than a Heart Can Stand/Try My True Love/I Got to Get to California/
It Don't Take Much to Keep Me

That's the Way Love Is
Gonna Give Her all the Love I've Got/Yesterday/Groovin'/I Wish It
Would Rain/That's the Way Love Is/How Can I Forget/Abraham, Martin and John/Gonna Keep On Tryin' Till I Win Your Love/No Time
for Tears/Cloud Nine/Don't You Miss Me a Little Bit Baby/So Long

Marvin Gaye and His Girls
a compilation of 12 previously released songs with Mary Wells, Kim
Weston, and Tammi Terrell

1971:   *What's Going On*
What's Going On/What's Happening, Brother/Flyin' High (in the Friendly
Sky)/Save the Children/God Is Love/Mercy Mercy Me (the Ecology)/
Right On/Wholly Holy/Inner City Blues (Make Me Wanna Holler)

An alternate version of God Is Love was released as a single and also
appeared on *Rock Gospel, The Key to the Kingdom*, with other artists

1972:   You're the Man (Part I), issued as a single, but available on 3-LP *Marvin
Gaye Anthology* (released in 1974), which also includes Pretty Little Baby
(originally issued in 1965) for the first time on an album

Save the Children, original motion picture soundtrack from Black Expo/
Operation Push Concert, with other artists
Save the Children/What's Going On/What's Happening, Brother

Trouble Man, Motion Picture Soundtrack
Main Theme from Trouble Man (2)/"T" Plays it Cool/Poor Abbey Walsh/The Break-in (Police Shoot Big)/Cleo's Apartment/Trouble Man/ Theme from Trouble Man/"T" Stands for Trouble/Main Theme from Trouble Man (1)/Life Is a Gamble/Deep-In-It/Don't Mess with Mr. "T"/ There Goes Mr. "T"

1973: *Diana and Marvin*, with Diana Ross
You Are Everything/Love Twins/Don't Knock My Love/You're a Special Part of Me/Pledging My Love/Just Say, Just Say/Stop, Look, Listen (To Your Heart)/I'm Falling In Love with You/My Mistake (Was to Love You)/Include Me in Your Life

Let's Get It On
Let's Get It On/Please Don't Stay (Once You Go Away)/If I Should Die Tonight/Keep Gettin' It On/Come Get to This/Distant Lover/You Sure Love to Ball/Just to Keep You Satisfied

1974: *Marvin Gaye Live!* from Oakland-Alameda County Coliseum
Trouble Man/Inner City Blues (Make Me Wanna Holler)/Distant Lover/ Jan/I'll Be Doggone/Try It Baby/Can I Get a Witness/You're a Wonderful One/Stubborn Kind of Fellow/How Sweet It Is (To Be Loved by You)/Let's Get It On/What's Going On

1976: *I Want You*
I Want You/Come Live with Me, Angel/After the Dance/Feel All My Love Inside/I Wanna Be Where You Are/All the Way Around/Since I Had You/Soon I'll Be Having You Again

Also sings as background vocalist on Holiday from Leon Ware's *Musical Massage* (Gordy Records)

1977: *Marvin Gaye Live at the London Palladium*, 2 LPs
All the Way Around/Since I Had You/Come Get to This/Let's Get It On/Trouble Man/Ain't That Peculiar/You're a Wonderful One/Stubborn Kind of Fellow/Pride and Joy/Little Darling (I Need You)/I Heard It through the Grapevine/Hitch Hike/You/Too Busy Thinking about My Baby/How Sweet It Is (To Be Loved by You)/Inner City Blues (Make Me Wanna Holler)/God Is Love/What's Going On/Save the Children/Distant Lover
Medley with Florence Lyles:
You're All I Need to Get By/Ain't Nothing Like the Real Thing/Your Precious Love/It Takes Two/Ain't No Mountain High Enough
Long studio version: Got to Give It Up

1978:   *Here, My Dear*
Here, My Dear/I Met a Little Girl/When Did You Stop Loving Me,
When Did I Stop Loving You/Anger/Is That Enough?/Everybody Needs
Love/Time to Get It Together/Sparrow/Anna's Song/A Funky Space
Reincarnation/You Can Leave, but It's Going to Cost You/Falling In
Love Again

1979:   *Pops, We Love You*
Gaye sings two versions of title song with Diana Ross, Smokey Robinson, and Stevie Wonder; album also contains previously unreleased
Marvin-Diana duet—I'll Keep My Light In the Window; and a third
alternate, slightly longer than the original, of God Is Love

Ego-Tripping Out (released only as single)

Untitled, unreleased ballad/big-band jazz album
I Would Still Choose You/She Needs Me/Funny/This Will Make You
Laugh/The Shadow of Your Smile/I Wish I Didn't Love You So/I Won't
Cry No More

1981:   *In Our Lifetime*
Praise/Life Is for Learning/Love Party/Funk Me/Far Cry/Love Me Now
or Love Me Later/Heavy Love Affair/In Our Lifetime

CBS

1982:   *Midnight Love*
Midnight Lady/Sexual Healing/Rockin' After Midnight/'Til Tomorrow/
Turn on Some Music/Third World Girl/Joy/My Love Is Waiting

1984:   At the time of writing—the fall of 1984—CBS tentatively planned to
issue a collection of unreleased Gaye material. Harvey Fuqua and Gordon Banks were employed by Larkin Arnold, the executive behind the
project, to co-produce the album. An early master I heard had the songs
lined up as follows: Life Story/Get Down/Savage in the Sack/Song about
Life/Masochistic Beauty/Ain't It Funny/Sanctified Lady/It's Madness/
The Devil's Trying to Do His Work/Our Father (The Lord's Prayer)/
Dream of a Lifetime
    Because of its historical importance, it's commendable that CBS is
considering releasing this album, just as, in the fifties, Savoy Records
performed a great service by releasing their treasure of Charlie Parker
out-takes, versions of songs Parker himself decided to re-do.
    I would guess, however, that Marvin would have been horrified to
see this work made public. After all, the tunes are all incomplete, the
vocals mere sketches. We're presented a series of early rough drafts. It
usually took Marvin 30 or 40 versions of a song—sometimes more—
before he was satisfied. Just as he was furious when Motown released
In Our Lifetime before its completion, there's no reason to think he
wouldn't have reacted similarly to this release.

It should also be noted that, while the record was designed to sound like a unified Marvin Gaye suite, it certainly is not. The album sorely lacks the cohesive flow of Gaye's great suites. The decision as to which songs to include, and in what order, was made by the producers. Furthermore, the use of certain devices—the voco der, for instance—to give the music a contemporary feel was done without Marvin's participation.

According to Art Stewart, the producer/engineer who worked with Gaye for nearly a decade, Life Story, Get Down, Song About Life, The Devil's Trying to Do His Work and The Lord's Prayer were part of the long composition begun in the seventies entitled *Life's Opera*. Marvin meant for these songs to run consecutively, yet here, even in fragmentary form, they are interrupted by material of radically clashing moods.

Savage in the Sack, for instance, was little more than an ongoing off-color joke Marvin had cooked up in the studio. Masochistic Beauty (recited in Gaye's evil English accent) and Sanctified Lady (conceived originally as Sanctified Pussy, another song about Marvin's search for the Holy Wife/Mother) were drawn from the dark, final year of Gaye's life. Ain't It Funny—"ain't it funny how things turn around," he sings— is a jazzy, philosophical statement typical of Marvin. The song was written in the Got to Give It Up period when Gaye was searching for a dance hit. The music for It's Madness ("I'm flirting with the mother of insanity," Marvin wrote) and Dream of a Lifetime date back to the late sixties/early seventies, the time of Distant Lover and other materials Marvin conceived for the Originals. The lyrics for both these songs, however, might have emerged from any of Gaye's many periods of acute depression and/or spiritual recommitment.

It remains to be seen whether CBS will actually release this material and, if they do, whether they'll dilute the lyrics. In Savage in the Sack, the background vocalists can distinctly be heard singing "dem niggers!" and Masochistic Beauty has Marvin cursing and beating that mythical Evil Woman he so long sought to crush. The album's final song, however, is touching, especially at the end of the syrupy, campy-sounding Dream of a Lifetime when Gaye rekindles the light of his original faith by, over and again, expressing gratitude to God for the miracle of his life.

Finally, the collection is a rare view of the artist's sketchbook—doctored by others—over a long period of time, an intriguing mixture of the profane and profound, the sex and the sacraments, an accurate— even if raw—reflection of Marvin Gaye's divided soul.

INDEX